2016

the best ca

SURREY

Compiled by: Alan Rogers Travel Ltd

Designed by: Vine Design Ltd

Additional photography: T Lambelin, www.lambelin.com
Maps created by Customised Mapping (01769 540044)
contain background data provided by GisDATA Ltd

Maps are © Alan Rogers Travel Ltd and GisDATA Ltd 2016

© Alan Rogers Travel Ltd 2016

Published by: Alan Rogers Travel Ltd,
Spelmonden Old Oast, Goudhurst, Kent TN17 1HE
www.alanrogers.com Tel: 01580 214000

British Library Cataloguing-in-Publication Data:
A catalogue record for this book is available
from the British Library.

ISBN 978-1-909057-82-1

Printed in Great Britain by Stephens & George Print Group

Contents

Alan Rogers - in search of 'the best'

Alan Rogers Guides were first published almost 50 years ago. Since Alan Rogers published the first campsite guide that bore his name, the range has expanded and now covers 27 countries in five separate guides. No fewer than 20 of the campsites selected by Alan for the first guide are still featured in our 2016 editions.

This guide contains impartially written reports on over 340 campsites in Italy, including many of the very finest, each being individually inspected and selected. We also feature reports on over 80 of the very best sites in Croatia and Slovenia, destination countries which have seen a substantial surge in interest in recent years. We aim to provide you with a selection of the best, rather than information on all – in short, a more selective, qualitative approach. New, improved maps and indexes are also included, designed to help you find the choice of campsite that's right for you.

We hope you enjoy some happy and safe travels – and some pleasurable 'armchair touring' in the meantime!

" ...the campsites included in this book have been chosen entirely on merit, and no payment of any sort is made by them for their inclusion."

Alan Rogers, 1968

How do we find the best?

The criteria we use when inspecting and selecting campsites are numerous, but the most important by far is the question of good quality. People want different things from their choice of site so we try to include a range of campsite 'styles' to cater for a wide variety of preferences: from those seeking a small peaceful campsite in the heart of the countryside, to visitors looking for an 'all singing, all dancing' site in a popular seaside resort. Those with more specific interests, such as sporting facilities, cultural events or historical attractions, are also catered for.

The size of the site, whether it's part of a chain or privately owned, makes no difference in terms of it being required to meet our exacting standards in respect of its quality and it being 'fit for purpose'. In other words, irrespective of the size of the site, or the number of facilities it offers, we consider and evaluate the welcome, the pitches, the sanitary facilities, the cleanliness, the general maintenance and even the location.

Expert opinions

We rely on our dedicated team of Site Assessors, all of whom are experienced campers, caravanners or motorcaravanners, to visit and recommend campsites. Each year they travel some 100,000 miles around Europe inspecting new campsites for the guide and re-inspecting the existing ones. Our thanks are due to them for their enthusiastic efforts, their diligence and integrity.

We also appreciate the feedback we receive from many of our readers and we always make a point of following up complaints, suggestions or recommendations for possible new campsites. Of course we get a few grumbles too – but it really is a few, and those we do receive usually relate to overcrowding or to poor maintenance during the peak school holiday period. Please bear in mind that, although we are interested to hear about any complaints, we have no contractual relationship with the campsites featured in our guides and are therefore not in a position to intervene in any dispute between a reader and a campsite.

Independent and honest

Whilst the content and scope of the Alan Rogers guides have expanded considerably since the early editions, our selection of campsites still employs exactly the same philosophy and criteria as defined by Alan Rogers in 1968.

'telling it how it is'

Firstly, and most importantly, our selection is based entirely on our own rigorous and independent inspection and selection process. Campsites cannot buy their way into our guides – indeed the extensive Site Report which is written by us, not by the site owner, is provided free of charge so we are free to say what we think and to provide an honest, 'warts and all' description. This is written in plain English and without the use of confusing icons or symbols.

Looking for the best

Highly respected by site owners and readers alike, there is no better guide when it comes to forming an independent view of a campsite's quality. When you need to be confident in your choice of campsite, you need the Alan Rogers Guide.

- Sites only included on merit
- Sites cannot pay to be included
- Independently inspected, rigorously assessed
- Impartial reviews
- Almost 50 years of expertise

Written in plain English, our guides are exceptionally easy to use, but a few words of explanation regarding the layout and content may be helpful. This guide is divided firstly by country, subsequently (in the case of Italy) by region. For a particular area the town index at the back provides more direct access.

Index town
Site name
Postal address (including region) T: telephone number. E: email address
alanrogers.com web address (including Alan Rogers reference number)

A description of the site in which we try to give an idea of its general features – its size, its situation, its strengths and its weaknesses. This section should provide a picture of the site itself with reference to the facilities that are provided and if they impact on its appearance or character. We include details on pitch numbers, electricity (with amperage), hardstandings etc. in this section as pitch design, planning and terracing affects the site's overall appearance. Similarly we include reference to pitches used for caravan holiday homes, chalets, and the like. Importantly at the end of this column we indicate if there are any restrictions, e.g. no tents, no children, naturist sites.

Facilities	Directions
Lists more specific information on the site's facilities and amenities and, where available, the dates when these facilities are open (if not for the whole season). Off site: here we give distances to various local amenities, for example, local shops, the nearest beach, plus our featured activities (bicycle hire, fishing, horse riding, boat launching). Where we have space we list suggestions for activities and local tourist attractions.	Separated from the main text in order that they may be read and assimilated more easily by a navigator en-route. Bear in mind that road improvement schemes can result in road numbers being altered.
Open: Site opening dates.	GPS: references are provided in decimal format. All latitudes are North. Longitudes are East unless preceeded by a minus sign e.g. 48.71695 is North, 0.31254 is East and -0.31254 is West.
	Charges guide

Maps, campsite listings and indexes

For this 2016 guide we include a map immediately after our Introduction to each region. These maps show the towns near which one or more of our featured campsites are located.

Within each regional section of the guide, we list these towns and the site(s) in that vicinity in alphabetical order.

You will certainly need more detailed maps for navigation, for example the Michelin atlas. We provide GPS coordinates for each site to assist you. Our indexes will also help you to find a site by region and site name or by the town where the site is situated.

Understanding the entries

Facilities

Toilet blocks

Unless we comment otherwise, toilet blocks will be equipped with WCs, washbasins with hot and cold water and hot showers with dividers or curtains, and will have all necessary shelves, hooks, plugs and mirrors. We also assume that there will be an identified chemical toilet disposal point, and that the campsite will provide water and waste water drainage points and bin areas. If not the case, we comment. We do mention certain features that some readers find important: washbasins in cubicles, facilities for babies, facilities for those with disabilities and motorcaravan service points. Readers with disabilities are advised to contact the site of their choice to ensure that facilities are appropriate to their needs.

Shop

Basic or fully supplied, and opening dates.

Bars, restaurants, takeaway facilities and entertainment

We try hard to supply opening and closing dates (if other than the campsite opening dates) and to identify if there are discos or other entertainment.

Children's play areas

Fenced and with safety surface (e.g. sand, bark or pea-gravel).

Swimming pools

If particularly special, we cover in detail in our main campsite description but reference is always included under our Facilities listings. We will also indicate the existence of water slides, sunbathing areas and other features. Opening dates, charges and levels of supervision are provided where we have been notified. There is a regulation whereby Bermuda shorts may not be worn in swimming pools (for health and hygiene reasons). It is worth ensuring that you do take 'proper' swimming trunks with you.

Leisure facilities

For example, playing fields, bicycle hire, organised activities and entertainment.

Dogs

If dogs are not accepted or restrictions apply, we state it here. Check the quick reference list at the back of the guide.

Off site

This briefly covers leisure facilities, tourist attractions, restaurants etc. nearby.

Charges

These are the latest provided to us by the sites. In those cases where 2016 prices have not been provided to us by the sites, we try to give a general guide.

Reservations

Necessary for high season (July/August) in popular holiday areas. You can reserve many sites via The Caravan Club Travel Service or through other tour operators. Or be wholly independent and contact the campsite(s) of your choice direct. However, do bear in mind that many sites are closed all winter.

Telephone Numbers

Italy: All numbers assume that you are phoning from within Italy. To phone Italy from outside that country, prefix the number shown with the relevant International Code: 00 39. Do NOT drop the first 0 of the area code.

Croatia and Slovenia: The numbers given assume you are actually IN the country concerned. If you are phoning from the UK remember that a first '0' is usually disregarded and replaced by the appropriate country code: Croatia 00 385, Slovenia 00 386.

Non-geographic telephone numbers

In this guide we do not include any numbers that impose an extra charge on callers to that number (e.g. 084x or 03xx). Where Freephone numbers appear (0800 or 0808), calls to these numbers are free of charge.

Opening dates

These are advised to us during the early autumn of the previous year – sites can, and sometimes do, alter these dates before the start of the following season, often for good reasons. If you intend to visit shortly after a published opening date, or shortly before the closing date, it is wise to check that it will actually be open at the time required. Similarly some sites operate a restricted service during the low season, only opening some of their facilities (e.g. swimming pools) during the main season; where we know about this, and have the relevant dates, we indicate it – again if you are at all doubtful it is wise to check.

Sometimes, campsite amenities may be dependent on there being enough customers on site to justify their opening and, for this reason, actual opening dates may vary from those indicated.

Some campsite owners are very relaxed when it comes to opening and closing dates. They may not be fully ready by their stated opening dates – grass and hedges may not all be cut or perhaps only limited sanitary facilities open. At the end of the season they also tend to close down some facilities and generally wind down prior to the closing date. Bear this in mind if you are travelling early or late in the season – it is worth phoning ahead.

The Camping Cheque low season touring system goes some way to addressing this in that many participating campsites will have all key facilities open and running by the opening date and these will remain fully operational until the closing date.

Taking a tent?

In recent years, sales of tents have increased dramatically. With very few exceptions, the campsites listed in this guide have pitches suitable for tents, caravans and motorcaravans. Tents, of course, come in a dazzling range of shapes and sizes. Modern family tents with separate sleeping pods are increasingly popular and these invariably require large pitches with electrical connections. Smaller lightweight tents, ideal for cyclists and hikers, are also visible on many sites and naturally require correspondingly smaller pitches. Many (but not all) sites have special tent areas with prices adjusted accordingly. If in any doubt, we recommend contacting the site of your choice beforehand.

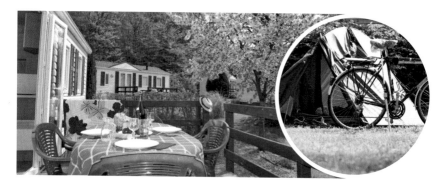

Our Accommodation section

222 Over recent years, more and more campsites have added high quality mobile home and chalet accommodation. In response to feedback from many of our readers, and to reflect this evolution in campsites, we have now decided to include a separate section on mobile homes and chalets. If a site offers this accommodation, it is indicated above the site report with a page reference where full details are given. We have chosen a number of sites offering some of the best accommodation available and have included full details of one or two accommodation types at these sites. Please note however that many other campsites listed in this guide may also have a selection of accommodation for rent.

You're on your way!

Whether you're an 'old hand' in terms of camping and caravanning or are contemplating your first trip, a regular reader of our Guides or a new 'convert', we wish you well in your travels and hope we have been able to help in some way.

We are, of course, also out and about ourselves, visiting sites, talking to owners and readers, and generally checking on standards and new developments.

We wish all our readers thoroughly enjoyable Camping and Caravanning

in 2016 – favoured by good weather of course! The Alan Rogers Team

The Alan Rogers Awards

The Alan Rogers Campsite Awards were launched in 2004 and have proved a great success.

Our awards have a broad scope and before committing to our winners, we carefully consider more than 2,000 campsites featured in our guides, taking into account comments from our site assessors, our head office team and, of course, our readers.

Our award winners come from the four corners of Europe, from Spain to Croatia, and this year we are making awards to campsites in ten different countries.

Needless to say, it's an extremely difficult task to choose our eventual winners, but we believe that we have identified a number of campsites with truly outstanding characteristics.

In each case, we have selected an outright winner, along with two highly commended runners-up. Listed below are full details of each of our award categories and our winners for 2015.

Alan Rogers Progress Award 2015

This award reflects the hard work and commitment undertaken by particular site owners to improve and upgrade their site.

Winner	
ES84800	Camping Resort Sanguli Salou *Spain*

Runners-up	
FR31000	Sites et Paysages Le Moulin *France*
UK2450	The Orchards Holiday Caravan and Camping Park *England*

Alan Rogers Welcome Award 2015

This award takes account of sites offering a particularly friendly welcome and maintaining a friendly ambience throughout readers' holidays.

Winner	
FR35080	Domaine du Logis *France*

Runners-up	
ES88020	Camping Cabopino *Spain*
NL5840	Veluwecamping de Pampel *Netherlands*

Alan Rogers Active Holiday Award 2015

This award reflects sites in outstanding locations which are ideally suited for active holidays, notably walking or cycling, but which could extend to include such activities as winter sports or watersports.

Winner

| AU0180 | Sportcamp Woferlgut *Austria* |

Runners-up

| DE30030 | Camping Wulfener Hals *Germany* |
| IT62040 | Camping Seiser Alm *Italy* |

Alan Rogers Innovation Award 2015

Our Innovation Award acknowledges campsites with creative and original concepts, possibly with features which are unique, and cannot therefore be found elsewhere. We have identified innovation both in campsite amenities and also in rentable accommodation.

Winner

| IT60200 | Camping Union Lido Vacanze *Italy* |

Runners-up

| FR29010 | Castel Camping Ty Nadan *France* |
| FR24350 | RCN Le Moulin de la Pique *France* |

Alan Rogers Small Campsite Award 2015

This award acknowledges excellent small campsites (less than 75 pitches) which offer a friendly welcome and top quality amenities throughout the season to their guests.

Winner

| IT64045 | Camping Tenuta Squaneto *Italy* |

Runners-up

| FR02020 | Camping Les Etangs du Moulin *France* |
| DE34380 | Camping Am Möslepark *Germany* |

Alan Rogers Seaside Award 2015

This award is made for sites which we feel are outstandingly suitable for a really excellent seaside holiday.

Winner

| FR17010 | Camping Bois Soleil *France* |

Runners-up

| NL6870 | Kennemer Duincamping de Lakens *Netherlands* |
| CR6782 | Zaton Holiday Resort *Croatia* |

Alan Rogers Country Award 2015

This award contrasts with our former award and acknowledges sites which are attractively located in delightful, rural locations.

Winner

| AU0265 | Park Grubhof *Austria* |

Runners-up

| FR12160 | Camping Les Peupliers *France* |
| SW2630 | Röstånga Camping & Bad *Sweden* |

Alan Rogers Family Site Award 2015

Many sites claim to be child friendly but this award acknowledges the sites we feel to be the very best in this respect.

Winner

| ES80400 | Camping Las Dunas *Spain* |

Runners-up

| UK0845 | Hillhead Caravan Club Site *England* |
| LU7620 | Europacamping Nommerlayen *Luxembourg* |

Alan Rogers Readers' Award 2015

We believe our Readers' Award to be the most important. We simply invite our readers (by means of an on-line poll at www.alanrogers.com) to nominate the site they enjoyed most.

The outright winner for 2015 is:

Winner

| FR38010 | Camping Le Coin Tranquille *France* |

Our warmest congratulations to all our award winners and our commiserations to all those not having won an award on this occasion.

The Alan Rogers Team

Getting the most from off peak touring

£14.95 night
outfit+ 2people

There are many reasons to avoid high season, if you can. Queues are shorter, there's less traffic, a calmer atmosphere and prices are cheaper. And it's usually still nice and sunny!

And when you use Camping Cheques you'll find great quality facilities that are actually open and a welcoming conviviality.

Did you know?

Camping Cheques can be used right into mid-July and from late August on many sites. Over 90 campsites in France alone accept Camping Cheques from 20th August.

Save up to 60% with Camping Cheques

Camping Cheque is a fixed price scheme allowing you to go as you please, staying on over 600 campsites across Europe, always paying the same rate and saving you up to 60% on regular pitch fees. One Cheque gives you one night for 2 people + unit on a standard pitch, with electricity. It's as simple as that.

Special offers mean you can stay extra nights free (eg 7 nights for 6 Cheques) or even a month free for a month paid! Especially popular in Spain during the winter, these longer-term offers can effectively halve the nightly rate. See Site Directory for details.

Check out our amazing Ferry Deals!

Why should I use Camping Cheques?

- It's a proven system, recognised by all 600+ participating campsites - so no nasty surprises.

- It's flexible, allowing you to travel between campsites, and also countries, on a whim - so no need to pre-book. (It's low season, so campsites are rarely full, though advance bookings can be made).

- Stay as long as you like, where you like - so you travel in complete freedom.

- Camping Cheques are valid at least 2 years - so no pressure to use them up. (If you have a couple left over after your trip, simply keep them for the following year, or use them up in the UK).

Tell me more... (but keep it brief!)

Camping Cheques was started in 1999 and has since grown in popularity each year (nearly 2 million were used last year). That should speak for itself. There are 'copycat' schemes, but none has the same range of quality campsites that save you up to 60%.

Ask for your **FREE** continental road map, which explains how Camping Cheque works
01342 336621

Order your 2016
Directory

Tourist Office

Italian State Tourist Board,
1, Princes Street, London W1B 2AY

Tel: 020 7408 1254 or 09065 508925 (brochures)
Fax: 020 7399 3567

E-mail: italy@italiantouristboard.co.uk
Internet: www.enit.it

Whether you want to explore historical cities, stroll around medieval hill towns, relax on sandy beaches or simply indulge in opera, good food and wine, Italy has it all. Roman ruins, Renaissance art and beautiful churches abound. The Italian Alps are a haven for winter sports and also offer good hiking trails.

Italy only became a unified state in 1861, hence the regional nature of the country today. With 20 distinct regions, each one has retained its own individualism which is evident in the cuisine and local dialects.

In the north, the vibrant city of Milan is great for shopping and home to the famous opera house, La Scala, as well as Leonardo's Last Supper fresco. It is also a good jumping-off point for the Alps; the Italian Lake District, incorporating Lake Garda, Lake Como and Lake Maggiore; the canals of Venice and the lovely town of Verona. Central Italy probably represents the most commonly perceived image of the country and Tuscany, with its classic rolling countryside and the historical towns of Florence, Siena, San Gimignano and Pisa, is one of the most visited areas. Further south are the historical capital of Rome and the city of Naples. Close to some of Italy's ancient sites such as Pompeii, Naples is within easy distance of Sorrento and the Amalfi coast.

Population
58 million

Capital
Rome (Roma)

Climate
The south enjoys extremely hot summers and mild, dry winters, whilst the mountainous regions of the north are cooler with heavy snowfalls in winter.

Language
Italian. There are several dialect forms and some German is spoken near the Austrian border.

Telephone
The country code is 00 39.

Currency
The Euro (€).

Banks
Mon-Fri 08.30-13.00 and 15.00-16.00.

Shops
Mon-Sat 08.30/09.00-13.00 and 15.30/16.00-19.30/20.00, with some variations in larger cities.

Public Holidays
New Year; Easter Mon; Liberation Day 25 Apr; Labour Day; Assumption 15 Aug; All Saints 1 Nov; Immaculate Conception 8 Dec; Christmas 25, 26 Dec; plus numerous special local feast days.

THE REGION IS MADE UP OF THE FOLLOWING PROVINCES: ALESSANDRIA, AOSTA, ASTI, BIELLA, CUNEO, IVREA, NOVARA, VERBANIA AND VERCELLI

Fringed by the French and Swiss Alps in the far north of the country, home to several ski resorts, with vine-clad hills in the south, Piedmont and Valle d'Aosta is renowned for its fine wines and local cuisine.

In the heart of Piedmont is Turin, home to the most famous holy relic of all time, the Turin Shroud, and the Fiat car company. It also boasts a superb Egyptian Museum, Renaissance cathedral, elegant piazzas plus designer shops and good restaurants. In the east, set in a vast plain of paddy fields along the River Po – which stretches right across northern Italy – is Vercelli, the rice capital of Europe. Further south are the wine producing towns of Alba, renowned for its white truffles and red wines; and Asti, the capital of Italy's sparkling wine industry, where the famous spumante is produced. There are numerous wine museums, vineyards and cantinas in the area, from where you can purchase wine, including those at Barolo, Annuziata and Costigliole d'Asti.

Studded with picturesque castles, the Valle d'Aosta offers great walking and skiing country with its dramatic mountains, beautiful valleys and lush meadows, most notably in the Gran Paradiso National Park. This huge park is also home to over 3,000 ibex, a relative of the deer family, 6,000 chamois, plus golden eagles and rare butterflies.

Places of interest

Aosta: attractive mountain town with Roman architecture and ruins.

Avigliana: small town perched beside two lakes surrounded by mountains, medieval houses.

Biella: renowned for its wool industry.

Domodossola: mountain town of Roman origin, arcaded medieval centre, starting point of a scenic train ride across to Switzerland.

Lake Orta: set among the foothills of the Alps, in the middle of the lake rises the Island of San Guilo, with a basilica.

Saluzzo: medieval town, Gothic church, castle.

Susa: medieval town, 11th-century castle and church.

Cuisine of the region

Bagna cauda: local variation on fondue, vegetables dipped into a sauce of oil, anchovies, garlic, cream and butter.

Fontina: a semi-hard cheese made in the Valle d'Aosta.

Manzo al Barolo: lean beef marinated in red wine and garlic and stewed gently.

Soupe à la cogneintze: soup with rice.

Spumone piemontese: a mousse of mascarpone cheese with rum.

Tora di Nocciole: nut tart including hazelnuts, eggs and butter.

Zabaglione: dessert made with a mixture of egg yolk, sugar and Marsala.

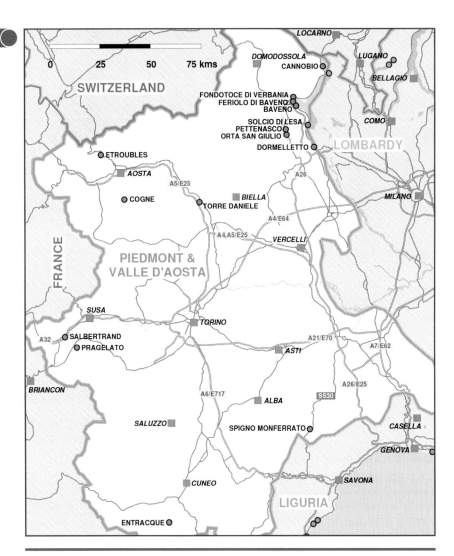

Baveno

Camping Tranquilla

Via Cave-Oltrefiume 2, I-28831 Baveno (Piedmont) T: 0323 923 452. E: info@campingtranquilla.it

alanrogers.com/IT62470

Tranquilla is a quiet family run site on the western slopes above Baveno, close to Lake Maggiore. The site is in two terraced sections, both with 6A electricity connections. The 55 touring pitches vary in size with trees offering plenty of shade. There is a very pleasant swimming pool with an attractive paddling pool. Reception is housed in a modern building together with a small bar and snack bar from where the Piralla family will welcome you. Some English is spoken. The site is an ideal base from which to explore this very attractive area.

Facilities

The sanitary block offers the usual facilities including those for disabled visitors. All are kept very clean. British and Turkish style WCs. Laundry. Motorcaravan services. Pizza ordering service. Swimming pool (10/5-30/9). Play area. Free WiFi over site. Off site: Restaurant 300 m. Fishing and bus service 800 m. Sailing 1.5 km. Golf and bicycle hire 3 km. Riding 3 km. Shops nearby. Excursions and boat trips from Baveno.

Open: 15 March - 15 October.

Directions

Baveno is 90 km. north west of Milan on the western shore of Lake Maggiore, and is on the SS33 road between Arona and Verbania. Site is well signed from SS33 in the northern part of the town. Follow site signs. Do not use sat nav for final approach. GPS: 45.91172, 8.49071

Charges guide

Per unit incl. 2 persons and electricity	€ 21.50 - € 33.50

Special discounts for campers with the latest Alan Rogers guide.

For latest campsite news, availability and prices visit
alanrogers.com

Baveno
Camping Parisi
Via Piave 50, I-28831 Baveno (Piedmont) T: 0323 923 156. E: info@campingparisi.it
alanrogers.com/IT62480

Camping Parisi is a quiet, family run site on the beautiful western shore of Lake Maggiore within the town of Baveno. The small and compact site has just 50 touring pitches, all with 6A electricity, which are shaded by mature trees. The site's real strength is the stunning views over the lake. It is possible to paddle and swim from the lake shore which is also good for sunbathing. A lifeguard is present. An early reservation would be necessary if you wish to occupy one of the lakeside pitches (extra charge, but well worth it!).

Facilities	Directions
Central sanitary facilities are clean with free hot showers and British style WCs but, as yet, no facilities for disabled campers. Washing machine and dryer. No shop (town is 100 m). Coffee machine. Freezer service. Play area. Bar in reception where bookings for local activities are made. Kayaks for hire. WiFi on part of site (free). Chalet and mobile home for hire. Off site: Shops nearby. Bus 200 m. Boat launching 1 km. Riding 3 km. Bicycle hire 4 km.	Baveno is 90 km. north west of Milan on western shore of Lake Maggiore, and on SS33 between Arona and Verbania. From A26 take Baveno exit and turn right on main road to site. GPS: 45.91245, 8.50555

Open: 22 March - 30 September.

Charges guide

Per unit incl. 2 persons and electricity	€ 24.00 - € 38.00
extra person	€ 5.50 - € 8.00

Cannobio
Camping Valle Romantica
Via Valle Cannobina, I-28822 Cannobio (Piedmont) T: 0323 712 49.
E: valleromantica@riviera-valleromantica.com **alanrogers.com/IT62400**

This site really lives up to its name! Situated in a wooded mountain valley, it was established about 60 years ago by the present owner's father, who planted some 20,000 plants, trees and shrubs. These are all now well established and maintained to make a delightful garden setting. The 164 numbered pitches for touring units are on flat grass among the trees, which provide good shade. All have 6/8A electricity, although long cables are necessary in some parts. The site's swimming pool is in a sunny position and there are two areas allowing river access where, except after heavy rain, children can play. The site is used by tour operators (24 pitches) and mobile homes are available to rent.

Facilities	Directions
Three sanitary blocks provide good facilities with free controllable showers. Washing machines. Gas supplies. Motorcaravan services. Small, well stocked supermarket. Pleasant bar/restaurant with waiter service and takeaway. Pizzeria. Swimming pool (1/5-11/9). Fishing (licence required). Sailing and windsurfing schools. Fridge box hire. WiFi throughout (charged). Off site: Bicycle hire, boat launching and sailing 1.5 km. Riding 25 km. Golf 35 km.	Cannobio is 4 km. from the Swiss border on the SS34 Locarno-Verbania road. Follow SS34 through Cannobio turning west, away from lake, at the southern outskirts of Cannobio, just past the church and 100 m. before Total filling station. Continue on 1.5 km. to site. GPS: 46.05758, 8.67737

Open: 18 March - 11 September.

Charges guide

Per unit incl. 2 persons and electricity	€ 32.50 - € 38.50

No credit/debit cards.

Cannobio
Camping Riviera
Via Casali Darbedo 2, I-28822 Cannobio (Piedmont) T: 0323 713 60. E: riviera@riviera-valleromantica.com
alanrogers.com/IT62450

With scenic views across the water and the surrounding mountains, this site is directly on the shore of Lake Maggiore. Under the same ownership as Valle Romantica, the site has a well cared for appearance. Over 250 numbered pitches are on flat grass, either side of hard surfaced access roads and divided by mature trees and shrubs giving good shade. There are 210 with 6A electricity (long cables may be needed). The site could make a suitable base for exploring the area, although progress on the winding lakeside road may be slow!

Facilities	Directions
Five sanitary blocks are of good quality and two of these include facilities for disabled visitors. Washing machines. Fridge boxes for hire. Gas supplies. Motorcaravan services. Well stocked shop. Bar/restaurants with covered terrace, providing waiter service and takeaway. Fishing (licence required). Boat slipway. New playground. WiFi over site (charged). Off site: Cannobio is only a short distance away. Bicycle hire 500 m.	Cannobio is 4 km. from the Swiss border on the SS34 Locarno-Verbania road. The site is north of the town, at the lakeside (on the east). Entrance is a few metres north of the bridge over the river, just before tennis courts. GPS: 46.05753, 8.67764

Open: 18 March - 16 October.

Charges guide

Per unit incl. 2 persons and electricity	€ 32.50 - € 39.50

For latest campsite news, availability and prices visit
alanrogers.com

Cogne

Camping Lo Stambecco

Valnontey, I-11012 Cogne (Valle d'Aosta) T: 0165 741 52. E: info@campeggiolostambecco.it
alanrogers.com/IT62150

Lo Stambecco (the Alpine ibex) is tucked away deep in the Gran Paradiso National Park. After an enthralling scenic mountain drive you will reach this small site with breathtaking views of the mountains and glaciers. The grass pitches are informally arranged on slopes and terraces (levelling aids are useful) and all have great views. Electricity is available (3A Europlug; long leads useful). Clean crisp air, beautiful views, the rushing clear mountain stream and the delightfully informal atmosphere make this a real destination site. You decide whether to hike, bike, raft or simply relax and let it all soak in.

Facilities

The two toilet blocks are mature but clean with a mixture of Turkish and British style WCs. Baby baths to borrow. Washing machine. Motorcaravan services. Bar and lounge with games and library. Torches useful. WiFi (free). Off site: Hotels and restaurants in the charming hamlet 200 m. Tiny but beautiful church. Riding 300 m. Bicycle hire 500 m. Alpine sports. Gran Paradiso National Park. ATM 8 km. Public transport almost opposite with hourly buses to Cogne in season. Mountain lift from Cogne.

Open: 20 May - 20 September.

Directions

Site is south of Aosta. From A5/E25 take Cogne exit south. (From the SS26, take the SR47). A long scenic drive will take you to the Cogne municipality. In town look for the right turn sign to Valnontey where site is clearly signed on the left.
GPS: 45.58855, 7.34293

Charges guide

Per unit incl. 2 persons and electricity	€ 23.00 - € 24.00
extra person	€ 7.00

Dormelletto

Camping Village Lago Maggiore

Via Leonardo da Vinci 7, I-28040 Dormelletto (Piedmont) T: 0322 497 193. E: info@lagomag.com
alanrogers.com/IT62435

This lively and happy site can be found on the south western shores of Lake Maggiore, close to the pretty town of Arona. There are 340 pitches here, the majority of which are occupied by seasonal units leaving around 60 available for touring. Pitches are all equipped with 6A electrical connections and have some shade. A number of mobile homes, apartments and bungalows are available for rent. There is direct access to the lake and sandy beach. Amenities include a well stocked shop and a bar/restaurant and there are many opportunities for sports and organised activities.

Facilities

Five toilet blocks in total, of which two are for touring units and a mix of Turkish and British style (hot water and showers charged). Private family bathrooms for rent. Motorcaravan services. Bar, restaurant/pizzeria. Shop. Games room. Adventure and play areas. Outdoor swimming pools (May-Aug). Beach bar. Children's pool. Sports field. Bicycle hire. Entertainment and activities (high season). Direct access to lake. Mobile homes and chalets for rent. WiFi on part of site (charged).

Open: 1 April - 30 September.

Directions

Leave the A26 motorway at the Sesto Calende exit and join the northbound SS33 as far as Dormelletto. The campsite is clearly signed from the village.
GPS: 45.73333, 8.57722

Charges guide

Per unit incl. 2 persons and electricity	€ 24.50 - € 44.00
extra person	€ 5.50 - € 9.50

Credit cards accepted in high season only.

Entracque

Camping Valle Gesso

Str. Provinciale per Valdieri 3, I-12010 Entracque (Piedmont) T: 0171 978 247.
E: info@campingvallegesso.com alanrogers.com/IT65030

Valle Gesso is situated in Entracque, a village near Cuneo in southern Piedmont. It borders on the Parco Naturale delle Alpi Marittime, the largest protected area in Piedmont and one of the biggest in Italy. There are 137 touring pitches, 70 of these have 3-6A Europlug, water and drainage. A dedicated area accommodates up to 70 tents. Rarely do we come across a site which appeals to such a wide variety of holiday styles. Valle Gesso offers a magnificent pool, a football and volleyball field, hiking and cycling for the more active, whilst maintaining a totally natural mountain retreat for those seeking a restful break.

Facilities

There are three sanitary blocks, one new, one below the pool and one in a utility building. All are kept very clean and offer a mixture of British and Turkish style WCs. Motorcaravan services. Laundry. Basic shop and bar (July/Aug). Three section swimming pool and whirlpool (July/Aug). Large screen TV. Video games. Billiard table. Playground and woods for exploring. Football. Volleyball. Communal barbecue. Bicycle hire. WiFi over site (free).

Open: All year.

Directions

From Turin, take A6 and A33 to Cuneo, then at Borgo S.D. turn onto S26 for Entracque. From south, use SS20 and turn at Borgo S.D. Site signed just after Valdieri. GPS: 44.25076, 7.38994

Charges guide

Per unit incl. 2 persons and electricity	€ 22.00 - € 28.80
extra person	€ 6.00 - € 7.50

For latest campsite news, availability and prices visit
alanrogers.com

Etroubles

Camping Tunnel

Via Chevrieres 4, I-11014 Etroubles (Valle d'Aosta) T: 016 578 292. E: info@campingtunnel.it

alanrogers.com/IT62160

This is a small, friendly site located near the southern exit of the Gran San Bernardo tunnel. The views from the site are really very pleasant with green hills and towering peaks all around. There is a distinct Italian feel about it and the young English-speaking owners, Silvia and Roberto, are most welcoming and helpful. The site sits on two sides of a quiet road and steady improvements are being made. There are 95 pitches, with 45 of mixed size for touring units, plus a special overnight area for motorcaravans, opposite the main gate. All have electricity (6A Europlug) with drainage and water taps nearby. Gas connections are also available. Some have shade and most are on terraces or gentle slopes.

Facilities

The main toilet block is beneath the restaurant building and has recently been refurbished, while the smaller block is central to the upper part of the site. WCs are mixed British and Turkish styles. Showers are modern in one block, outdoor in the other. Good facilities for disabled visitors. Laundry room with washer/dryer and baby changing. Motorcaravan services. Bar and restaurant (1/6-15/9). New lounge with TV, games and library. Torches and long leads useful. Playground. Pétanque. Communal barbecue. WiFi (charged). Nightstop area for motorcaravans with electricity and access to toilets. Off site: Fishing 2 km. Golf 7 km. Riding 16 km. Walking, climbing. Skiing in season. Historic village of Etroubles.

Open: All year. Closed two weeks Jan. and three in May and November (phone to confirm dates).

Directions

From A5-E25 take Aosta turn and travel north on E27 towards Col de Gran San Bernardo. At Etroubles, site is signed on left, on a bend, just before the bridge. From the north, ignore first Campeggi sign as you descend the hill. In the village, cross river bridge, turn immediately right. GPS: 45.81840, 7.22891

Charges guide

Per person	€ 6.00 - € 6.50
child (3-11 yrs)	€ 4.50 - € 5.00
pitch incl. electricity	€ 11.00 - € 14.00
dog	€ 2.50 - € 3.00

Feriolo di Baveno

Camping Holiday

Via 42 Martiri 28, I-28835 Feriolo di Baveno (Piedmont) T: 0323 281 64. E: welcome@camping-holiday.info

alanrogers.com/IT02400

Camping Holiday is located on Lake Maggiore's western shores, close to the resort of Baveno and larger town of Stresa. This is a small site with direct access to a sandy beach. There are just 41 touring pitches, all of which are equipped with 6A electricity and satellite TV connections. Premium pitches are available with direct lake access. A number of pitches with shade are suitable for small tents and eight mobile homes are available to rent. Although the site is small, there is a bar/restaurant and a well stocked shop. A cycle track leads from the site to the village of Feriolo, 600 m. away, and beyond to Baveno. Lake Maggiore is rightly renowned for its lush gardens and magnificent mountain scenery. The Borromean islands are a popular excursion and easily accessible from Stresa.

Facilities

The single, clean sanitary block has both British and Turkish style toilets and good showers. Bar with terrace and shop (all season). Direct access to lake and sandy beach. Small play area. Boat launching. Fishing. WiFi on part of site (charged). Riding and bicycle hire. Off site: Feriolo 600 m. Golf 2 km. Baveno 3 km. Stresa 7 km. Walking and cycle routes. Watersports. Fishing.

Open: 20 April - 22 September.

Directions

Leave the A26 motorway at the Casale exit and join the eastbound S33 as far as Feriolo. Site is clearly signed from the village. GPS: 45.93602, 8.48635

Charges guide

Per unit incl. 2 persons and electricity	€ 30.00 - € 55.00
extra person	€ 5.00 - € 8.00
child (2-12 yrs)	€ 4.50 - € 7.00
dog	€ 3.00 - € 6.00

For latest campsite news, availability and prices visit

alanrogers.com

Feriolo di Baveno
Camping Orchidea

Via Quarantadue Martiri 20, I-28831 Feriolo di Baveno (Piedmont) T: 032 328 257.
E: info@campingorchidea.it **alanrogers.com/IT62465**

Camping Orchidea is an immaculate family owned site on the western bank of Lake Maggiore, 35 km. south of the Swiss border and 8 km. from Stresa. This site has direct access to the lake and the banks of the River Stronetta, and has a sandy beach. Orchidea has a good range of modern amenities, including a shop, bar and restaurant. Watersports are understandably popular here and pedaloes and kayaks can be rented on site. The 234 touring pitches are grassy and generally well shaded, all with 6A electrical connections. Some pitches are available facing the lake (a supplement is charged in mid and peak season). There are apartments and mobile homes available for rent. Stresa, nearby, is an important town with 5,000 inhabitants and has a harbour with regular boat trips to the Borromean islands, and also a cable car to the summit of Monte Mottarone, passing the stunning Giardino Botanico Alpinia, world renowned mountain gardens. This site would suit families who prefer a simple and peaceful holiday.

Facilities

Two toilet blocks are kept clean and have hot and cold water throughout. Special facilities for children and provision for disabled visitors. Laundry facilities. Shop. Restaurant. Bar. Takeaway. Direct lake access. Pedalo and kayak hire. Fishing. Boat launching. Playground. Children's club. Mobile homes for hire. Bicycle hire. WiFi on part of site (charged). Off site: Walking and cycle trails. Tennis. Golf 3 km. Stresa 5 km. Riding 15 km. Excursions.

Open: 19 March - 9 October.

Directions

Take the Baveno/Stresa exit from the A26 (autostrada dei Trafori) and head north on the Via Sempione. In Feriolo follow signs to the campsite. GPS: 45.9334, 8.4812

Charges guide

Per unit incl. 2 persons	
and electricity	€ 21.00 - € 44.50
extra person	€ 5.20 - € 9.20
child (2-12 yrs)	€ 3.60 - € 6.10
dog	€ 2.60 - € 5.50

PIEMONTE
NUOVO PER SEMPRE
REGIONE
PIEMONTE

camping Residence
ORCHIDEA
FERIOLO

Lago Maggiore

via 42 Martiri, 20
Feriolo di Baveno
28831 (VB)
tel +39 0323 28257
fax +39 0323 28573
info@campingorchidea.it

www.campingorchidea.it
www.residenceorchidea.net

Feriolo di Baveno
Camping Miralago

Via 42 Martiri 24, I-28831 Feriolo di Baveno (Piedmont) T: 0323 282 26. E: welcome@camping-miralago.info
alanrogers.com/IT62464

Miralago is a small site located on the western banks of Lake Maggiore and the bank of the Stronetta river where it runs into the lake, offering many waterfront pitches. It is very close to the little resort of Feriolo which can be accessed via a cycle track. There are 72 neat and easily accessed touring pitches here, all of which have 6A electricity connections. Miralago is a simple site with few on-site amenities and would suit those who prefer a quiet and peaceful holiday without all the entertainment and activities of the larger sites.

Facilities

A single sanitary block provides a mix of British and Turkish style toilets and facilities for disabled visitors. Shop. Bar with terrace (all season). Play area. Direct access to lake and sandy beach. Boat launching ramp. WiFi on part of site (charged). Off site: Feriolo and riding 500 m. Golf and bicycle hire 2 km. Baveno 3 km. Stresa 7 km. Walking and cycle routes. Watersports. Fishing.

Open: 1 April - 3 October.

Directions

Leave the A26 motorway at the Casale exit and join the eastbound S33 as far as Feriolo. Site is clearly signed from the village. GPS: 45.93388, 8.48471

Charges guide

Per unit incl. 2 persons	
and electricity	€ 23.00 - € 40.00
extra person	€ 5.00 - € 8.00
child (3-12 yrs)	€ 4.50 - € 6.50
dog	€ 4.50 - € 6.00
Low season discounts.	

Feriolo di Baveno
Camping Conca d'Oro

Via 42 Martiri 26, I-28835 Feriolo di Baveno (Piedmont) T: 0323 281 16. E: info@concadoro.it
alanrogers.com/IT62485

Conca d'Oro is a delightful site with spectacular views across Lake Maggiore to the distant mountains. The first impression is one of spaciousness and colour. There are 13 mobile homes for rent, the rest of the 210 grass plots provide good sized touring pitches. All have 6A electrical connections, some have shade and many have spectacular views, especially at night. The land slopes gently down to a fine sandy beach. An attractive terraced restaurant serves a range of regional dishes and there is a pleasant bar and pizzeria plus a well stocked shop. The owners, Maurizio and Alessandra, are sure to give you a warm welcome. The site is close to the lakeside town of Baveno from where boat trips are available to the three small islands on this part of Lake Maggiore. Fishing is possible from the beach at the site (only in evenings, licence required), with sailing and other watersports available. There are nature reserves nearby and the surrounding mountains provide opportunities for walkers, cyclists and climbers.

Facilities

Three toilet blocks provide all necessary facilities kept in immaculate condition, including controllable showers and open style washbasins; some toilets with washbasins. En-suite unit for disabled visitors. Laundry. Motorcaravan services. Bar, restaurant, pizzeria and shop. Swimming, fishing and boat launching from beach. Bicycle hire. Dogs must be pre-booked and are not allowed 5/7-22/8. WiFi over site (charged). Off site: Shops, bars and restaurants. Riding 700 m. Golf 1 km. Sailing 7 km. Excursions to nearby attractions.

Open: 26 March - 29 September.

Directions

Baveno is 90 km. north west of Milan on the western shore of Lake Maggiore. Site is off the SS33 road between Baveno and Fondotoce di Verbania, 1 km. south of the junction with the SS34 and is well signed. GPS: 45.93616, 8.48649

Charges guide

Per unit incl. 2 persons	
and electricity	€ 25.00 - € 45.00
extra person	€ 5.40 - € 9.80
child (6-11 yrs)	€ 3.80 - € 6.90
dog	€ 3.80 - € 4.90

Fondotoce di Verbania
Camping Lido Toce

Via per Feriolo 41, I-28924 Fondotoce di Verbania (Piedmont) T: 0323 496 220. E: info@campinglidotoce.eu
alanrogers.com/IT62455

This small family owned site is the type that some will love – camping as a back-to-nature experience. The facilities here are of a very high quality and the Perucchini family team, with 50 years' experience, are all very keen to make your stay enjoyable. The 80 touring pitches are between 80-140 sq.m, with 6A electricity and larger outfits can access the site easily. There is plenty of shade and greenery, and the beach frontage is attractive with fine views. There is much to do in the local area.

Facilities

Two sanitary blocks with spotless, modern facilities. Good showers. Baby room. Facilities for disabled visitors. Washing machines. Motorcaravan services. Small shop. Bar. Takeaway (from April). Play area with climbing frames. Beach frontage onto lake. River alongside (through small wood). WiFi over part of site (charged). Off site: Riding 500 m. Public bus 1 km. Golf 3 km. Bicycle hire 9 km. Excursions to tourist attractions.

Open: Mid March - mid October.

Directions

Leave A26 autostrada at the Casale exit and join the eastbound S33 as far as Feriolo. Site is signed from village and is on the right just before crossing the river bridge. GPS: 45.939232, 8.485774

Charges guide

Per unit incl. 2 persons	
and electricity	€ 15.00 - € 32.00
extra person	€ 4.90 - € 6.80
child (3-13 yrs)	€ 3.50 - € 5.00
dog	€ 1.50 - € 4.00

For latest campsite news, availability and prices visit
alanrogers.com

Fondotoce di Verbania
Camping Continental Lido
Via 42 Martiri 156, I-28924 Fondotoce di Verbania (Piedmont) T: 0323 496 300.
E: info@campingcontinental.com **alanrogers.com/IT62490**

Continental Lido is a large, bustling site situated on the shore of the charming little Lake Mergozzo, about one kilometre from the better known Lake Maggiore. The 343 average size touring pitches are back to back in rows on grass and although a little close together, the rest of the site has a more open feel. All have 6A electricity, TV connections, water, drainage and there is some shade. There are also 287 mobile homes and 14 apartments available to rent. There is an impressive pool complex and a small sandy beach slopes gently into the lake where swimming and watersports can also be enjoyed (no powered craft may be used). A bustling entertainment programme is provided, centred around a very large amphitheatre. Pine-clad mountains and a pretty village directly opposite the beach provide a pleasing, scenic background. An unusual feature here is the nine-hole golf course. There is a busy programme of activities from May to September. Under the same ownership as Camping Village Isolino, this site is managed by the son, Gian Paolo, who speaks good English.

Facilities

Five high standard toilet blocks have free hot water. Facilities for disabled visitors. Washing machines and dryers. Mini-fridges. Well stocked shop and bar/restaurant with terrace and takeaway. Swimming pool complex (23/4-18/9) with slides, rapids and waves, plus free sun loungers and parasols. Snack bars by pool and lake. Large amphitheatre. TV. Tennis. Golf course (9 holes). Playground. Fishing. Windsurfing, pedaloes, canoes, kayaks. Games room. Bicycle hire. Entertainment and activities (24/3-3/4 and 23/4-18/9). Bus on request to Verbania. Internet access and free WiFi. Bookings for dogs must be made in high season. Off site: Riding 1 km. Sailing 5 km. 18-hole golf 12 km. Excursions.

Open: 23 March - 19 September.

Directions

Verbania is 100 km. north west of Milan, on western shore of Lake Maggiore. Site is off the SS34 road between Fondotoce and Gravellona, 200 m. west of junction with SS33. GPS: 45.94960, 8.48058

Charges guide

Per unit incl. 2 or 3 persons	
and electricity	€ 22.65 - € 54.75
extra person	€ 5.95 - € 9.35
child (6-11 yrs)	€ 4.00 - € 7.70

Fondotoce di Verbania
Camping Village Isolino
Via per Feriolo 25, I-28924 Fondotoce di Verbania (Piedmont) T: 0323 496 080. E: info@isolino.com
alanrogers.com/IT62460

Lake Maggiore is one of the most attractive Italian lakes and Isolino is an impressive site and one of the largest in the region. Most of the 442 touring pitches have shade from a variety of trees. They vary in size, all have 6A electrical connections, 216 with water, drainage and satellite TV, some with lake views. The bar and restaurant terraces overlook the very large, lagoon-style swimming pool with its island sun deck area, water games and a canyon river, and stunning views across the lake to the fir-clad mountains beyond. Often the social life of the campsite is centred around the large bar/terrace which has a small stage inside, sometimes used for musical entertainment. A huge and impressive amphitheatre is where an extensive programme of activities and entertainment takes place throughout the season. The large poolside terrace outside the bar provides an ideal casual eating area for pizzas and ice cream. In the restaurant on the floor above you can enjoy an excellent menu and the magnificent views across the lake. The site is well situated for visiting the many attractions of the region which include the famous gardens on the Borromeo islands in the lake and at the Villa Taranto, Verbania. The site is owned by the friendly Manoni family who also own Camping Continental Lido at nearby Lake Mergozzo.

Facilities

Six well built toilet blocks have hot water for showers and washbasins but cold for dishwashing and laundry. Good baby room. Laundry facilities. Motorcaravan services. Supermarket, bar and takeaway. Boutique. Gelateria. Swimming pool (23/4-18/9). Entertainment (24/3-3/4 and 23/4-18/9). Amphitheatre. Football field. Tennis court. Table tennis. Fishing. Watersports. Boat launching. Bicycle hire and guided mountain bike tours. Long beach. Free WiFi on part of site. Good English is spoken. Bookings for dogs must be made in high season. Off site: Golf 2 km. Sailing 5 km. Riding 12 km. Swiss mountains and resort of Locarno.

Open: 23 March - 19 September.

Directions

Verbania is 100 km. north west of Milan on the western shore of Lake Maggiore. From A26 motorway, leave at exit for Stresa/Baveno, turn left towards Fondotoce. Site is well signed off the SS33 north of Baveno and 300 m. south of the junction with the SS34 at Fondotoce. GPS: 45.93835, 8.50008

Charges guide

Per unit incl. 3 persons	
and electricity	€ 28.25 - € 56.60
extra person	€ 4.10 - € 9.35
child (6-11 yrs)	€ 4.00 - € 7.90
dog	€ 4.00 - € 9.35

For latest campsite news, availability and prices visit
alanrogers.com

Fondotoce di Verbania

Camping la Quiete

Via Turati 72, I-28040 Fondotoce di Verbania (Piedmont) T: 0323 496 013. E: info@campinglaquiete.it

alanrogers.com/IT62495

La Quiete is a small site, attractively located on the shore of Lake Mergozzo, a small lake to the west of the much larger Lake Maggiore. There are 180 pitches here, mostly well shaded and with 6A electrical connections, many of which have fine views across the lake. A number of mobile homes are available for rent. On-site amenities include a shop and bar/restaurant, as well as a sports field and volleyball court. This is excellent mountain biking and walking country and the site owners will be pleased to recommend possible routes, although little English is spoken. The site does appear to be predominantly used by Italian families.

Facilities

Three small, clean and modern sanitary facilities are well placed along the length of the site. Washing machines. Bar/restaurant. Shop. Sports field. Games room. Play area. Direct access to Lake Mergozzo. WiFi on part of site (charged). Off site: Verbania. Golf and riding 1 km. Bicycle hire 5 km. Lake Maggiore. Watersports. Fishing. Motorboats are not allowed on the lake. Walking and cycle routes.

Open: Easter - 20 September.

Directions

Leave the A26 motorway at the Casale exit and join the eastbound S34 as far as Fondotoce. Head north here on SP54 and the campsite is clearly signed. GPS: 45.9535, 8.47745

Charges guide

Per unit incl. 2 persons and electricity	€ 17.00 - € 42.00
extra person	€ 5.50 - € 9.50
child (0-12 yrs)	free - € 6.00

Orta San Giulio

Camping Orta

Via Domodossola 28, I-28016 Orta San Giulio (Piedmont) T: 0322 902 67. E: info@campingorta.it

alanrogers.com/IT62420

Lake Orta is a delightful, less visited small lake just west of Lake Maggiore. The site is on a considerable slope and most of the 90 touring pitches (all with 6A electricity) are on the top grass terrace with spectacular views across the lake to the mountains beyond. There are some superb lakeside pitches across the main road (linked by a pedestrian underpass) although there is some traffic noise here. Amenities include a large games and entertainment room and a traditional Italian bar and restaurant serving good value family meals. Some English is spoken by the Guarnori family, who take pride in maintaining their uncomplicated site to a high standard. Book ahead to enjoy the lakeside pitches. If you are anxious about towing a large caravan to the top terraces, the owner will help out with his tractor!

Facilities

Four modern sanitary blocks are clean and well maintained providing mainly British style toilets, coin operated showers and an excellent unit for disabled visitors. Laundry facilities. Motorcaravan services. Good quality shop, bar and restaurant with basic menu serving good value Italian family meals (also takeaway, all season). Playground. Large games/TV room. WiFi in reception/bar area (charged). Fishing. Bicycle hire. Boat launching. Lake swimming and watersports. Accommodation to rent all year. Off site: Riding and sailing 4 km. Golf 10 km.

Open: 1 March - 31 December.

Directions

Lake Orta is 85 km. north west of Milan, just west of Lake Maggiore. Site is on the SR229 between Borgomanero and Omega, 600 m. north of the turn to Orta San Giulio. Parking area for arrivals is on lake side of the road, with reception and main entrance on the opposite side. GPS: 45.80188, 8.42047

Charges guide

Per unit incl. 2 persons and electricity	€ 23.50 - € 40.10
extra person	€ 5.75 - € 8.80
child (3-11 yrs)	€ 4.25 - € 5.75
dog	€ 3.70 - € 5.75

For latest campsite news, availability and prices visit
alanrogers.com

Pettenasco
Camping Royal

Via Pratolungo, 32, I-28028 Pettenasco (Piedmont) T: 0323 888 945. E: info@campingroyal.com
alanrogers.com/IT62419

It would be difficult to find a more beautiful lake than Orta, surrounded by wooded hills and mountains and fringed with ancient towns and villages. Camping Royal, family owned and run, sits on a hillside overlooking the lake. There are 60 pitches, 20 for touring, set on level terraces, each with 5A Europlug and a water point nearby. Although professionally managed, this site has maintained the typical relaxed informality for which Italy is famous. Popular with campers from all over Europe, many return year after year. Nothing seems to be too much trouble to ensure a memorable stay. A new pool was installed in 2014, which will make this site even better for family holidays, but there may be noise in high season. At other times, those seeking a relaxing holiday will enjoy sitting out overlooking the lake. The shop and bar are well stocked, and a village restaurant is 100 m. away. Bigger shopping will need a trip to Omegna. In season, the site runs a shuttle service (€ 2 return) to Orta San Giulio, whose history goes back to the 7th Century. The monastery and basilica on the Isola San Giulio should not be missed. Rates are very attractive, especially off peak.

Facilities

Refurbished toilet block has hot showers (20c tokens) and a mixture of British and Turkish style toilets. New wet room for disabled campers by reception. Washing machine and dryer. Laundry and dishwashing sinks. Fridges. Shop with takeaway pizzas. Bar. New swimming pool. Playground. Football field. Room with games, library, cooking hobs and TV. Children's activities (daily in July/August) and some entertainment for adults. Shuttle bus to San Giulio in season (€ 2 return). Bicycle, scooter and car hire arranged. Internet cabin. WiFi (charged). Off site: Restaurant 100 m. Supermarkets in Omegna. Ancient villages and towns all around the lakeshore. Medieval town of Orta and the Isola San Giulio. Ferry boats and boat cruises. Watercraft hire. Lake swimming. Fishing 3 km. Riding 6 km. Golf 15 km.

Open: 1 March - 30 November.

Directions

From A26 Autostrada, take SP229 and follow signs to Lake Orta. This road continues along eastern shore of lake to Pettenasco. Opposite church on left, turn right signed Camping Royal. Some sat navs miss this turn. Do not go past Pettenasco, as back road to site is extremely narrow with sharp bends. From the north, drive into village and turn left opposite church. Road up to site is steep and needs care (unsuitable for units over 7 m). GPS: 45.82331, 8.41398

Charges guide

Per unit incl. 2 persons and electricity	€ 24.00 - € 34.50
extra person	€ 6.00 - € 8.50
child (2-12 yrs)	€ 4.50 - € 6.00
dog	€ 4.00 - € 5.00

BETWEEN LANDSCAPE AND NATURE

Located just a few miles from Orta San Giulio, an area of 15,000 m2 terraced, in a quiet and panoramic zone. It has 60 spacious pitches, surrounded by hedges and green areas. Open from March to November, suitable for lovers of the lake (3 km) and mountain (Mottarone 15 km), ideal for families it is also a meeting point for young people. It offers services such as a grocery shop, bar, swimming pool, soccer field, playground, meeting room with summer entertainment, internet point, library, barbecue area and bicycle hire. Restaurant and pizzeria are next door. Free bus service with Alan Rogers guide to Orta San Giulio and beaches.

Pragelato
Gofree Villaggio Turistico Camping

Via Nazionale 52, I-10060 Pragelato (Piedmont) T: 0122 780 45. E: info@villaggiogofree.com
alanrogers.com/IT65050

Gofree, an unusual name for a campsite, is owned by Patrizia Laurent. She will be pleased to welcome you to this site which is primarily an alpine chalet village. It is open all year for touring and the supporting facilities are of a high quality for all to enjoy. It is one of the very few camping sites hereabouts. The 40 undefined pitches with 10A electricity are sited in three separate, level areas close to the site entrance. Tents are placed in a separate area. A two storey modern building houses reception, a good restaurant and a bar which are at your disposal all year.

Facilities

One modern, well appointed, very clean sanitary block. British style WCs. Basic facilities for disabled visitors. Washing machines. Two bungalows for hire, adapted for visitors with disabilities. Pleasant bar, restaurant/pizzeria and takeaway (July/Aug, Dec-March). Small play area. Regular bus service at gate. Electric barbecues permitted. WiFi in bar. Ski chalets for hire. Off site: Fishing 100 m. Town and bicycle hire 1 km. Riding 2 km. Golf 3 km. All mountain sports including skiing. Shuttle bus to ski lifts in Pragelato from the site.

Open: All year.

Directions

Site is west of Torino and south east of the Fréjus tunnel exit. From A32 take S24 towards Sestriere. Pass Sestriere and head east for Torino on the R23. Site is 8 km. along this road just past the village of Pragelato and well signed. GPS: 45.01667, 6.93333

Charges guide

| Per unit incl. 2 persons and electricity | € 15.00 - € 21.50 |
| person (over 8 yrs) | € 8.00 |

For latest campsite news, availability and prices visit
alanrogers.com

Salbertrand

Camping Gran Bosco

SS 24 del Monginevro km 75, I-10050 Salbertrand (Piedmont) T: 0122 854 653. E: info@campinggranbosco.it
alanrogers.com/IT65000

This is a modern and efficiently run site very near the Fréjus tunnel. The site was chosen to host guests for the winter Olympics of 2006, thus the amenities are very good in an area of notoriously poor campsites. A family site, now being run by the keen younger generation, Gran Bosco has many attractive features, including a smart bar/restaurant with terrace within the clean, modern building just inside the entrance, and everything is open all year. The 60 undefined touring pitches are at both ends of the site, all have 6A electricity and are on flat ground with some shade. Long leads may be required. Some entertainment is offered in July and August and there is also a popular children's club operated by professionals. This is a great site for visiting the area, skiing in winter or just taking a break before tackling the Fréjus tunnel or relaxing after the taxing journey.

Facilities

Two modern, well appointed toilet blocks (with piped music) are well placed on the site. Clean WCs are mainly Turkish with some British style. Showers are excellent. Superb facilities for disabled visitors. Washing machines. Motorcaravan services. Large bar and pleasant restaurant open every day and used by local people. Play area. Games/wet weather room. Entertainment in high season. Children's club. Electric barbecues are not permitted. WiFi close to reception. Torches useful. Off site: Public transport 100 m. Distance to beach and fishing 1 km. Bicycle hire and ATM 3 km. Riding and skiing in season 5 km. Golf 20 km.

Open: All year.

Directions

Site is east of the Italian exit of the Fréjus tunnel. From A32 Torino-Fréjus autoroute take Oulx East exit. Turn east towards Turin on the SS24 and site is at km. 75 which is 2 km. from the Oulx exit. GPS: 45.06187, 6.866667

Charges guide

Per unit incl. 2 persons and electricity	€ 27.00
extra person (over 3 yrs)	€ 8.00
child (under 3 yrs)	free

Solcio di Lesa

Camping Solcio

Via al Campeggio, I-28040 Solcio di Lesa (Piedmont) T: 0322 749 7. E: info@campingsolcio.com
alanrogers.com/IT62440

Camping Solcio is a family run site on the lakeside and has lovely views over the lakes and the surrounding green hills. The 105 neat touring pitches are 60-90 sq.m. with 6A electricity and mostly shaded by trees. A very pleasant restaurant and a bar back onto a large building alongside the site, and there are some views of the lake from the terraces. All manner of watersports are available here and the beach is of coarse sand. The lake is fine for safe swimming. An ambitious entertainment programme is arranged for children in high season, and there is adventure sport for the over tens. This is a pleasant site with modest facilities and it may suit those who do not seek the luxuries of the larger sites. English and Dutch are spoken and the site is very popular with Dutch campers.

Facilities

One main central toilet block is smart and clean. Toilets here are British style. An older block nearer reception has mixed Turkish and British style toilets. Facilities for disabled visitors. Baby room. Washing machine and dryer. Restaurant and bar with terrace. Basic shop. Full entertainment programme in season. Play areas. Baby club. Slipway for boat launching. WiFi throughout (charged). Torches useful. Off site: Public transport 50 m. Town facilities 1 km. ATM 2 km. Riding 5 km. Golf 10 km.

Open: 7 March - 20 October.

Directions

Site is on the west side of Lake Maggiore. From A4 (Milan-Torino) take the A8 to Castelletto Sticino. Then north on SS33 towards Stresa and look for site sign in town of Lesa. Take the access road towards the lake and to the site. GPS: 45.81586, 8.54962

Charges guide

Per unit incl. 2 persons and electricity	€ 25.00 - € 29.00
extra person	€ 5.70 - € 8.90
child (3-11 yrs)	€ 4.90 - € 6.80
dog	€ 3.80 - € 8.70
Low season discounts.	

For latest campsite news, availability and prices visit
alanrogers.com

Spigno Monferrato
Camping Tenuta Squaneto

Frazione Squaneto, I-15018 Spigno Monferrato (Piedmont) T: 014 491 862.
E: info@tenutasquaneto.it **alanrogers.com/IT64045**

After years of experience in the camping industry, Barbara and Pieter Witschge have built their dream – Tenuta Squaneto, natural camping with brilliant facilities. It is deep in the countryside with no villages, shops or restaurants in the immediate area. The 68 grassy, level touring pitches (100-120 sq.m) have wonderful views and 35 have water, waste water and TV connections. The site is in a small valley with trees all around, there is a river to walk along, fish or simply swim and play in. A lovely lake is central to the site and the nearby swimming pool is stunning with a large whirlpool and a children's shallow play pool with wonderful frogs and turtles that spray water. Tenuta Squaneto is a tranquil site; background noise comes mainly from insects and birds. The experience here is about the beauty of the setting and how good it is to be in harmony with nature. The surrounding countryside is idyllic and it is hard to imagine anyone not embracing the experience at Tenuta Squaneto.

Facilities

Two sparkling new sanitary blocks offer full and luxurious facilities including those for disabled visitors. Some pitches have private facilities including cooker, fridge and luxury facilities (small extra daily charge). Fresh bread available to order. Quality restaurant and bar. Attractive swimming pool and paddling pool. Large children's play area. Beach volleyball. Barbecues allowed subject to local restrictions. Cooking groups in low season, wine tastings in high season. River swimming. WiFi in reception (free). Off site: The famous Acqui Terme thermal baths and the Monferrato wine region are close by. Riding 7 km. Golf 20 km. River fishing 30 m. Walking and cycling routes.

Open: End April - end September.

Directions

From north (Milan) take A7 for Genova then A21 towards Torino and the exit for Alessandria South. Take R30 to Acqui Terme and then Sivona. Site is signed at 25 km. on R30 at Spigno Monferrato. Follow site signs and after 7 km. turn right for a further 5 km, through village of Squaneto. Do not use sat nav after Spigno Monferrato. GPS: 44.488978, 8.347126

Charges guide

Per unit incl. 2 persons and electricity	€ 23.00 - € 40.00
extra person (over 2 yrs)	€ 7.50
dog	€ 4.00

Torre Daniele
Camping Mombarone

Settimo Vittone Reg., I-10010 Torre Daniele (Piedmont) T: 0125 757 907. E: info@campingmombarone.it
alanrogers.com/IT62200

This is a small, friendly, all-year site alongside the SS26 road and close to the motorway from the Mont Blanc tunnel and the Saint Bernard Pass, providing a useful stop if entering or leaving Italy via these routes. It has 130 pitches accommodating about 50 touring units on the grass areas between the permanent units. The Peretto family take pride in looking after their guests and English is spoken. The site has a small bar and a simple, inexpensive restaurant is 50 metres away. The site is thoughtfully laid out in a valley with attractive plants, shrubs and trees for shade and is surrounded by high mountains and wooded hills, with vines bedecking the eastern slopes. If you are here in October help the family pick their own grapes, make the wine (in the Nebbiolo style) and share the fun; the wine is sold at the bar – it is rather good! Being close to main roads, there is inevitably some traffic noise.

Facilities

The sanitary facilities are adequate and kept clean, with both British and Turkish style toilets and free hot showers. A new, high quality toilet block with facilities for disabled visitors has been opened on the upper level of the site. Washing machine and dryer. Bar (Easter-30/9). Outdoor free-standing pool (1/6-31/8). Free bicycle hire. Fishing. WiFi (free). Off site: Shops and restaurants nearby. Casino opposite. Riding 5 km. Golf 30 km. Just north is the ancient Forte di Bard, an old fortress, now a museum.

Open: All year.

Directions

Settimo Vittone is 75 km. north of Turin. From A5 motorway take Quincinetto exit onto SS26 turning right; the site is almost immediately on the left. On SS26 Aosta-Turin road, the site is between the 45 and 46 km. markers between Pont St Martin and Settimo Vittone. GPS: 45.5655, 7.8157

Charges guide

Per person	€ 6.00
child (under 10 yrs)	€ 4.50
pitch	€ 3.00 - € 6.00
electricity	€ 2.50

Major credit cards now accepted.

For latest campsite news, availability and prices visit
alanrogers.com

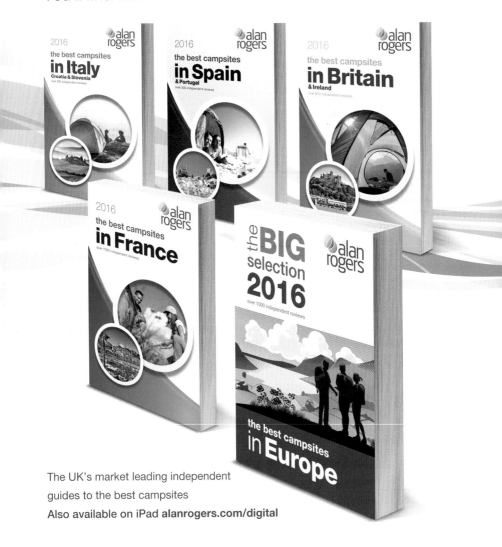

THE REGION HAS FOUR PROVINCES: GENOVA, IMPERIA, LA SPEZIA AND SAVONA

Ligúria is a long, thin coastal strip nestling at the foot of olive- and vine-clad mountains. The Italian Riviera boasts an abundance of sandy beaches and charming seaside villages, while inland the mountain resorts offer plenty of walking and a respite from the crowds.

Ligúria divides neatly into two distinct stretches of coastline: to the west is the Riviera di Ponente and to the east is the Riviera Levante. Between the two lies Genoa, Italy's biggest port. It has a fascinating old town with medieval alleyways, and numerous palaces and churches to explore. It was also once the home of Christopher Columbus. The surrounding hills offer a quiet retreat from the city: the picturesque Valle Scrivia has several hiking routes and is easily accessible from the small town of Casella. Stretching across to the French border, the Riviera di Ponente has a number of places of interest: the pretty wine producing town of Dolceacqua; the pleasant resort of San Remo; the charming seafront village of Cervo; and the medieval hilltown of Toirano. There are more coastal resorts along the Riviera Levante including Portofino, the most exclusive harbour and resort town in Italy. With sandy beaches and small coves, this attractive area also offers good walking. Further along is the coastline of the Cinque Terre (Five Lands). The name refers to five tiny villages which appear to cling dramatically to the edge of sheer cliffs: Monterosso al Mare, Vernazza, Corniglia, Manrola and Riomaggiore.

Places of interest

Albenga: small market town.

Camogli: attractive resort.

Cinque Terre: wine growing region, picturesque villages, sandy coves and beaches.

Dolceacqua: medieval stone bridge and ruined castle.

La Spezia: museum with medieval and Renaissance art, ferry trips to Bastia in Corsica.

Lévanto: beachside resort.

Portovénere: village with three islets offshore.

Toirano: caves at the Grotte della Basura and Grotta di Santa Lucia.

Villa Hanbury: impressive botanical gardens.

Cuisine of the region

The best known speciality is *pesto:* made with chopped basil, garlic, pine nuts and grated cheese with olive oil, it was invented by the Genoese to help their long term sailors fight scurvy. Fish and seafood are readily available, often eaten with pasta. Chickpeas grow in abundance, and make *farinata*, a kind of chickpea pancake. Genoa is famous for its *pandolce*, a sweet cake laced with dried fruit, nuts and candied peel.

Burrida di seppie: cuttlefish stew.

Cacciucco: rich stew of mixed fish and seafood cooked with wine, garlic and herbs.

Carpione: fish marinated in vinegar and herbs.

Cima alla Genovese: cold stuffed veal.

Torta pasqualina: spinach and cheese pie.

Trenette al Pesto: noodles with pesto.

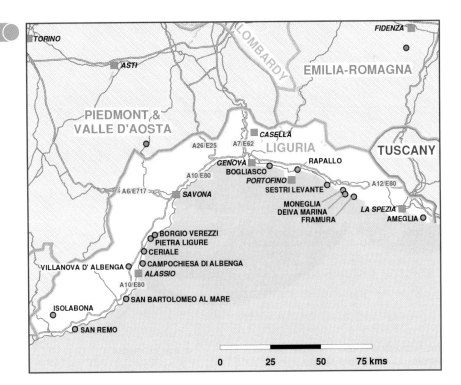

Bogliasco
Camping Genova Est

Via Marconi, localitá Cassa, I-16031 Bogliasco (Ligúria) T: 0103 472 053. E: info@camping-genova-est.it

alanrogers.com/IT64100

This wooded site is set on very steep slopes close to the Genoa motorways and is east of the city. It has very limited facilities but runs a free bus service to connect with local transport for visiting Genoa. If you are extremely fit, a set of steep stairs (125 m. elevation) will take you there in 15 minutes. The approach from the main road twists and climbs steeply with a tight final turn at the site entrance. There are 54 pitches for tents and mobile units with electricity (3/6A) available to the vehicle pitches. The site is not suitable for disabled visitors. The restaurant/bar with terrace commands fine views over the sea and offers a simple menu, which changes daily. The Buteros, who own the site, both speak good English and are very enthusiastic and anxious to ensure you enjoy your stay. This is a site to be used for exploring Genova and Riviera di Levante, rather than for extended stays. It is the only site in the area.

Facilities

Two dated sanitary blocks provide free hot showers and en-suite cabins (WC, washbasin and shower). Washing machine. Basic motorcaravan services. Shop providing essentials. Bar/restaurant and takeaway (Easter-30/9). Towing vehicle available. Gas supplies. Free WiFi in reception/bar area. Free bus shuttle to local town. Scooters for hire. Off site: Beach 500 m. Fishing and boat launching 1.5 km. Bicycle hire 2 km. Golf and riding 20 km.

Open: 19 March - 10 October.

Directions

From autostrada A10 take Nervi exit and turn towards La Spezia on the SS1. In Bogliasco look for a very sharp left turn with a large sign for the site. Follow narrow winding road for 2 km. to site. GPS: 44.38453, 9.07308

Charges guide

Per unit incl. 2 persons and electricity	€ 21.40 - € 29.50
extra person	€ 6.00 - € 7.00
child (3-10 yrs)	€ 4.10 - € 4.60
dog	€ 2.20

No credit cards.
Less 5% for holders of the current Alan Rogers Guide.

For latest campsite news, availability and prices visit

alanrogers.com

Ameglia
Camping River

Localitá Armezzone, I-19031 Ameglia (Ligúria) T: 0187 659 20. E: info@campingriver.com
alanrogers.com/IT64190

Camping River is a large oblong site on the banks of the Magna river but only the swimming pool and entertainment area has river views. It provides 100 level, 75-100 sq.m. touring pitches (all 3A electricity) mostly under a canopy of tall trees with much welcome shade on hot days. They are mostly separated from the equal number of permanent pitches. It is possible to launch your boat into the Magra river from the campsite and there are good fishing opportunities further up river. A busy entertainment programme is provided from mid June until September. Camping River has something for all the family; we saw fishermen setting off for the afternoon, families playing in the pool, and small children enjoying the large play area while their parents relaxed with a cup of coffee on the terrace. This is a wonderful area to explore with the Cinque Terre nearby, its beautiful coastline and interesting hill top villages. Ligúria is also a well known wine growing area.

Facilities

Two unisex sanitary blocks provide toilets (some Turkish style), washbasins and showers. Facilities for disabled visitors. Motorcaravan services. Shop, restaurant and bar, pizzeria (1/5-30/9). Swimming pool (1/5-15/9) and sun deck. Play area. Football. Hydro massage. Boat launching. Fishing. Mobile homes and bungalows to rent. Entertainment area. Beach shuttle bus. Lessons organised (scuba diving, swimming, dancing). Kayak, windsurf board, bicycle hire. WiFi (free). Off site: Tennis and riding 200 m. Archery. Sailing. Scuba diving. La Spezia.

Open: 1 April - 30 September.

Directions

Take Sarzana exit on A12 (Genoa-Livorno). Follow signs initially towards Lerici. After 3 km. follow signs to Bocca di Magra and Ameglia where site is signed to left. Avoid other less good sites (one claiming to be 'formerly Camping River'). Final access road is a little narrow. GPS: 44.07556, 9.96972

Charges guide

Per unit incl. 2 persons and electricity	€ 18.50 - € 43.00
extra person	€ 5.00 - € 11.00
child (2-10 yrs)	€ 2.00 - € 8.00

RiverVillage Camping

CAMPING BETWEEN LIGURIA AND TUSCANY

www.campingriver.com

Numero Verde Toll-free
800 953 253 *Fast Line*

Borgio Verezzi
Camping Park Mara

Via Trento Trieste, 83, I-17022 Borgio Verezzi (Ligúria) T: 0196 104 79. E: info@campingparkmara.it
alanrogers.com/IT64055

Set into a hillside with wonderful views of the town and the rocky coastline of the Ligurian Sea, roughly halfway between Genoa and the French border, Park Mara is a compact site with 147 pitches. Of these, only eight are suitable for touring units up to 5.5 m, 28 are for tents and the remainder are occupied by seasonal caravans and rental chalets. The touring pitches are on the small side (40-70 sq.m) with steep access roads. All have 4A Europlugs and nearby water points. Park Mara is not suitable for campers with mobility problems. The shingle beach is just a 400-metre walk down the hill, whilst the shops, bars and restaurants of Borgio and Borgio Verezzi are also within easy reach.

Facilities

The sanitary blocks provide a mixture of British and Turkish style WCs, and hot water (payment card). Washing machines, dryers and ironing facilities. Small shop. Bar. Restaurant and takeaway (April-Sept). Bread available. Swimming pool and children's pool. Games room. Playground. Miniclub and organised activities and entertainment (high season). Fridge hire. Safes. WiFi over part of site (charged).

Open: 15 March - 31 December.

Directions

From west leave A10 at Pietra Ligure exit and follow signs for Viale Riviera to join SS1 east to Borgio Verezzi. Turn north across railway (traffic lights) towards village, then immediately right, then second left following site signs. GPS: 44.161536, 8.312659

Charges guide

Per unit incl. 3 persons and electricity	€ 21.00 - € 38.00
extra person	€ 6.00 - € 8.00

For latest campsite news, availability and prices visit
alanrogers.com

Campochiesa di Albenga
Camping Bella Vista

Reg. Campore 23, I-17031 Campochiesa di Albenga (Ligúria) T: 0329 592 3683. E: info@campingbellavista.it

alanrogers.com/IT64060

Owned and run by the multilingual, Dutch Kox family, this site has 63 level pitches, separated in places by hedges and trees. The pitches are in rows, loosely ringed by bungalows. Two sizes of pitch are offered: 50 and 80 sq.m. with a sink and tap for every four pitches. Electricity (6A) is available. Large units will experience manoeuvring difficulties and must phone ahead to use alternative entrance. This is an inexpensive and thus crowded site in high season.

Facilities

The single modern block is clean with British style toilets. Shower water is solar heated, washbasins have cold water only. Single facility for disabled campers although the unit doubles as a baby room with a washing machine and ironing equipment. Shop (1/5-1/10). Bar. Takeaway with restrictions (1/5-1/10). Swimming pool and separate paddling pool. Limited entertainment in season. Play area. Aviary. Free WiFi throughout. Off site: Beach 1.5 km.

Open: 20 March - 15 November.

Directions

Exit at Borghetto San Spirito onto the SS1 (via Aurelia) towards Ceriale. In Ceriale follow blue signs for Peagna and the campsite. Look for the small signs at regular intervals. GPS: 44.08333, 8.21033

Charges guide

Per unit incl. 2 persons	
and electricity	€ 19.00 - € 37.00
extra person	€ 5.00 - € 9.00
child (3-12 yrs)	€ 4.00 - € 6.00

Ceriale
Camping Baciccia

Via Torino 19, I-17023 Ceriale (Ligúria) T: 0182 990 743. E: info@campingbaciccia.it

alanrogers.com/IT64030

This friendly, family run site is a popular holiday destination. Baciccia was the nickname of the present owner's grandfather who grew fruit trees and tomatoes on the site. Tall eucalyptus trees shade the 111 flat touring pitches (all with electricity 6A). Laura and Mauro work tirelessly to ensure that you enjoy your stay here and we have watched the growth of a very effective campsite over the years. An informal restaurant, overlooking the swimming pool and sports area, is cheerfully and efficiently run by Flavio and Pamela who serve delightful seasonal Italian dishes.

Facilities

Two very clean and modern sanitary blocks near reception have British and Turkish style WCs and hot water throughout. Laundry. Motorcaravan services. Combined restaurant/bar/pizzeria/takeaway and shop, swimming pool and paddling pool (all season) and private beach. Tennis. Volleyball. Excellent play area. Wood-burning stove and barbecue. Fishing. Diving. Entertainment for all (July/Aug). Excursions. Bicycle hire. WiFi over site. Off site: Supermarket 200 m. Aquapark 500 m. Golf 5 km.

Open: 27 March - 20 October, 4 December - 10 January.

Directions

From the A10 between Imperia and Savona, take Albenga exit. Follow signs Ceriale/Savona and Aquapark Caravelle (which is 500 m. from site) and then site signs. Site is just south of Savona. GPS: 44.08165, 8.21763

Charges guide

Per unit incl. up to 3 persons	
(over 2 yrs) and electricity	€ 23.00 - € 51.00
extra person	€ 6.50 - € 11.00
dog	€ 3.00 - € 5.00

Deiva Marina
Villaggio Camping Valdeiva

Localitá Ronco, I-19013 Deiva Marina (Ligúria) T: 0187 824 174. E: camping@valdeiva.it

alanrogers.com/IT64120

A mature and cheerful site, 3 km. from the sea between the famous Cinque Terre and Portofino, Valdeiva is open for most of the year. The 40 touring pitches, with 3A electricity, are in a square at the bottom of the site, some with shade and views, and cars are parked separately. There are 100 permanent pitches on the upper reaches of the site. Camping Valdeiva does have a small swimming pool, which is very welcome if you do not wish to take the free bus to the beach. A small busy bar/restaurant offers food at realistic prices. There was late night noise from residents when we stayed in high season.

Facilities

The toilet block nearest the touring pitches provides cramped facilities. A new block is in the centre of the site. WCs are mainly Turkish, but there are some of British style. Washing machines and dryers. Shop (15/6-10/9). Bar/restaurant and takeaway with reasonable menu and pizzas cooked in a traditional oven (15/6-10/9). Small swimming pool. Play area. Excursions. Free bus to the beach. Torches required. Bicycle hire. Camping gas. No electric barbecues. WiFi on part of site (charged).

Open: All year excl. 10/1-10/2 and 4/11-4/12.

Directions

Leave A12 at Deiva Marina exit and follow signs to Deiva Marina. Site signs are prominent at the first junction and site is on left 3 km. down this road. GPS: 44.22470, 9.55168

Charges guide

Per unit incl. 2 persons	
and electricity	€ 23.00 - € 36.00
extra person (over 6 yrs)	€ 6.50

For latest campsite news, availability and prices visit
alanrogers.com

Deiva Marina
Camping la Sfinge

Localitá Gea, I-19013 Deiva Marina (Ligúria) T: 0187 825 464. E: info@campinglasfinge.com
alanrogers.com/IT64160

La Sfinge is peacefully located in the famous area of Cinque Terre and stylish Portofino, in a landscape of pine and acacia trees, with some panoramic views. Most of the 65 touring pitches are located at the lower level with tent pitches on pleasant terraces, some with views. There are permanent residents on the site but they are separated from the touring pitches. A set evening meal is prepared at a good price with barbecues in high season. There is a free private shuttle service to the beach and to the railway station to explore the region. The owners, Tania and Guido, are keen to please and speak good English.

Facilities

Clean and modern sanitary facilities including a locked WC for disabled visitors. Washing machines, spin dryers and ironing area. Communal fridge. Small but well stocked shop. Snack bar producing evening menu. Sports ground and safe play area for children. Free mobile phone charging facility. International phone. Animation for children at weekends in July/Aug. 27 tents for hire. Bus to beach. No electric barbecues. Free WiFi over site.

Open: 15 March - 15 November.

Directions

From A12/E80 Genova-Livorno motorway take Deiva Marina exit and follow road to Deiva Marina (4 km). Site is on the right as you approach the village. GPS: 44.22625, 9.5502

Charges guide

| Per unit incl. 2 persons and electricity | € 21.00 - € 31.00 |
| extra person | € 6.00 - € 8.00 |

Framura
Camping Framura

Localitá La Spiaggetta, I-19014 Framura (Ligúria) T: 0187 815 030. E: hotelriviera@hotelrivieradeivamarina.it
alanrogers.com/IT64180

Framura is an unusual, small, cliff-side site of 170 pitches including just 15 pitches for touring units and ten for tents. Positioned on the site of the old railway, the pitches themselves are fabulous as they are directly above the crystal clear waters here, but there is no shade. Access to the site is through the old railway tunnel. The supporting amenities are basic but have a certain charm, some being cut into the rock face. Direct access to a narrow but pleasant beach is via a steep stairway. The site is considered unsuitable for children and the infirm and has no facilities for disabled visitors.

Facilities

Five very mixed blocks offer clean but basic toilets, mostly Turkish but some British style. Innovation has been used here and one very small shower block is carved into the rock face. Cold water at sinks. Washing machine. Motorcaravan services. Simple snack bar and takeaway (1/6-15/9). Bar (1/4-30/10). Small shop (15/6-15/9). Canoeing and windsurfing is possible. Fishing. Dogs are not accepted. Off site: Sister hotel with restaurant 400 m. Town 500 m. Boat launching 1 km. Bicycle hire 3 km.

Open: 1 April - 15 October.

Directions

From A12 take Deiva Marina exit. In town centre take care to find campsite signs! Cross narrow bridge and negotiate narrow approach road then narrow railway tunnel (check for cyclists in the dark interior and drive to site!). If avoiding height restricted (3 m) tunnels to the west, note that road to north is difficult for larger units. GPS: 44.21150, 9.52262

Charges guide

| Per unit incl. 2 persons and electricity | € 27.00 - € 34.50 |

No credit cards.

Isolabona
Camping Delle Rose

Via Provinciale, Regione Prati Gonter 4, I-18035 Isolabona (Ligúria) T: 0184 208 130.
E: info@campingdellerose.eu **alanrogers.com/IT64015**

Camping Delle Rose is close to the French border, and a few miles inland from the Italian Riviera. This is a peaceful spot, set deep in the Maritime Alps, with many unspoilt medieval towns, picturesque churches and bustling markets. This is a friendly, family site where Lorena, Mauro and Lorenzo will guarantee a warm welcome. The site is located on a steeply terraced hillside, surrounded by eucalyptus and mimosa. The 80 touring pitches are 40-80 sq.m, and most have 3A electricity connections. A number of mobile homes and apartments are available for rent. Many improvements are being made to the site and those already completed are of a high standard.

Facilities

One basic toilet block, recently refurbished, has some washbasins with hot water, pushbutton showers (no dividers) and baby changing mat. No facilities for disabled visitors. Swimming pools (15/6-15/9). Bar (15/6-15/9). Restaurant and pizzeria (July/Aug). Small play area. Activities for children, live music for adults (July/Aug). Communal barbecues only. Torch useful. WiFi.

Open: 18 April - 31 October.

Directions

From Ventimiglia, head north on SP54 to Dolceacqua and continue to Isolabona. The site is well signed from here. GPS: 43.894573, 7.646905

Charges guide

| Per unit incl. 2 persons and electricity | € 15.00 - € 30.50 |

No credit cards.

For latest campsite news, availability and prices visit
alanrogers.com

Moneglia
Camping Villaggio Smeraldo

Localitá Preata, I-16030 Moneglia (Ligúria) T: 0185 493 75. E: info@villaggiosmeraldo.it
alanrogers.com/IT64075

Camping Smeraldo is a unique and simple site near the seaside town of Moneglia. It has been formed out of a cliff face and was once the site for railway workers. Touring pitches (25) and tent pitches (35) are provided on hard terraces overlooking the sea. Electricity (3A) and artificial shade are available. A number of two- and three-bedroom chalets are also available for rent. On-site amenities are limited; a basic shop and a café/restaurant. The restaurant and its terrace provide fine sea views which are extra special on moonlit evenings. The owners are very friendly and helpful and English is spoken.

Facilities

Fairly basic sanitary facilities. Washing machines. Basic shop. Bar/restaurant with snack bar. Chalets for rent. Dogs are not accepted in July/Aug. Barbecues allowed on pitches (with care, not electric). Torches necessary. WiFi on part of site (charged). Off site: Shops, restaurants and cafés in Moneglia. Walking and cycling routes. Sub-aqua diving.

Open: All year excl. November.

Directions

Site is between Genova and La Spezia. Note height restriction through site approach tunnel. Approach road from west on coast road has a 3 m. restriction tunnel so be prepared to make short winding inland diversion. On coast road in Moneglia ignore consent sign on tunnel. GPS: 44.238611, 9.477778

Charges guide

Per unit incl. 2 persons and electricity	€ 27.00 - € 46.00

No credit cards.

Pietra Ligure
Camping Dei Fiori

Viale Riviera 17, I-17027 Pietra Ligure (Ligúria) T: 0196 256 36. E: info@campingdeifiori.it
alanrogers.com/IT64040

This is a small, family owned site with limited facilities, situated some 550 metres from the beach in an old olive orchard and charging average prices for your stay. A road runs past the entrance and the restaurant terrace is partly overlooked by an elevated section of this road. There are 232 pitches, some very small, with lots of seasonal pitches for Italian campers, and some bungalows. The 60 level touring pitches are mainly on the lower terraces of the site, with some shade and 6A electricity. Some of the smallest pitches may be challenging when manoeuvring with large units.

Facilities

Two blocks, one refurbished, provide a mixture of British and Turkish style toilets. However a prefabricated unit offers better showers and toilets although the majority are Turkish. Water is solar heated and free throughout. The facilities can be under pressure at peak times. Sinks have cold water only. Motorcaravan services. Fridges for use by campers. Bar/snack bar. Pizzeria (June-Sept). Shop. Swimming pool (May-Sept) and fabric paddling pool. Limited entertainment programme in season. Play area. Bicycle hire. No barbecues. WiFi on part of site (charged).

Open: 1 January - 25 October.

Directions

From A10/E80 take Pietra Ligure exit between Finale Ligure and Loano. Site is just north of Pietra Ligure town, and clearly signed off the beach road onto a minor road off the roundabout to the west of the town centre. GPS: 44.14769, 8.26833

Charges guide

Per unit incl. 3 persons and electricity	€ 23.50 - € 43.50
extra person	€ 5.00 - € 9.00

No credit cards.

Pietra Ligure
Camping Pian dei Boschi

Viale Riviera 114, I-17027 Pietra Ligure (Ligúria) T: 0196 254 25. E: info@piandeiboschi.it
alanrogers.com/IT64107

Camping Pian dei Boschi can be found on the Ligurian Riviera, 700 m. from the sea, close to the resort of Pietra Ligure. There are 215 pitches available for touring. They are well shaded and most have electrical connections (5-6A). A number of mobile homes are available for rent, as well as apartments (for 4-6 people). There is a large swimming pool surrounded by a wide sun terrace, with a paddling pool adjacent. The campsite restaurant includes a wood-fired pizza oven and offers an enticing range of Mediterranean cuisine. Other on-site amenities include a tennis court and sports field.

Facilities

Two sanitary blocks with mainly Turkish style toilets, some hot water to open style washbasins, preset showers (token). Facilities for disabled visitors. Washing machines. Motorcaravan services. Shop. Bar/restaurant/pizzeria. Takeaway. Swimming pool (caps compulsory). Paddling pool. Play area. Tennis. Sports field. Entertainment and activities. Mobile homes and apartments for rent.

Open: Easter - end September.

Directions

From France (Menton) on A10 motorway, leave at the exit to Pietra Ligure and head south on Viale Riviera towards the town centre, from where the site is well signed. GPS: 44.14906, 8.26856

Charges guide

Per unit incl. 3 persons and electricity	€ 26.00 - € 42.00
extra person (over 2 yrs)	€ 5.20 - € 8.50

Rapallo
Camping Miraflores
Via Savagna 10, I-16035 Rapallo (Ligúria) T: 0185 263 000. E: camping.miraflores@libero.it
alanrogers.com/IT64110

Camping Miraflores is close to the famous resort of Portofino and the Cinque Terre. It is a small, uncomplicated site with a tiny restaurant and bar offering pizzas and a reasonable menu of the day. The 87 pitches are flat and arranged around the lower levels of the site with separate terraced areas for tents (small pitches). Caravans and motorcaravans are provided with electricity (6A). A small swimming pool is free to campers (hats required). Rapallo is an attractive resort in its own right with an interesting old town centre. An A12 motorway junction is very close to the site but is shielded from sight and sound.

Facilities

Single, central, traditional sanitary block with a small number of toilets (some Turkish style). Showers. Washing machine. Shop, restaurant/pizzeria and takeaway meals (all 1/5-10/9). Basic games room. Playground. Swimming pool (hats compulsory). Mobile homes for rent. Tours and visits booked by reception. WiFi over site (free). Off site: Golf 500 m. Tennis and riding 1 km. Beach, fishing and boat launching 1.5 km. Rapallo centre 1.5 km.

Open: All year.

Directions

Site is extremely close to the Rapallo exit from the A12 motorway. From here, follow signs to Rapallo town and immediately at first complex roundabout look for signs to site. GPS: 44.35772, 9.20964

Charges guide

Per unit incl. 2 persons
and electricity   € 29.50 - € 32.00
No credit cards.

San Bartolomeo al Mare
Camping Il Frantoio
Via Pairola, 65, I-18016 San Bartolomeo al Mare (Ligúria) T: 0183 401 098. E: info@ilfrantoiocamping.it
alanrogers.com/IT64095

Camping Il Frantoio can be found on the Ligurian Riviera, at San Bartolomeo al Mare, between the larger towns of Alassio and San Remo. The site has an extensively terraced hillside setting and is surrounded by olive trees. It is around 1.5 km. from the sea, easily accessible with the site's free shuttle bus (mid June to mid September). Unfortunately, an elevated autoroute section dominates the sea views. Pitches here are predominantly occupied by accommodation units for hire, leaving just 20 fairly tight touring pitches on the lower level and a further 100 tent pitches on the upper level. Electricity is not available for the tent pitches. Additionally, a number of cabins and bungalows are privately owned.

Facilities

Sanitary blocks have a mixture of British and Turkish toilets, showers on payment (hot water 08.00 00.00). Facilities for disabled visitors. Washing machine. Motorcaravan services. Outdoor swimming pool (1/6-15/9, limited hours, hats compulsory). Play area. Bar with TV. Restaurant/pizzeria (June-Sept). Entertainment and activity programme (July/Aug). Miniclub. Shuttle bus to beach. Mobile homes for rent. WiFi. Off site: Beach 1.5 km.

Open: All year excl. 15 October - 5 December.

Directions

Approaching from France (Menton) on A10 motorway, leave at the exit to San Bartolomeo al Mare and head for the town centre, from where the site is well signposted. GPS: 43.9324, 8.09744

Charges guide

Per unit incl. 2 persons
and electricity   € 22.00 - € 33.00
extra person   € 7.00 - € 9.00
No credit cards.

San Remo
Camping Villaggio dei Fiori
Via Tiro a Volo 3, I-18038 San Remo (Ligúria) T: 0184 660 635. E: info@villaggiodeifiori.it
alanrogers.com/IT64010

Open all year round, this open and spacious site is a member of the Sunêlia group and maintains very high standards. It is excellent for exploring the Italian and French Rivieras, a guided tour to Monte Carlo in particular, or for just relaxing by the enjoyable, filtered seawater pools or on the private beach. Unusually, all of the pitch areas at the site are totally paved, with huge pitches for large units. Electricity (3/6A) is available to all 107 pitches. Water, drainage and an outside sink with cold water is available for every four pitches in one area. There is ample shade on some pitches from mature trees and shrubs, which are constantly watered and cared for in summer. The seafront pitches enjoy great views.

Facilities

Four clean and modern toilet blocks have British and Turkish style WCs and hot water throughout. Controllable showers. Baby rooms. Facilities for disabled campers. Private cabins. Laundry facilities. Motorcaravan services. Gas. Bar sells limited essential supplies. Large restaurant. Pizzeria and takeaway. Sea water swimming pools and heated whirlpool spa. Tennis. Excellent play area. Fishing. Bicycle hire. Free WiFi. Dogs are not accepted.

Open: All year.

Directions

From autostrada A10 take San Remo exit. Use SS1 (Ventimiglia-Imperia), site is on right just before San Remo. There is a very sharp right turn into site if approaching from the west. Site is well signed. GPS: 43.80117, 7.74867

Charges guide

Per unit incl. 4 persons
and electricity   € 29.00 - € 71.00

For latest campsite news, availability and prices visit
alanrogers.com

Sestri Levante

Camping Mare Monti

Via Aurelia km 469, I-16039 Sestri Levante (Ligúria) T: 0185 443 48. E: info@campingmaremonti.com

alanrogers.com/IT64130

Mare Monti is a neat and tidy site with 140 pitches. It is set high in the hills with spectacular views overlooking the small town of Sestri Levante. The owner and his staff are relaxed and very friendly. The site has 140 pitches, 40 of which are for touring with 6A electricity, all set on terraces. The remaining pitches are taken by seasonal units. A small shop and a bar with its impressive terrace and wonderful views overlook a neat swimming pool. Access to the site and within is difficult and the site is therefore more suitable for smaller units. The rural location, together with good facilities offers a quiet and relaxing atmosphere for your stay. We would not recommend this site for disabled visitors. The owners speak very good English and have spent much time and effort to ensure your stay will be enjoyable. There are many charming restaurants and shops in Sestri Levante, 2 km. away, along with many other tourist attractions. The site provides a free minibus link to the town in high season.

Facilities

Two refurbished toilet blocks are modern, bright and spotlessly clean. British and Turkish style WCs. Hot showers. Washing machine and dryer. Small shop, bar with takeaway (April-Oct). Outdoor swimming pool with separate pool for children (June-Oct). Volleyball. Communal barbecues. Minibus to town (July/Aug). English is spoken. WiFi on part of site (free). Off site: Bars, restaurants, shops and ATM in Sestri Levante 2 km. Fishing 2 km. Bicycle hire 4 km. Riding 5 km. Sailing 5 km. Golf 20 km.

Open: 15 March - 1 November.

Directions

From autostrada A12 take exit for Sestri Levante. Follow road SP1 in an easterly direction to km. 469. Site entrance is on the left set back from road and difficult to see. The road is steep in places and winding. It is not suitable for large units. GPS: 44.26365, 9.441901

Charges guide

Per unit incl. 2 persons and electricity	€ 25.00 - € 33.00
extra person	€ 6.00
child (3-12 yrs)	€ 3.00

Villanova d'Albenga

Camping C'era una Volta

Localitá Fasceti, I-17038 Villanova d'Albenga (Ligúria) T: 0182 580 461. E: info@villaggioceraunavolta.it

alanrogers.com/IT64050

An attractive campsite, C'era una Volta is about 6 km. back from the sea, situated on a hillside with panoramic views. The 165 touring pitches are on terraces in different sections of the site. Varying in size, most have shade from the young trees which harbour crickets with their distinctive noise. Some of the upper pitches have good views. Cars are required to park in separate areas at busy times. There are electricity connections with water and drainage close by. Charges are high in season but the site has an enjoyable atmosphere and is a good choice for families. A private beach 7 km. away is serviced by a bus in July and August.

Facilities

The main toilet block is modern and above average with hot water throughout. Four additional smaller blocks are spread around the site. Maintenance can be variable. Shop. Bar and pizzeria (15/5-10/9). Restaurant. Takeaway (evenings only). Disco (July/Aug). Swimming pools (15/5-20/9). Small gym. Fitness track. Miniclub. Health centre with Finnish sauna. Hydromassage bath/shower. Turkish bath. Hydrojet massage bed. Tennis. Large adventure playground. Boules. WiFi over part of site (free). Satellite TV. Communal barbecue. Off site: Riding 500 m. Golf 2 km. Lake fishing 4 km. Beach, boat launching and sailing 6 km.

Open: 1 April - 30 September.

Directions

Leave A10 at Albenga, turn left and left again at roundabout for the SS453 for Villanova. At T-junction turn left (Garlenda), turn right in 200 m. and follow signs up a long winding narrow road beyond the Stadium. GPS: 44.04433, 8.1137

Charges guide

Per unit incl. up to 3 persons	€ 28.00 - € 49.00
tent pitch	€ 24.00 - € 38.00
extra person	€ 8.00 - € 12.00
child (3-6 yrs)	€ 4.00 - € 6.00

Discounts for longer stays in low season. No credit cards.

THE REGION IS MADE UP OF THE PROVINCES: BERGAMO, BRESCIA, COMO, CREMONA, LECCO, LODI, MANTOVA, MILANO, PAVIA, SONDRIO AND VARESE. WE FEATURE LAKE GARDA SEPARATELY.

The region of Lombardy stretches from the Alps on the border with Switzerland, down past the romantic lakes of Como and Maggiore to the broad, flat plain of the River Po.

Lombardy is one of the most developed tourist destinations in Italy, its major draw being the beautiful scenic lakes. Surrounded by abundant vegetation, Lake Como is set in an idyllic landscape of mountains, tall peaks that seem to rise directly from the water's edge. With a number of places to visit along the shores, including the prosperous towns of Como and Lecco, the area is also great for walking and in most places the lake is clean enough for swimming. Lake Maggiore has a Mediterranean atmosphere, with citrus trees and palms lining the shores, and offers a more sedate pace. There are good walks in the surrounding hills. Lying in the centre of the lake, near Stresa, are the Borromean Islands, of which Isola Bella is the most popular. It is home to the 17th-century Palazzo Borromeo and its splendid garden of landscaped terraces, fountains, peacocks and statues. A lesser known lake, Lake Iseo, is the fifth largest in northern Italy. Situated in wine producing country, surrounded by mountains and waterfalls, it is popular for its watersports and boasts the largest lake-island in Italy, Monte Isola. All three lakes are well served by ferries which zig-zag from shore to shore, and are within easy reach of the vibrant city of Milan.

Places of interest

Bellagio: beautiful town by Lake Como, hilly old centre with steep, cobbled streets.

Bergamo: hill-top town, medieval and Renaissance buildings.

Brescia: Roman ruins, 12th-century church.

Certosa di Pavia: magnificent Renaissance Charterhouse.

Cremona: where the violin was developed, home of famous violin maker Stradivarius.

Lodi: charming medieval town of pastel coloured houses with pretty courtyards.

Milan: fashion capital, great for shopping, art museums, home of famous opera house La Scala and Leonardo Da Vinci's *Last Supper* fresco.

Cuisine of the region

Food varies considerably from town to town. Risotto is popular (the short grain rice is grown in the paddy fields of the Ticino Valley) as are green pasta and polenta. Lombardy is one of the largest cheese making regions in the country – Gorgonzola and Mascarpone are produced here.

Biscotti: biscuits flavoured with nuts, vanilla and lemon.

Cotolette alla Milanese: veal escalope.

La Casoêula: pork stew.

Ossobuco: shin of veal.

Panettone: light yeast cake with candied fruit.

Pizzoccheri: buckwheat noodles.

Risotto alla Milanese: rice cooked in meat stock with white wine, onion, saffron and grated parmesan.

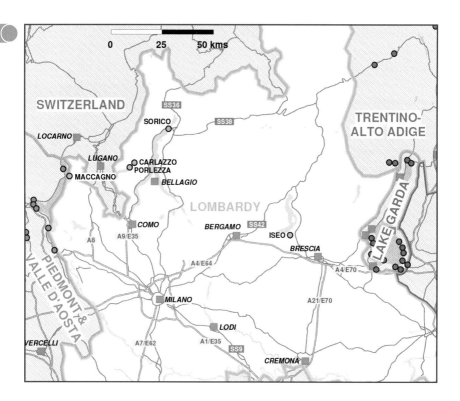

Carlazzo

Camping Ranocchio

Via Al Lago N7, localitá Piano Porlezza, I-22010 Carlazzo (Lombardy) T: 0344 703 85.
E: campingranocchio@ngi.it **alanrogers.com/IT62515**

This is a delightful site next to a small lake in a wetland nature reserve, surrounded by tree-clad slopes with views of distant mountain peaks. Such peaceful locations are rare. The very friendly Cremella family are all involved in the running of the site and their welcome is warm and genuine. The 195 touring pitches (all with 3-6A electricity) are on gravel hardstanding or grass. The restaurant, with a bar and terrace, offers a range of Italian dishes and pizzas to eat in or take away. There is a well maintained swimming pool and a paddling pool with safety precautions. A short walk along the lakeside takes you to the visitor centre and a bar/restaurant; if you prefer not to drive to the nearby supermarket, it is possible to reach it by continuing along the shore of Lake Piano.

Facilities

Two sanitary blocks provide excellent, modern facilities with warm water to some washbasins; showers are token operated. Good facilities for disabled visitors. Baby rooms. Motorcaravan services. Washing machines. Bar (15/4-30/9). Restaurant/takeaway (15/4-15/9). Pool is charged for (€ 1) but always supervised (15/6-15/9). Gas supplies. Fishing, swimming from small shingle beach (fence and gate, but young children would need watching). WiFi in reception (charged). Off site: Bicycle hire 600 m. Supermarket 800 m. Riding 2 km. Sailing and golf 4 km.

Open: 1 April - 30 September.

Directions

Carlazzo is on the SS340, 6 km. from Porlezza. Ranocchio is clearly signed. Turn right in the centre of the village, keep right, the site is at the bottom of the lane. The SS340 is very narrow and winding, especially on the Porlezza-Lugano section. The road from Menággio is better. GPS: 46.04078, 9.16828

Charges guide

Per unit incl. 2 persons	
and electricity	€ 21.00 - € 25.00
extra person	€ 5.50 - € 6.50
child (2-8 yrs)	€ 3.00 - € 3.50
dog	€ 2.00

No credit cards.

For latest campsite news, availability and prices visit
alanrogers.com

Iseo

Camping del Sole

Via per Rovato 26, I-25049 Iseo (Lombardy) T: 0309 802 88. E: info@campingdelsole.it
alanrogers.com/IT62610

Camping del Sole is, in our opinion, one of Italy's best family sites. It lies on the southern edge of Lake Iseo, just outside the pretty lakeside town of Iseo. The site has 306 pitches, of which 180 are for touring, all with 3A electricity and some fine views of the surrounding mountains and lake. Pitches are generally flat and of a reasonable size, but cars must park in the car park. The site has a wide range of excellent leisure amenities, including a large swimming pool. There is a bar and restaurant with a pizzeria near the pool and an entertainment area. The site is near the delightful waterfront area of the town (cycle path from the site gate) where you can enjoy classic Italian architecture, stroll around the shops or enjoy a meal in one of the many restaurants. There is a boat launching facility at the lakeside. There is a lively entertainment programme and excursions around the lake are organised, notably to Lake Iseo's three islands where you can sit at a street café or take a walk while enjoying the magnificent scenery. Excursions are also organised to the wine cellars of Franciacorta.

Facilities

Sanitary blocks are modern and well maintained, including special facilities for children and disabled visitors. Washing machines and dryers (€ 4). Bar, restaurant, pizzeria, snack bar and excellent shop. Motorcaravan services. Bicycle hire. Swimming pool with children's pool (21/5-10/9). Tennis. Football pitch. Fitness area. Canoe and pedal boat hire. WiFi (free). Dog exercise area. Entertainment in high season. Off site: Golf 5 km. Riding 6 km.

Open: 16 April - 25 September.

Directions

Lake Iseo is 50 km. west of Lake Garda. From A4 (Milan-Venice) take Rovato exit and at roundabout go north on SPX1 following signs for Lago d'Iseo for 12 km. Site is well signed to left at large roundabout. From Brescia on SS510, turn north before Iseo towards Rovato and turn right to site.
GPS: 45.65708, 10.03740

Charges guide

Per unit incl. 2 persons and electricity	€ 23.90 - € 46.10
extra person	€ 6.20 - € 10.80
child (5-12 yrs) or senior (over 60 yrs)	€ 3.20 - € 9.30
dog	€ 2.40 - € 5.00

Reductions in low season.

Campsite Del Sole is a 4 stars village tailor made for you and for your family, located just 5 minutes' walk from the historic center of Iseo. Relaxation, quietness and fun for teenagers and for those travelers who are devoted to hi-tech.
The wi-fi is entirely free.
Our staff makes an effort to treat carefully every detail of your holiday: quality and courtesy are the order of the day !
Il Camping Sun Village is located directly on the lake and has a private beach. We invite you to enjoy breakfast with a breathtaking panoramic view that you will hardly forget: our bar is, in fact, opposite the largest lake island in Europe.
Not to forget mentioning our specialties of Franciacorta, which you can find at the mini-market and the restaurant / pizzeria at the campsite.
Camping Village del Sole offers different types of accommodation, equipped tents, glamping, mobile homes, stone houses, pitches for tents and caravans and has an area of sports and entertainment with two swimming pools, tennis, volleyball, mini-football, playground for children and mini-club. A team of animation staff will take care of your children all day.
You can also rent bikes, canoes, pedal boats and motorboats.
2016 will be remembered thanks to Christo Vladimirov, an American artist of worldwide fame that will realize in June - and available to visitors for 15 days - a temporary bridge called "The Floating Piers".

CAMPING DEL SOLE - Via per Rovato, 26 - 25049 Iseo (BS)
tel. +39 030 980288 fax +39 030 9821721
www.campingdelsole.it - info@campingdelsole.it

For latest campsite news, availability and prices visit
alanrogers.com

Iseo

Camping Punta d'Oro

Via Antonioli 51-53, I-25049 Iseo (Lombardy) T: 0309 800 84. E: info@camping-puntadoro.com

alanrogers.com/IT62590

Camping Punta d'Oro, just outside the town of Iseo in the south east corner of the lake, is a small, tranquil campsite. It has been run by the Zatti-Brescianini family for the last thirty years and you will receive a very warm welcome on arrival. The very pretty site slopes gently down to the lake. It has 62 grass pitches (plus two static caravans for hire) all with 3-5A electricity connections. Trees and shrubs provide some shade and there are lovely views across the lake to the mountains. Lakeside pitches are a little more expensive. There is some occasional noise from the nearby railway.

Facilities

The two small sanitary blocks have been refurbished to a high standard with a mix of British and Turkish style WCs and hot water in washbasins and showers. Suite for disabled visitors. All facilities are kept very clean. Laundry facilities. Motorcaravan services. Shop. Small bar serving a limited range of snacks. Social room. TV in bar. Access to lake for swimming and fishing with two narrow slipways for boat launching. Bicycle hire arranged. Internet access and free WiFi. Off site: Town within walking distance.

Open: 27 March - 18 October.

Directions

Leave A4 Milan-Venice autostrada at Rovato, turn left to roundabout and go north on SPXI following signs for Lago di Iseo. Avoid town centre and continue to the roundabout where several campsites are signed. Take the exit leading back into town, right at next roundabout, over the railway and first right. Well signed. GPS: 45.66392, 10.05583

Charges guide

Per unit incl. 2 persons, electricity and water	€ 20.00 - € 55.00

Iseo

Camping Covelo

Via Covelo 18, I-25049 Iseo (Lombardy) T: 0309 8213 05. E: info@campingcovelo.it

alanrogers.com/IT62595

Covelo has a superb lakeside location and is one of the friendliest family sites we have visited in Italy. It is three hundred metres long, with grassy pitches and mature trees. The average sized, level pitches are in rows parallel with the shores of the lake. As the site is just four pitches deep, all have excellent access to the water plus brilliant views of the mountains across the lake and the tree-clad escarpment to the rear of the site. The owners take great pride in their site, insisting on high levels of simple family-style enjoyment for their guests.

Facilities

Three refurbished sanitary blocks of differing sizes provide pleasant facilities including those for disabled visitors. Baby cubicle. Motorcaravan services. Shop. Bar. Restaurant. Small play area. Entertainment. TV room. Big screen movies at night. Free bicycles for guests. Fishing. Boat launching. Buoys for boats. Free WiFi. Off site: Town of Iseo 1 km. Golf 2 km. Cycle track into Iseo.

Open: 1 April - 31 October.

Directions

From Milan/Verona A4 autostrada approach Lake Iseo on SPX1 from Seriate travelling east, or from any of the many approach roads travelling west from Brescia. At Iseo, site is well signed 800 m. south of town on the lakeside. GPS: 45.66667, 10.06694

Charges guide

Per unit incl. 2 persons and electricity	€ 24.00 - € 35.00
extra person	€ 6.00 - € 7.50

Maccagno

Parkcamping Maccagno Lagocamp

Via Corsini 3, I-21010 Maccagno (Lombardy) T: 0332 560 203. E: maccagno@lagocamp.com

alanrogers.com/IT62390

Newly renovated for the 2015 season, Parkcamping Maccagno Lagocamp is a delightful small site with immediate access to the shores of Lake Maggiore and a shingle beach. With hills on each side, the views over the lake are spectacular. There is no entertainment or infrastructure, so the site will suit those who just wish to relax on a traditional style campsite. The 115 relatively level pitches vary in size (40-80 sq.m), most have been re-turfed and many have shade. They are numbered but demarcation is somewhat informal. The bar and shop have been refurbished, with a few snacks added to the menu. English is spoken and the site staff are keen to ensure you have a pleasant stay.

Facilities

The toilet block is old but has been re-fitted inside to provide clean and modern facilities including those for babies (in ladies' toilet) and disabled visitors (key). Laundry facilities. Motorcaravan services. Newly refurbished bar and shop selling bread and basics. Terrace seating. Basic snacks. Simple play areas and sandpit. WiFi around reception (charged). Off site: Buses 500 m. Golf 20 km.

Open: 18 March - 13 November.

Directions

Site is on the eastern side of Lake Maggiore, a little to the north of the town of Luino. Follow the SS394 towards Maccagno and Locarno. Site is well signed. GPS: 46.038862, 8.734728

Charges guide

Per unit incl. 2 persons and electricity	€ 24.00 - € 47.00
extra person	€ 5.50 - € 9.00

Porlezza
Camping Darna

Via Osteno 50, I-22018 Porlezza (Lombardy) T: 0344 615 97. E: campingdarna@hotmail.it
alanrogers.com/IT62505

At the eastern end of Lake Lugano, Camping Darna is in a broad valley with a great view down the lake and mountains on all sides. It is a well run, family owned site which becomes lively in high season with plenty of entertainment for young and old; in low season it is much more relaxed. The 304 touring pitches are on flat ground, all with 3A electricity. There are 46 seasonal pitches (not along the lakeside). A restaurant serves a full range of Italian dishes and has a bar and an extensive terrace. There is an excellent swimming pool and a paddling pool. Porlezza is just 12 km. from Menággio on Lake Como with boat connections to many points on that lake.

Facilities

Five sanitary blocks, some with controllable showers, are kept very clean. Facilities for disabled visitors. Washing machines and dryers. Motorcaravan services. Good shop and bakery. Bar/restaurant with takeaway and large terrace (all season). Swimming pool (open to public, free to campsite guests Mon-Fri, € 5 at weekends) and paddling pool (1/6-30/9). Fishing, swimming and boating. WiFi (charged). Off site: Riding 1 km. Bicycle hire, shops, bars and restaurants 1.5 km. Sailing 3 km. Golf 10 km.

Open: 1 April - 31 October.

Directions

Porlezza is 14 km. east of Lugano on SS340 to Menággio. Turn right at traffic lights in Porlezza (Via Osteno). Site is 1.5 km. on right. NB: SS340 is narrow and winding, especially on the Porlezza-Lugano section (not for large units). The Como-Menággio road is least congested between 12.00 and 14.00! GPS: 46.02514, 9.12603

Charges guide

Per unit incl. 2 persons	
and electricity	€ 24.00 - € 38.00
extra person	€ 6.00 - € 10.00
child (3-12 yrs)	€ 4.00 - € 8.00

No credit cards.

Sorico
Camping La Riva

Via Poncione 3, I-22010 Sorico (Lombardy) T: 0344 945 71. E: info@campinglariva.com
alanrogers.com/IT62510

La Riva lies on a waterway at the northern end of Lake Como. It is surrounded by mountains, close to the nature reserve of Pian di Spagna and within walking distance of Sorico, a pretty town with bars, restaurants and shops. The site is beautifully laid out, with 70 level touring pitches on well tended grass, and an average size of 80 sq.m. Many have attractive views across the river to the mountains and most have 6A electrical connections. Reception houses a small bar, with limited snack bar and takeaway. Bread and milk to order. The excellent outdoor pool has a sunbathing terrace. Camping La Riva has a happy, friendly atmosphere. This most attractive site is popular with British and Dutch visitors, many having found it through Alan Rogers. The owners strive to maintain its tranquillity.

Facilities

The centrally located sanitary building contains modern showers (token), British style toilets and washbasins and is kept very clean. Excellent suite for disabled visitors. Washing machine. Swimming pool. Small playground. Bicycle hire. Fishing. Water skiing. Canoe and pedalo hire. Free WiFi in reception area. Off site: Guided walks. Cycling/walking track from site to Sorico. Riding. Golf 25 km. Sailing 1 km. Local market.

Open: 1 April - 3 November.

Directions

Sorico is at the northern tip of Lake Como. Approach via the free SS36 dual carriageway from Lecco; just after end of motorway section turn east to Sorico. From Como the SS340 is narrow and winding. Site is on eastern edge of town and well signed. GPS: 46.17067, 9.39268

Charges guide

Per unit incl. 2 persons	
and electricity	€ 27.00 - € 40.00
extra person	€ 7.00 - € 11.00
dog	€ 4.00

No credit cards.

For latest campsite news, availability and prices visit
alanrogers.com

IN THIS POPULAR TOURIST REGION WE HAVE INCLUDED THE LAKESIDE AREAS OF THE REGIONS OF VENETO, LOMBARDY AND TRENTINO-ALTO ADIGE

The largest and cleanest of the Italian lakes, Lake Garda is also the most popular. The low-lying countryside of the southern stretches gives way to the dramatic, craggy mountains of the north, while the western shore is fringed with olive groves, vines and citrus trees.

The lake's largest town, Desenzano del Garda, lies on the southern shore. Bars and restaurants line the lakefront and a walk to the town's castle affords spectacular views. Nearby, Sirmione is popular with those seeking cures in its sulphurous springs. It has the remains of a Roman spa plus a 13th-century fairytale castle, which is almost entirely surrounded by water. Along the sheltered stretch of the western shore, otherwise known as the Riviera Bresciana, are lush groves and fruit trees; Salò is a good place to stock up on the local produce. Gardone is best known for its exotic botanical garden and Il Vittoriale, the home of the notorious writer Gabriel D'Annunzio, which is filled with curiosities. Up in the mountains behind Gardone is the little alpine village of San Michele, and there are good walks to the springs and waterfalls in the surrounding hills. At the north west tip of the lake, Riva del Garda is one of the best known resorts and a favourite with windsurfers, as is Torbole, where sailing and mountain biking are popular too. On the eastern shore, Malcesine boasts a 13th-century turreted castle and a funicular which climbs to the summit of Monte Baldo giving panoramic views. Near the lively resort of Garda are white shingle beaches.

Places of interest

Bardolino: home of the light, red Bardolino wine. Festival of the Grape is held between Sept-Oct.

Gargano: olive factory, 13th-century church, good place for sailing.

Peschiera: attractive enclosed harbour and fortress.

Puegnago del Garda: home of Comincioli vineyard that has been producing wine since the 16th century.

Torri del Benaco: considered to be the prettiest lakeside town, with old centre, cobbled streets and a castle.

Cuisine of the region

Fish is popular; there are 40 different species in the lake including carp, trout, eel and pike. Regional dishes include trout filled with oranges and lemons, risotto with tench, and *sisam,* a traditional way of preparing lake minnows. The fruits grown on the western shore are used to make olive oil, citrus syrups and Bardolino, Soave and Valpolicella wines.

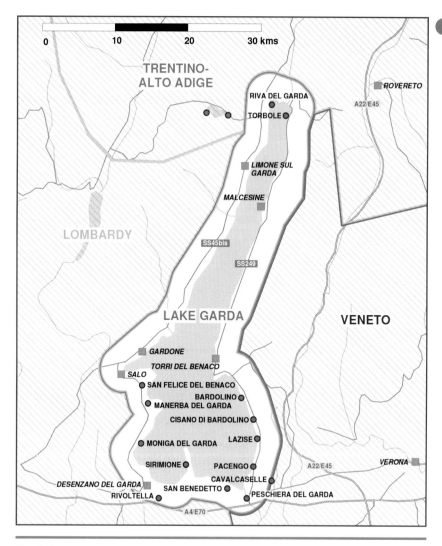

Bardolino
La Rocca Camp

Localitá San Pietro, I-37011 Bardolino (Lake Garda) T: 0457 211 111. E: info@campinglarocca.com
alanrogers.com/IT63600

This site was one of the first to operate on the lake and the family has a background of wine and olive oil production. La Rocca is in two areas, each side of the busy A249, the upper part being used mostly for bungalows and these have great lake views. The remaining touring pitches are on the lower part of the site, along with the main facilities. There is access between the two parts via a tunnel. The 400 pitches are mostly on terraces with shade, 10-16A electricity and access from narrow tarmac roads. Sixteen pitches are available with full services.

Facilities

Four toilet blocks, two on each side of the site. Mixed British and Turkish style WCs and controllable showers. Facilities for disabled visitors. Children's facilities. Washing machines. Motorcaravan services. Shop and bakery. Restaurant, bar and takeaway with large terrace. Swimming and paddling pools (lifeguard). Whirlpool. Sun terrace with views. Pool bar. Play area. Entertainment programme in season. Miniclub. Internet. Bicycle hire. Games room. Watersports. WiFi throughout (charged). Torches useful. Only gas barbecues permitted.

Open: 1 April - 15 October.

Directions

Site is on the east side of Lake Garda, on the lake ring road 249. From A4 take Pescheria exit and 249 north for Garda (there are many signs for Gardaland). Site is well signed approaching Bardolino. GPS: 45.5645, 10.7129

Charges guide

Per unit incl. 2 persons	
and electricity	€ 20.80 - € 45.70
extra person	€ 4.90 - € 10.90
child (2-10 yrs)	free - € 9.70

No credit cards.

For latest campsite news, availability and prices visit
alanrogers.com

Bardolino
Camping Serenella

Localitá Mezzariva 19, I-37011 Bardolino (Lake Garda) T: 0457 211 333. E: serenella@camping-serenella.it

alanrogers.com/IT63590

Situated alongside Lake Garda, Serenella has 297 average size pitches, some with good lake views. Movement around the site may prove difficult for large units (look for the wider roads). The pitches are shaded and have 6A electricity. A long promenade with brilliant views of the mountains and lake runs the length of the campsite. It is dotted with grassy relaxation areas and beach bars where snacks are served and the atmosphere is charming. The pleasant pool complex is near a traditional-style restaurant where delicious, sensibly priced food is served. There is some road noise at some of the amenities and the pool. Serenella is popular with Italians and international guests. Gardaland is nearby.

Facilities

Five clean, well equipped sanitary blocks include three that are more modern with laundry facilities. British style toilets, free hot water throughout. Facilities for families and disabled visitors. Washing machines and dryer. Freezer. Bar/restaurant, takeaway and shop. Watersports. Outdoor swimming pool (1/5-18/9). Entertainment and sporting programme for all in high season. Play area. Bicycle hire. Internet and WiFi on part of site (charged). Dogs are not accepted. Off site: Beach with fishing and watersports. Town and golf 3 km. Riding 3.5 km. Verona 35 km.

Open: 21 March - 25 October.

Directions

From E70/A4 Milan-Venice autostrada take Pescheria exit and follow signs to Bardolino. Site is on lakeside between Bardolino and Garda, 1 km. south of Garda. GPS: 45.55920, 10.71655

Charges guide

Per unit incl. 2 persons and electricity	€ 18.50 - € 41.00
per person	€ 4.50 - € 10.50
child (0-5 yrs)	free - € 5.00

Cavalcaselle
Camping Gasparina

Via Gasparina 13, I-37010 Cavalcaselle (Lake Garda) T: 0457 550 775. E: info@gasparina.com

alanrogers.com/IT62660

Gasparina is of average size for this area and of reasonable quality, but a little away from the towns around the lake. It is in a peaceful location and has the feeling of being in the countryside. As the site slopes gently towards the lake, levellers are needed in some parts. There are 363 grass touring pitches in back-to-back rows separated by gravel roads. Many trees and flowers adorn the site, with shade in most parts. The pleasant swimming pools are separated from the restaurant terraces by a neat, well clipped hedge. Just beyond the site fence is a beach and pleasant promenade. Boats can be launched here. Near reception are the supermarket and a bar/restaurant with three terraces and good prices.

Facilities

One refurbished and one new toilet block have the usual facilities with warm water. Facilities for disabled visitors. Washing machines and dryer. Shop. Bar/restaurant with terrace. Swimming pool (15/5-20/9). Playground. Watersports. Entertainment in high season. Dogs and other pets are not accepted in rentals. Off site: Bicycle hire 2 km. Riding 3 km.

Open: 1 April - 1 October.

Directions

Leave A4 Milan-Venice motorway at exit for Peschiera, go north on east side of lake on the SS249 towards Lazise for entrance road on your left. GPS: 45.45539, 10.7017

Charges guide

Per unit incl. 2 persons and electricity (3A)	€ 20.00 - € 36.00
extra person	€ 4.00 - € 9.00
child (6-10 yrs)	€ 2.00 - € 6.00

For latest campsite news, availability and prices visit
alanrogers.com

Cisano di Bardolino
Campings Cisano & San Vito

Via Peschiera 48, I-37011 Cisano di Bardolino (Lake Garda) T: 045 622 9098. E: cisano@camping-cisano.it
alanrogers.com/IT63570

This is a combination of two sites, each with its own reception. Some of the 700 touring pitches have superb locations along the 1 km. of shaded lakeside in Cisano. Some are on sloping ground and most are shaded, but the San Vito pitches have no lake views. Both sites are family orientated and much effort has been taken in the landscaping to provide maximum comfort, even for the largest units. San Vito is the smaller and more peaceful location, and shares many of the facilities of Cisano. A security fence separates the pitches from the beach, so access involves a short walk. Visitors with disabilities should select their pitch carefully to ensure an area appropriate to all their needs (there are some slopes in Cisano). On the San Vito site there is a pleasant family style restaurant (some road noise) which also sells takeaway food. San Vito is accessed via a tunnel under the road. The friendly staff speak English.

Facilities

Plentiful, good quality sanitary facilities are provided in both sites (nine blocks at Cisano and two at San Vito). Facilities for disabled visitors. Baby room. Washing machines. Fridge hire. Shop, two bar/restaurants and takeaway. Swimming pool (May-Sept). Whirlpool. Play area. Fishing and sailing. Free windsurfing and canoeing. Archery. Football. Minigolf. Boat launching. WiFi on part of site (charged). Car wash. Dogs are not accepted (cats are). Motorcycles not allowed on site (parking provided).

Open: 29 March - 12 October.

Directions

Leave A4 autoroute at Pescheria exit and head north towards Garda on lakeside road. Pass Lazise and site is signed (small sign) on left halfway to Bardolina. Site is 12 km. beyond the Gardaland theme park. GPS: 45.52290, 10.72760

Charges guide

Per unit incl. 2 persons	
and electricity	€ 18.50 - € 44.00
extra person	€ 4.50 - € 11.00
child (2-5 yrs)	free - € 5.00

Lazise
Camping Piani di Clodia

Via Fossalta 42, I-37017 Lazise (Lake Garda) T: 0457 590 456. E: info@pianidiclodia.it
alanrogers.com/IT62530

Piani di Clodia is one of the largest sites on Lake Garda and it has a positive impression of space and cleanliness. It is located on a slope between Lazise and Peschiera in the south east corner of the lake, with lovely views across the water to Sirmione's peninsula and the mountains beyond. The site slopes (in some parts, quite steeply) down to the water's edge and has 968 pitches, all with 6/16A electricity, 290 with electricity, water and drainage, terraced where necessary and back-to-back off hard access roads. There is some shade from both mature and young trees. The pool complex is truly wonderful with a range of pools, a pleasant sunbathing area and a bar. A member of Leading Campings group.

Facilities

Seven modern, immaculate sanitary blocks have British and Turkish style WCs, facilities for disabled visitors and one has a baby room. Washing machines, dryers and laundry service. Motorcaravan services. Shopping complex with supermarket and general shops, two bars, self-service restaurant with takeaway (all season). Pizzeria. Ice cream parlour. Swimming pools (28/3-10/10). Tennis. Gymnastics. Fishing. Boat launching. Large playground. Outdoor theatre with entertainment programme. WiFi over part of site (charged). Dog area and shower.

Open: 21 March - 11 October.

Directions

Lazise is on south east side of Lake Garda 30 km. west of Verona. From north on A22 (Trento-Verona) take Affi exit then follow signs for Lazise and site. From south on A4 (Brescia-Venice) take Peschiera exit and site is 6 km. towards Lazise and Garda on SS249. GPS: 45.48272, 10.72932

Charges guide

Per unit incl. 2 persons	
and electricity	€ 20.40 - € 52.90
extra person	€ 5.10 - € 13.40

For latest campsite news, availability and prices visit
alanrogers.com

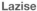

Lazise
Camping du Parc

Via Gardesana, 110, I-37017 Lazise sul Garda (Lake Garda) T: 045 758 0127.
E: duparc@campingduparc.com **alanrogers.com/IT62535**

Camping du Parc is a very pleasant, family owned site which resembles a Tardis, in that it extends and extends as you progress further through the site. Olive groves are interspersed with the pitch areas which gives an open and green feel. The site is set on a slope that goes down to the lakeside beach of soft sand. The 242 touring pitches are terraced and all have 5A electricity. Units above 10 m. long will be challenged by some of the corners here. Pitches are separated by trimmed hedges and some have shade, others have fine views of the lake. The restaurant is on the lower level, with a terrace to catch the sunsets, and the pizzeria also has a patio with sea views. Relax by the beach bar or in the pool whilst the children enjoy the slides and paddling pool. This is a very good site for those who prefer peace and quiet to the noisier atmosphere of the larger sites hereabouts. Buses stop by the gate to take you to Gardaland and other tourist attractions. As a site which caters for families, there is no disco or excessive noise and when we visited there were many happy customers.

Facilities

Four modern sanitary blocks are heated, well placed and have free hot water throughout. Three blocks have facilities for disabled visitors, one for children and babies. Washing machines and dryers. Motorcaravan services. Well stocked mini-market, restaurant with lake views, pizzeria with terrace and views, takeaway (19/3-31/10). Beach bar. Pool bar. Outdoor heated swimming pool (26/3-20/10). Large paddling pool with slides. Children's entertainment programme. Baby club. Play area. Tennis. Fitness suite. Multisports court. Fishing. WiFi (free).

Open: 4 March - 6 November.

Directions

Leave A4 Venice-Milan autostrada by taking the Brennero exit to Lake Garda and then on to Lazise. At the lakeside in town turn left and follow signs for site. GPS: 45.49833, 10.7375

Charges guide

Per unit incl. 2 persons	
and electricity	€ 23.10 - € 52.10
extra person	€ 5.80 - € 11.80
child (2-6 yrs)	€ 1.50 - € 6.00

No credit cards.

Lazise
Camping la Quercia

I-37017 Lazise sul Garda (Lake Garda) T: 045 647 0577. E: laquercia@laquercia.it
alanrogers.com/IT62550

La Quercia is a spacious, popular site on a slight slope leading down to Lake Garda and is decorated by palm trees and elegantly trimmed hedges. Accommodating up to 850 touring units, pitches are mostly in regular double rows between access roads, all with 6A electricity. Most are shaded by mature trees, although those furthest from the lake are more open to the sun. Much of the activity centres around the impressive pool complex with its fantastic slides and the terrace bar, restaurant and pizzeria which overlook the entertainment stage.

Facilities

Six toilet blocks are of a very high standard. Laundry. Supermarket. General shop. Bar, restaurant, self-service restaurant and pizzeria. Swimming pools (small charge). Tennis. Aerobics, judo and yoga. Scuba club. Playground with water play. Organised events and free courses. Canoeing. Roller-blading. Archery. Minigolf. Evening entertainment or dancing. Babysitting service. WiFi (charged). ATM. Free weekly excursion.

Open: 25 March - 4 October.

Directions

Lazise is on the south east side of Lake Garda 30 km. west of Verona. From north on A22 (Trento-Verona) take Affi exit then follow signs for Lazise and site. GPS: 45.49318, 10.73337

Charges guide

Per unit incl. 2 persons	
and electricity	€ 22.50 - € 65.60
extra person	€ 5.70 - € 13.20

For latest campsite news, availability and prices visit
alanrogers.com

Lazise
Camping Le Palme

Via del Tronchetto, I-37017 Lazise (Lake Garda) T: 0457 590 019. E: info@lepalmecamping.it

alanrogers.com/IT63015

On the southern shore of Lake Garda, Le Palme is a quiet site on the attractive Riviera degli Olivi, yet within easy reach of numerous attractions including several theme parks. There are 133 touring pitches, all with electricity (6-10A), water and waste water connections. Trees provide some shade throughout and a few pitches have spectacular views across the lake, for which a supplement is payable. Some mobile homes and chalets are available for hire. Nearby Lazise and Peschiera del Garda are both attractive towns with plenty of history, as well as shops, bars and restaurants. The ancient city of Verona is an easy drive away. There are several shopping centres and outlet villages in the area.

Facilities

Three heated sanitary blocks provide hot showers, baby and laundry rooms. Motorcaravan services. Swimming pool with terrace, bar, slides and children's pool. Restaurant, pizzeria and bar with entertainment in high season. Shop with bazaar. Playground. Football. Volleyball. Rent of bicycles, fridges, private bathrooms, boat moorings and parking for boat trailers. WiFi over site (charged). Underground car parking available. Doctor daily in middle and high season. Direct lake access. Off site: Sailing and water sports nearby. Walking and cycle tracks. Boat hire and excursions. Riding and golf 5 km. Bus services including Bus Walk & Bike. Amusement parks, museums and Spas. Lazise and Peschiera del Garda both 5 km. Verona 28 km.

Open: 4 April - 27 October.

Directions

From A4 (Milano/Verona) motorway leave at exit for Peschiera and follow signs for Peschiera Centro then turn north along riverside. At roundabout take first exit and follow SR249 for Lazise. Site is signed to left 1 km. after passing Gardaland.
GPS: 45.46472, 10.71476

Charges guide

Per unit incl. 2 persons and electricity, water and drain	€ 17.50 - € 42.40
extra person	€ 4.50 - € 9.70
child (1-7 yrs)	€ 2.50 - € 6.00
dog	€ 1.50 - € 5.50

Lazise
Camping Park Delle Rose

Strada San Gaetano 20, I-37017 Lazise (Lake Garda) T: 045 647 1181. E: info@campingparkdellerose.it

alanrogers.com/IT63580

An orderly, well designed site with a feeling of spaciousness, Delle Rose is on the east side of Lake Garda, three kilometres from the attractive waterside village of Peschiera. The 455 pitches are of average size, most with grass and shade, and laid out in 30 short, terraced avenues. The ratio of recreational area to pitches is unusually high, particularly for sites at Lake Garda. Unusually, reception is located one third of the way into the site. On approach one sees the attractive restaurant, gardens and comprehensive sporting facilities including the pool complex with its stylish terraced bar and entertainment area close by. There is a large car park at the modern reception centre where many languages including English and Dutch are spoken.

Facilities

Five very clean, modern sanitary blocks have hot water throughout and British style toilets, some in cabins with washbasins. Private bathrooms for hire. Good baby rooms. Facilities for disabled visitors. Washing machines. Motorcaravan services. Fridge hire. Bar/restaurant, takeaway and pool bar serving snacks. Shops. New swimming pool with flumes (mid April-Sept). Tennis. Archery. Minigolf. Play area and miniclub. Fishing (with permit). Beach at site. Watersports. Kayaking. Windsurfing. Daily medical services. Entertainment programme in high season. Excursions. Dogs and motorbikes are not accepted. Torches useful. WiFi on part of site (charged). Off site: Peschiera with ATM and usual town amenities 2 km. Golf 6 km. Riding 8 km. Gardaland close by.

Open: 21 April - 30 September.

Directions

From A4 Milan-Venice autostrada take exit for Pescheria, west of Verona. Travel north towards Lazise. The campsite is on the south eastern lakeside 2.5 km. north of Pescheria and well signed.
GPS: 45.48300, 10.73183

Charges guide

Per unit incl. 2 persons and electricity	€ 20.00 - € 50.50
extra person	€ 5.00 - € 11.00
child (4-9 yrs)	€ 1.50 - € 6.00
No credit cards.	

For latest campsite news, availability and prices visit
alanrogers.com

Lazise

Camping Spiaggia d'Oro

Via Sentieri 2, I-37017 Lazise (Lake Garda) T: 0457 580 007. E: info@campingspiaggiadoro.com

alanrogers.com/IT62545

Spiaggia d'Oro is a well equipped family site near Lazise on Lake Garda's eastern bank. This is a large site with 765 grassy touring pitches and a selection of chalets and mobile homes for rent. The site has its own sandy beach with a beach volleyball court. A fitness centre is a recent addition and has been developed with a good range of high specification equipment. The impressive swimming pool complex has three pools, one for children with a slide and water games. This is a lively site in high season with a varied activity programme and a club for children. Other on-site amenities include a snack bar with a terrace overlooking the lake and a well stocked supermarket. Lazise and Peschiera are both within easy reach and are amongst the most attractive towns around the lake. A little further afield, Verona is, of course, well worth a visit and Italy's premier theme park, Gardaland, is also close by.

Facilities

Five modern, suitably positioned toilet blocks provide open style washbasins and showers. Good facilities for disabled visitors. Laundry. Motorcaravan services. Supermarket. Bar. Snack bar. Swimming pools with waterslide. Separate children's pool. Fitness centre. Tennis. Playground. Children's club and entertainment programme. Direct access to beach. Mobile homes and chalets for rent. WiFi on part of site (charged). Off site: Shops, cafés and restaurants in Lazise and Peschiera. Verona 35 km.

Open: 20 March - 18 October.

Directions

Leave the A4 (Milan-Venice) autostrada at exit for Castelnuovo del Garda. Head north on the SR450. Leave this road at Ca Isidoro and join the westbound SP5 to Lazise. Site is clearly signed from here. GPS: 45.49716, 10.73806

Charges guide

Per unit incl. 2 persons	
and electricity	€ 20.00 - € 59.00
extra person	€ 5.00 - € 11.00
child (3-7 yrs)	free - € 6.50
dog	€ 2.50 - € 7.00

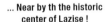

Lazise

Camping Belvedere

Via Belvedere 9, I-37017 Lazise (Lake Garda) T: 0457 590 228. E: info@campingbelvedere.com

alanrogers.com/IT62555

Belvedere is a pleasant, family site located between Pacengo and Lazise at the south eastern corner of Lake Garda. There is a good selection of amenities here including a restaurant with an attractive terrace overlooking the lake. Other facilities include a swimming pool, supermarket and renovated toilet blocks. Pitches are of varying sizes and are grassy, with reasonable shade. This is a popular corner of the lake and Belvedere is just 200 m. from the Caneva water park, and also very close to Gardaland, Italy's largest theme park. A lively entertainment and activities programme for children is run during July and August, and includes a miniclub. The site is popular with school groups visiting the theme parks.

Facilities

Modern sanitary facilities with free controllable hot showers, baby room and shower and WC for disabled visitors. Laundry. Motorcaravan services. Bar. Restaurant. Snack bar. Supermarket. Swimming pool. Children's pool. Volleyball. Tennis. Play area (2-7 yrs). Direct access to lake and sandy beach. Mobile homes and chalets for rent. Entertainment and activity programme. WiFi (charged). Off site: Nearest town is Lazise with bars, shops and restaurants. Caneva water park 200 m. Gardaland 3 km.

Open: 18 March - 2 October.

Directions

Leave the A4 (Milan-Venice) autostrada at the Castelnuovo del Garda exit. Head north on the SR450. Leave this road at Ca Isidoro and join the westbound SP5 to Lazise. Site is clearly signed to the south of the town. GPS: 45.47951, 10.72278

Charges guide

Per unit incl. 2 persons	
and electricity	€ 18.00 - € 43.00
extra person	€ 4.00 - € 10.50
child (1-8 yrs)	€ 2.00 - € 5.50

For latest campsite news, availability and prices visit

alanrogers.com

Manerba del Garda
Camping Romantica

Via G Verdi 17, I-25080 Manerba del Garda (Lake Garda) T: 0366 564 444. E: info@campingromantica.com

alanrogers.com/IT62820

Camping Romantica is a tranquil site with some lakeside pitches that have beautiful views across the lake to the mountains. The glittering lights across the lake at night are quite romantic and it is a pleasure to sit out and enjoy balmy summer evenings here. The 280 pitches are of 70-80 sq.m, mostly on grass and with tarmac access roads, many having shade. The lake is accessed through a security fence and across a public promenade. It is great here for swimming, watersports and boat launching. A stylish, bistro-style restaurant is at the front of the site serving good food in a very attractive, modern setting.

Facilities

Seven toilet blocks, all clean and pleasant with mixed British and Turkish style WCs and very good, spacious showers. Facilities for disabled visitors. Washing machines. Quality restaurant and bar with large terrace. Large supermarket and bazaar. Play areas. Boat parking and launching. Watersports. WiFi on part of site (charged). No electric barbecues. Torches useful. Off site: Public transport 100 m. in high season. Bicycle hire, ATM 2 km.

Open: One week before Easter - 30 September.

Directions

Site is on the western side of Lake Garda near the town of Manerba. From the E70 east of Brescia, take Desenzano exit and turn north for Saló on P572. Then take road to Manerba di Garda and site is well signed. GPS: 45.56639, 10.54972

Charges guide

Per unit incl. 2 persons	
and electricity	€ 30.00 - € 48.00
extra person	€ 7.00 - € 13.00

Manerba del Garda
Camping la Rocca

Via Cavalle 22, I-25080 Manerba del Garda (Lake Garda) T: 0365 551 738. E: info@laroccacamp.it

alanrogers.com/IT62830

Set high on a peninsula, on the quieter western shore of Lake Garda, la Rocca is a very friendly, family orientated campsite. The 180 attractive touring pitches enjoy shade from the tree canopy and 20 are on open terraces with lake views. In addition, there are 25 mobile homes to rent. Visitors have the choice of two pebble lakeside beaches with a jetty. The beaches can be accessed from the site and there is a pleasant pool complex. The site has all modern amenities without losing its distinctive Italian ambience with an open feel. Nothing is too much trouble for the management. The owner, Livio, is charming and very engaging with his pleasant, halting English.

Facilities

Two sanitary blocks with smart new units for disabled campers and baby changing areas which are kept in a clean condition at all times. Washing machines. Small shop. Bar with terrace also offers basic meals. Swimming pools. Tennis. Play area. Fishing (permit). Boat launching. Music in the evenings. Miniclub (high season). Torches required on beach steps and tunnel. WiFi in some areas (free). Off site: Bars and restaurants a short walk away.

Open: 15 April - 28 September.

Directions

From A4 autostrada take Desenzano exit and follow SS572 towards Saló for 11 km. and look for site signs. Turn right off main road, then right again along Via Belvedere and it is the second site on Via Cavalle. GPS: 45.56118, 10.56383

Charges guide

Per unit incl. 2 persons	
and electricity	€ 21.00 - € 45.00
extra person	€ 5.00 - € 10.00

Manerba del Garda
Camping Zocco

Via del Zocco 43, I-25080 Manerba del Garda (Lake Garda) T: 036 555 1605. E: info@campingzocco.it

alanrogers.com/IT62850

Camping Zocco is an excellent, professionally run site in a quiet, scenic location sloping gently down towards the lake where there is a jetty, buoys for your boat and a long pleasant shingle beach with a bar. The Sandrini family, who run this site, give British and Dutch visitors a warm welcome and English is spoken. There are 244 pitches for touring units, all with 6A electricity either on slightly sloping ground or terraced. The position and quality of the facilities make Zocco a most attractive option if you prefer a smaller, quieter site which improves year on year.

Facilities

Three tiled sanitary blocks are clean and well cared for. Two are very modern with spacious showers and toilets (some Turkish). Facilities for disabled visitors. Washing machines. Motorcaravan services. Well stocked shop. Bar overlooking beach (limited hours in low season), good restaurant/pizzeria with terrace and bar. Pool complex (22/4-3/10). Fishing. Tennis. Play area. Bocce. Children's entertainment (July/Aug). Bicycle hire arranged. WiFi.

Open: 22 April - 3 October.

Directions

From A4 Milan-Venice take Desenzano exit and head north on SS572 towards Saló for 10 km. Zocco is well signed to right through Manerba. GPS: 45.53967, 10.55595

Charges guide

Per unit incl. 2 persons	
and electricity	€ 17.00 - € 37.50
extra person	€ 6.00 - € 9.50

49

For latest campsite news, availability and prices visit

alanrogers.com

Manerba del Garda
Camping Village Baia Verde

Via del Edera 19, I-25080 Manerba del Garda (Lake Garda) T: 0365 651 753. E: info@campingbaiaverde.com
alanrogers.com/IT62860

Baia Verde is a smart, luxurious and peaceful campsite located in the south western corner of Lake Garda. The 145 touring pitches are in regular rows on flat, open ground where the young trees are giving some shade. The pitches are all fully serviced (16A electricity) and 12 have superb private facilities. The remaining 46 pitches are used for mobile homes to rent and there are apartments available too. The excellent restaurant block and the building housing the other facilities are designed by an architect and it shows. A great deal of thought and loving care has gone into Baia Verde. We were impressed!

Facilities

Full range of high quality sanitary facilities in an impressive three storey building in the style of an Italian villa. Rooms for babies and children. Superb facilities for disabled visitors. Washing machines and dryers. TV lounge. Rooftop sunbathing area with jacuzzi. Entertainment and activity programme (high season). WiFi over site (charged). Only some breeds of dog accepted. Off site: Beach with fishing, swimming and boat launching 400 m.

Open: 12 April - 11 October.

Directions

Manerba is on western shore of Lake Garda at the southern end. From A4 Milan-Venice autostrada take Desenzano exit and head north on SS572 towards Saló for 12 km; then turn right following signs to site. GPS: 45.56155, 10.55352

Charges guide

Per unit incl. 2 persons	
and electricity	€ 26.50 - € 74.00
extra person	€ 6.00 - € 12.50

Manerba del Garda
Camping San Biagio

Via Cavalle 19, I-25080 Manerba del Garda (Lake Garda) T: 036 555 1549. E: info@campingsanbiagio.net
alanrogers.com/IT62870

San Biagio is a great site at the tip of an attractive green peninsula surrounded by Lake Garda. Trees, shrubs and flowers have been planted and it has a pleasant, peaceful ambience. Steeply terraced in some parts to maximise views over the water, the 161 pitches are shaded in places, whilst others are in more open lakeside positions. All have 16A electricity. A good bar/restaurant is located on the water's edge in a charming old building with views of the small connected island which has a second bar. You can walk there when the level of the lake is low. This site has one of the best positions on the lake and has great charm.

Facilities

The large central toilet block is of a high standard and provides excellent facilities which are kept very clean. Supermarket, large restaurant/takeaway and bar (all season). Island bar/snack bar. Play area. Fishing. Boat launching, moorings for boats. WiFi throughout (free). Off site: Bars and restaurants within walking distance. Bicycle hire, tennis, golf and riding 5 km. Sailing 10 km.

Open: Week before Easter - 30 September.

Directions

From A4 (Milan-Venice) take Desenzano exit, head north on SS572 towards Saló for 10 km. and look for site signs. Turn right off main road, then keep left along Via Valtanesi, Via Panoramico, Via Belvedere then Via Cavalle to site. GPS: 45.56352, 10.56638

Charges guide

Per unit incl. 2 persons and	
electricity (on meter)	€ 31.00 - € 56.00
extra person	€ 8.00 - € 12.00

Moniga del Garda
Camping Fontanelle

Via del Magone 13, I-25080 Moniga del Garda (Lake Garda) T: 0365 502 079. E: info@campingfontanelle.it
alanrogers.com/IT62770

Camping Fontanelle, a new member of the HG Hotels group, is situated near the historic village of Moniga and enjoys excellent views across the lake. The site sits on the south west slopes of Lake Garda and has 166 touring pitches on slightly sloping and terraced ground. A further 50 pitches are used by tour operators but there is little impingement. All are marked and have 6A electricity connections (36 are fully serviced) and there are some very pleasant lakeside pitches (at extra cost). Some for tents and touring units are very secluded, being distant from the campsite facilities, although small blocks with toilets are close by. This is a peaceful, friendly site. Good English is spoken.

Facilities

The two main toilet blocks and two smaller blocks are modern and clean with hot water throughout. Facilities for disabled campers. Washing machines and dryers. Motorcaravan services. Large shop. Bar/restaurant. Takeaway. Swimming pools (15/5-15/9, supervised). Tennis. Electronic games. Play area. Live entertainment in high season. Fishing. Boat launching. WiFi (free).

Open: 18 April - 4 October.

Directions

From A4 Milan-Venice autostrada take Desenzano exit and head north on SS572 towards Saló for 10 km. and watch for campsite signs, turning right then right again in 3 km. GPS: 45.5253, 10.5434

Charges guide

Per unit incl. 2 persons	
and electricity	€ 23.80 - € 40.60
No credit cards.	

For latest campsite news, availability and prices visit
alanrogers.com

Pacengo
Camping Lido

Via Peschiera 2, I-37017 Pacengo (Lake Garda) T: 0457 590 030. E: info@campinglido.it
alanrogers.com/IT62540

Camping Lido is one of the largest and amongst the best of the 120 campsites around Lake Garda and is situated at the south east corner of the lake. There is quite a slope from the entrance down to the lake, so many of the 561 grass touring pitches are on terraces which afford lovely views across the lake. They are of varying sizes, separated by hedges, all have 6A Europlug electricity connections. A number of pitches by the lake have 10A electricity, water and two hours free WiFi daily. This is a most attractive site with tall, neatly trimmed trees standing like sentinels on either side of the broad avenue that runs from the entrance right down to the lake.

Facilities

New toilet blocks for 2015 include provision for disabled visitors (key access) and family rooms. Private sanitary facilities can be booked. Washing machines and dryer. Motorcaravan services. Fridge rental. Restaurant, bars, pizzeria, takeaway and well stocked supermarket (all season). Swimming pools, paddling pool and slides. Superb fitness centre. Playground. Tennis. Bicycle hire. Fishing. Activity programme (high season). WiFi (charged).

Open: 27 March - 11 October.

Directions

Leave A4 Milan-Venice motorway at exit for Peschiera. Head north on east side of lake on the SS249. Site entrance on left after Gardaland theme park. GPS: 45.46996, 10.72042

Charges guide

Per unit incl. 2 persons	
and electricity	€ 18.40 - € 45.50
extra person	€ 4.70 - € 11.00

Peschiera del Garda
Camping del Garda

Via Marzan 6, I-37019 Peschiera del Garda (Lake Garda) T: 0457 550 540.
E: prenotazioni@camping-delgarda.com **alanrogers.com/IT62560**

Camping del Garda is directly on the lake with access through gates which provide security at night. This is one of the largest campsites around Lake Garda and is more of a self contained holiday village with many pitches used by tour operators and permanent units, although they are generally separate from the touring pitches. The mature trees provide shade for the 659 grass pitches of which 337 are for touring units. Arranged in numbered rows, all have 4A electrical connections and hedges have been cleverly trimmed for maximum attractiveness. Hard roads give access. This is a well kept site with colour added by attractive flower beds.

Facilities

Eleven good quality toilet blocks have the usual facilities with free hot water in sinks, washbasins and showers. Facilities for disabled visitors in two blocks. Washing machines and dryers. Bars, restaurant and takeaway. Supermarket. Swimming pools. Tennis courts and tennis school. Minigolf. Watersports including windsurf school. Fishing. Play area. Organised activities (July/Aug). Bowls. Dogs and motorcycles are not accepted. WiFi (charged).

Open: 1 April - 30 September.

Directions

Leave the A4 (Milan-Venice) at Peschiera exit and travel through the town towards Garda. Follow signs for Lasize on SS249. After 500 m. turn left at Famila supermarket roundabout where site is signed. GPS: 45.44797, 10.70125

Charges guide

Per unit incl. 2 persons	
and electricity	€ 22.50 - € 57.00
extra person	€ 5.50 - € 15.00

Peschiera del Garda
Camping Butterfly

Lungolago Garibaldi 11, I-37019 Peschiera del Garda (Lake Garda) T: 045 640 1466.
E: info@campingbutterfly.it **alanrogers.com/IT62620**

Camping Butterfly is in the town of Peschiera and has been owned by the same family for 40 years. Giorgio, the younger generation owner, is keen to make your holiday a success. The site is associated with IT62630 Bella Italia. There are 292 flat pitches on grass and sand of which 50 are for touring with 6A electricity and with some shade from mature trees. Many mobile homes are dotted around the camping area. A pleasant swimming pool with a paddling pool (and lifeguard) is available for cooling off and fun. The site is keen to welcome children under 12 years of age accompanied by their parents.

Facilities

Three toilet blocks are light and bright. WCs are mainly British style with some Turkish. Facilities for disabled visitors. Washing machines. Shop. Bar and restaurant plus takeaway. Swimming and paddling pools with lifeguard (hats compulsory). Play area. Multisports court. Entertainment. Miniclub. WiFi on part of site (charged).

Open: 12 March - 6 November.

Directions

From A4 take Peschiera exit and immediately pick up signs for site as you cross the attractive waterways on the 249. Take care as the signs are not that obvious. GPS: 45.44524, 10.69444

Charges guide

Per unit incl. 2 persons	
and electricity	€ 21.00 - € 56.00
No credit cards.	

For latest campsite news, availability and prices visit
alanrogers.com

Peschiera del Garda

Camping Bella Italia

Via Bella Italia 2, I-37019 Peschiera del Garda (Lake Garda) T: 045 640 0688. E: info@camping-bellaitalia.it

alanrogers.com/IT62630

Peschiera is a picturesque village on the southern shore of Lake Garda, and Camping Bella Italia is a very attractive, large, well organised and very busy site in the grounds of a former farm, just west of the centre of the village. Half of the 1,200 pitches are occupied by the site's own mobile homes and chalets and by tour operators; there are some 330 touring pitches, most towards the lakeside and reasonably level on grass under trees. All have 16A electricity, water and waste water and are separated by shrubs. There are some fine views across the lake to the mountains beyond. A superb promenade allows direct access to the town. Bella Italia collaborates with Cisano/San Vito (IT63570) and Butterfly (IT62520). The site slopes gently down to the lake with access to the water for watersports and swimming. A feature of the site is the group of pools of varying shapes and sizes with an entertainment area and varied sports provision nearby. A range of supervised activities is organised. Regulations are in place to ensure that the site is peaceful. English and Dutch are spoken by the friendly staff. Although large, this site has not lost its personal touch, and their sixty years of experience has been wisely used.

Facilities

Six modern toilet blocks have British style toilets, washbasins and showers. Baby rooms and facilities for disabled visitors. Washing machines. Motorcaravan services. Infirmary. Shops. Gelateria. Bars. Waiter service restaurant and terrace and two other restaurants (one in the old farm building). Swimming pools. Tennis. Archery. Playgrounds (small). Games room. Watersports. Fishing. Bicycle hire. Organised activities and entertainment. Mini club. WiFi over part of site (charged). ATMs. Dogs are not accepted. Off site: Fishing 1 km. Golf 2.5 km. Riding 3 km. Gardaland, Italy's most popular theme park, is about 2 km. east of Peschiera, with others nearby. Verona 40 minutes.

Open: 12 March - 23 October.

Directions

Peschiera is 32 km. west of Verona. From A4 take exit for Peschiera del Garda and follow SS11 towards Brescia. Site is at the large junction at the western entrance to the village. GPS: 45.44165, 10.67920

Charges guide

Per unit incl. 2 persons and electricity	€ 27.20 - € 56.50
extra person	€ 6.60 - € 15.00
child (3-5 yrs)	free - € 5.80

Four charging seasons.
No credit/debit cards.

Riva del Garda

Camping Brione

Via Brione 32, I-38066 Riva del Garda (Lake Garda) T: 0464 520 885. E: info@campingbrione.com

alanrogers.com/IT62350

Brione is a municipal site situated on the edge of the small town of Riva at the head of Lake Garda. It is about 500 m. from the town centre and lakeside. There are 110 level pitches, 78 with 6A electricity and trees provide some shade. Some also have water and a waste water point. Terraces on the hillside take 21 tents. There are 39 mobile homes to rent, two equipped for disabled visitors. The site is neat and well tended with spectacular views of the mountains from all pitches. Riva is recognised as one of Europe's windsurfing Meccas due to a combination of strong winds with flat water. The nearby town has many good restaurants.

Facilities

Two refurbished sanitary blocks, one at either end of the site, have mixed Turkish and British style WCs, washbasins in cabins, and facilities for disabled visitors. New baby/children's room. 8 private en-suite shower rooms for hire. Motorcaravan services. Shop for basics (1/4-15/10). Bar/breakfast room with buffet breakfast. Good sized swimming pool (15/6-15/9). Minigolf. TV/video. Bicycle hire. Two play areas. WiFi over site (charged). Off site: Tennis nearby. Fishing, boat launching, sailing 800 m. Restaurants, bars and shops in resort and many more in town centre 2 km. Riding 5 km.

Open: 7 April - 18 October.

Directions

Site is on the north east tip of Lake Garda. From A22 Brenner-Modena motorway, leave at Roverto Sud exit for Lake Garda north, and take SS240 for Nago, Torbole and Riva del Garda. Just before Riva, go through two short tunnels, then immediately turn right at site signs. GPS: 45.88133, 10.86148

Charges guide

Per unit incl. 2 persons and electricity	€ 27.50 - € 35.00
extra person	€ 7.00 - € 9.00
child (4-12 yrs)	€ 4.50 - € 6.50
dog	€ 2.00 - € 4.00

For latest campsite news, availability and prices visit
alanrogers.com

Rivoltella

Camping Village San Francesco

Strada Vicinale San Francesco, I-25015 Rivoltella (Lake Garda) T: 0309 110 245.
E: moreinfo@campingsanfrancesco.com **alanrogers.com/IT62520**

San Francesco is a large, very well organised site situated to the west of the Sirmione peninsula, on the south east shores of Lake Garda. The 323 touring pitches are generally on flat gravel and sand and enjoy shade from mature trees. There are three different sizes of pitch to choose from, with 6A electricity; 76 are fully serviced. They are marked by stones but there is no division between them. A wooded beach area of about 400 m. on the lake is used for watersports and there is a jetty for boating. There are delightful lake views from the restaurant and terrace.

Facilities	Directions
Sanitary facilities are in two large, modern, centrally located buildings. Spotlessly clean and well equipped. Excellent facilities for disabled campers. Shop (sells gluten-free products). Restaurant. Bar. Pool bar. Pizzeria. Takeaway and snacks. In a separate area across the road: swimming pools (26/4-14/9; disability hoist), jacuzzi, sports centre and tennis. Playground. Entertainment, organised activities and excursions. Bicycle hire arranged. Torches required in some areas. WiFi (charged).	From autostrada A4, between Brescia and Verona, exit towards Sirmione and follow signs to Sirmione and site. GPS: 45.46565, 10.59443

Open: 1 April - 30 September.

Charges guide

Per unit incl. 2 persons and electricity	€ 25.00 - € 62.00
extra person	€ 6.50 - € 13.50
child (0-10 yrs)	free - € 9.70
dog	free

San Benedetto

San Benedetto Villaggio Turistico

Strada Bergamini 14, I-37019 San Benedetto (Lake Garda) T: 0457 550 544. E: info@campingsanbenedetto.it
alanrogers.com/IT62640

Overlooking Lake Garda and in a position central to local historic attractions and theme parks, San Benedetto is on a slope and has 371 pitches. Of these, there are 80 reasonably sized, grass touring pitches with shade and some with lakeside views. The restaurant and bar has a large covered terrace area and there is a comprehensive and reasonably priced menu. Additionally, a beach bar serving simple meals is in a pleasant traditional building at one end of the site. A long pathway with reed beds and alternating beach and grass areas for relaxation makes an attractive promenade towards the marina and boat launching area. Two swimming pools provide a welcome cooling alternative to lake swimming.

Facilities	Directions
Four toilet blocks provide mainly British style WCs. Washing machines and dryers. Motorcaravan services. Restaurant and beach snack bar. Two swimming pools. Aerobics. Play areas. Small boat launching. Canoe, motorcycle and bicycle hire. Sub aqua club. Miniclub and entertainment programme all season. WiFi (charged).	Leave autostrada A4 at Pescheria de Garda exit and take lakeside road to Desenzano. At San Benedetto site is well signed on the right. GPS: 45.4482, 10.6697

Open: 15 March - 1 October.

Charges guide

Per unit incl. 2 persons and electricity	€ 33.60 - € 46.00

San Felice del Benaco

Camping Europa Silvella

Via Silvella 10, I-25010 San Felice del Benaco (Lake Garda) T: 0365 651095. E: info@europasilvella.it
alanrogers.com/IT62600

This large, traditional, lakeside site is a slightly confusing merger of two different sites with the result that the 345 pitches (about 108 for touring units) appear randomly dispersed around the site. However, those alongside the lake are in small groups and close together; the main bar, restaurant and shop are also located at the lower level. The main area is at the top of a fairly steep hill on slightly sloping or terraced grass and has slightly larger pitches. There is reasonable shade in many parts and all pitches have 4A electricity. Nine new pitches of 120 sq.m. with 10A electricity have been added. An attractive swimming pool complex also has a daytime bar and a restaurant which serves lunch.

Facilities	Directions
Toilet blocks include washbasins in cabins, facilities for disabled visitors and a superb children's room with small showers. Laundry. Shop. Restaurant/pizzeria. Swimming pools (11/5-13/9, hats required) with bar. Tennis, volleyball and five-a-side soccer. Playground. Bowling alley. Entertainment (every night in July/Aug). Disco for children. Bicycle hire. Tournaments. Fishing and boat launching. First aid room. WiFi on part of site (charged).	From A4 Milan-Venice autostrada take Desenzano exit and go north on SS572 towards Saló for 14 km. Turn right for San Felice and follow brown tourist signs with site name (about 3 km). Enter Manerba del Garda for sat navs. GPS: 45.574474, 10.54857

Open: 29 April - 21 September.

Charges guide

Per unit incl. 2 persons and electricity	€ 23.00 - € 48.00

No credit cards.

San Felice del Benaco
Camping Ideal Molino

Via Gardiola 1, I-25010 San Felice del Benaco (Lake Garda) T: 0365 620 23. E: info@campingmolino.it
alanrogers.com/IT62650

Molino is a small, garden-like site with much charm and character beside Lake Garda. It is in two main areas divided by the site buildings, and the 85 pitches vary in character, some well shaded on level ground by the lake, some for tents on terraces, and many in rows with pergolas and flowering shrubs. All have electricity, water and drainage. The excellent restaurant has superb lake views and serves traditional Italian food. A friendly family atmosphere is maintained at the site by the daughter of the original owners. Ingeborg is delightful and speaks perfect English.

Facilities

Three small sanitary blocks are of a very high standard and include British style WCs (some en-suite with washbasins), adjustable hot showers and hot water to all washbasins. Facilities for disabled visitors. Laundry (attended). Motorcaravan services. Shop, restaurant and bar. Bicycle and canoe hire. Fishing. Free organised entertainment in season. Boat launching. Boat excursions. Boat and caravan storage. WiFi throughout (charged).

Open: 19 March - 9 October.

Directions

From A4 (Milan-Venice) take Desenzano exit and head north on SS572 towards Saló for 13 km; turn right towards San Felice. Pass Guardiola sign then follow brown signs bearing site name, turning right and right again. GPS: 45.5785, 10.5542

Charges guide

Per unit incl. 2 persons
and electricity   € 24.40 - € 53.30
No credit cards.

San Felice del Benaco
Villaggio Turistico La Gardiola

Via Gardiola 36, I-25010 San Felice del Benaco (Lake Garda) T: 0365 559 240. E: info@baiaholiday.com
alanrogers.com/IT62700

Located at the end of a narrow lakeside road, this small neat site has just 25 touring pitches, five are fully serviced. The touring pitches are close to the lake with mobile homes on the slope above. The reception, bar and café with a terrace are modest but attractive and overlook the lake. The sanitary amenities are of a high standard and discretely built underground, preventing any intrusion on the beautiful views. We found this a delightful, friendly site with cheerful staff who give you a chance to practise your Italian. The lakeside beach is just five metres from the closest pitches and is brilliant for peaceful picnics in sight of your pitch.

Facilities

The sanitary block is just below ground level and has a mixture of Turkish and British style WCs. Lift system for disabled visitors. The facilities are quite small but are adequate. Free hot water. Laundry. Motorcaravan services. Small kiosk with terrace for coffee and snacks. Small playground. Fishing. Diving. Bicycle hire. WiFi (charged). Off site: Restaurants, shops, pizzerias nearby. Golf and riding 1 km.

Open: 1 April - 12 October.

Directions

From A4 (Milan-Venice) take Desenzano exit and head north on SS572 towards Saló for 13 km; turn right towards San Felice. Site is well signed (La Gardiola) before town. Access is via a long, narrow lane. GPS: 45.57861, 10.55388

Charges guide

Per unit incl. 2 persons,
water and electricity   € 21.00 - € 47.50
extra person   € 6.00 - € 12.50

San Felice del Benaco
Fornella Camping

Via Fornella 1, I-25010 San Felice del Benaco (Lake Garda) T: 036 562 294. E: fornella@fornella.it
alanrogers.com/IT62750

Fornella Camping is one of the few campsites on Lake Garda still surrounded by farmed olive trees and retaining a true country atmosphere. Parts of the crisp, clean site have great lake views, others a backdrop of mountains and attractive countryside. The 266 touring pitches are on flat grass, terraced where necessary and most have good shade, all with 6/10A electricity; 101 have water and a drain as well. The remaining pitches are used for mobile homes to rent. The staff speak excellent English and Dutch. A superb lagoon pool complex is here, along with a more traditional pool.

Facilities

Three very clean, modern toilet blocks have mainly British type WCs and hot water in washbasins (some in cabins), showers and sinks. Facilities for disabled visitors. Laundry. Motorcaravan services. Shop. Bar/restaurant. Pizzeria and takeaway. Supervised swimming pools and paddling pool (7/5-19/9). Tennis. Two playgrounds and entertainment for children in season. Beach. Bicycle hire (high season). Beach. Fishing. Small marina. WiFi throughout (charged).

Open: 23 April - 25 September.

Directions

From A4 Milan-Venice autostrada take Desenzano exit and head north on SS572 towards Saló for 13 km; turn right towards San Felice and follow signs. GPS: 45.58497, 10.56582

Charges guide

Per unit incl. 2 persons
and electricity   € 26.00 - € 63.00
extra person   € 6.50 - € 13.00

55

For latest campsite news, availability and prices visit
alanrogers.com

San Felice del Benaco
Camping Villaggio Weekend

Via Vallone della Selva 2, I-25010 San Felice del Benaco (Lake Garda) T: 0365 437 12. E: info@weekend.it
alanrogers.com/IT62800

Created among the olive groves and terraced vineyards of the Château Villa Louisa, which overlooks it, this modern, well equipped site enjoys some superb views over the small bay which forms this part of Lake Garda. On reaching the site you will pass through a most impressive pair of gates. There are 248 pitches, all with 6/10A electricity, of which 79 are used by tour operators and for mobile homes. The touring pitches are in several different areas and many enjoy superb views. Some pitches for larger units are set in the upper terraces on steep slopes, so manoeuvring can be challenging and low olive branches may cause problems for long or high units.

Facilities

Three sanitary blocks, one below the restaurant/shop, are modern and well maintained. Mainly British style WCs, a few washbasins in cabins and facilities for disabled visitors in one. Baby room. Laundry. Shop. Bar/restaurant (waiter service). Takeaway. Supervised swimming pool and paddling pool. Entertainment programme all season. TV. Barbecues. All facilities are open throughout the season. Two playgrounds. English spoken. WiFi in some areas (charged). Off site: Beach and fishing 400 m.

Open: 12 April - 5 October.

Directions

From Milan-Venice autostrada take Desenzano exit towards Saló and Localitá Cisano-San Felice. Watch for narrow right fork after Cunettone roundabout. Pass petrol station on left, then turn right towards San Felice for 1 km. Site is next left. GPS: 45.59318, 10.53088

Charges guide

Per unit incl. 2 persons	
and electricity	€ 15.50 - € 70.00
extra person	€ 4.00 - € 12.50

Sirmione
The Garda Village

Via Coorti Romane, 47, I-25019 Sirmione (Lake Garda) T: 0309 904 552. E: info@gardavillage.it
alanrogers.com/IT62523

Camping Garda Village is a large (16 hectares), well equipped, modern Holiday Village with over 450 apartments, bungalows and mobile homes. There are no pitches for touring units. It is situated on the southern end of beautiful Lake Garda, on the Sirmione peninsula between Peschiera del Garda and Desenzano del Garda, and has its own private sandy beach. There is an extensive bar/restaurant complex and three separate swimming pools including one for children. The sun terraces have dramatic views of the lake and mountains overlooking the village. Breakfast, half- and full board available.

Facilities

Launderettes. Restaurant/pizzeria, international menu, large terrace bar with panoramic views over the lake, with shows and cabaret (May-Sept). Two cafés. Supermarket (June-Sept). Swimming pool complex including children's pool and play area with slide (16/5-15/10). Hairdresser. Tennis. Multisports court. Volleyball. Minigolf. Football. Riding. Archery. Fishing. Play area. Watersports equipment and bicycle hire. WiFi. Dogs are not accepted.

Open: 28 March - 25 October.

Directions

Leave the A4, Turin–Venice motorway at Sirmione junction. At roundabout take SP13 north west for approx. 4 km. to roundabout. Take SPB811 west for 800 m. to roundabout then take Vialle Francesco Agello north east for 800 m. to site. GPS: 45.4658, 10.59558

Charges guide

Contact the site.

Torbole
Camping Al Porto

Via al Cor, 3, I-38069 Torbole sul Garda (Lake Garda) T: 0464 50 5891. E: info@campingalporto.it
alanrogers.com/IT62370

This is a small pleasant site built on what was the owner's family farm 50 years ago. It is peaceful, set back from the main road, and a short stroll from the very attractive promenade with its bars and restaurants. The grass pitches are level with mature trees providing shade. Hedges separate the two camping areas, one with 80 touring pitches with 6/16A electricity. The other area is primarily for tents (no electricity) and has a secure hut for windsurfing equipment. Near the modern reception (with wonderful historic photos on the wall) is a small bar with a terraced area where basic snacks are served.

Facilities

The clean, modern toilet block has British and Turkish style WCs and hot water throughout. Facilities for disabled campers. Washing machines and dryers. Motorcaravan services. Bar with snacks including light breakfasts (all season). Boat launching. Play area with adventure unit. WiFi throughout (charged). Off site: Shops and cafés a short walk. Fishing and bicycle hire 100 m. Riding 3 km.

Open: 19 March - 9 October.

Directions

From A22 (Brenner-Modena), leave at Roverto Sud exit for Lake Garda north, and take SS240 for Nago and Riva del Garda. At roundabout in Torbole, turn right (Riva). Site is signed to left in 200 m. before bridge over river. GPS: 45.87210, 10.87292

Charges guide

Per unit incl. 2 persons	
and electricity	€ 24.50 - € 33.00

For latest campsite news, availability and prices visit
alanrogers.com

THERE ARE TWO PROVINCES IN THE REGION: BOLZANO AND TRENTO

Trentino-Alto Adige is a region of mixed Austrian and Italian influences, and much of it has only been part of Italy since 1919. The landscape is dominated by the majestic Dolomites, snow-clad in winter and carpeted with Alpine plants in summer.

Before 1919, Alto Adige was known as the South Tyrol and formed part of Austria. However, at the end of the First World War, Austria ceded it to the Italians. As a result there are marked cultural differences between the provinces as reflected in the cuisine, architecture and language (both German and Italian are spoken).

The landscape of Trentino-Alto Adige is dramatic and amongst the most beautiful in the country. With only a couple of snow-free months a year, the region is a winter sports haven, and there is also a good network of well established trails which vary in length from a day's walk to a two week trek or longer. Covering the whole Ortles range and topped by one of Europe's largest glaciers is the Stelvio National Park. One of Italy's major parks, it is popular with skiers, walkers and cyclists; the annual Giro d'Italia, Italy's answer to the Tour de France, passes through here. It also boasts an abundant wildlife, with red deer, elk, chamois, golden eagles and ibex. There are several other parks in the region including the Panevéggio National Park, a predominantly forested area with numerous nature trails and a lake.

Places of interest

Bolzano: 15th-century church, archaeology museum with a 5,300-year-old preserved mummy.

Canazei: mountainside town, good place for exploring the Dolomites.

Cembra: wine producing town.

Merano: attractive spa town.

Ortisei: major centre for wood carving.

Roverto: 15th-century castle converted into a war museum.

Trento: attractive town with 13th/15th-century church, Romanesque cathedral, impressive city square.

Cuisine of the region

The food is a mix of Germanic and Italian influences. Traditional dishes include game and rabbit with polenta, sauerkraut, and sausages with horseradish sauce (*salsa al cren*). Desserts are often based on apples, pears or plums, readily available from the local orchards. The region also produces a variety of wines including the famous Pinot Grigios and Chardonnays.

Apfel strudel: apple pastry.

Canederli: bread dumplings flavoured with smoked ham.

Soffiato alla Trentino: meringue trifle.

Strangolapreti: bread and spinach gnocchi.

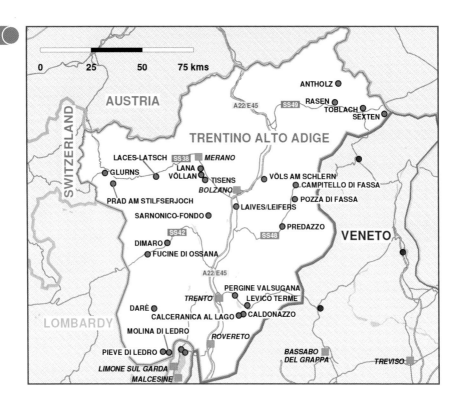

Antholz

Camping Antholz

Artholz Obertal 34, I-39030 Antholz (Trentino - Alto Adige) T: 0474 492 204. E: info@camping-antholz.com

alanrogers.com/IT62010

Camping Antholz is an all-year campsite in the heart of the Dolomites, with picturesque meadows, forests and impressive mountain views. The 120 pitches, numbered but only roughly marked out, have at least 4A electricity and 50 have 16A electricity, water and waste water. Just inside the entrance is a traditional building with a welcoming reception and a smart restaurant. High up in the Anterselva valley, there are splendid views of near and distant peaks. This is good skiing country in winter (ski bus, ski school, ski lifts) and nearby is an internationally important Biathlon Centre. In summer, with a new national park nearby, Camping Antholz is a great place for walkers, cyclists, mountain bikers and for those who prefer to explore the valleys and mountain roads of this wonderful region by car.

Facilities

The sanitary facilities are of an extremely high standard, with underfloor heating in addition to the normal facilities. Hair salon. Cosmetics room with infra-red sauna. Baby room. Washing machine and dryer. Motorcaravan services. Bar, restaurant and takeaway (all year). Shop for basics. Playground. TV room. Bicycle hire. Limited entertainment programme for children in high season. WiFi (charged). Off site: Skiing and biathlon 1 km. Fishing 3 km. Riding and golf 13 km. Many waymarked tracks for walking and cycling.

Open: All year.

Directions

Antholz/Anterselva is 90 km. north east of Bolzano. From Bressanone/Brixen exit on A22 (Brenner-Modena), go east on SS49 for 50 km, then turn north (signed Antholz) for 12 km. Pass upper Antholz village and site is on right. GPS: 46.86442, 12.10937

Charges guide

Per unit incl. 2 persons	
and electricity (4A)	€ 17.00 - € 31.00
extra person	€ 6.00 - € 10.00
child (3-16 yrs)	€ 4.50 - € 7.50
dog	€ 3.50 - € 4.00

For latest campsite news, availability and prices visit
alanrogers.com

Calceranica al Lago
Camping Fleiola

Via Trento 42, I-38050 Calceranica al Lago (Trentino - Alto Adige) T: 0461 723 153. E: info@campingfleiola.it
alanrogers.com/IT61975

Celebrating its fiftieth anniversary in 2012, this family run campsite is attractively located on one of the smaller and most easterly of the Italian lakes. The 92 touring pitches are moderately sized (65 sq.m), with those on the lakeside costing a little more, and 3A electricity included. There are four modern, well equipped mobile homes and 11 old and very basic bungalows for hire. The private 300 m. beach, made up partly of pebbles and partly of fine gravel, slopes gently at one end and falls away sharply at the other. Children's activities are organised daily (except Sundays) in high season.

Facilities

New high quality toilet block includes washbasins and showers and good facilities for disabled visitors. Small bar with terrace and TV (from end May). Small shop sells fresh bread and basics. Play area. Organised activities for children (high season). Fishing. WiFi. Off site: Water skiing, sailing, windsurfing and canoeing on lake. Numerous cycle tracks. Hiking, mountain biking, hang-gliding and paragliding. Trains to Trento and beyond from adjacent station.

Open: 24 March - 30 September.

Directions

From A22 Verona-Brenner, leave at Trento-Nord, follow signs for SS47 (Valsugana, Padova). 3 km. after Pergine follow signs for S. Cristoforo, along lake to Calceranica. At 2nd roundabout turn left onto Viale Trento. Site is just after railway bridge (height limit 3.25 m). GPS: 46.006828, 11.245252

Charges guide

Per unit incl. 2 persons, electricity, water and drainage	€ 19.00 - € 45.00

No credit cards.

Calceranica al Lago
Camping Spiaggia Lago di Caldonazzo

Viale Venezia 14, I-38050 Calceranica al Lago (Trentino - Alto Adige) T: 0461 723 037.
E: info@campingspiaggia.net **alanrogers.com/IT62230**

Camping Spiaggia is a welcoming, family run site with private beach access on Lake Caldonazzo. The bar and snack bar is situated on the lakeshore with a beautiful panorama of the lake and surrounding mountains. There are 104 touring pitches (80-100 sq.m), some with shade and all with 6A electricity. On-site activities are limited, although a wellness centre is planned. Swimming is possible in the lake and there are plenty of opportunities nearby for watersports. Other more adventurous sports can also be organised such as rafting, canyoning or hydro speed.

Facilities

One modern sanitary block with some private cabins for hire. Facilities for disabled visitors. Laundry facilities. Motorcaravan services. Shop. Bar/restaurant and pizzeria. Wellness centre planned. Direct lake access. Lake swimming. Fishing. Windsurfing. Beach volleyball. Play area. Bicycle hire. WiFi over site (charged). Mobile homes for rent. Off site: Cafés and shops in nearby Caldonazzo.

Open: 3 April - 27 September.

Directions

Lake Caldonazzo is to the east of the A22. From Levico Terme, head west on SP1 to Caldonazzo and then follow signs to the site which is on the busy lakeside road. GPS: 46.004343, 11.259763

Charges guide

Per unit incl. 2 persons and electricity	€ 21.00 - € 37.00
extra person	€ 6.00 - € 11.00

Calceranica al Lago
Camping Punta Lago

Via Lungo Lago 70, I-38050 Calceranica al Lago (Trentino - Alto Adige) T: 0461 723 229.
E: info@campingpuntalago.com **alanrogers.com/IT62260**

Camping Punta Lago is in a beautiful setting on Lago di Caldonazzo. This attractive family run campsite, with easy lake access across a main road, has 140 level, shaded pitches on grass. Of a good size, all have 3/6A electricity and 50 are serviced with water and drainage. The campsite first opened 50 years ago and brothers Gino and Mauro continue the friendly family tradition of ensuring you enjoy your holiday. As a former President of the Consortia Trentino Outdoors, Gino knows all about the range of activities available locally including fishing, lake swimming, windsurfing, sailing and canoeing.

Facilities

One central sanitary block has superb facilities with hot water throughout. Well designed bathroom and washbasin area. Excellent facilities for babies and disabled visitors. Private units for rent. Washing machines and dryer. Freezer. Small shop. Bar/snack bar. Fishing (with permit). Modern play area. Entertainment programme (July/Aug). Internet access. WiFi over site (charged). Cinema. TV. Off site: Bicycle hire, town and ATM 1 km. Watersports. Train (1 km) to Venice and other cities.

Open: 1 May - 13 September.

Directions

From A22 Bolzano-Trento take SS47 for Padova. After 15 km. turn for Lago di Caldonazzo and Calceranica al Lago. Approaching from west by the railway, continue along Via Donegani, turn left at Esso station into Via al Lago and right at lakeside into Via Lungo Lago. GPS: 46.00230, 11.25450

Charges guide

Per unit incl. 2 persons and electricity	€ 17.00 - € 42.00
extra person	€ 7.00 - € 11.00

For latest campsite news, availability and prices visit
alanrogers.com

Calceranica al Lago
Camping Al Pescatore

Via dei Pescatori 1, I-38050 Calceranica al Lago (Trentino - Alto Adige) T: 0461 723 062.
E: trentino@campingpescatore.it **alanrogers.com/IT62270**

The enchanting small lake of Calceranica lies just to the east of Trento, in the foothills of the Dolomites, amidst splendid scenery. Camping Al Pescatore is a small, very pretty, family campsite with a long tradition of camping and where daughter, Giulia, speaks excellent English. The site has a pool complex, attractive landscaping and a small poolside café with terrace. There are 244 touring pitches, all with 6A electricity (long leads required on some), on grass under tall trees. A separate area immediately opposite the entrance has one third of these pitches; however, many of the toilets here are of Turkish style. The lake is very popular and busy at weekends and during the summer season.

Facilities

Three renovated toilet blocks on the main site provide the usual facilities and there is a single unisex block in the overflow section. Facilities for disabled visitors. Baby rooms. Washing machines. Motorcaravan services. Shop, bar and restaurant. Swimming pools with spa, paddling pool and slides (24/5-15/9). Playground. Organised activities for children and music and dancing for adults in July/Aug. WiFi (charged).

Open: 9 May - 13 September.

Directions

Leave A22 (Brenner-Modena) motorway at Trento Nord, follow SS47 towards Padova to San Cristoforo and follow signs to Calceranica and site. Do not follow GPS as this will take you to a no through road. GPS: 46.01000, 11.24100

Charges guide

Per unit incl. 2 persons and electricity	€ 18.00 - € 39.00
extra person	€ 9.00 - € 12.00

Caldonazzo
Camping Mario Village

Via Lungolago, 4, I-38052 Caldonazzo (Trentino - Alto Adige) T: 0461 723 341.
E: direzione@campingmario.com **alanrogers.com/IT62255**

Camping Mario is a family site, across a small road from Lake Caldonazzo, one of the most attractive small Italian lakes where swimming, fishing and other water-based activities can be enjoyed. The 160 grassy touring pitches (80-150 sq.m) have 6/10A electricity and a further 52 also have water and drainage. Mobile homes are also available for rent. There is a large swimming pool with a new bar/pizzeria/restaurant adjacent and new play areas for children. There is also a good mini-market. This region is popular for mountain sports, particularly mountain biking, trekking and rafting.

Facilities

Two well maintained toilet blocks provide all the usual facilities including an area for children and two rooms for disabled visitors (key access). Laundry facilities. Motorcaravan services. Well stocked shop selling fresh bread. Bar. Restaurant/pizzeria. Large swimming pool with children's pool. New play areas. Miniclub, teenage club and evening entertainment for adults in high season. Bicycle hire. Mobile homes to rent. WiFi over site (free in low season). Off site: Fishing 200 m. Bicycle hire 1.5 km.

Open: 23 April - 20 September.

Directions

Leave A22 motorway at Trento Nord and follow SS47 towards Padova. After Pergine and Valsugana, follow signs to Calceranica/Caldonazzo. After Caldonazzo railway station turn left and after level crossing turn left again towards the lake and site is well signed. GPS: 46.004662, 11.260619

Charges guide

Per unit incl. 2 persons and electricity	€ 12.00 - € 68.00
extra person	€ 6.00 - € 10.00

Campitello di Fassa
Camping Miravalle

Strèda de Greva 39, I-38031 Campitello di Fassa (Trentino - Alto Adige) T: 0462 750 502.
E: info@campingmiravalle.it **alanrogers.com/IT62095**

Miravalle has a wonderful mountain backdrop in a peaceful location, but unusually is within the very pretty mountain village of Campitello with entertainment and services. The 135 touring pitches are neat and very grassy, all with 3/6A electricity, 40 are fully serviced. Some are terraced and others are at the level of the river (minimal fencing). All the site facilities are of modern construction and top quality, located in the centre of the site. We liked the clean freshness of this place and the views from anywhere on the site are fabulous.

Facilities

Excellent modern sanitary facilities are fully equipped and of a very high standard. Provision for babies and disabled campers is very good. Laundry facilities. Motorcaravan services. Bar, snacks and takeaway. Restaurant (July/Aug). Play area. Entertainment (15/7-25/8). Communal barbecue. Fishing. WiFi over site (charged). Apartments for rent. Off site: Village centre 50 m.

Open: 1 December - 30 March, 1 June - 30 September.

Directions

From A22, take Egna/Ora exit and follow SS48 for 40 km. (towards Val di Fiemme). Site is clearly signed in Campitello. GPS: 46.474828, 11.740726

Charges guide

Per unit incl. 2 persons and electricity	€ 25.00 - € 37.00
extra person	€ 8.00 - € 12.50

For latest campsite news, availability and prices visit
alanrogers.com

Darè
Camping Val Rendena

Via Civico 117, I-38080 Darè (Trentino - Alto Adige) T: 0465 801 669. E: info@campingvalrendena.com
alanrogers.com/IT62135

Set in the Adamello Brenta National Park, a refuge of the European brown bear, Camping Val Rendena, is an enthusiastically run family site with a very friendly feel. There are 62 level grass touring pitches with some tree shade, all with 6A electricity and spread out between the seasonal pitches. The site's location makes it an ideal base from which to explore this beautiful region, rich in flora and fauna, where wooded hills with many marked paths reach up to 1,800 m. Beside the site runs the Sarca river, bordered for much of its journey by a cycleway.

Facilities

Two sanitary units, a small one in the reception block, a larger one at centre of site, have hot water, controllable showers and washbasins in cabins. Facilities for disabled visitors. Baby room. Laundry. Motorcaravan service area. Shop selling essentials. Solar heated swimming pool with adjoining children's pool (1/6-30/9). Large playing field. Play area with table tennis and play room. Bicycle hire. Communal barbecue. Massage and other treatments by appointment. Apartments and mobile homes to rent. WiFi at reception (free). Off site: Pizza restaurant adjoins site.

Open: 16 May - 30 September.

Directions

From A22 (E45) Brenner-Verona take exit for Trento-Centro. Then travel westerly on SS45b to Sarche, then SS237 to Ponte Arche and Tione di Trento. From here head north on SS239 towards Madonna di Campiglio for 10 km. to Darè. On entering Darè take descending slip road to right then follow camping signs to site by river. Ignore sat nav. GPS: 46.07440, 10.71718

Charges guide

Per unit incl. 2 persons
and electricity   € 18.00 - € 35.00

Dimaro
Dolomiti Camping Village & Wellness Resort

Via Gole 105, I-38025 Dimaro (Trentino - Alto Adige) T: 0463 974 332. E: info@campingdolomiti.com
alanrogers.com/IT61830

Dolomiti di Brenta is open for separate winter and summer seasons. It is situated at an altitude of 800 m. in an attractive, open valley surrounded by the rugged Dolomite Mountains, and is only 100 m. from the River Noce. It is an ideal base to explore this fantastic region. There are 190 level and grassy pitches, all with 4/6A electricity and some fully serviced. Young trees offer a little shade. The pitches range in size from small (25 sq.m), suitable for small tents, to large (120 sq.m), suitable for medium sized outfits. Cars must be parked away from pitches.

Facilities

Modern, heated toilet block with all necessary facilities including private bathrooms for rent. Washing machine, dryer. Motorcaravan services. Small shop (1/6-10/9). Bar, restaurant, pizzeria. Heated outdoor swimming pool (30/5-10/9). Excellent wellness centre. Large play area. Communal barbecues. Football. Volleyball. Bicycle hire. Free WiFi over site. Dogs are not accepted (July/Aug).

Open: 23 May - 28 September, 5 December - 10 April.

Directions

Leave A22 Brenner motorway at San Micholo All'Adige, 40 km. south of Bolzano. Follow signs for SS43 through Cles, then SS42 through Malè. 19 km. after Cles turn left in Via Gole, site is on right. GPS: 46.325278, 10.863056

Charges guide

Per unit incl. 2 persons
and electricity   € 28.20 - € 42.30

Fucine di Ossana
Camping Cevedale

Via di Sotto Pila 4, I-38026 Fucine di Ossana (Trentino - Alto Adige) T: 046 375 1630.
E: info@campingcevedale.it **alanrogers.com/IT62110**

Nestled under a castle and close to a tiny village, Camping Cevedale has a European atmosphere with very little English spoken. You will be made welcome by Maura who owns the site. The 197 pitches are grouped in two areas on either side of a fast flowing river (fenced) which generates a pleasant, natural sound. The touring pitches, all with electricity (only 2A), are shaded, on grass and slope somewhat; they are in various areas among the well kept seasonal caravans. Some campers come here every holiday and most have built complex wooden chalets next to their caravans. We loved it here.

Facilities

Two sanitary blocks with mainly Turkish style WCs are well maintained, modern and spotlessly clean. Heated in winter, there is hot water to showers and washbasins. Washing machine and dryer. Small shop. Pleasant bar serves snacks. Large play area. Picnic area with tables and gas/charcoal barbecues. Bicycle hire. Entertainment. Education area for children. Free ski bus. Adventure sport courses arranged. Internet access. WiFi throughout (free). Dogs are not accepted. Off site: Ossana village 500 m.

Open: All year.

Directions

From A22 (Brenner-Modena) take exit for San Michele, north of Trento, then SS43 north for 43 km. to Cles. Turn east on SS42 for 26 km. to Fucine. Go through village, turn south on SP202 (Ossana). Follow signs for campsite (not sat nav!). Entrance is next to bridge. GPS: 46.30834, 10.73361

Charges guide

Per unit incl. 2 persons
and electricity   € 25.00 - € 35.00

For latest campsite news, availability and prices visit
alanrogers.com

Glurns

Campingpark Gloria Vallis

Wiesenweg 5, I-39020 Glurns (Trentino - Alto Adige) T: 0473 835 160. E: info@gloriavallis.it
alanrogers.com/IT62130

Gloria Vallis is a style setter. The 92 terraced pitches are well grassed, level and all have 8A electricity, water and drainage. All have lovely mountain views and young trees provide some shade. The whole site is most attractive with flowers and landscaping. There is an elegant curved restaurant and bar with a spectacular panorama across the valley with its thousands of apple trees and snow capped mountains beyond. Another more casual eating area is across a grass field alongside a small lake which is stocked with fish. A very modern building houses the excellent sanitary facilities and a new, sympathetically designed, outdoor swimming pool opened in 2015.

Facilities

The sanitary block with underfloor heating is equipped to the highest possible standard including showers with basin, WC and hairdryer. Excellent en-suite facilities for disabled visitors. Five private rooms for hire (from € 15 per day) with shower, toilet, basin, bidet, hairdryer, safe and music system. Excellent laundry area. Motorcaravan services. Bar, restaurants and shop (bread can be ordered for the following morning). Outdoor swimming pool. Lake for fishing. Play area. Internet access.

Open: 1 April - 31 October.

Directions

Glurns/Glorenza is 50 km. west of Merano via the SS38 then the SS40. Follow signs for the Reschenpass. In Sluderno/Sluderns turn west onto the SS41. Site is in 1 km. (signed). Can be approached from north on SS40 from Austria, on good roads. GPS: 46.67317, 10.57013

Charges guide

Per unit incl. 2 persons and electricity	€ 36.80 - € 43.90
extra person	€ 9.70 - € 12.00

Laces-Latsch

Camping Latsch an der Etsch

Reichstrasse 4, via Nazionale 4, I-39021 Laces-Latsch (Trentino - Alto Adige) T: 0473 623 217.
E: info@camping-latsch.com **alanrogers.com/IT62120**

This site has splendid views to the surrounding mountains. Some of the 100 shaded touring pitches are alongside the river, others are set on slopes. All have 6A electricity and 50 also have water and drainage. The site and its adjoining hotel reveal an array of amenities when explored and campers may use all the facilities of the hotel. Two interconnected swimming pools, one in the hotel, the other outside, are a great feature. Mountain walkers and anyone with adventurous ambitions will be in their element here and several chair lifts give access to higher slopes. This is an unusual site with a huge variety of things to do and a very pleasant ambiance.

Facilities

The sanitary block, refurbished in 2014, is on two floors and is heated in cool weather. Private bathrooms for hire. Facilities for disabled visitors. Washing machine and dryer. Motorcaravan services. Shop, bar and lovely restaurant. Heated indoor pool, sauna, solarium and fitness room. Larger, outdoor pool with marble surrounds. Playground. Indoor bowls and pool. Use of hotel facilities.

Open: 1 January - 10 November.

Directions

Latsch/Laces is 28 km. west of Merano on the SS38 Bolzano-Silandro road. Site entrance is by the Hotel Vermoi. GPS: 46.622592, 10.864921

Charges guide

Per unit incl. 2 persons and electricity	€ 29.90 - € 36.00
extra person	€ 7.80 - € 8.80
child (3-11 yrs)	€ 6.50 - € 7.80

Laives/Leifers

Camping-Park Steiner

J. F. Kennedy Str. 32, I-39055 Laives/Leifers (Trentino - Alto Adige) T: 0471 950 105.
E: info@campingsteiner.com **alanrogers.com/IT62100**

The very welcoming Camping Steiner is very central for touring with the whole of the Dolomite region within easy reach. With a happy atmosphere and much on-site activity, one could spend an enjoyable holiday here. The 180 individual touring pitches, mostly with good shade and hardstanding, are in rows with easy access and all have 6A electricity. There is a pleasant, family style pizzeria/restaurant with a great menu, plus indoor and outdoor pools with a sunbathing area. The Steiner Park Hotel at the entrance to the site provides another restaurant, café and full hotel facilities.

Facilities

The two sanitary blocks are equipped to a high standard and can be heated in cool weather. Facilities for disabled campers. Shop. Bar/pizzeria/restaurant with takeaway (11/4-30/10). Outdoor swimming pool with paddling pool (11/4-30/9). Aquagym. Smaller covered heated pool (11/4-30/10). Playground. Entertainment incl. wine tastings. Dogs are not accepted in July/Aug. WiFi (free).

Open: 21 March - 31 October.

Directions

From north, at Bolzano-Süd exit from A22 (Brenner-Modena) follow Trento signs for 7 km. then signs for 'centre' Leifers/Laives. GPS: 46.42950, 11.3434

Charges guide

Per unit incl. 2 persons and electricity	€ 28.00 - € 36.00
extra person	€ 7.00 - € 9.00

For latest campsite news, availability and prices visit
alanrogers.com

Lana
Komfortcamping & Resort Schlosshof

Feldgatterweg, I-39011 Lana (Trentino - Alto Adige) T: 0473 561 469. E: info@schlosshof.it
alanrogers.com/IT61860

Komfortcamping Schlosshof is a hotel with its own campsite of 134 pitches. The site is open from March to mid November and offers hotel standard facilities with the aim of making your stay special. The level touring pitches are between 80-130 sq.m. on either shale or grass, all with 16A electricity and many are fully serviced. The site is close to Lana, one of the largest villages in the South Tirol and famous for its Mediterranean climate. This is a German-speaking area of Italy and a good base for active families wishing to explore this region of natural beauty.

Facilities

Three well equipped sanitary blocks are all of a very high standard. Facilities for disabled visitors and families. Laundry facilities. Motorcaravan service point. Restaurant, bar and takeaway (all from 16/3). Bread available mornings. Indoor and outdoor swimming pools (from 16/3). Jacuzzi. Sauna. Solarium. Massage. Fenced play area. WiFi throughout (free). Off site: Bus stop 200 m. Golf and bicycle hire 2 km. Fishing 3 km. Hiking. Tennis.

Open: 1 March - 13 November.

Directions

Leave A22 Brenner motorway at Bozen Süd. Take expressway towards Meran. At the Lana-Burgstall exit turn left. Continue across first roundabout for about 500 m. and turn right at Gasthof Tennis where site is signed. GPS: 46.61192, 11.16846

Charges guide

Per unit incl. 2 persons	
and electricity (plus meter)	€ 38.00
extra person	€ 10.00

Lana
Camping Arquin

Feldgatterweg 25, I-39011 Lana (Trentino - Alto Adige) T: 0473 561 187. E: info@camping-arquin.it
alanrogers.com/IT61865

Camping Arquin is in the South Tirol (Alto Adige) where the majority of the population speak German. It is open from early March to mid November and lies in an open valley surrounded by orchards, beyond which are high mountains. This is a region of natural beauty and is famous for its flowery meadows. The site is close to the village of Lana, one of the largest in the South Tirol and famous for its Mediterranean climate. There are 120 sunny, level, grass pitches up to 100 sq.m, all with 6A electricity and many are fully serviced. The interesting old town of Meran is only 7 km. away and is accessible by bus.

Facilities

Modern toilet block with all necessary facilities including those for babies and disabled visitors. Motorcaravan corviooo. Small shop (15/3-5/11). Restaurant and bar (30/3-31/10). Small heated outdoor swimming pool (1/4-30/9). Play area. WiFi throughout (free). Charcoal barbecues not permitted. Off site: Bus stop 200 m. Large swimming pool 200 m. (May onwards; free to campers). Historical town of Meran 7 km. Museums. Golf 2 km.

Open: 1 March - 15 November.

Directions

Leave A22 Brenner motorway at Bozen Süd. Take expressway towards Meran. At the Lana-Burgstall exit turn left. After 250 m. take first right and follow signs to site. GPS: 46.611151, 11.174434

Charges guide

Per unit incl. 2 persons	
and electricity	€ 33.00 - € 37.00
extra person	€ 7.00
child (5-10 yrs)	€ 4.00

Levico Terme
Camping Due Laghi

Localitá Costa 3, I-38056 Levico Terme (Trentino - Alto Adige) T: 0461 706 290. E: info@campingclub.it
alanrogers.com/IT62250

Due Laghi has a new entrance and reception with very helpful and welcoming staff. This attractive site with flowers and trees is close to the main road but it is quiet, with mountain views and only five minutes walk from Lake Levico, where it has a small private beach. There are over 400 level touring pitches on grass, all with 3/10A electricity. The site has a good pool and excellent facilities for adults and children. A new Camperstop with services, Internet access and restaurant is open all year.

Facilities

The central toilet block is very large and of good quality with British and Turkish style WCs, some washbasins in cubicles, a baby room and a unit for disabled visitors. Private facilities to rent. Laundry. Motorcaravan services. Shop (7/6-7/9). Bar (21/5-6/9). Restaurant, pizzeria and café/bar with takeaway. Heated swimming pool (over 300 sq.m) and paddling pool. Entertainment and music (high season). Playground. Tennis. Bicycle hire. Free WiFi. Off site: Fishing (for children) 600 m. Sailing 1 km.

Open: 25 April - 6 September.

Directions

Levico Terme is 20 km. south east of Trento and the site is west of the town, just off the SS47 Trento-Bassano-Padova road. Take exit for Caldonazzo, Levico Terme. Site has a new entrance opposite petrol station (Due Laghi and Camperstop 47). Look for campsite signs immediately on leaving the main road. GPS: 46.00396, 11.28865

Charges guide

Per unit incl. 2 persons	
and electricity	€ 22.00 - € 40.00
extra person	€ 8.00 - € 11.00

For latest campsite news, availability and prices visit
alanrogers.com

Levico Terme

Camping Lago di Levico

Località Pleina, I-38056 Levico Terme (Trentino - Alto Adige) T: 046 170 6491. E: info@campinglevico.com

alanrogers.com/IT62290

Camping Lago di Levico, by a pretty lakeside in the mountains, was formed from the merging of two popular sites. An impressive new reception has efficient systems and you are soon on one of 430 grassy and shaded pitches. All pitches have 6A electricity, 150 also have water and drainage and 12 have private facilities. The lakeside pitches are really quite special. Staff are welcoming and fluent in English. The swimming pool complex is popular, as is the summer family entertainment. A small shop and a mini-market are on site and it is a short distance to the local village. The restaurant, bar, pizzeria and takeaway are open all season. Improvements continue steadily at this site which is great for families.

Facilities	Directions
Four modern sanitary blocks provide hot water for showers, washbasins and washing. Mostly British style toilets. Single locked unit for disabled visitors. Laundry facilities. Freezer. Motorcaravan services and stopover pitches. Good shop. Bar/restaurant and takeaway. Outdoor swimming pool. Play area. Miniclub and entertainment (high season). Small zoo. Watersports. Kayak hire. Fishing. Tennis. Bicycle hire. Torches useful. Max. 1 dog in high season. WiFi throughout (free).	From A22 Verona-Bolzano road take turn for Trento on S47 to Levico Terme where campsite is very well signed. GPS: 46.00799, 11.28454

Open: 20 March - 16 October.

Directions

From A22 Verona-Bolzano road take turn for Trento on S47 to Levico Terme where campsite is very well signed. GPS: 46.00799, 11.28454

Charges guide

Per unit incl. 2 persons and electricity	€ 19.00 - € 52.00
extra person	€ 4.50 - € 9.90
child (3-11 yrs)	€ 4.00 - € 6.50
dog	€ 2.00 - € 5.00

Molina di Ledro

Camping Al Sole

Via Maffei 127, I-38060 Ledro (Trentino - Alto Adige) T: 0464 508 496. E: info@campingalsole.it

alanrogers.com/IT62320

Lake Ledro is only 9 km. from Lake Garda, its sparkling waters and breathtaking scenery offering a low key alternative for those who enjoy a natural setting. The drive from Lake Garda is a real pleasure and prepares you for the treat ahead. This site has been owned by the same friendly family for over 40 years and their experience shows in the layout of the site, with its mature trees and the array of facilities provided. The 180 touring pitches (70-110 sq.m) all have 6A electricity. Situated on the lake with its own sandy beach, pool and play area, the facilities include an outstanding wellness centre.

Facilities	Directions
Superb toilet block with well appointed facilities. Five private bathrooms with shower, toilet, basin and safe. Excellent facilities for disabled visitors. Baby room. Laundry facilities. Freezer. Motorcaravan services. Well stocked mini-market. Pleasant restaurant/pizzeria with terrace. Bar serving snacks and takeaway. Swimming pool. Play area. Bicycle hire. Boating, windsurfing, fishing and canoeing. Children's club. TV room. WiFi over site (charged). Torches needed in some areas.	From autostrada A22 exit for Lake Garda North to Riva del Garda. In Riva follow sign for Ledro valley. Site is well signed as you approach Lago di Ledra. GPS: 45.87805, 10.76773

Open: 28 March - 30 September.

Charges guide

Per unit incl. 2 persons and electricity	€ 24.00 - € 41.00
extra person	€ 7.50 - € 11.00
child (2-11 yrs)	€ 5.00 - € 7.00

Pergine Valsugana

Camping San Cristoforo

Via dei Pescatori, I-38057 Pergine Valsugana (Trentino - Alto Adige) T: 0461 512 707. E: info@campingclub.it

alanrogers.com/IT62300

This part of Italy is becoming popular with those wishing to spend time by a lake in splendid countryside, but away from the more crowded, better known resorts. Lake Caldonazzo is one of the smaller Italian lakes, but is excellent for watersports. Camping San Cristoforo is a relatively new site on the edge of the small town of the same name and is separated from the lake by a minor road, but with easy access. There are 133 pitches on flat grass with tarmac access roads, separated by shady trees. The pitches are of a good size and all have 6A electricity. Diego, the manager, speaks excellent English.

Facilities	Directions
The large, modern sanitary block has some washbasins in cabins and pushbutton showers (with plenty of changing room). Facilities for disabled visitors. Washing machine and dryer. Motorcaravan services. No shop (but village nearby). Bar/restaurant with takeaway. Swimming pool (20x20 m) and children's pool. Play area. Beach volleyball. Bicycle hire. Minigolf. Activities (high season).	Site is just off the SS47 Trento-Bassano-Padova road, 2 km. south of Pergine Valsugana town, near village of San Cristoforo. Site is signed from main road or via village. GPS: 46.03855, 11.23698

Open: 18 May - 8 September.

Charges guide

Per unit incl. 2 persons and electricity	€ 16.00 - € 40.00
extra person	€ 5.00 - € 12.00

For latest campsite news, availability and prices visit

alanrogers.com

Pergine Valsugana
Camping Punta Indiani

Valcanover, I-38057 Pergine (Trentino - Alto Adige) T: 046 154 8062. E: info@campingpuntaindiani.it
alanrogers.com/IT62310

Punta Indiani is a small peninsula on the north western shore of Lake Caldonazzo, one of the smaller and most easterly of the Italian lakes. This simple, family run campsite is split into three camping areas. Two are split by a railway line (the trains only run during the day – great for train spotters). There are 115 pitches here which vary in size, all with 3/4A electricity, some with shade. Many have a superb position being right on the shores of this beautiful lake. There are limited amenities on the site, but a rear gate gives access to the town which has all the usual facilities and these compensate for the site's simplicity. This site is very popular with windsurfers and offers simple camping at reasonable prices.

Facilities

Two modernised toilet blocks with mixed British and Turkish style toilets and hot water. Washing machine and dryer. Freezer. High season family activities including al fresco eating. Simple play area. Beach. Dogs accepted by prior arrangement only. Off site: Watersports and sailing on lake, including at Calceranica-al-Lago 3 km. Pergine Valsugana 4 km. Trento 16 km.

Open: 1 May - 30 September.

Directions

From A22 Verona-Brenner motorway, leave at Trento-Nord, follow signs for SS47 Valsugana and Padova. After Pergine Valsugana, take exit for Lago di Caldonazzo on SP1. Site is signed to left within 1 km. Watch for bridge (3.5 m) and sudden left turn into site road. GPS: 46.02773, 11.231444

Charges guide

Per unit incl. 2 persons and electricity	€ 22.00 - € 41.00
extra person	€ 11.00

Pieve di Ledro
Camping Al Lago

Via Alzer 7/9, I-38067 Pieve di Ledro (Trentino - Alto Adige) T: 0464 591 250. E: info@camping-al-lago.it
alanrogers.com/IT62330

This small, family owned campsite has been lovingly rebuilt and refurbished to a very high standard. There are great views over the lakes and of the towering mountains surrounding Al Lago. The 105 pitches are of average size, on grass or gravel, with tarmac roads. Some pitches have a slight slope to the lake while others are flat. English and Dutch are spoken at reception and the Penner family is keen that guests enjoy their stay. The small restaurant serves excellent regional food. This site is ideal for watersports, hiking, cycling or for a quiet holiday in a spectacular setting.

Facilities

Two sanitary blocks provide clean facilities with a mixture of Turkish and British toilets. Washing machines and dryers. Basics at the mini-market. Very pleasant new bar/restaurant with balcony. Snacks and takeaway. TV. Limited entertainment in high season. Play area. Bicycle and canoe hire. Boat launching. WiFi (charged). Off site: Riding 6 km. Hiking. Canyoning. Canoeing.

Open: 2 April - 4 October.

Directions

From Brescia-Verona on the A4 take the S45 or the P572 north to Saló, then the S45 for Riva del Garda. Take the S240 west to Saló and Pieve di Ledro where the site is well signed. Be prepared for narrow winding last section. GPS: 45.8851, 10.7313

Charges guide

Per person	€ 6.00 - € 11.00
pitch incl. electricity	€ 8.00 - € 13.00

Pozza di Fassa
Camping Vidor – Family & Wellness Resort

Strada de Ruf de Ruacia 15, I-38036 Pozza di Fassa (Trentino - Alto Adige) T: 0462 760 022.
E: info@campingvidor.it **alanrogers.com/IT62090**

This very smart, family run site is in a beautiful mountainous setting and has the most fabulous infrastructure. The 160 pitches are of average size with 16A electricity connections, some also with water, drainage and hardstanding. Vidor has excellent facilities including a super new reception, camping shop, high quality restaurant and pizzeria (serving local cuisine with special menus for children), and a café with terrace and lounge. There is a wellness centre with an indoor heated swimming pool with whirlpool etc. (charged), plus a superb beauty centre offering a large variety of modern treatments.

Facilities

Two truly excellent, hotel standard heated sanitary blocks provide hot water throughout and very good showers with private bathrooms for hire. Facilities for disabled visitors. Washing machines, drying room and dryer. Fridge and freezer. Bar/restaurant with superb views, takeaway and shop. Beauty and wellness centre, heated indoor pool and gym (charged). TV room and cinema. Miniclub. Bicycle hire. Entertainment. WiFi throughout (charged).

Open: All year except November.

Directions

From A22 Trento-Bolzano road take S48 to Pozza di Fassa. In centre of town, at the roundabout take first exit towards Meida and Valle San Nicolo. Site is well signed in 2 km. GPS: 46.41987, 11.70754

Charges guide

Per unit incl. 2 persons and electricity	€ 19.00 - € 41.00
extra person	€ 6.00 - € 11.00

For latest campsite news, availability and prices visit
alanrogers.com

Prad am Stilfserjoch
Camping Kiefernhain

Kiefernhain 37, I-39026 Prad am Stilfserjoch (Trentino - Alto Adige) T: 0473 616 422.
E: kiefernhain@rolmail.net **alanrogers.com/IT62060**

The Stelvio National Park is arguably Italy's premier Alpine park. Camping Kiefernhain lies within the park in the Val Venosta. There are 160 touring pitches here – some well shaded by pine trees, others with much sunnier settings. Many pitches have fine views across to the Otztaler Alps and the Ortler glaciers. All have 6A electrical connections. A public swimming pool is adjacent to the site with free access for campers. Other amenities are available in a nearby sports centre or in the village, five minutes away on foot. The village of Prad am Stilfserjoch (900 m) provides shops, restaurants and essential services.

Facilities

Two modern, clean sanitary blocks with controllable hot showers, some washbasins in cabins, and provision for disabled visitors. Nine individual units available for rent. Baby room in ladies. Laundry facilities. Motorcaravan services. Bar/café and small shop. Play area. Children's club (July/Aug). Guided walking excursions. WiFi throughout (free by bar). Off site: Swimming pool (free access). Bus stop 100 m. Village centre 300 m. Fishing.

Open: 1 May - 4 October.

Directions

From the A22 autostrada take the Bozen (south) exit and join the S38 passing Merano and Silandro. Spondigna head south (still on the S38) to the village of Prato allo Stelvio, from where the site is well signed. GPS: 46.62536, 10.59485

Charges guide

Per unit incl. 2 persons and electricity	€ 29.10 - € 42.10
extra person	€ 7.50 - € 12.50

Prad am Stilfserjoch
Camping Residence Sägemühle

Dornweg 12, I-39026 Prad am Stilfserjoch (Trentino - Alto Adige) T: 0473 616 078.
E: info@campingsaegemuehle.com **alanrogers.com/IT62070**

This very attractive, well maintained site with beautiful mountain views is alongside a little village. The 160 grass touring pitches are neat and level, some have shade and most have electricity, water and drainage. The high standard indoor pool area is welcoming to cool oneself in the summer and relax in warm water after skiing in winter. The excellent facilities are cleverly placed under the pool area. New for the season is an enlarged reception, well equipped gym and a coffee bar with terrace leading to a very good restaurant. The friendly owners speak some English and Dutch.

Facilities

The main and very modern sanitary facilities are under the pool complex. All WCs are British style and the showers are of high quality. Private cabins for hire. Facilities for disabled visitors. Children's facilities and baby baths. Washing machines. Restaurant and bar. Coffee bar with terrace. Indoor swimming pool with waves, jacuzzi and waterfall. Gym and sauna (charged). Entertainment in season. Miniclub. Play areas. WiFi (free). Torches useful.

Open: All year excl. 8 November - 19 December.

Directions

From A38/S40 west of Bolzano, take exit for Pso dello Stelvio/Stilfserjoch (also marked S38) and village of Prad am Stilfserjoch. Site is well signed from here. GPS: 46.617628, 10.595317

Charges guide

Per unit incl. 2 persons	€ 30.00 - € 36.00
extra person	€ 9.50 - € 12.00
electricity (per kWh)	€ 0.60

Predazzo
Camping Valle Verde

Localitá Ischia 2, Sotto Sassa, I-38037 Predazzo (Trentino - Alto Adige) T: 0462 502 394.
E: info@campingvalleverde.it **alanrogers.com/IT62105**

Beautifully located in the Dolomites, at a height of just over 1,000 metres, Camping Valle Verde is an attractive family run site. There are 125 level pitches with mountain views, set on shallow, grassy terraces with some tree shade; all have 3A electricity. From the site there is plenty of walking in the forests alongside rushing mountain streams enclosed in small rocky canyons, with waterfalls and an abundance of flora and fauna. The site produces its own map of suggested rambling/cycle routes, however a detailed map of the area is an added advantage. The comfortable site restaurant, with its wood-fired pizza oven and terrace, is a very welcoming refuge after a day spent in the mountains.

Facilities

Modern toilet block with all necessary facilities including those for babies and campers with disabilities. Washing machine/dryer. Motorcaravan services. Restaurant, snack bar, takeaway (mid May-mid Sept). Play area. Sports area. Volleyball. Football. Paddling in adjacent stream. Bicycle hire. WiFi over site (charged). Off site: Indoor pool, tennis, rock climbing, pony trekking, shops, bars and restaurants in Predazzo 2 km. Hang-gliding. Rafting.

Open: 1 May - 30 September.

Directions

Leave Brenner motorway, A22, south of Bolzano, (Ora). From Ora take SS48 to Calvalese (20 km), then SS232 to Predazzo. Pass the Alpine School of Financial Police then first right (Bellamonte and Paneveggio). After minigolf take first right to site. GPS: 46.310565, 11.631764

Charges guide

Per unit incl. 2 persons and electricity	€ 21.40 - € 33.90
extra person	€ 6.20 - € 8.20

For latest campsite news, availability and prices visit
alanrogers.com

Rasen
Camping Residence Corones

Niederrasen 124, I-39030 Rasen (Trentino - Alto Adige) T: 0474 496 490. E: info@corones.com
alanrogers.com/IT61990

Situated in a pine forest clearing at the foot of the attractive Antholz valley in the heart of German-speaking Südtirol, Corones is ideally situated both for winter sports enthusiasts and for walkers, cyclists, mountain bikers and those who prefer to explore the valleys and mountain roads of the Dolomites by car. There are 135 level pitches, all with 16A electricity and many also with water, drainage and satellite TV. The Residence offers luxury apartments and there are authentic Canadian log cabins for hire. From the site you can see slopes which in winter become highly rated skiing pistes.

Facilities	Directions
The central toilet block is traditional but well maintained and clean. Additional facilities below the Residence are of the highest quality including individual shower rooms with washbasins, washbasins with all WCs, a delightful children's unit and an excellent facility for disabled visitors. Fully equipped private shower rooms for hire. Wellness centre with saunas, solarium, jacuzzis, massage, therapy pools and heat benches. Heated outdoor swimming and paddling pools (4/5-20/10). Play area. WiFi (charged).	From Bressanone/Brixen exit on A22 Brenner-Modena motorway, go east on SS49 for 50 km. then turn north (signed Rasen/Antholz). Turn immediately west at roundabout in Niederrasen/Rasun di Sotto to site on left in 100 m. GPS: 46.7758, 12.0367

Open: 9 May - 27 October, 6 December - 7 April.

Charges guide

Per unit incl. 2 persons, (electricity on meter)	€ 23.50 - € 33.80
extra person	€ 5.70 - € 8.90

No credit cards.

Sarnonico-Fondo
Camping Park Baita Dolomiti

Via Cesare Battisti 18, I-38010 Sarnonico-Fondo (Trentino - Alto Adige) T: 0463 830 109.
E: info@baita-dolomiti.it alanrogers.com/IT61980

Baita Dolomiti is a family campsite located in a splendid mountain region. It was very quiet when we visited in early June, but apparently becomes quite lively in high season, with plenty of organised entertainment for young and old. There is a rustic bar and restaurant providing typical local meals. The 130 grass touring pitches all have 3-6A electricity and, although they are not large, there is a great sense of space. The Val di Non is a wonderful area for walking and cycling and the more adventurous can explore the canyons on foot or by boat.

Facilities	Directions
Two toilet blocks are well equipped and maintained, with a mixture of British and Turkish style WCs, controllable showers, baby room and hot water to all washbasins and sinks. Facilities for disabled visitors. Laundry facilities. Motorcaravan services. Bar/restaurant. Swimming and paddling pools (1/6-30/9). Play area. Dogs are not accepted 1/8-15/9. Off site: Tourist train from site to various local villages. Golf and bicycle hire 1 km. Fishing 3 km. Riding 4 km. Canoeing. Canyoning.	From S Michele/Mezzocorona exit on A22 (Bronner Modena), turn right on SS43 (Val di Non) and follow signs for Cles. In 20 km. turn north east on SS43D (Fondo). Continue 14 km. to Sarnonico where site is signed. Avoid the route from Bolzano via the Mendel Pass, especially if towing. GPS: 46.42134, 11.13929

Open: 27 May - 30 September.

Charges guide

Per unit incl. 2 persons and electricity	€ 33.60 - € 36.80

No credit cards.

Sexten
Caravan Park Sexten

Saint Josef Strasse 54, I-39030 Sexten (Trentino - Alto Adige) T: 0474 710 444. E: info@caravanparksexten.it
alanrogers.com/IT62030

Caravan Park Sexten is 1,520 metres above sea level and has 268 pitches, some very large and all with electricity (16A), TV connections and water and drainage in summer and winter (underground heating stops pipes freezing). Some pitches are in the open to catch the sun, others are tucked in forest clearings by the river. They are mostly gravelled to provide an ideal all year surface. It is the facilities that make this a remarkable site; no expense or effort has been spared to create a luxurious environment that matches that of any top class hotel. A member of Leading Campings group.

Facilities	Directions
The three main toilet blocks are remarkable in design, fixtures and fittings. Heated floors. Controllable showers. Hairdryers. Luxurious private facilities to rent. Children and baby rooms. En-suite facilities for disabled visitors. Laundry. Motorcaravan services. Shop. Bars. Restaurant. Play areas. Tennis. Bicycle hire. Climbing wall. Fishing. Adventure activity packages. WiFi (whole site).	From Bressanone/Brixen exit on A22 (Brenner-Modena) follow SS49 east for 60 km. Turn south on SS52 at Innichen/S Candido and follow signs to Sexten. Site is in 5 km. GPS: 46.66727, 12.40221

Open: All year.

Charges guide

Per unit incl. 2 persons	€ 29.00 - € 44.50
extra person	€ 10.50 - € 16.00
electricity (per kWh)	€ 0.70

For latest campsite news, availability and prices visit
alanrogers.com

Tisens

Naturcaravanpark Tisens

I-39010 Tisens (Trentino - Alto Adige) T: 0473 927 131. E: info@naturcaravanpark-tisens.com

alanrogers.com/IT61844

Naturcaravanpark Tisens is a new site, open all year and located amidst orchards in tranquil Alpine surroundings. It can be found 10 minutes walk from the centre of Tesimo (Tisens) and midway between Merano and Bolzano (both 14 km. distant). The 89 touring pitches are of a good size (around 90 sq.m), all with 6A electricity, water and drainage. A number of larger pitches and 'panoramic' pitches (120 sq.m) are also available. The site's 25 m. heated swimming pool and the smaller children's pool (also heated) are surrounded by meadows, ideal for sunbathing, with fine mountain views on all sides. Off site, there are miles of excellent walking and cycle tracks close at hand, and cycle hire is available on site. The village of Tisens (Tesimo) is located on a plateau 650 m. above sea level. This is a peaceful spot, surrounded by chestnut groves and some of Europe's most ancient vineyards.

Facilities	Directions
Impressive heated toilet block. En-suite facilities for disabled visitors. Small, well stocked shop, bar/restaurant with open terrace and takeaway (all March-Nov). Heated swimming pool and paddling pool (April-Oct). Bicycle hire. Playground. WiFi over site (charged). Off site: Walking and cycling. Tennis. Golf. Riding. Merano and Bolzano 14 km.	Approaching from the A22 motorway and Brenner Pass, take the Merano Sud exit and follow signs to Lana. From there go towards Palade/Gampenpass as far as Tesimo/Tisens, from where the site is well signed. GPS: 46.56218, 11.17608

Open: All year.

Charges guide

Per unit incl. 2 persons,
electricity, water and drainage   € 32.00 - € 34.00
extra person   € 7.00
child (5-10 yrs)   € 4.00
dog   free

Toblach

Camping Olympia

Camping 1, I-39034 Toblach (Trentino - Alto Adige) T: 0474 972 147. E: info@camping-olympia.com

alanrogers.com/IT62000

In the Dolomite mountains, Camping Olympia continues to maintain its high standards. The 300 pitches are set out in a regular pattern and the tall pine trees, shrubs and hedges make this a very pleasant and attractive site. There are tree-clad hills on either side and craggy mountains beyond. The 230 mainly level touring pitches all have 6-16A electricity and a TV point. There are 63 fully serviced pitches with water, waste water, gas (21), telephone and satellite TV points. Some accommodation is available for rent, and there are 62 seasonal caravans which are mainly grouped at one end of the site. A little fish pond with a fountain and surrounded by flowers makes an attractive central feature, whilst on the far side of the site, a gate leads out into the woods where there is a little play area and a small zoo with meerkats, black swans and other small animals.

Facilities	Directions
The toilet block is of a very high standard. Rooms with WC, washbasin and shower to rent. Baby room. Facilities for disabled visitors. Two small blocks provide further WCs and showers. Motorcaravan services. Shop. Attractive bar, restaurant and pizzeria (all year). Bar with grill and terrace by pool (10/6-30/9; 20/12-Easter). Heated swimming pool (20/5-15/9). Sauna, solarium, steam bath and whirlpools. Massage and Kneipp treatments. Fishing. Bicycle hire. Play area. WiFi over site (free). Activities and excursions. Entertainment in high season. Off site: Tennis and minigolf nearby. Riding 3 km. Golf 6 km. Skiing 2 km.	Toblach/Dobbiaco is 100 km. north east of Bolzano. Site is west of town. From the A22 (Innsbruck-Bolzano), take Bressanone/Brixen exit and travel east on SS49 for 60 km. Site signed to left just after a short tunnel. From Cortina take SS48 and SS51 northwards then turn west on SS49 for 1.5 km. GPS: 46.734449, 12.194266

Open: All year.

Charges guide

Per unit incl. 2 persons
and electricity   € 27.00 - € 37.50
extra person   € 9.50 - € 12.50
child (3-11 yrs)   € 5.50 - € 9.50
dog   € 3.00 - € 5.50
Supplement for serviced pitch (14/7-19/8).

For latest campsite news, availability and prices visit

alanrogers.com

Völlan
Camping Völlan
Zehentweg 6, I-39011 Völlan (Trentino - Alto Adige) T: 0473 568 056. E: info@camping-voellan.com
alanrogers.com/IT61850

A small, family campsite attractively located among orchards and woods, Camping Völlan stands on a hillside above the town of Meran/Merano in the Südtirol/Alto Adige region. There are spectacular views over the surrounding valleys with mountain peaks beyond, and the area offers many opportunities for walking, cycling, mountain biking and motoring excursions visiting Alpine villages, ancient fortresses and picturesque castles. The 55 touring pitches are moderately sized (80-90 sq.m) and are generally level, although the site itself is on a slope; electricity connections are available. There is a small swimming pool and the site shop provides 'all you need for your camping holidays'.

Facilities

One modern toilet block with showers and washbasins. Washing machine and dryer. Motorcaravan services. Shop providing basic supplies. Swimming pool with terrace (May-Sept). Small adventure playground. TV room. Free WiFi on part of site. Off site: Shops, bars and restaurants in the village of Lana 6 km. Meran 15 km. Bozen 30 km. Museums in Völlan, Lana and Meran.

Open: 24 March - 4 November.

Directions

Völlan/Lana is 30 km. north west of Bozen/Bolzano. Leave A22 Verona/Brenner motorway at exit for Bozen Süd and follow signs for Merano. In 20 km. take exit to Lana and then follow signs up hillside to Völlan and campsite. GPS: 46.5989, 11.14558

Charges guide

Per unit incl. 2 persons and electricity	€ 29.00 - € 34.00
extra person	€ 7.00

No credit cards.

Völs am Schlern
Camping Seiser Alm

Saint Konstantin 16, I-39050 Völs am Schlern (Trentino - Alto Adige) T: 0471 706 459.
E: info@camping-seiseralm.com **alanrogers.com/IT62040**

What an amazing experience awaits you at Seiser Alm! Elisabeth and Erhard Mahlknecht have created a superb site in the magnificent Südtirol region of the Dolomite mountains. Towering peaks provide a wonderful backdrop when you dine in the charming, traditionally-styled restaurant on the upper terrace. Here you will also find the bar, shop and reception. The 150 touring pitches have 16A electricity; most comfort pitches have gas, water, drainage, satellite connection and WiFi also. Guests were delighted with the site when we visited, many coming to walk or cycle, some just to enjoy the area. There are countless things to see and do here, including a full entertainment programme and a brilliant new pool. Enjoy the grand 18-hole golf course by the site or join the organised excursions and activities. Local buses and cable cars provide an excellent service for summer visitors and skiers alike (discounts are available). In keeping with the natural setting, the majority of the luxury facilities are set into the hillside. The children's bathrooms are in a magic forest setting complete with a giant mushroom and elves! A family play park with animals is at the lower part of the site where goats also roam. If you wish for quiet, quality camping in a crystal clean environment, then visit this immaculate site.

Facilities

One spotless, luxury underground block is in the centre of the site. 16 private units are available. Excellent facilities for disabled visitors. Fairy tale facilities for children. Infrared sensors, underfloor heating and gently curved floors to prevent slippery surfaces. Washing machines and large drying room. Rooms for sick equipment. Supermarket. Quality restaurant and bar with terrace. Swimming pool (heated in cool weather). Sauna. Entertainment programme six days a week. Miniclub. Children's adventure park and play room. Animal enclosure. WiFi (charged). Apartments, mobile homes and maxi-caravans for rent. Off site: Riding alongside site. 18-hole golf course (discounts) and fishing 1 km. Bicycle hire and lake swimming 2 km. ATM 3 km. Paragliding.

Open: 20 December - 2 November.

Directions

From A22-E45 take Bolzano Nord exit. Take road for Prato Isarco/Blumau, then road for Fie/Völs. Road divides suddenly – if you miss the left fork as you enter a tunnel (Altopiano dello Sciliar/Schlerngebiet) you will pay a heavy price in extra kilometres. Enjoy the climb to Völs am Schlern and site is well signed. GPS: 46.53344, 11.53335

Charges guide

Per unit incl. 2 persons	€ 19.60 - € 47.00
extra person	€ 7.80 - € 11.20
child (2-16 yrs)	€ 4.40 - € 6.80
electricity (per kWh)	€ 0.60
dog	€ 3.50 - € 5.50

For latest campsite news, availability and prices visit
alanrogers.com

Want independent campsite reviews at your fingertips?

You'll find them here...

With over 8,000 campsites listed
and 4,000 in-depth reviews at
alanrogers.com

THE REGION HAS FOUR PROVINCES: GORIZIA, PORDENONE, TRIESTE AND UDINE

Friuli-Venézia Giúlia is a beautiful border region nudging Slovenia on the east, Austria and the Carnic Alps to the north with the Adriatic to the south – forming a bridge between the Mediterranean world and central Europe.

Near the Slovenian border lies the atmospheric city of Trieste, with its long bustling harbour. The prime tourist site is the hill of San Giusto; at the summit is the castle and a walk along the ramparts offers sweeping views over the Gulf of Trieste. Across the bay, Múggia is only a short ferry ride from Trieste, whilst outside the city is an area of limestone uplands, known as the Carso. With an abundance of caves, including the Grotta Gigante, the world's largest accessible cave and second largest natural chamber in the world, the Carso can be easily reached by the tranvia (cable tramway). Sitting on a group of low islands in the middle of the Adriatic lagoon, Grado is attached to the mainland by a long, narrow causeway. A popular seaside resort, it has a long sandy beach and harbour plus a historic centre. A short distance from here is Aquileia, now a small town but once an important city of the Roman Empire and further inland, Udine boasts galleries, fine churches and well preserved historic buildings. Towards the Austrian border in the north is Carnia. With its lush valleys and flower-filled meadows, which give way to Alpine peaks, it is an area popular with walkers.

Places of interest

Aquileia: Basilica, with mosaic pavement dating from the 4th century.

Cividale del Friuli: market town, medieval walls, archaeology museum.

Forni di Sopra: thickly wooded area, popular for mountain biking, horse riding and hiking.

Gorizia: major shopping town, numerous parks and gardens, castle.

Pordenon: preserved historic centre.

Tarvisio: small mountain resort.

Cuisine of the region

Fish broths made from squid, octopus, mackerel, sardines and clams are common. Gnocchi is a Trieste speciality; gnocchi the size of eggs are stuffed with a pitted prune, rolled in breadcrumbs, browned in butter and sprinkled with cinnamon and sugar. Local wines include Tocai, Ribolla Gialla, Merlot and Cabernet Sauvignon.

Brodo di Pesce: fish soup, sometimes flavoured with saffron.

Cialzons: ravioli from Carnia, usually stuffed with spinach and ricotta.

Jota: a soup of sauerkraut and barley.

Spaghetti alle Vongole: spaghetti with fresh clams in a chilli-pepper sauce.

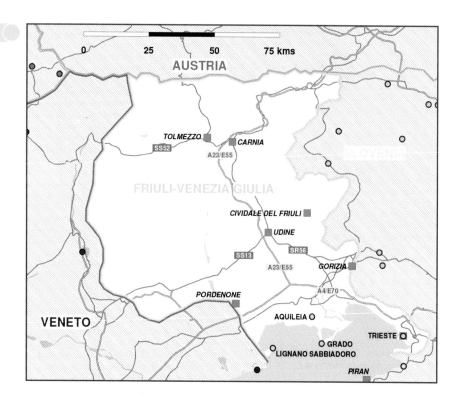

Grado
Villaggio Turistico Europa

Via Monfalcone 12, I-34073 Grado (Friuli - Venézia Giúlia) T: 043 180 877. E: info@villaggioeuropa.com
alanrogers.com/IT60050

This large, flat, high quality site is beside the sea and has 500 pitches, with 400 for touring units. They are all neat, clean and marked, most with shade and 6/10A electricity; 300 are fully serviced. The terrain is undulating and sandy in the areas nearer the sea, where cars have to be left in parking places. A huge, impressive aquatic park covers 1,500 sq.m. with two long slides, a whirlpool and many other features, including a pool bar. This is a very pleasant site with a spacious feel which families will enjoy. There is direct access to the beach, where local tidal activity presents a large, protected area for children to play and paddle under the gaze of the lifeguards. The beach bar is pleasant and a narrow wooden jetty gives access to deeper water and the tour boats. This is a neat, well managed site setting high standards.

Facilities

Five excellent, refurbished toilet blocks are well designed and kept very clean. Free hot water in all facilities, mostly British style WCs with excellent facilities for disabled visitors. Baby showers and baths. Washing machines. Dishwashers. Freezer. Motorcaravan services. Large supermarket, small general shop (all season). 3 bars and 2 restaurants with takeaway (all season). Gelateria. Swimming pools (1/5-17/9). Tennis. Fishing. Bicycle hire. Playground. Full entertainment programme in season. Miniclub. Football. Basketball. Minigolf. Archery. Watersports. Dancing lessons. WiFi (charged). Dogs are restricted to specific areas and not allowed on the beach. Off site: Golf 500 m. Riding 10 km. Bus and boat excursions.

Open: 21 April - 18 September.

Directions

Site is 4 km. east of Grado on road to Monfalcone. Venice-Trieste motorway exit at Reipuglia-Monfalcone, first roundabout take second exit towards airport and follow Grado signs for 13 km. Site is on the left opposite a golf course. GPS: 45.69649, 13.45595

Charges guide

Per unit incl. 2 persons and electricity	€ 20.50 - € 43.50
extra person	€ 6.00 - € 11.00
child (3-16 yrs)	€ 4.00 - € 10.00
dog	€ 3.20 - € 6.20

Less 10% for longer stays out of season.

For latest campsite news, availability and prices visit
alanrogers.com

Aquileia
Camping Aquileia

Via Gemina10, I-33051 Aquileia (Friuli - Venézia Giúlia) T: 0431 910 42. E: info@campingaquileia.it

alanrogers.com/IT60020

Situated in former parkland, under mature trees providing plenty of welcome shade in summer, Camping Aquileia, with 115 level, grass touring pitches, is a quiet site 10 km. away from the bustling coastal beaches. The pitches, all with 4/6A electricity, are separated from the entrance, swimming pool and play areas by tall hedges, and the more peaceful part of the site with the newer sanitary block is at the rear of the site. The now small town of Aquileia, founded in 181 BC, became one of the most important Roman military and trading posts and is now a UNESCO World Heritage Site. In the basilica, only a short walk from the campsite along the former harbour, lays one of the world's most magnificent mosaic floors. The campsite is popular with families and for those who seek a quiet base from which to visit the beaches or tour this interesting region. From reception, tours can be organised with the town's tourist office to the region's archaeological sites, and not surprisingly a weekly mosaic course is also on offer.

Facilities

Two sanitary blocks with free hot water, controllable showers and washbasins in cabins. Facilities for disabled visitors. Folding baby changing bench. Laundry facilities. Motorcaravan services. Restaurant, bar and automat for drinks and ice-cream. Large playing field with playground. Swimming and paddling pools. Bicycle hire. Mobile homes and chalets for rent. WiFi (charged). Off site: Supermarket opposite entrance. Riding 12 km. The historic towns of Trieste, Gorizia and the beach resort of Grado.

Open: Easter - 30 September.

Directions

Site is 30 km. west north west of Trieste. From the A4 (Venice-Trieste) take exit for Palmanova and travel south for 20 km. towards Grado. Just after entering Aquileia turn left at traffic lights, signed Trieste and Goriza and site is 400 m. on the right. GPS: 45.77585, 13.37084

Charges guide

Per unit incl. 2 persons	
and electricity	€ 24.00 - € 41.00
extra person	€ 7.00 - € 8.50
child (3-11 yrs)	€ 4.00 - € 6.00
dog	€ 2.00 - € 3.00

Grado
Camping Residence Punta Spin

Via Monfalcone 10, I-34073 Grado (Friuli - Venézia Giúlia) T: 0431 807 32. E: info@puntaspin.it

alanrogers.com/IT60055

Punta Spin is a large, well maintained site, set between the road and a soft sand beach. The 250 flat touring pitches vary in size (65-100 sq.m), all with 6A electricity, and with some on the beach front (book early for these). A bicycle is an asset here to access the furthest sanitary blocks. The comprehensive amenities are clustered near the entrance and include three pools, one of which is a sophisticated paddling complex, another is covered and heated. The restaurant and bar terraces overlook the lit pools, making a great setting for dinner. This site has a distinct Italian feel and will suit all families.

Facilities

Three modernised sanitary blocks have free hot water and mainly British style toilets. Facilities for disabled campers. Washing machines and dryers. Motorcaravan services. Large supermarket and other shops. Bars and restaurant (April-Sept). Pizzeria. Takeaway. Three swimming pools. Beauty and fitness centre. Minigolf. Disco. Entertainment team in high season. Playground. Tennis. WiFi (charged). Bicycle hire. Bungalows and mobile homes for hire.

Open: 1 April - 22 September.

Directions

Site is 3.5 km. east of Grado. Take the 35L road to Grado Pineto and continue to site on same road. Note: 3 m. height restriction at barrier – alternative entrance available. GPS: 45.69467, 13.45255

Charges guide

Per unit incl. 2 persons	
and electricity	€ 20.00 - € 41.00
extra person	€ 6.00 - € 12.00

For latest campsite news, availability and prices visit

alanrogers.com

Grado

Camping Tenuta Primero

Via Monfalcone 14, I-34073 Grado (Friuli - Venézia Giúlia) T: 0431 896 900. E: info@tenuta-primero.com
alanrogers.com/IT60065

Tenuta Primero is a large, attractive, well run, family owned site with direct access to its own private beach, marina and golf course. It offers a wealth of facilities and activities and caters for all members of the family. The 740 pitches are all level, with 6A electricity, some separating hedges and ample tree shade. The site has several restaurants and bars, and the large, elevated, flower decked Terrazza Mare, overlooking the sea, is great for eating and drinking whilst enjoying views over the romantic Adriatic.

Facilities

Nine traditional sanitary blocks, seven with facilities for disabled visitors. Washing machines and dryers. Motorcaravan services. Swimming pools and paddling pool. Shop, bars and restaurants, pizzeria, takeaway (all May-Sept). Beauty salon. Aerobics. Water gymnastics. Football pitch. Tennis. Boules. Skateboarding. Play areas. Windsurfing. Marina, sailing, boat launching and boat hire. Bicycle hire. Children's and family entertainment. Live music, disco, dancing. Private beach with sunshades, deck chairs and jetty. Internet corner and WiFi (free). Dogs are not accepted. Courses now available for many activities. Off site: 18-hole golf course opposite entrance (reduced fees). Grado 5 km. Riding 7 km. Trieste. Palmanova. Aquileia. World Heritage Centres.

Open: 14 April - 28 September.

Directions

Leave the A4 autostrada at the Palmanova exit and head towards Grado. In Grado, after crossing the causeway turn left towards Monfalcone on the SP19. Site is on the right after 5 km. opposite a large golf course. GPS: 45.7051, 13.4640

Charges guide

Per unit incl. 2 persons	
and electricity	€ 27.00 - € 51.00
extra person	€ 9.00 - € 13.00
child (4-15 yrs. acc. to age)	free - € 11.00

Grado

Camping Village Belvedere Pineta

Localitá Belvedere, I-33051 Grado (Friuli - Venézia Giúlia) T: 0431 910 07. E: info@belvederepineta.it
alanrogers.com/IT60070

Belvedere Pineta is situated on the edge of an almost entirely land-locked lagoon, 5 km. from Grado on the northern Adriatic Sea. A minor road runs between the site and the lagoon and a bridge over this connects the site with the beach of fine sand. It is a large site with 900 touring pitches arranged in regular rows with most under shade provided by the many tall pine trees which cover the site. Most are of reasonable size and all have electricity. An area of accommodation to let is to one side of the camping area. In high season a large programme of sport and entertainment for children and adults is organised.

Facilities

Most of the six toilet blocks have been refurbished to a good standard with all the usual facilities including some for children and free hot water in all washbasins, showers and sinks. Facilities for disabled visitors. Motorcaravan services. Range of shops. Restaurant, pizzeria and takeaway. Swimming pools. Sports facilities. Play areas. Organised entertainment in high season. Bicycle hire. WiFi (charged). Off site: Riding and golf 10 km.

Open: 30 April - 30 September.

Directions

Site is 5 km. north of Grado. Leave A4 Venice-Trieste motorway at exit for Palmanova and go south on SS352 towards Grado. Site is signed after Aquileia on the left. GPS: 45.72867, 13.40109

Charges guide

Per unit incl. 2 persons	
and electricity	€ 20.10 - € 41.10
extra person	€ 4.80 - € 9.80
child (2-10 yrs)	free - € 7.00
dog	€ 3.80 - € 7.60

For latest campsite news, availability and prices visit
alanrogers.com

Lignano Sabbiadoro
Camping Sabbiadoro

Via Sabbiadoro 8, I-33054 Lignano Sabbiadoro (Friuli - Venézia Giúlia) T: 043 171 455.
E: campsab@lignano.it **alanrogers.com/IT60080**

Sabbiadoro is a large, top quality site that caters very well for children. It is divided into two parts with separate entrances and efficient receptions. It has 974 touring pitches and is ideal for families who like all their amenities to be close by. The level, grassy pitches vary in size, are shaded by attractive trees and have electricity (6-10A) and TV connections. The facilities are all in excellent condition and well thought out, especially the pool complex, and everything here is very modern, safe and clean. The site's private beach (with 24-hour guard) is only 250 m. away and has its own showers, toilets and baby rooms. Open in high season, the smaller and quieter part of the site, with an entrance from Viale Central, is only a few metres away from the main site entrance in Via Sabbiadoro. It has four new sanitary blocks, 232 fixed pitches for touring units, an area for tents and a selection of mobile homes to rent. Shopping and nightlife can be found in Sabbiadoro itself, more so in Lignano Pineta about 1.5 km. away.

Facilities

Well equipped sanitary facilities with free showers and superb facilities for disabled visitors. Washing machines and dryers. Motorcaravan services. Huge supermarket. Bazaar. Good restaurant, snack bar and takeaway. Heated outdoor pool complex with separate fun pool area, slides and fountains. Heated indoor children's pool. Swimming courses. Play areas. Tennis. Fitness centre. Boat launching. Windsurfing school. Activity centre for children with well organised entertainment (July/Aug) and language school. WiFi throughout (charged). Bicycle hire.

Open: 19 March - 9 October.

Directions

Leave A4 at Latisana exit, west of Trieste. From Latisana follow road to Lignano, then Sabbiadoro. Site is well signed as you approach the town. GPS: 45.68198, 13.12577

Charges guide

Per unit incl. 2 persons	
and electricity	€ 24.40 - € 44.80
extra person	€ 6.50 - € 12.00
child (3-12 yrs)	€ 4.00 - € 6.80
dog	free - € 3.10

Trieste
Camping Mare Pineta

Sistiana 60 D, Duino-Aurisina, I-34011 Trieste (Friuli - Venézia Giúlia) T: 040 299 264.
E: info@marepineta.com **alanrogers.com/IT60000**

This site is 18 km. north west of Trieste, at the top of an 80 metre cliff, and it has superb views over the Sistiana Bay from the bar and pool areas. Of the 500 pitches, 340 are reserved for touring units, all with 4/6A electricity and water nearby. Some are in light woodland. Everyone is friendly and English is spoken. Enjoy a drink and the fabulous views at the cliff-top bar, or a meal in the restaurant overlooking the attractive pool complex. The site is used by tour operators.

Facilities

Five toilet blocks have been thoughtfully refurbished (two with solar panels for hot water) and offer some washbasins in cabins. WCs are of both British and Turkish style. Facilities for disabled visitors. Laundry. Motorcaravan services. Shop (all season). Bars. Pizzeria with terrace. Entertainment and disco. Swimming pool (1/5-20/9). Fitness studio. New playground. Tennis. Bicycle hire. Fishing. Organised entertainment in season. WiFi (charged). Information point. Dogs permitted in certain areas only and not allowed on the beach.

Open: 1 April - 16 October.

Directions

From the west on the A4 take Sistiana exit and turn right on S14 towards Sistiana and then Duino. Site is 1 km. on the left past Sistiana. From the east approach on the S14. Site is well signed. GPS: 45.7725, 13.62444

Charges guide

Per unit incl. 2 persons,	
water and electricity	€ 19.60 - € 46.00
extra person	€ 5.80 - € 12.50
child (3-9 yrs)	€ 4.80 - € 11.50

For latest campsite news, availability and prices visit
alanrogers.com

THE REGION HAS SEVEN PROVINCES: BELLUNO, PADOVA, ROVIGO, TREVISO, VENEZIA, VERONA AND VICENZA

Home to the unique city of Venice, the historic towns of Verona, Padua and Vicenza, plus several fortified settlements, Veneto has an abundance of sights to keep you entertained. Situated in the north east of Italy, it stretches from the flat river plains to the Dolomites.

Built on a series of low mud banks amid the tidal waters of the Adriatic, the main thoroughfare through Venice is the Grand Canal. At nearly four kilometres long, 30 to 70 metres wide, it divides the city in half and palaces, churches and historic monuments line the waterway. The Piazza San Marco is the main focal point of the city, with the Oriental splendour of the Basilica di San Marco, the Palazzo Ducale and the Bridge of Sighs. With another famous bridge and bustling markets, the district of Rialto is one of the liveliest spots, while the lagoon islands offer an escape from the crowds. Murano comprises a cluster of small islands, connected by bridges, and has been the centre of the glass-blowing industry since 1291; Burano is the most colourful with brightly painted houses and a long lace-making tradition, while Torcello boasts a 7th-century cathedral, the oldest building on the lagoon. Outside Venice, the old university town of Padua is rich in art and architecture, and Verona is renowned for its Roman ruins including the amphitheatre, which is the third largest in the world. It is also home to Casa di Giulietta, Juliet's house, a restored 13th-century inn with a small marble balcony, immortalised in Shakespeare's Romeo and Juliet.

Places of interest

Bassano del Grappa: well known for its majolica products and Grappa distilleries.

Conegliano: a wine producing region, renowned wine growers' school, grape festival in September, wine routes.

Euganean Hills: hot sulphur springs and mud baths.

Montagnana: fortified settlement with medieval town walls.

Padua: Basilica di Sant'Antonio, one of the most important pilgrimage destinations in Italy.

Treviso: attractive town with medieval, balconied houses overlooking willow-fringed canals.

Vicenza: Roman-Renaissance architecture, home of Europe's oldest surviving indoor theatre, 17th-century stone bridges.

Cuisine of the region

Risottos are popular, especially with seafood, plus pork dishes, polenta and heavy soups of beans, rice and vegetables. The region is also home to Italy's famous dessert *tiramisu,* a rich blend of coffee-soaked sponge cake and mascarpone cheese. Locally produced wines include Soave, Merlot, Cabernet, Pinot Grigio and Chardonnay. Grappa is made from grape husks, juniper berries or plums.

Brodo di Pesce: fish soup.

Bussolia: ring shaped cinnamon flavoured biscuits.

Radicchio alla Griglia: red salad leaves lightly grilled.

Risi e Bisi: soft and liquid risotto with fresh peas and bacon.

Risotto alle Seppie: contains cuttlefish ink.

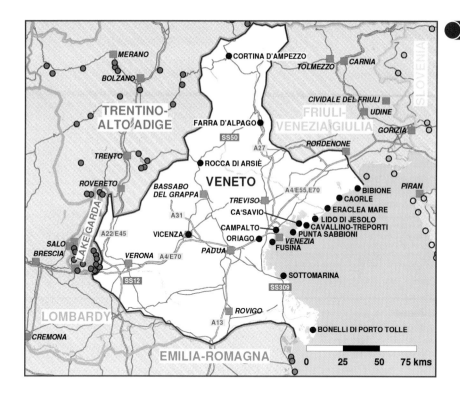

Bibione

Camping Capalonga

Via della Laguna 16, I-30028 Bibione-Pineda (Veneto) T: 0431 438 351. E: capalonga@bibionemare.com
alanrogers.com/IT60100

A quality site surrounded by water, Capalonga is large with 787 shaded touring pitches (70-90 sq.m) with 6/10A electricity, 35 fully serviced. The site is pleasantly laid out and permanent pitches are unobtrusive. The lagoon swimming pool and regular pools are excellent. Additionally, the wide, soft sand beach is very safe. Quality entertainment tops off the enjoyment here and the site has something for everyone. It has a spacious feel and bicycles are a real boon here. The site has a great location between the sea and a large lagoon, offering some fabulous waterside pitches. Boating (motor or sail) can be undertaken; a landing stage, crane and moorings are available. Security is handled well and all staff are cheerful and attentive. Capalonga is an excellent site, with comprehensive facilities. It is affiliated with Il Tridente (IT60150) and Lido (IT60130) nearby, and a short walk or bike ride gives you access to their facilities.

Facilities

Nine toilet blocks are of a high standard and frequently cleaned. There are facilities for disabled visitors and great children's rooms. Some washbasins in private cabins. Launderette. Dishwashers (€ 1). Motorcaravan services. Large supermarket. Bazaar. Self-service restaurant and separate bar (all season). Two swimming pools (from 24/4). Boating (170 moorings). Fishing (sea or lagoon). Watersports, tennis and karate schools. Archery. Gym. Outdoor cinema. Football. Volleyball. Bicycle hire. Three playgrounds. Entertainment programme. WiFi (charged). Late arrival parking with electricity. Dogs are not accepted. Off site: Bus by entrance. Riding 2 km. Golf 10 km. Touring and excursions. Boat hire.

Open: 24 April - 22 September.

Directions

Bibione is 80 km. east of Venice, well signed from afar on approach roads. 1 km. before Bibione turn right towards Bibione-Pineda and follow site signs. GPS: 45.63035, 12.99450

Charges guide

Per unit incl. 2 persons	
and electricity	€ 28.00 - € 53.00
extra person	€ 7.50 - € 12.50
child (1-11 yrs. acc. to age)	free - € 10.20

For latest campsite news, availability and prices visit
alanrogers.com

Bibione
Camping Lido

Via dei Ginepri 115, I-30028 Bibione-Pineda (Veneto) T: 0431 438 480. E: lido@bibionemare.com

alanrogers.com/IT60130

Camping Village Lido is a quiet, green site with direct access to the seafront in the centre of the town of Bibione-Pineda. Of 663 pitches, 388 are for touring units. Mostly shaded, there are three sizes, all with 6A electricity. There is convenient access to the long white sandy beach with its slowly shelving water, ideal for swimming/paddling. This is an impressive site with all manner of sporting and children's facilities, and an informal bar and restaurant. There are welcoming swimming pools for adults and children to relax in, although the site's main strength is the excellent beach and its central location, convenient to Bibione-Pineda's shopping area.

Facilities

Six sanitary blocks are conveniently located and are of a high standard. Car wash. Motorcaravan services. Bar, restaurant, supermarket and bazaar. Double swimming pool. Archery. Canoeing. Children's play park. Football. Volleyball. Basketball. Entertainment. Open-air cinema. Tennis and windsurfing schools. Boat mooring. Bicycle hire. WiFi (charged). Dogs and other animals are not accepted. Off site: Town of Bibione-Pineda. Marina.

Open: 12 May - 16 September.

Directions

Bibione is 80 km. east of Venice. Leave the E55 at Latisana exit and take the 354 for Bibione. Site is well signed from afar on approach roads. 1 km. before Bibione turn right towards Bibione-Pineda and follow site signs. GPS: 45.63222, 13.00132

Charges guide

Per unit incl. 2 persons and electricity	€ 18.70 - € 40.00
extra person	€ 5.10 - € 10.50

Bibione
Villaggio Turistico Internazionale

Via Colonie 2, I-30020 Bibione (Veneto) T: 0431 442 611. E: info@vti.it

alanrogers.com/IT60140

This is a large, professionally run tourist village which offers all a holiday maker could want. The Granzotto family have owned the site since the sixties and the results of their continuous improvements are very impressive. There are 300 clean pitches with electricity (10/16A), fully serviced, including TV hook-up, shaded by mature trees and mostly on flat ground. The site's large sandy beach is excellent (umbrellas and loungers are available for a small charge). All facilities are well thought out, in peak condition, and there is something for everyone. The tourist village is split by a main road (bridge for pedestrians) with the main restaurant, gym, laundry, disco, cinema and children's club, play areas and pleasant wooded spaces on the very smart chalet side.

Facilities

Seven modern toilet blocks house excellent facilities with mainly British style toilets. Facilities for children and disabled campers. Private bathrooms (€ 10/day). Laundry. Motorcaravan services. Car wash. Supermarket. Bazaar. Two good restaurants. Pizzeria. Snack bar. Pool complex. Hydromassage. Pool bar. Fitness centre. Disco. Cinema. Theatre. Bicycle hire. WiFi (charged). Play areas. Tennis. Electronic games. TV. Beach with bar.

Open: 28 March - 10 October.

Directions

Leave A4 east of Venice at Latisana exit on Latisana road. Take road 354 towards Lignano, after 12 km. turn right to Bevazzana and then left to Bibione. Site is well signed entering town. GPS: 45.6351, 13.0374

Charges guide

Per unit incl. 2 persons and electricity	€ 21.50 - € 51.00
extra person	€ 5.50 - € 13.00
child (1-9 yrs. acc. to age)	free - € 10.50

Bibione
Camping Residence Il Tridente

Via Baseleghe 12, I-30028 Bibione-Pineda (Veneto) T: 0431 439 600. E: tridente@bibionemare.com

alanrogers.com/IT60150

This is an unusual site in that it has huge open spaces. Formerly a holiday centre for deprived children, it occupies a large area of woodland. It is divided into two parts by the hotel and apartment block. The 199 touring pitches (6/10A) are located among tall, shading pines in the area between the entrance and the hotel. The other section is a pleasant open area leading to the sea. It is used for many sports facilities and two excellent swimming pools. Dogs are not accepted.

Facilities

Three sanitary blocks have a mixture of British and Turkish style WCs in cabins with washbasins. Facilities for disabled visitors. Laundry. Motorcaravan services. The Residence has an excellent restaurant, pizzeria, takeaway and bar. Supermarket. Swimming pools. 2 playgrounds. 5-a-side football. Bocce. Watersports. Tennis. Gym. Fishing. WiFi (charged). Entertainment in high season.

Open: 12 May - 16 September.

Directions

From A4 Venice-Trieste autostrada, take Latisana exit and follow signs to Bibione and then Bibione-Pineda and site signs. GPS: 45.63476, 13.01687

Charges guide

Per unit incl. 2 persons and electricity	€ 20.00 - € 45.00
extra person	€ 6.00 - € 11.50

For latest campsite news, availability and prices visit
alanrogers.com

Bonelli di Porto Tolle
Villaggio Barricata
Via Strada del Mare 74, I-45010 Bonelli di Porto Tolle (Veneto) T: 0426 389 198.
E: info@villaggiobarricata.com **alanrogers.com/IT60590**

Villaggio Barricata is a pleasant site, located within the large nature reserve at the mouth of the Po Delta. A drive through many rows of mobile homes brings you to 70 touring pitches, all with 6A electricity and water connections, and protected in the main by expensive artificial shading. On-site amenities are impressive and include a fabulous swimming pool complex, a bar/restaurant and a well stocked supermarket. A lively entertainment and activity programme is on offer during the peak season, including a children's club. A short walk leads to a long, gently shelving sandy beach.

Facilities

Heated sanitary facilities include provision for disabled visitors. Laundry. Bazaar. Bar. Restaurants. Takeaway. Shop. Swimming pools. Pool bar. Children's pool and lagoon. Wellness and spa. Aerobics. Tennis. Miniclub. Entertainment. Disco. Dancing classes. Play area. TV/games room. Bicycle hire. Riding. Archery. 5-a-side football. Canoeing. Dog beach. Accommodation and glamping. Max. 1 dog. Off site: Beach (lifeguards) 200 m.

Open: 15 May - 20 September.

Directions

From the A13 (Bologna-Padova), take Monselice exit and join the SS309 Romea-Venice road to Porto Tolle exit, and follow signs to Porto Tolle then Scardovari. Site is well signed from here. GPS: 44.84613, 12.4633

Charges guide

Per unit incl. 2 persons and electricity	€ 23.00 - € 44.00

No credit cards.

Ca'Savio
Camping Ca'Savio
Via di Ca'Savio 77, 30013 Cavallino-Treporti, I-30013 Ca'Savio (Veneto) T: 0419 660 17. E: info@casavio.it
alanrogers.com/IT60440

Ca'Savio is a very large, family owned site of almost 50 years standing. It is in traditional Italian style and is set on a wide, sandy, Blue Flag beach which is safe for swimming. The beach is separated from the pitches by a pleasant open area and a row of bungalows. There are many activities here, some needing additional payment. There are 800 touring pitches (all with 10A electricity), 256 mobile homes/bungalows and around 400 tour operator pitches. Rows of pitches lead off a very busy central avenue and they are shaded, mostly flat and varying in size (90-100 sq.m). Many are a long way from water and sanitary facilities. Customers are left to find their own pitches, so leave someone there while you fetch your unit!

Facilities

Three large toilet blocks include many shower, toilet and washbasin units. The toilets are in cabins with showers and washbasins, so at busy periods there may be a long wait. Supermarket, bazaar and other shops. Restaurants, pizzeria, café and pub. Two very large pool complexes (free). Miniclub. Bicycle hire. Minigolf. Good adventure style playground. Car hire. Internet and WiFi (in restaurant; charged). Dogs are not accepted.

Open: 26 April - 2 October.

Directions

From A4 autostrada take Tessera exit and follow signs to Jesolo then Cavallino. Pass through Cavallino, Ca'Ballarin and Ca'Pasquali. After 3 km. in centre of Ca'Savio turn left towards beach and site. GPS: 45.44543, 12.46127

Charges guide

Per person	€ 5.50 - € 9.50
pitch and electricity	€ 9.50 - € 19.50

Min. stay 3 nights (7 from 7/7-18/8).

Campalto
Camping Rialto
Via Orlanda 16, I-30173 Campalto (Veneto) T: 0415 420 295. E: info@campingrialto.com
alanrogers.com/IT60510

Camping Rialto is a family run site with a pleasant atmosphere. Its main attraction is its close proximity to Venice, which can be reached by bus from the gate (€ 2.60 return). There are 89 pitches (6A, Europlug) for tourers, under mature trees and in rows between hard roads allowing easy access. They are situated further into the site past the rental accommodation and tents. A pizza restaurant/takeaway with a bar is close to the entrance, along with all other administrative buildings. English is spoken.

Facilities

One sanitary block is offset nearer the entrance. It is of traditional design but has modern equipment and facilities for disabled visitors. Washing machines and dryer. Motorcaravan services. Freezer for gel packs. Shop. Bar with TV. Pizzeria and takeaway. Communal barbecue area. WiFi (charged). Off site: Venice. Boat trips on the Brenta canal.

Open: 1 February - 20 October.

Directions

From Milan take Mestre Villabona exit and A57 (Tangenziale di Mestre). Then take Terraglio exit. At roundabout take SS13s (Venice). At next roundabout take Campalt/Aeroporto exit (third). Site is just after Lidl store on left. GPS: 45.48421, 12.28313

Charges guide

Per unit incl. 2 persons and electricity	€ 25.50 - € 30.50

For latest campsite news, availability and prices visit
alanrogers.com

Caorle
Camping San Francesco

Via Selva Rosata, 1, I-30021 Caorle (Veneto) T: 0421 29 82. E: info@villaggiosanfrancesco.com

alanrogers.com/IT60110

Camping San Francesco is a large, beachside site in a quiet location close to the coastal town of Caorle (Little Venice), known for its connection with Ernest Hemingway. Although there are over 600 mobile homes to rent, 370 level, grassy pitches are reserved for tourers. They are close to the beach, shaded, and all have electricity (10A) and fresh and waste water connections. The site has every facility for a comfortable holiday, with swimming pools, an attractive aquapark (extra charge), a good beach for swimming, a large supermarket etc. However, some touring in the area from the site and a trip to Venice are also worthwhile. The large, well organised reception is supplemented by a separate information office at the flower-decked entrance to the site. At the end of the entrance road, near the fountain, are some shops and an ice cream parlour. The shop selling Murano glass will be of particular interest, especially if you are not already acquainted with the colourful products from the islands just north of Venice. The islands and glassworks are well worth visiting. The site has three restaurants, one at the beachside pool, and during summer there are entertainment programmes for children.

Facilities

Five sanitary blocks with all the usual facilities including free, controllable showers, washbasins in cabins, facilities for disabled visitors, children's area and baby room. Motorcaravan services. Bars, restaurants, pizzeria and ice-cream parlour. Supermarket and shopping centre plus first aid centre and a Murano glass shop. Swimming pools, paddling pools and hydromassage centre. Aquapark with waterslides (charged). Fitness centre. Solarium. Gym. Bowls. Tennis. Playground. Windsurfing school. Diving school. Games room. Entertainment and activity programme. Children's club. Excursions. Mobile homes and chalets for rent. Free WiFi throughout. Off site: Golf and riding 5 km. Venice and Caorle.

Open: 21 April - 24 September.

Directions

From A4 motorway (Venice-Trieste) take exit to Ste Stino di Livenza and follow signs to Caorle joining the P59. Site is signed from Caorle on the continuation of this road to Porto Santa Margherita. GPS: 45.56709, 12.7943

Charges guide

Per unit incl. 2 persons and electricity	€ 16.00 - € 59.00
extra person	€ 4.00 - € 14.00
child (3-6 yrs)	free - € 7.50

For latest campsite news, availability and prices visit

alanrogers.com

Caorle

Centro Vacanze Pra' Delle Torri

Viale Altanea, 201, localitá Pra' delle Torri, I-30021 Caorle (Veneto) T: 042 129 9063. E: info@pradelletorri.it

alanrogers.com/IT60030

Pra' Delle Torri is a superb Italian Adriatic site which has just about everything! Pitches for camping, hotel accommodation and two very large, superbly equipped pool complexes which may be rated among the best in the country. There is also a full size golf course. Of the 1,000 pitches, 800 are available for touring and are arranged in zones, with 5A electricity and shade. There is an amazing choice of quality restaurants, bars, shops and services placed strategically around an attractive square. Although a very large site, there is a great atmosphere here that families will enjoy. The fabulous lagoon pool complex with islands, slides and sunbathing areas is the site's crowning glory, plus indoor (Olympic size) and outdoor lane pools. Other super amenities include a large grass area for ball games, playgrounds, a children's car track, and a whole range of sports, fitness and entertainment programmes, along with a medical centre, skin care and other therapies. The site has its own sandy beach with bars and beach restaurants, while Porto, Santa Margherita and Caorle are nearby. One could quite happily spend an entire holiday here without leaving the site, but the attractions of Venice, Verona, etc. might well tempt campers.

Facilities

Sixteen high quality, spotless toilet blocks with excellent facilities including very attractive children's bathrooms. Units for disabled visitors. Laundry facilities. Motorcaravan services. Large supermarket and wide range of shops, restaurants, bars and takeaways. Indoor and outdoor pools. Disco with music selected by mobile phone app. Tennis. Minigolf. Fishing. Watersports. Archery. Diving. Fitness programmes and keep fit track. Crèche and supervised play area. Bowls. Mountain bike track. Wide range of organised sports and entertainment. Road train to town in high season. Dogs are not accepted. Off site: Riding 3 km. Beach fishing. Tours.

Open: 21 April - 25 September.

Directions

From A4 Venice-Trieste motorway leave at exit for Santo Stino di Livenze and follow signs to Caorle then Santa Margherita and signs to site. GPS: 45.57312, 12.81248

Charges guide

Per unit incl. 2 persons and electricity	€ 18.70 - € 52.50
extra person	€ 4.90 - € 10.80
child (3-11 yrs. acc. to age)	free - € 8.90
Min. stay 2 nights.	

See advertisement on the back cover.

Caorle

Camping Marelago

Viale dei Cigni 18, I-30021 Caorle (Veneto) T: 0421 299 025. E: info@marelago.it

alanrogers.com/IT60040

This site is relatively new and is in pristine condition, set between the road and the beach. There are two types of pitches available here, some having a private kitchen and bathroom, others are more standard. The 150 touring pitches have 16A electricity and are slowly gaining shade from the trees. The site has high quality facilities and sits within a huge holiday complex which has everything a holidaymaker would wish for. All facilities are impeccably clean and the site is well organised. The pool has a separate, safe, shallow paddling area. The sandy beach is accessed through a secure gate (the beach is shared with two hotels). There are loungers and umbrellas for hire, lifeguards throughout the high season and a beach bar.

Facilities

One spotless central modern sanitary block has free hot water throughout. All British style toilets and facilities for disabled campers. Superb separate unit for children. Baby room. Washing machines and dryers. Small shop. Snack bar. Beach bars. Takeaway. Swimming pool. Fishing (permit required). Entertainment team (high season). Basic playground. WiFi (free). Dogs are not accepted. Off site: Golf and bicycle hire 500 m. Caorle seaside town 5 km. Shuttle train around resort. Excursions to Venice and other areas.

Open: 22 April - 15 September.

Directions

From A4 motorway (Venice-Trieste) take Stino di Livenza exit and follow signs for Caorle, then Lido Altanea West. Site is clearly signed in 7 km. GPS: 45.57869, 12.82704

Charges guide

Per unit incl. 2 persons and electricity	€ 16.00 - € 43.00
extra person	€ 5.00 - € 10.50
child (6-11 yrs)	€ 3.00 - € 7.00
No credit cards.	

For latest campsite news, availability and prices visit

alanrogers.com

Cavallino-Treporti
Camping Union Lido Vacanze

Via Fausta 258, I-30013 Cavallino-Treporti (Veneto) T: 041 257 5111.
E: info@unionlido.com **alanrogers.com/IT60200**

This amazing site is very large, offering absolutely everything a camper could wish for. It is extremely professionally run and we were impressed with the whole organisation. It lies along a 1.2 km. long, broad sandy beach which shelves very gradually and offers a huge number of sporting activities. The site itself is regularly laid out with parallel access roads under a covering of poplars, pine and other trees. There are 2,200 pitches for touring units, all with 6/10/16A electricity and 1,969 also have water and drainage. Because of the size of the site, there is an internal road train and amenities are repeated across the site (cycling is permitted on specific roads). You do not need to leave this site during your stay – everything is here, including a smart and sophisticated wellness centre. Overnight parking is provided outside the gate with electricity, toilets and showers for those arriving after 21.00. There are two aqua parks, one with fine sandy beaches and both have swimming pools, lagoon pools for children, a whirlpool and a 160 m. 'Wild River'. Another water park is planned for 2016. A huge selection of sports and activities are offered, along with luxury amenities too numerous to list. Entertainment and fitness programmes are organised in season. A diving centre offers lessons and open water diving. Union Lido is, above all, an orderly and clean site. This is achieved by implementing reasonable regulations to ensure peaceful, comfortable camping under good management. A member of Leading Campings group.

Facilities

Fourteen facilities superb, fully equipped toilet blocks; 11 have facilities for disabled visitors. Launderette. Motorcaravan services. Gas supplies. Comprehensive shopping areas set around a pleasant piazza (all open till late). Eight restaurants each with a different style plus 11 pleasant and lively bars (all services open all season). Impressive aqua parks (all season). Tennis. Riding. Minigolf. Skating. Bicycle hire. Archery. Two fitness tracks in 4 ha. natural park with play area and supervised play. Diving centre and school. Windsurf school in season. Exhibitions. Boat excursions. Recreational events. Hairdressers. Internet cafés. ATM. Dogs are accepted in designated areas. WiFi throughout (free). Off site: Boat launching 3.5 km. Aqualandia (special rates). Excursions.

Open: 21 April - 3 October.

Directions

From Venice-Trieste autostrada leave at exit for airport or Quarto d'Altino and follow signs first for Jesolo and then Punta Sabbioni, and site will be seen just after Cavallino on the left.
GPS: 45.467883, 12.530367

Charges guide

Per unit incl. 2 persons	
and electricity	€ 19.80 - € 51.70
with services	€ 22.20 - € 70.90
extra person	€ 4.90 - € 12.20
child (1-11 yrs. acc. to age)	€ 2.90 - € 9.90

Three different seasons: (i) high season 29/6-31/8; (ii) mid-season 18/5-29/6 and 31/8-14/9, and (iii) off-season, outside these dates.

Cavallino-Treporti
Italy Camping Village

Via Fausta 272, I-30013 Cavallino-Treporti (Veneto) T: 041 968 090. E: info@campingitaly.it
alanrogers.com/IT60210

Italy Camping Village, under the same ownership as the adjacent and better known Union Lido, is a good choice for those who prefer a smaller, more compact site. The 180 touring pitches (60-80 sq.m) are on either side of sand tracks, off hard access roads, under a cover of trees. All have electricity connections (10A, Europlug) and 126 are fully serviced. Access is impossible for large units, particularly in high season when cars are parked everywhere. There is direct access to a gently sloping, sandy beach. A pleasant, heated, swimming pool has a slide and a whirlpool at one end, but for those who want a greater choice of activities, guests can use the facilities at Union Lido for a small additional charge. Strict regulations regarding undue noise make this a fairly peaceful site and with lower charges than some in the area, it is ideal for families with young children. Advance booking is possible.

Facilities

Two high quality, fully equipped sanitary blocks include private cabins, family shower rooms and facilities for disabled visitors. Washing machines. Shop. Restaurant with TV. Bar beside beach. Heated swimming pool with flumes (May-Sept). Small playground, miniclub and children's disco. Bicycle hire. WiFi throughout (free). Only gas and electric barbecues permitted on individual pitches; charcoal only permitted in the designated area. Dogs are not accepted. Off site: Use of facilities at IT60200 Union Lido (extra charge for pool). Sports centre, golf and riding 400 m. Venice.

Open: 28 April - 25 September.

Directions

From Venice-Trieste A4 autostrada leave at exit for airport or Quarto d'Altino and follow signs for Jesolo and Punta Sabbioni. Site well signed on left after Cavallino. GPS: 45.46836, 12.53338

Charges guide

Per unit incl. 2 persons	
and electricity	€ 18.10 - € 46.20
extra person	€ 4.90 - € 10.20
child (1-5 yrs)	free - € 7.30

Three charging seasons.

For latest campsite news, availability and prices visit
alanrogers.com

UNION LIDO
Vacanze
★★★★★

CAMPING
LODGING
HOTEL

NEW
WATER GAMES

THE FIRST 5-STAR
CAMPING IN ITALY

LeadingCampings

FREE WIFI

DOG
CAMP
UNION LIDO
★★★★★

OPEN FROM 21ST APRIL
TO 3RD OCTOBER 2016

UNION LIDO CAMPING LODGING HOTEL
30013 CAVALLINO VENEZIA ITALIA
Camping Tel. +39 0412575111
Art&Park Hotel Tel. +39 041968043 Fax +39 0415370355
info@unionlido.com - booking@unionlido.com

UNIONLIDO.COM

Cavallino-Treporti
Residence Village
Via F Baracca 47, I-30013 Cavallino-Treporti (Veneto) T: 0419 680 27. E: info@residencevillage.com
alanrogers.com/IT60250

Camping Residence is a stylish site with a sandy beach directly on the Adriatic. It is well kept and has many floral displays. The 265 touring pitches are marked out with small fences or pines, and some have excellent shade. The pitches are in regular rows on level sand and vary in size (60-80 sq.m). All have 6/10A electricity connections. There are strict rules regarding noise with quiet periods required between 13.00-15.00 and no unaccompanied under 18s. A pleasant restaurant offering fine food is located in an impressive building. The beach runs the whole length of the site and shelves gradually into the sea making it safe for children. A super lagoon-style pool has a large separate paddling area for children.

Facilities	Directions
Three large, clean and modern toilet blocks, plus a smaller one near the beach, have good facilities including British style WCs. Supermarket, separate shops for fruit and other goods. Well appointed restaurant with separate bar. Takeaway. Swimming pools with sunbathing areas. Playground. Tennis. Fitness programme. Games room. Entertainment programme. Miniclub. Bicycle hire. WiFi in some areas (charged). Dogs are not accepted.	From A4 Venice-Trieste autostrada take exit for airport or Quarto d'Altino. Follow signs for Jesolo, then Punta Sabbioni. Take first left after Cavallino bridge and site is 800 m. on the left. GPS: 45.48002, 12.57395

Open: 7 May - 18 September.

Charges guide

Per unit incl. 2 persons and electricity	€ 21.20 - € 68.00
extra person	€ 5.40 - € 10.50

Cavallino-Treporti
Camping Vela Blu
Via Radaelli 10, I-30013 Cavallino-Treporti (Veneto) T: 0419 680 68. E: info@velablu.it
alanrogers.com/IT60280

Thoughtfully landscaped within a natural wooded coastal environment, the tall pines here give shade, while attractive flowers enhance the setting and paved roads give easy access to most pitches. The 261 pitches (130 for tourers) vary in size (55-90 sq.m) and shape, but all have 10/16A electricity, water and drainage. Vela Blu is a smaller, family style site and a pleasant alternative to some of the other massive sites on Cavallino. It is a popular destination for Italian families, booking is essential for high season and national holidays. There is a pleasant swimming pool with a mini water park. A clean, fine sandy beach with lifeguards runs the length of one side of the site with large stone breakwaters.

Facilities	Directions
Two modern, well maintained toilet blocks include baby rooms and good facilities for disabled visitors. An attendant is on hand to maintain high standards. Laundry facilities. Motorcaravan services. Medical room. Shop. Bar. Gelateria. Restaurant and takeaway. New swimming pool complex. Games room. Satellite TV room. Pedalos. Fishing. Bicycle hire. Entertainment. WiFi (charged).	Leave A4 Venice-Trieste motorway at exit for Aeroporto and follow signs for Jesolo and Punta Sabbioni. Site is signed after village of Cavallino. GPS: 45.45681, 12.5072

Open: 28 March - 26 September.

Charges guide

Per unit incl. 2 persons and all services	€ 19.90 - € 50.40
extra person	€ 4.70 - € 10.70

Cavallino-Treporti
Camping Villa al Mare
Via del Faro 12, I-30013 Cavallino-Treporti (Veneto) T: 0419 680 66. E: info@villaalmare.com
alanrogers.com/IT60290

A small, pleasant family site, Villa al Mare enjoys an unusual location close to Cavallino's lighthouse and harbour, on the western bank of the River Sile. The 100 shaded touring pitches (50-75 sq.m) each have 4/6A electricity, satellite TV connections, water and drainage. There is direct access to a pretty beach and during high season a range of activities are organised there. The pleasant and homely restaurant has a covered area and a large patio, both with sea views. A small pool for children is on a raised area just inside the site and there is an elevated spa pool giving great local views.

Facilities	Directions
Two modernised toilet blocks are kept very clean and have hot water throughout. Facilities for disabled visitors. Washing machines. Bar, restaurant and pizzeria, shop (all season). Swimming pool (1/5-15/9). Jacuzzi. Playground. Children's club. Entertainment and activity programme. Excursion programme. Direct access to the beach. Fishing. Bicycle hire. Mobile homes and apartments for rent. WiFi over site (charged). Dogs are not accepted.	From A4 (from Milan) take Mestre exit. Follow signs for Venice airport and then Jesolo. From Jesolo, follow signs to Cavallino. Cross large bridge in Cavallino, take first left (Via F Baracca). In 600 m. left into Via del Faro to site. GPS: 45.47933, 12.58103

Open: 16 April - 17 October.

Charges guide

Per person	€ 3.50 - € 9.90
child (2-10 yrs)	free - € 8.50
pitch	€ 8.50 - € 25.00

For latest campsite news, availability and prices visit
alanrogers.com

Cavallino-Treporti
Camping Dei Fiori

Via Pisani 52, I-30013 Cavallino-Treporti (Veneto) T: 0419 664 48. E: fiori@vacanze-natura.it

alanrogers.com/IT60300

Dei Fiori stands out among the other sites in the area. As its name implies, it is ablaze with colourful flowers and shrubs in summer and presents a neat and tidy appearance whilst providing a relatively quiet atmosphere. The 279 touring pitches are fully serviced with 6/10A electricity, water and drainage. Some pitches are in woodland where space varies according to the trees, which have been left in their natural state. Others are beneath artificial shade, where regular shaped pitches are of reasonable size (70-85 sq.m). A great pool complex plus a separate water play park and spa is a superb feature. This is a lovely site for family holidays.

Facilities

Three sanitary blocks are of exceptional quality with British style WCs, family rooms, well equipped baby rooms. Facilities for disabled visitors. Washing machines and dryers. Family rooms (key from reception). Motorcaravan services. Shops. Restaurant. Snack bar. Swimming pools and whirlpool. Fitness centre, gym, hydro-massage bath (free in low season) and programmes (1/5-30/9). Tennis. Minigolf. Play area. Organised activities and entertainment. Satellite TV. Bicycle hire. WiFi (charged). No dogs.

Open: 1 May - 30 September.

Directions

Leave A4 Venice-Trieste autostrada either by taking exit for airport or Quarto d'Altino and follow signs for Jesolo and then Punta Sabbioni and site signs just after Ca'Ballarin. GPS: 45.45263, 12.47127

Charges guide

Per unit incl. 2 persons and electricity	€ 17.10 - € 58.80
extra person	€ 4.40 - € 11.40

Min. stay 3 days in high season (3/7-21/8).

Cavallino-Treporti
Camping Silva

Via F Baracca 53, I-30013 Cavallino-Treporti (Veneto) T: 0419 680 87. E: info@campingsilva.it

alanrogers.com/IT60310

If simple and peaceful camping is for you, Silva may fit the bill. Owned by the same family for many years, it is set alongside the excellent Cavallino beach. The site offers 256 touring pitches (45-60 sq.m), all with 6A electricity available. They are on sand and grass with a canopy of mature trees providing shade. Some of the pitches are superbly placed, just feet from the beach. There is no sophisticated entertainment here, but there is a pleasant bar and restaurant/pizzeria, and a basic shop. A simple play area is at the beach end of the site and there are umbrellas and loungers for hire on the safe beach. We enjoyed our stay here away from the noise generated by the larger sites nearby.

Facilities

Three refurbished toilet blocks provide simple, clean facilities. A mix of British and Turkish style toilets and hot water throughout. Separate facilities for disabled visitors. Motorcaravan services. Washing machine. Shop. Bar, restaurant/pizzeria. Play area. Direct access to excellent beach. Accommodation to rent. WiFi in bar area (free). Off site: Buses every 30 minutes from entrance to Venice and Jesolo. Bicycle hire 1 km. Golf 4 km. Riding 5 km.

Open: 9 May - 15 September.

Directions

Travelling east on A4 (Milan-Trieste) take Quarto d'Altino exit. Follow directions for Portegrandi and Jesolo. In Jesolo follow the signs for Cavallino. Site is signed from there. GPS: 45.47929, 12.56887

Charges guide

Per unit incl. 2 persons and electricity	€ 18.00 - € 36.00

No credit cards.

Cavallino-Treporti
Camping Village Cavallino

Via delle Batterie 164, I-30013 Cavallino-Treporti (Veneto) T: 0419 661 33. E: info@campingcavallino.com

alanrogers.com/IT60320

This large, well ordered site is part of the Baia Holiday Group. It lies beside the sea with direct access to a superb beach of fine sand, which is very safe and has lifeguards. The site is thoughtfully laid out with the 457 large touring pitches shaded by olives and pines. All pitches have 6/10A electricity, some have water and they are generally flat and enjoy shade from mature pines. The pleasant pool, restaurant, entertainment and most other services are at the centre of the site. We enjoyed the hubbub from this area, but also the ability to find peace on the periphery. You should have a great family holiday here.

Facilities

Two remarkable, modern toilet blocks are well spaced and can be heated. Facilities for disabled campers. Dog shower. Launderette. Motorcaravan services. Bazaar. Supermarket. Restaurant with large terrace. Takeaway. Pizzeria. Swimming pools and whirlpool (May-Sept). Minigolf. Playground. Bicycle hire. Fishing. Entertainment. ATM. WiFi (charged). Dogs are accepted in certain areas.

Open: 24 March - 31 October.

Directions

From Venice-Trieste autostrada leave at airport or Quarto d'Altino exit. Follow signs, first for Jesolo, then Punta Sabbioni. Site signs will be seen just after Cavallino on the left. GPS: 45.45666, 12.50055

Charges guide

Per unit incl. 2 persons and electricity	€ 23.00 - € 49.90

Min. stay in high season one week.

For latest campsite news, availability and prices visit
alanrogers.com

Cavallino-Treporti
Camping Mediterraneo

Via delle Batterie 38, I-30010 Cavallino-Treporti (Veneto) T: 0419 667 21. E: mediterraneo@vacanze-natura.it

alanrogers.com/IT60350

This is a lively site near Punta Sabbioni from where boats depart for Venice. Mediterraneo is directly on the Adriatic Sea with a 480 metre long beach of fine sand which shelves gently and also two large pools and a whirlpool. Of the 766 pitches, 496 are for touring, all with electricity (4-9A); 300 also have water and drainage. They are zoned with artificial shade, others are in unmarked zones under natural woodland, reserved for tents, and equipped with electric hook-ups. Tour operators use 145 pitches. This is a well organised and efficient site.

Facilities	Directions
Eight modern sanitary blocks are of high quality with British type WCs and free hot water. Laundry facilities. Motorcaravan services. Commercial centre with supermarket and other shops with a restaurant, bars and a pizzeria near the pools. Gelateria. Swimming pool (heated low season). Playground. Tennis. Bicycle hire. Sports, games, excursions etc. Dancing in main season. Windsurfing and sailing schools. No dogs. WiFi (charged).	Site is well signed from Jesolo-Punta Sabbioni road near its end after Ca'Ballarin and before Ca'Savio. Follow site signs, not those for Treporti which is some way from the site. GPS: 45.45413, 12.48173

Charges guide

Per unit incl. 2 persons and electricity	€ 17.10 - € 58.80
extra person	€ 4.40 - € 11.40

Open: 24 April - 27 September.

Cavallino-Treporti
Camping Ca'Pasquali

Via A Poerio 33, I-30013 Cavallino-Treporti (Veneto) T: 0419 661 10. E: info@capasquali.it

alanrogers.com/IT60360

Situated on the pretty, natural woodland coast of Cavallino with its wide, safe, sandy beach, Ca'Pasquali is a high quality holiday resort with easy access to Venice. The fine sandy beach was alive with families playing games, flying kites and enjoying themselves when we watched from the renovated restaurant at sunset. This is a large site affiliated with nos. IT60280 and IT60140. Detail is important to the site owners and it shows everywhere. There are great pools, a fitness area, an arena for the ambitious entertainment programme and a beachside restaurant. The 371 touring pitches (10-16A electricity) are shaded and flat (80-90 sq.m) and some have spectacular sea views. This is a superb site for a family holiday.

Facilities	Directions
Three spotless modern units have excellent facilities with superb amenities for disabled campers and babies. Washing machines and dryers. Motorcaravan services. Restaurant. Pizzeria. Crêperie. Cocktail bar. Snack bar. Supermarket. Bazaar. Boutique. Superb pool complex with slides, fun pool and fountains (all services open all season). Fitness centre. Play areas. Bicycle hire. Canoe hire and lessons. Excellent entertainment. Amphitheatre. Miniclub. WiFi (charged). Excursions. No animals.	Leave autostrada A4 at Noventa exit in San Doná di Piave and head towards Jesolo and to Cavallino-Treporti. Site is well signed shortly after town of Cavallino. GPS: 45.45237, 12.48905

Charges guide

Per unit incl. 2 persons and electricity	€ 19.20 - € 52.40
extra person	€ 5.10 - € 11.40
No credit cards.	

Open: 27 April - 21 September.

Cavallino-Treporti
Sant'Angelo Village

Via F Baracca 63, I-30013 Cavallino-Treporti (Veneto) T: 0419 68 882. E: info@santangelo.it

alanrogers.com/IT60390

Sant'Angelo Village is aptly named. It is a large site, concentrated around a central square where a restaurant/pizzeria, shops, bar and an information centre with booking service for excursions can be found. The site is well planned and includes a beach snack bar with its own square, which supports the sports areas, and a fine sandy beach with lifeguards. There are 600 mostly shaded, level pitches which are mainly around the perimeter of the site. Although large, the site has a friendly atmosphere and is ideal for families with young children and campers with mobility problems.

Facilities	Directions
Five modern toilet blocks provide excellent facilities with mainly British toilets and very good facilities for children and disabled campers. Laundry. Motorcaravan services. Supermarket. Restaurant and snack bar. Pizzeria. Crêperie. Gelateria. Takeaway. Pool complex with slide, and fun pool. Aerobics. Fitness centre. Play areas. Games room. Tennis. Bicycle and boat hire. Small boat launching. Beach volleyball. Miniclub. WiFi (charged). Fridge box.	Leave autostrada A4 at San Doná Noventa exit and head for San Doná di Piave, Jesolo, then peninsula of Cavallino and Punta Sabbioni. Site is well signed shortly after Cavallino. GPS: 45.47681, 12.55509

Charges guide

Per unit incl. 2 persons, electricity and water	€ 21.40 - € 48.80
extra person	€ 5.00 - € 11.00

Open: 4 May - 15 September.

For latest campsite news, availability and prices visit
alanrogers.com

Cavallino-Treporti
Camping Village Garden Paradiso
Via F. Baracca 55, I-30013 Cavallino-Treporti (Veneto) T: 0419 680 75. E: info@gardenparadiso.it
alanrogers.com/IT60400

Garden Paradiso is a great name for this site as it describes what it resembles. Colour from abundant flowers and attractive gardens give a very pleasant feel to this seaside site. It has three excellent, centrally situated pools with fun water features, a fitness centre, minigolf, a train to the local weekly market and many other activities for children. All 752 pitches have 6/10A electricity, satellite connection, water and drainage points. They are shaded by trees. A smart reception provides a professional welcome and the service is impressive. The site is directly beside the sea with a beach of fine sand.

Facilities

Four smart, clean toilet blocks are fully equipped. Mixture of British and Turkish style toilets. Facilities for babies. Washing machines and dryers. Motorcaravan services. Shopping complex. Restaurant, snack bar and takeaway (all season). Pizzeria and crêperie. Aqualandia pool complex. Fitness centre. Tennis. Minigolf. Play area. Organised entertainment and excursions (high season). Bicycle hire. Windsurfing. Communal barbecue area. WiFi over site (charged). Dogs are not accepted.

Open: 23 April - 27 September.

Directions

Leave Venice-Trieste autostrada either by taking airport or Quarto d'Altino exits; follow signs to Jesolo and Punta Sabbioni. Take first road left after Cavallino roundabout and site is a little way on the right. GPS: 45.47897, 12.56359

Charges guide

| Per unit incl. 2 persons, electricity, water and drainage | € 22.00 - € 54.00 |
| extra person | € 5.00 - € 11.50 |

Cavallino-Treporti
Camping Village Europa
Via Fausta 332, I-30013 Cavallino-Treporti (Veneto) T: 0419 680 69. E: info@campingeuropa.com
alanrogers.com/IT60410

Europa is a smart, modern site in a great position with direct access to a fine, sandy, Blue Flag beach with lifeguards. There are 450 touring pitches, all with 8A electricity, water, drainage and satellite TV connections. The site is kept beautifully clean and neat and there is an impressive array of restaurants, bars, shops and leisure amenities. These are cleverly laid out along a central avenue and include a jeweller, a doctor's surgery, Internet services and much more. All manner of leisure facilities are arranged around the site. The touring area, with some great beachside pitches, is surprisingly peaceful for a site of this size. This site would be ideal for families.

Facilities

Three toilet blocks are kept pristine and have hot water throughout. Facilities for disabled visitors. Washing machines. Large supermarket and shopping centre, bars, restaurants, cafés and pizzeria (takeaway 15/5-30/9). Excellent pool complex with slide and spa centre. Tennis. Games room. Playground. Miniclubs. Entertainment. Beach access. WiFi (charged). Accommodation for rent.

Open: 30 March - 30 September.

Directions

From A4 autostrada (from Milan) take Mestre exit and follow signs initially for Venice airport and then Jesolo. From Jesolo, follow signs to Cavallino from where site is well signed. GPS: 45.47380, 12.54903

Charges guide

| Per unit incl. 2 persons and electricity | € 20.00 - € 52.70 |
| extra person | € 5.00 - € 11.60 |

Cavallino-Treporti
Camping Village Al Boschetto
Via della Batterie 18, Ca'Vio, I-30013 Cavallino-Treporti (Veneto) T: 0419 661 45. E: info@alboschetto.it
alanrogers.com/IT60455

Al Boschetto is a lovely and peaceful, family owned, beachside site which prides itself on offering a thoughtful service to its customers and has a particular appeal to families. It has an open green and pleasant feel and everything is well maintained. Of 335 pitches, 240 are for touring units (6A Europlug) and 190 of the flat, variable sized pitches (55-100 sq.m) are fully serviced. The remaining pitches are taken by seasonal units, which do not affect the touring areas. An abundance of flowers and trimmed foliage gives the site a pleasant garden atmosphere. This is a great site for families who do not want the razzamatazz and noise of the bigger sites and it is perfect for a relaxing holiday.

Facilities

Three modern sanitary blocks have free hot water throughout. Mostly British style WCs and good facilities for disabled campers. Baby room. Laundry. Motorcaravan services. Well stocked supermarket. Bar. Restaurant, pizzeria and takeaway. Entertainment team in high season. Playground. Tennis. Bicycle hire. Beach volleyball. Windsurfing. ATM. Gym. WiFi (charged). No dogs.

Open: 1 May - 15 September.

Directions

Leave A4 Venice-Trieste autostrada either by taking the airport exit or the Quarto d'Altino exit. Follow signs to Jesolo and Punta Sabbione. Site is well signed from here. GPS: 45.45186, 12.47631

Charges guide

| Per unit incl. 2 persons and electricity | € 19.50 - € 44.50 |
| extra person | € 5.50 - € 10.00 |

For latest campsite news, availability and prices visit
alanrogers.com

Cavallino-Treporti
Camping Miramare

Punta Sabbioni, I-30010 Cavallino-Treporti (Veneto) T: 0419 661 50. E: info@camping-miramare.it

alanrogers.com/IT60460

This small, neat, family owned site (since 1962) is well located, being the closest site to the Punta Sabbioni ferry to Venice. The site provides a free bus service to the ferry and to the local beach. It has an unusually long season compared with other sites in the area. Miramare is ideally located for exploring Venice and its islands, as well as the Lido di Venezia. There are 100 level pitches here, all with 6A electricity. The shop is superb for a small site and the restaurant, 50 m. out of the gate, is renowned for its excellent regional meals.

Facilities	Directions
Two toilet blocks (one heated in low season) with facilities for disabled campers and babies. Washing machines and dryers. Motorcaravan services. Excellent supermarket. Bar, restaurant and pizzas from the oven in the restaurant. Takeaway. Library. Play area. Bicycle hire. Dogs are only accepted on 15 specific pitches. Free shuttle bus to Punta Sabbioni square (departure point for trips to Venice and the islands) and to the nearest beach. WiFi (charged).	Leave the A4 autostrada at exit for Venezia Mestre and follow signs to Jesolo and Punta Sabbioni, where the site is signed. GPS: 45.44035, 12.42110

Open: 23 March - 3 November.

Charges guide

Per unit incl. 2 persons and electricity	€ 23.50 - € 30.00
extra person	€ 5.20 - € 7.20
child (1-10 yrs)	€ 3.40 - € 5.30

Cavallino-Treporti
Camping Scarpiland

Via A Poerio 14, I-30013 Cavallino-Treporti (Veneto) T: 0419 664 88. E: info@scarpiland.com

alanrogers.com/IT60470

Scarpiland is a family owned site which has a fine sandy beach and is directly on the Adriatic. It is a medium sized site with touring pitches under the shade of mature pines and scattered amongst mobile homes. The 147 touring pitches are level, vary in size (60-90 sq.m) and all have 6A electricity. Some are hedged and most have water. Most of the facilities are just outside the site entrance; the road is pleasant but has some traffic. The site will suit campers who prefer smaller establishments with excellent beaches and competitive prices. Excursions are organised to local attractions and into Venice.

Facilities	Directions
Two sanitary blocks, one large, clean and modern with the main site services. The second smaller unisex block has almost all Turkish style toilets. Facilities for babies in the large block plus one unit for disabled visitors. Washing machines and dryers. Fridge/freezer. Restaurant/pizzeria. Ice cream parlour. Newsagent. Supermarket. Butcher. Souvenir shop. Greengrocer and local produce (all on the main site road). Bicycle hire. Riding. Beach umbrella and lounger hire. WiFi (charged). Off site: Golf 3 km.	From Milan, take A4 to Venice and continue towards Trieste as far as A27 intersection, then follow signs to airport. At end of bypass, follow signs to Jesolo then Cavallino and Punta Sabbioni. From here the site is clearly signed. GPS: 45.45507, 12.48874

Open: 12 April - 27 September.

Charges guide

Per unit incl. 2 persons and electricity	€ 15.50 - € 35.90
extra person	€ 4.50 - € 8.70

Minimum stay 2 nights.

Cortina d'Ampezzo
Camping International Dolomiti

Via Campo di Sotto, I-32043 Cortina d'Ampezzo (Veneto) T: 0436 2485. E: campeggiodolomiti@tin.it

alanrogers.com/IT62050

Cortina is a pleasant provincial town with many interesting shops and restaurants and, nestling below wonderful sunlit peaks, this site enjoys a peaceful setting for its visitors. Dedicated to touring units, the site does not take reservations so arrive early in the day in the first three weeks of August to improve your chance of obtaining a pitch. There are 390 informally arranged pitches, all with 2A electricity and some with shade. A heated swimming pool is on site, but otherwise this is a simple and uncomplicated site with fairly basic facilities. It is a pleasant centre for touring the Dolomites.

Facilities	Directions
The two toilet blocks have been refurbished. WCs are British and Turkish style. Washbasins have hot water. The smaller heated block is open all season and kept very clean. Facilities for disabled visitors. Washing machines. Gas supplies. Coffee/drinks bar and shop (20/6-10/9). Heated swimming pool (5/7-25/8). Playground (hard base). WiFi throughout (free). Off site: Restaurant 600 m. Supermarket 1 km. Golf 2 km. Bicycle hire 3 km.	Cortina is 60 km. north of Belluno. Site is 3 km. south of town off the SS51 from Toblach/Dobbiaco to Belluno and Veneto. Follow signs to site, turning right towards Campo from north or left in Zuel from south. GPS: 46.51623, 12.13600

Open: 1 June - 20 September.

Charges guide

Per unit incl. 2 persons and electricity	€ 21.00 - € 27.00
extra person	€ 7.00 - € 9.00

For latest campsite news, availability and prices visit
alanrogers.com

Cortina d'Ampezzo
Camping Rocchetta
Via Campo 1, I-32043 Cortina d'Ampezzo (Veneto) T: 0436 5063. E: camping@sunrise.it
alanrogers.com/IT62055

Within walking distance of one of Europe's most well known winter ski and summer holiday resorts, Camping Rocchetta is an attractive, medium sized, family run site set largely under pines beside a stream. The pitches are level, on grass and all have 3A electricity and views of the surrounding mountains, some over 3,000 m. high. The site is well maintained, all-year-round facilities. Good English is spoken at the helpful reception and whether your interests are walking, cycling or something more strenuous, there is plenty of information and advice available, ensuring you make the most of your stay in this beautiful region.

Facilities

Heated sanitary block, with all facilities under cover, has free, controllable showers and some washbasins in cabins. Facilities for disabled visitors. Washing machines and dryers. Dishwashing. Motorcaravan services. Small shop. Bar with snacks. Outdoor jacuzzi. Playground. WiFi over site (charged). Off site: Cortina 1.5 km. (bus stop at site entrance). Winter sports. Dolomite mountains.

Open: 1 June - 20 September, 5 December - 7 April.

Directions

From the south travel north on A27, after Belluno take exit Cadore/Cortina joining the SS51. Continue to outskirts of Cortina (passing Olympic ski jump). Site is signed to the left. GPS: 46.52262, 12.13406

Charges guide

Per unit incl. 2 persons	
and electricity	€ 22.00 - € 29.00
extra person	€ 7.50 - € 9.00

Eraclea Mare
Camping Village Portofelice
Viale dei Fiori 15, I-30020 Eraclea Mare (Veneto) T: 0421 664 11. E: info@portofelice.it
alanrogers.com/IT60220

Portofelice is an efficient and attractive coastal site, with a sandy beach which is a short walk through a protected pine wood. The beach is very safe and has lifeguards. There is a total of 422 pitches, half of which are available for touring. These flat and shady pitches have 6/8A electricity (70 also have water, drainage and TV sockets), are well kept and cars are parked separately. Some 302 pitches are dedicated to rental accommodation. The social life of the site is centred around the stunning pool complex where the shops, pizzeria, bar, café and restaurant are also located. This is a great family site.

Facilities

Three modern sanitary blocks with slightly more Turkish style WCs than British. Children's block (0-12 yrs). Facilities for disabled campers. Very large supermarket and bazaar. Pizzeria and takeaway. Bar/restaurant. American diner. Gelateria. Crêperie. Three superb pools with waterfalls, slides and an area equipped for disabled guests. Playgrounds. Go-kart track. Pedalos. Water dodgems. Tennis. 5-a-side football. Basketball. Volleyball. Sandy beach. Bicycle hire. ATM. Organised activities and entertainment. Miniclub. WiFi (charged). No dogs.

Open: 7 May - 18 September.

Directions

From A4 Venice-Trieste take S Dona/Noventa exit. After Noventa di Piave toll booth, turn right towards S Doná di Piave. At roundabout (before town centre) keep right and follow signs to Eraclea. At Eraclea turn left (river on right), at first roundabout turn right for Eraclea Mare. Continue for 9-10 km. and turn left at roundabout just before Eraclea Mare. Site is on right in 2 km. GPS: 45.55357, 12.76752

Charges guide

Per unit incl. 2 persons	
and electricity	€ 16.20 - € 48.50
extra person	€ 3.80 - € 11.00

Farra d'Alpago
Camping Sarathei
Lago di Santa Croce, viale al Lago 13, I-32016 Farra d'Alpago (Veneto) T: 0437 454 937. E: info@sarathei.it
alanrogers.com/IT61700

Camping Sarathei is a friendly, family owned site on the banks of Santa Croce lake. It is very popular with windsurfers due to the constant wind, combined with flat water, and is renowned in windsurfing circles. Nestling below the surrounding mountains there are 236 touring pitches, all with 5A electricity. Some are shaded and some have views of the lake. Sarathei caters for those interested in outdoor pursuits and offers peaceful camping for all. The restaurant is very pleasant, as is the beach bar.

Facilities

One sanitary block has hot showers (one per day free) and some hot water for laundry. A mixture of British and Turkish style toilets. Separate facility for disabled campers. Washing machines and a dryer. Freezer. Motorcaravan services. Restaurant with terrace (sells basics). Pizzeria. Takeaway. Beach bar. Play areas. Tennis. Beach. Bicycle hire. Beach. Boat launching. Watersports. WiFi (charged).

Open: 1 April - 30 September.

Directions

Leave A4 Venice-Padova and take A27 Belluno road. Then take exit for Farra d'Alpago. Site is at eastern end of lake. GPS: 46.1190, 12.3534

Charges guide

Per unit incl. 2 persons	
and electricity	€ 23.50 - € 30.50
extra person	€ 7.00 - € 9.00
child (3-10 yrs)	€ 4.00 - € 6.00

For latest campsite news, availability and prices visit
alanrogers.com

Fusina

Camping Fusina

Via Moranzani 93, I-30176 Fusina (Veneto) T: 0415 470 055. E: info@campingfusina.com

alanrogers.com/IT60530

This is traditional camping, but what fun. Choose from 500 well shaded, flat and grassy informal pitches or an unrivalled position directly by the water with amazing views over the lagoon to the towers in Saint Mark's Square. Huge ships pass within 50 metres of the site and delight the children. With water on three sides there are welcoming cool breezes. The ferry to Venice is just outside the gate, so this is an ideal site for visiting the city. As a short-stay site, there are few luxuries, but a busy bar and restaurant are at the heart of the site, along with a small shop. We enjoyed the informality here, where you are left alone to either travel to Venice or just relax watching the sunset over the lagoon from your pitch.

Facilities

Modern, well equipped facilities include units for disabled visitors, along with some existing older units. Many washing machines and dryers. Motorcaravan services. Shop (15/3-31/10). Restaurant. Pizzeria and beer garden. Very lively bar. TV with satellite. Small playground. Boat hire. Marina with cranes, moorings and maintenance facilities. Air-conditioned London cyber bus (really!). Bicycle hire. ATM. Torches useful. WiFi (charged).

Open: All year.

Directions

From SSII Padua-Venice road follow site signs on road east of Mira, turning right as signed. Site is in Fusina at end of peninsula and is well signed. Keep a keen watch for brown camping signs for Fusina and ferry terminal. GPS: 45.4195, 12.2563

Charges guide

Per unit incl. 2 persons and electricity	€ 33.00 - € 35.00
extra person	€ 9.50 - € 10.50

Lido di Jesolo

Villaggio Turistico Malibu Beach

Viale Oriente 78, I-30016 Lido di Jesolo (Veneto) T: 042 136 2212. E: info@campingmalibubeach.com

alanrogers.com/IT60330

This is a family site with direct access to a beach. There are 220 pitches for touring units, all with 6A electricity. Some are well shaded by pine trees and there are some fully serviced pitches. The beach is of soft sand, shelves gently and has lifeguards plus sunshades and loungers for hire. The central complex incorporates a bright, cheery self-service restaurant topped by a very smart restaurant and cocktail patio with views. A large entertainment theatre offers all manner of delights in high season. Other amenities include a large swimming pool, plus a paddling pool with slide and fountains. Everything around this site was clean and smart and the visitors we spoke to were happy.

Facilities

Three very clean blocks provide very good facilities with some Turkish style toilets. Facilities for disabled visitors and children. Bar, self-service restaurant and formal restaurant and cocktail patio. Pizzeria. Shop. Games room. Fitness centre. Hairdresser. Massage. Swimming pool, jacuzzi and paddling pool (hats compulsory). Playground. Miniclub. Entertainment. Beach access. Fridge box hire. WiFi throughout (charged). No dogs.

Open: 13 May - 27 September.

Directions

From A4 autostrada (from Milan) take Mestre exit and follow signs initially for Venice airport and then Jesolo. From Jesolo, follow signs to Jesolo Pineta and site is well signed. GPS: 45.5241, 12.7004

Charges guide

Per unit incl. 2 persons and electricity	€ 20.50 - € 48.50
extra person	€ 5.50 - € 10.50
No credit cards.	

Lido di Jesolo

Camping Waikiki

Viale Oriente 144, I-30016 Lido di Jesolo (Veneto) T: 0421 980 186. E: info@campingwaikiki.com

alanrogers.com/IT60340

Waikiki is twinned with IT60330 Malibu Beach which is close by. This site has direct access to a broad, soft, sandy beach across a 300 m. grass area which has a boarded walkway. The beach shelves slowly, so swimming is safe for children; there are sunshades and loungers to hire and lifeguards on the beach. The touring pitches are on soft sand and shaded by pines and other trees, some close to the beach fence but without sea views. Relatively flat, all have 6A electricity and some have water. On-site amenities include an attractive water park with games and lifeguards.

Facilities

Two refurbished sanitary blocks are clean and well equipped and have a separate area for children. Facilities for disabled visitors in one block. Shop and bazaar. Bar. Restaurant/pizzeria. Swimming and paddling pools. Playground. Children's club. Entertainment programme. Direct access to the beach. Dogs are accepted in a designated area. WiFi (charged).

Open: 13 May - 27 September.

Directions

From A4 autostrada (from Milan) take Mestre exit and follow signs initially for Venice airport and then Jesolo. From Jesolo, follow signs to Jesolo Pineta and site is well signed. GPS: 45.53125, 12.72213

Charges guide

Per unit incl. 2 persons and electricity	€ 18.90 - € 39.90
extra person	€ 4.20 - € 9.20

For latest campsite news, availability and prices visit

alanrogers.com

Lido di Jesolo
Camping Jesolo International

Viale A. da Giussano, I-30016 Lido di Jesolo (Veneto) T: 0421 971 826. E: info@jesolointernational.it
alanrogers.com/IT60370

This is an absolutely brilliant, family oriented, resort-style site that we loved, especially for its positive value for money approach. The truly amazing array of top quality on-site activities is included in the price, some off-site attractions are free (Aqualandia, etc) and others are discounted. Jesolo International is located on a beautiful promontory with 700 m. of white sandy beach and slowly shelving waters. The 368 pitches are flat, mostly shaded and with 10/20A electricity, water and drainage, WiFi and satellite TV connection. Some have private bathrooms. The superb pool complex, where a great entertainment programme is presented each night, rounds off this outstanding site. The dynamic director, Sergio Comino, works long hours to maintain and ever improve this high quality site. A bus service to the ferry to Venice leaves from outside the site. The ferry takes you to Saint Mark's Square in the heart of the city.

Facilities

Sanitary facilities include 72 very modern, continually cleaned bathroom units (shower, WC and basin). Rooms for babies, seniors and disabled campers. Washing machines and dryers. Dishwashers. Motorcaravan services. Supermarket. Family-style restaurant. Pizzeria. Meals and shopping delivery to pitch. Beach bar with snacks. Pool bar serving light lunches. Sports centre. Miniclub. Indoor gym. Tennis (free courts and lessons). Golf (lessons and fees all free). Large play area with adventure-style equipment. Sailing (tuition), banana boat, canoes, pedal boats, loungers and sunshades (all free). Offshore pirate ship. Scuba diving (free; introductory lesson). Language course (free). Pony riding (free). Doctor on site (free). More free activities, too numerous to list here. WiFi free. Dogs are not accepted. Off site: Bus to Venice ferry. Jesolo promenade with shops, restaurants and bars 500 m. Aqualandia 1.5 km. (free). Golf 2 km. Go-kart racing (free) and riding 4 km.

Open: 24 April - 27 September.

Directions

From A4 Venice-Trieste autostrada take Dona di Piave exit and follow signs to Jesolo then Punta Sabbioni. Turn off to Lido di Jesolo just before the Cavallino bridge where the site is well signed. GPS: 45.48395, 12.58763

Charges guide

Per unit incl. 2 persons	
and electricity	€ 28.50 - € 61.50
extra person	€ 6.00 - € 14.50
child (1-5 yrs)	free - € 6.00

Oriago
Camping della Serenissima

Via Padana 334/a, I-30176 Mancontenta (Veneto) T: 0419 218 50. E: info@campingserenissima.it
alanrogers.com/IT60500

The charming Alberti family own this delightful little site of some 155 pitches (all with 16A electricity) where one could stay for a number of days whilst visiting Venice (12 km), Padova (24 km), Lake Garda (135 km) or the Dolomites. There is a good service by bus to Venice (€ 2.60 return) and the site is situated on the Riviera del Brenta, at a section with some very large, old villas. A long, rectangular, flat site with numbered pitches on each side of a central road, there is shade in most parts with many trees, plants and grass. English is spoken and the family pride themselves on the cleanliness of their site. The site is busy with many European visitors travelling to and from Venice on a daily basis. The restaurant/bar is great for a livener after a hot, sticky day in the City of Lovers. It is a calm and quiet site which may suit some campers for longer stays.

Facilities

Sanitary facilities are modern and spotless and include those for disabled visitors. Additional quality toilet facilities adjacent to restaurant. Motorcaravan services. Gas supplies. Shop (all season). Bar. Restaurant and takeaway (1/6-31/10). Play area. Fishing. Bicycle hire. Local markets are well publicised. Off site: Golf and riding 3 km. Brenta canal (boat trips). Historic villas. Venice.

Open: 30 March - 6 November.

Directions

Approaching Venice on the A4 take exit for Oriago-Mira then signs for Ravenna, Padova (SS11) to Oriago. On A27 or SS309 take exit for Venezia-Mestre then signs for Ravenna, Padova and Milano. After Padova-Riviera del Brenta follow signs to Oriago. Site is well signed. GPS: 45.451769, 12.183784

Charges guide

Per unit incl. 2 persons	
and electricity	€ 29.00 - € 33.00
extra person	€ 7.50 - € 9.00
child (3-12 yrs)	€ 4.50 - € 5.50

For latest campsite news, availability and prices visit
alanrogers.com

Punta Sabbioni
Marina di Venezia Camping Village

Via Montello 6, I-30013 Punta Sabbioni (Veneto) T: 041 530 2511. E: camping@marinadivenezia.it
alanrogers.com/IT60450

This is an amazingly large site (2,881 pitches) with every conceivable facility. It has a pleasant feel, with cheerful staff and no notion of being overcrowded, even when full. Marina di Venezia has the advantage of being within walking distance of the ferry to Venice. It will appeal in particular to those who enjoy an extensive range of entertainment and activities and a lively atmosphere. Individual pitches are spacious and set on sandy or grassy ground; most are separated by trees or hedges. All are equipped with 10A electricity and water. The site's excellent sandy beach is one of the widest along this stretch of coast and has five pleasant beach bars. This is an efficiently run site with committed management and staff.

Facilities

Nine modern toilet blocks are maintained to a very high standard with hot showers and a high proportion of British style toilets. Pleasant facilities for disabled visitors. Laundry. Range of shops. Several bars, restaurants and takeaways. Five beach bars/snack bars. Enormous swimming pool complex with slides and flumes. Several play areas. Tennis. Surfboard and catamaran hire. Wide range of organised entertainment. WiFi throughout (free). Special area and facilities for dog owners (also beach area). Off site: Fishing 1 km. Riding 7 km. Golf 10 km.

Open: 23 April - 2 October.

Directions

From A4 motorway, take Jesolo exit. After Jesolo continue towards Punta Sabbioni. Site is clearly signed to the left towards the end of this road, close to the Venice ferries. GPS: 45.43750, 12.43805

Charges guide

Per unit incl. 2 persons	
and electricity	€ 22.10 - € 52.10
extra person	€ 4.90 - € 11.70
child or senior (2-5 yrs, over 60s)	€ 4.00 - € 8.90
dog	€ 1.80 - € 5.80

Rocca di Arsiè
Camping Al Lago di Arsiè

Via Campagna 14, Rocca, I-32030 Rocca di Arsiè (Veneto) T: 0439 585 40. E: info@campinglago.com
alanrogers.com/IT61500

This small, quiet site with its beautiful lakeside setting, surrounded by steep, tree-clad hills is now under the same ownership as IT62290. It is located at the southern edge of the Dolomites and is only 110 km. from Venice and the Adriatic. This is an ideal site to spend some time just relaxing, walking or cycling in this most attractive region. The main camping area slopes gently down to the lake and has some shade; it has 118 touring pitches, all with 4/6A electricity. There is a large area catering for both tents and caravans, plus a separate 'Sosta' area for motorcaravans stopping over. We enjoyed the restaurant which is also used by locals.

Facilities

Two central toilet blocks have controllable showers and a mixture of Turkish and British style toilets. Washbasins (open-style) and sinks (under cover) have only cold water, but there are taps from which to collect hot water. Washing machines and dryer. Motorcaravan services. Facilities for disabled visitors. Bar (with Sky TV). Restaurant/pizzeria with takeaway (all season). Play area. Games room. WiFi throughout (free). Off site: Walking, cycling and mountain biking. Riding 5 km.

Open: 1 April - 30 September.

Directions

Arsiè is 45 km. south west of Belluno and 65 km. east of Trento on the SS50/SS50bis which links Belluno to the SS47 Padua-Trento road. Site is near Rocca di Arsiè, alongside the Corlo lake, and is signed to the south off the SS47. GPS: 45.96405, 11.75913

Charges guide

Per unit incl. 2 persons	
and electricity	€ 19.00 - € 35.00
extra person	€ 6.00 - € 8.00
child (2-10 yrs)	€ 4.00 - € 6.00
dog	€ 2.00 - € 3.50

For latest campsite news, availability and prices visit
alanrogers.com

Sottomarina
Camping Miramare

Via Barbarigo 103, I-30015 Sottomarina di Chioggia (Veneto) T: 0414 906 10.
E: info@miramarecamping.com **alanrogers.com/IT60560**

Camping Miramare is a pleasant, fairly shady site with beach access, a swimming pool and a busy entertainment programme. The site is kept beautifully clean and is divided by a road with reception on the beach side, along with most of the amenities. The other side is spacious and very peaceful with just sports amenities and a sanitary block. The 230 touring pitches are separated from the permanent units. All have 6A electricity and some have water and drainage. The beach is great, with soft sand and a lifeguard. You can hire sunshades and loungers. The restaurant offers traditional food and pizzas which can be enjoyed on the terraces overlooking the pools. Children have several play areas and there is entertainment on site all season. The swimming and paddling pool is excellent with two diving boards and a lifeguard. The site lies close to the ancient city of Chioggia, famous for its fishing and Venice-like construction. It is well worth a visit on a bicycle to investigate its amazing history. This is a pleasant, family oriented site which has a distinct Italian feel. English is spoken.

Facilities

Three identical, modern, very clean blocks, one in the permanent campers' area. Pushbutton hot showers and mainly Turkish style toilets. Facilities for disabled visitors. Baby room. Laundry rooms. Motorcaravan services. Pleasant bar. Restaurant, pizzeria and takeaway, smart shop (all open all season). Excellent swimming pool and separate paddling pool (9/5-21/9). Several great play areas. Multisports court. Bicycle hire. Entertainment and children's activities (high season). WiFi over site (charged). Mobile homes to rent. No dogs in high season.

Open: 4 April - 21 September.

Directions

Site is off S309 south of Chioggia. Follow signs to Sottomarina, crossing the Laguna del Lusenzo, then look for site signs. Site is off Viale Mediterranneo road to the right. Site is the second of many along this narrow road. GPS: 45.19018, 12.30341

Charges guide

Per unit incl. 2 persons	
and electricity	€ 20.50 - € 35.50
extra person	€ 5.00 - € 8.50
child (1-6 yrs)	€ 2.50 - € 4.00

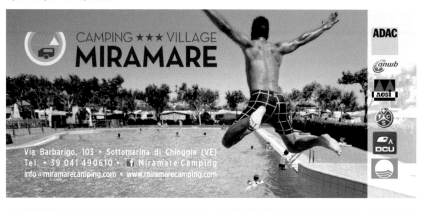

Sottomarina
Camping Village Oasi

Via A Barbarigo 147, I-30015 Sottomarina di Chioggia (Veneto) T: 0415 541 145. E: info@campingoasi.com
alanrogers.com/IT60540

Camping Oasi is a traditional, friendly, family site where many Italian families return for the summer – you could certainly practise your Italian language skills here. The Tiozzi family will make you feel very welcome. The 100 flat, grass pitches for touring units are in separate areas from the permanent units, and have the choice of shade or sun, all have 6A electricity, water and drainage. The private, soft sand beach has a second bar and restaurant, umbrellas and loungers, plus all manner of watersports. This tardis of a site has a huge range of holiday options for families.

Facilities

Two clean sanitary blocks with mostly British style toilets and free hot showers. Facilities for babies and disabled visitors. Private cabins (€5/day). Pleasant swimming pool and paddling pool with flumes (disability hoist available). Adventure play area. Multisports pitch. Tennis. Bicycle hire. Riding. Watersports. Marina with secure parking for motorcaravans and caravans with boats. Fishing. Late arrival area. WiFi on part of site (charged).

Open: 28 March - 28 September.

Directions

Site is off S309 south of Chioggia. Follow signs to Sottomarina, crossing Laguna del Lusenzo, then look for signs. Site off this road (V. Mediterranneo) to right. Site is at end of this narrow road. GPS: 45.18148, 12.30755

Charges guide

Per unit incl. 2 persons	
and electricity	€ 21.20 - € 37.50

No credit cards.

For latest campsite news, availability and prices visit
alanrogers.com

Sottomarina
Villaggio Turistico Isamar

Isolaverde, via Isamar 9, I-30010 Chioggia (Veneto) T: 0415 535 811. E: info@villaggioisamar.com
alanrogers.com/IT60550

This is a very large, high quality site with many shops and restaurants and a huge range of leisure facilities. The camping areas are beneath pine trees and within easy reach of the two excellent pool complexes and covered entertainment centre. The pitches are arranged on either side of hard access roads and all have 6A electrical connections. There are many other areas containing well constructed chalets and holiday bungalows. The site has its own beautiful soft sand beach and is a great destination for families as it caters for all tastes. Entertainment and activity programmes are organised in several languages. There is a much higher proportion of Italian holidaymakers than many other sites. It is also popular with German and Dutch campers and may become crowded in high season.

Facilities

Four large, spotlessly clean sanitary blocks are arranged around the main camping area. Fully equipped and of superb quality with facilities for children and disabled visitors. Laundry. Motorcaravan services. Gas supplies. Hairdresser. Beauty centre. Supermarket and shopping centre. Ice cream shop. Pastry shop. Restaurant. Large bar/pizzeria and self-service restaurant. Swimming pools. Tennis. Gym. Playground. Games room. Riding. Volleyball. Archery. Football. Bicycle hire. Extensive entertainment and fitness programme. Supervised play for over 4s. Miniclub. ATM. Boat launching. WiFi (charged). Dogs are not accepted. Off site: Disco with bar/restaurant adjacent. Boat launching 500 m. Excursions.

Open: 15 May - 20 September.

Directions

Turn off the main 309 road towards sea just south of Adige river 10 km. south of Chioggia, and proceed 5 km. to site. GPS: 45.16236, 12.32477

Charges guide

Per unit incl. 2 persons	
and electricity	€ 24.00 - € 54.00
extra person	€ 8.00 - € 12.00
child (under 12 yrs)	free - € 10.00

Vicenza
Camping Vicenza

Strada Pelosa, I-36100 Vicenza (Veneto) T: 0444 582 311. E: info@campingvicenza.it
alanrogers.com/IT60275

This is a very pleasant site with a difference, in that it is paired with a quality hotel close to Vicenza. As such, it is able to offer use of the hotel facilities including the pool, bar/restaurant and spa (charge for spa). The 77 pitches (80 sq.m) are attractively laid out with bricked hardstandings and brick access roads, plenty of shade from trees, and privacy from neat and mature hedges. They are smart, clean and equipped with 3/6A electricity. The hotel and site are alongside an autoroute exit, but a tall soundproofing fence along one side of the site minimises its impact. It is peaceful here despite the proximity of the autoroute, and the bus service is brilliant for visiting Vicenza, a beautiful Italian city in miniature with Palladian architecture, taking just two hours to cover. This site is ideal for visiting the area, and will suit some campers for longer stays.

Facilities

The single sanitary block is initially quite forbidding (concrete, post WW2 styling), but the facilities within are neat and comprehensive. Baby room with bath. Children's bathroom. Facilities for disabled visitors. Washing machine. Drying area under cover. Fridge freezer. Motorcaravan services. No shop. Restaurant and takeaway (1/4-20/9). Drinks machine. Hotel wellness centre with pool and bar. TV room. Entertainment in the hotel on Fridays. Communal barbecues. Public bus service. WiFi (free). Off site: Shops and ATM 1 km.

Open: 1 April - 30 September.

Directions

From A4 Verona-Padova autoroute take Vincenz est exit and you will immediately see campsite sign on your right as you exit the autoroute. Take a series of right turns at mini roundabouts following campsite signs bringing you to Hotel Vieste and campsite entrance. GPS: 45.518002, 11.602544

Charges guide

Per unit incl. 2 persons	
and electricity	€ 26.50 - € 34.50
extra person	€ 6.50 - € 8.50
child (3-8 yrs)	€ 3.00 - € 5.00

For latest campsite news, availability and prices visit
alanrogers.com

EMILIA-ROMAGNA COMPRISES NINE PROVINCES: BOLOGNA, FERRARA, FORLI, MODENA, PARMA, PIACENZA, RAVENNA, REGGIO EMILIA AND RIMINI

Once two regions, Emilia-Romagna stretches from the Adriatic coast almost to the shores of the Mediterranean. A prosperous area with historical cities and thriving industry, it is also home to two of Italy's most famous food exports: Parma ham and Parmesan cheese.

One of the richest regions of Italy, Emilia and Romagna only became united in 1947. Its landscape is varied, with the flat fields of the northern plain giving way to the forest-covered Apennine mountains in the south. Carving a route through the heart of the region is the Via Emilia, a Roman military road built in 187 BC that links the garrison town of Piacenza to Rimini on the coast. Most of the major towns lie along this route including Bologna, the region's capital. The historic city boasts a rich cultural heritage with its famous porticos, old university buildings and medieval palaces clustered around bustling town squares. North of Bologna, Ferrara is one of the most important Renaissance centres in Italy, while further inland Modena and Parma are home to some of the region's finest architecture. Parma also boasts one of the country's top opera houses. In the east, Ravenna is renowned for the Byzantine mosaics that decorate its churches and mausoleums, and along the Adriatic coast lie various beaches and the seaside resorts of Cervia, Cesenatico and Rimini. A popular summer destination, Rimini has sandy beaches, a lively nightlife, an abundance of bars and restaurants.

Places of interest

Faenza: home of faïence ceramic-ware.

Ferrara: walled town with impressive medieval castello.

Modena: the home of fast cars: both Ferrari and Maserati have factories on the outskirts.

Montese: wild black cherry festival in July, medieval singing, dancing and classical concerts in August.

Piacenza: historic Roman town, medieval and Renaissance architecture.

Valli di Comacchi: a wetland area, good for birdwatching.

Vignola: best known for its cherries and cherry blossom, spring festival, 15th/16th-century castle.

Cuisine of the region

Bologna is regarded as the gastronomic capital of Italy. Famous regional specialities include parmesan cheese (*parmigiano-reggiano*), egg pasta, Parma ham (*prosciutto di Parma*) and balsamic vinegar. Local dishes include *lasagne*, *tortellini* stuffed with ricotta and spinach, *bollito misto* (boiled meats), *zampone* (stuffed pig's trotter). Fish is also popular along the coast of Romagna.

Cannelloni: large pasta tubes stuffed with meat or cheese and spinach, covered in tomato or cheese sauce.

Ciacci: chestnut flour pancakes filled with ricotta cheese and sugar.

Spaghetti al Ragù: pasta with beef and tomato sauce.

Torta di Limone: tart made with lemon and fresh cream.

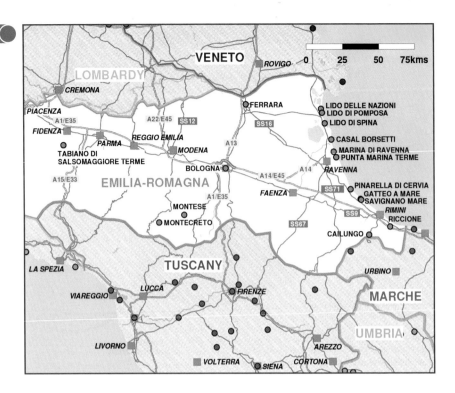

Bologna

Camping Hotel Cittá di Bologna

Via Romita 12-4A, I-40127 Bologna (Emilia-Romagna) T: 0513 250 16. E: info@hotelcamping.com

alanrogers.com/IT66020

This spacious city site was established in 1993 on the edge of the Trade Fair Centre of this ancient and historic city and is very clean and modern. The 120 pitches, with 6A electricity, are numbered and marked out in a very orderly manner and shaded by trees. All pitches are on level 'grasscrete' hardstandings. There are two main areas plus a separate section for very long units. You will always find space here as there is huge over capacity. There is an unassuming restaurant and bar in a central location and the pleasant swimming pool with paddling area is very welcome after a day exploring the city. The site is excellent for an overnight stop or for longer stays to explore the most attractive and unusual city of Bologna. The reception is impressively efficient and friendly with excellent English spoken. There is a little daytime aircraft noise, but the site is surrounded by fields and trees giving a peaceful atmosphere. The intention was not only to make a campsite, but to provide high quality motel-type rooms for use by those visiting trade fairs. There are now 92 chalets for rent. Bologna has a beauty of its own and we believe a visit is a must.

Facilities

Modern sanitary blocks include excellent provision for disabled visitors (with British style WCs, free showers and alarms that ring in reception). Washing machines. Motorcaravan services. Restaurant and bar with adjoining terrace where quality meals are offered. Large swimming pool with shallow area for children. Basic play area. Minigolf. Fitness centre. WiFi over site (first 15 mins. free). Off site: Bus service to city centre from site. Fast rail links to major cities. Shops and restaurant 500 m. Bicycle hire 5 km. Fishing 10 km.

Open: 9 January - 20 December.

Directions

Site is well signed from Bologna Fiera exit on the autostrada on the north east of the city. Look for brown signs. GPS: 44.52366, 11.3741

Charges guide

Per unit incl. 2 persons and electricity	€ 24.00 - € 33.00
extra person	€ 6.50 - € 9.00
child (5-9 yrs)	€ 4.50 - € 5.50
dog	€ 2.00

For latest campsite news, availability and prices visit

alanrogers.com

Cailungo
Centro Vacanze San Marino

Strada San Michele 50, Cailungo, I-47893 Repubblica di San Marino (Emilia-Romagna) T: 0549 903 964.
E: info@centrovacanzesanmarino.com **alanrogers.com/IT66230**

Centro Vacanze San Marino, at 400 m. above sea level and positioned on an attractive hillside, has lovely views of the Adriatic. This excellent, modern site has a variety of well tended trees offering shade. On level terraces, the main grass pitches are roomy and accessed from tarmac or gravel roads. Separated by hedges, all have electricity (5A). Smaller pitches on lower terraces are for tents. There is a pleasant open feel to this site. Mobile homes and bungalows are available to rent and the site is used by a tour operator (30 pitches). The large swimming pool has a section for children and a broad sunbathing terrace. Make sure you visit the ancient city of San Marino at the top of the mountain (4 km).

Facilities

Four high quality, heated toilet blocks are kept very clean and have British and Turkish style WCs. Facilities for disabled visitors at the upper level to avoid slopes. Laundry facilities. Motorcaravan services. Kitchen. Gas supplies. Shop (April-Sept). TV room (satellite). Restaurant/pizzeria. Large swimming pool (1/6-1/9) with jacuzzi and solarium. Large enclosed play area. Games room. Free WiFi over part of site. Tennis. Bicycle hire. Mini zoo. Entertainment programme for children (high season). Off site: Bus service to town from outside gate (site runs Sun. service). San Marino.

Open: All year.

Directions

Leave autostrada A14 at exit Rimini-Sud (or SS16 where signed), follow SS72 west to San Marino. Site is signed from 15 km. GPS: 43.95957, 12.46126

Charges guide

Per unit incl. 2 persons and electricity	€ 22.00 - € 42.00
extra person	€ 7.50 - € 10.00
child (3-9 yrs)	€ 3.00 - € 8.00
dog	€ 2.00 - € 5.00

Casal Borsetti
Camping Village Adria

Via Spallazzi 30, I-48010 Casal Borsetti (Emilia-Romagna) T: 0544 445 217. E: adria@camping.it
alanrogers.com/IT60790

Adria is a modest site at first glance, however one soon realises this is a real gem. Unusually for the Adriatic, the setting is tranquil as there is no road or rail noise. Alongside the pretty beach, the site is surrounded by fields and a nature reserve. The pitches (50-100 sq.m) are level and have 10A electricity. Well shaded in the older area, the trees in the new area are beginning to provide welcome shade. The exciting new pool complex is a fun setting for both day and evening entertainment. This family oriented site really does give value for money. When we visited, children of all ages were having great fun with the entertainment staff.

Facilities

Six toilet blocks, four with showers. Facilities for disabled visitors in every block. Very good facilities for children. Washing machines. Three bars including a beach bar, restaurant, separate snack bar and pizzeria with large terrace. Two swimming pools. Excellent entertainment programme in season. Miniclub. Three excellent play areas. Archery. Boules. Multisports courts. Watersports. Bicycle hire. WiFi (charged). Off site: Beach 180 m. ATM 1 km. Riding 3 km. Golf 40 km.

Open: 23 April - 15 September.

Directions

Site is north of Ravenna. From the A13 take the Ferrara road towards the coast at Comacchio and then south on the S309 towards Ravenna. Continue to town of Casal Borsetti and site is well signed. From south, use S309, turning right after crossing new bridge. GPS: 44.55910, 12.27965

Charges guide

Per unit incl. 2 persons and electricity	€ 16.60 - € 40.80
extra person	€ 4.90 - € 9.60
child (3-10 yrs)	free - € 7.00
dog	€ 2.50 - € 4.00

For latest campsite news, availability and prices visit
alanrogers.com

Ferrara

Camping Comunale Estense

Via Gramicia 76, I-44123 Ferrara (Emilia-Romagna) T: 0532 752 396. E: campeggio.estense@libero.it
alanrogers.com/IT60600

Ferrara is an interesting and historic city, well worth a short visit. This pretty municipal campsite on the northern outskirts offers comfortable facilities for all types of units and includes 25 fairly large, grass pitches with numerous electrical connections. Trees are used to provide shade and to screen the site. Unusual concrete portals are covered in roses, shrubs and other flowers giving a cheerful atmosphere. On-site facilities are limited with machines for snacks and cold drinks, but there is an excellent trattoria within walking distance (1 km) and a wide choice of other eating places in the city itself.

Facilities	Directions
Two acceptable, adjacent toilet blocks are fully equipped, one heated with British and Turkish style toilets. Separate facilities for disabled visitors. Drink and snack machines. Torches required in places. Off site: Restaurant close by. Golf 100 m. Fishing 500 m. Riding 3 km. **Open:** 25 February - 10 January.	Site is well signed from the city and is on the northern side of the ring road. GPS: 44.85217, 11.63417

Charges guide

Per unit incl. 2 persons and electricity	€ 21.50 - € 24.50
extra person	€ 5.00 - € 6.00

No credit cards.

Gatteo a Mare

Villaggio Camping Delle Rose

Via Adriatica 29, I-47043 Gatteo a Mare (Emilia-Romagna) T: 0547 862 13. E: info@villaggiorose.com
alanrogers.com/IT66210

On the Cesanatico coastline of Emilia-Romagna, this site is unusually located in a shaded park area just 450 m. from the beautiful sandy beach. It is a site with a very Italian flavour and when we visited we were made very welcome. The 200 touring pitches, with 3/10A electricity, are cosily positioned and most have shade. There is a large swimming pool and paddling pool and an ambitious programme of activities and entertainment takes place throughout the day and during the evening. The bar and restaurant facilities on site are very good, as is the pool bar. A nearby railway line (300 m) can be heard.

Facilities	Directions
Modern sanitary facilities are very clean and well spaced around the site. Motorcaravan services. Shop. Restaurant, pizzeria and snack bar with takeaway (all 1/5-20/9). Swimming pool with pool bar (30/5-13/9). Paddling pool. Hydro-massage. Playgrounds. Games room. TV room. Miniclub. Entertainment. Sports field. Free shuttle bus and use of bicycles to beach. WiFi on part of site (free). Off site: Retail centre including supermarkets nearby. **Open:** 1 May - 19 September.	Take the Cesena exit from the A14 Bologna-Ancona motorway. Head east to join the SS16 and then south to Gatteo a Mare. Site is clearly signed. GPS: 44.16597, 12.43196

Charges guide

Per unit incl. 2 persons and electricity	€ 26.00 - € 66.00
extra person	€ 4.00 - € 9.50
child (4-10 yrs)	free - € 7.50

Lido delle Nazioni

Tahiti Camping & Terme Bungalow Park

Viale Libia 133, I-44020 Lido delle Nazioni - Comacchio (Emilia-Romagna) T: 053 337 9500.
E: info@campingtahiti.com alanrogers.com/IT60650

Tahiti is an excellent, extremely well run, family owned site, thoughtfully laid out 800 m. from the sea (a continuous, fun road-train link is provided). An abundance of flowers and shrubs enhance the site's appearance. The 450 touring pitches are of varying sizes, back to back from hard roads, defined by trees with shade in most areas and all with 10A electricity. There are six types, from a basic pitch to those with kitchens plus a shower. Several languages, including English, are spoken by the friendly staff. The Thermal Oasis is luxurious and there is a 50% discount for campers. This award-winning site has a great atmosphere and everyone was cheerful when we visited. Torches are needed in some areas.

Facilities	Directions
All toilet blocks are of a very high standard. British and Turkish style WCs. Baby room. Large supermarket, two restaurants, bar, pizzeria, takeaway, heated swimming pools (all season). Thermal Oasis (charged). Fitness and beauty centre. Playgrounds. Miniclub. Gym. Tennis. Minigolf. Riding. Entertainment and excursions (July/Aug). 'Disco-pub'. ATM. Bicycle hire. WiFi (charged). Free transport to beach. Archery. Bowls. Dogs accepted 12/5-19/6 and 28/8-18/9 only. **Open:** 12 May - 18 September.	Turn off SS309 35 km. north of Ravenna to Lido delle Nazioni (north of Lido di Pomposa) and follow site signs. GPS: 44.73457, 12.22178

Charges guide

Per unit incl. 2 persons and electricity	€ 22.70 - € 46.80
extra person	€ 5.90 - € 11.90
child (under 8 yrs)	free

For latest campsite news, availability and prices visit
alanrogers.com

Lido di Pomposa
Camping Village Vigna sul Mar

Via Capanno Garibaldi 20, I-44020 Lido di Pomposa (Emilia-Romagna) T: 0533 380 216.
E: info@vsmcampingvillage.com **alanrogers.com/IT60700**

This quietly situated site, about 8 km. north of Ravenna, has everything required for a happy and active family holiday. Tall, mature trees mark out pitches and give excellent shade in all parts. Some 400 pitches have 6A electricity and satellite TV connections. The private beach is about 100 m. from the centre. The campsite's own beach has a bar with snacks and beach equipment for hire. The site also has an excellent double swimming pool and many sports and recreational facilities, including a small theatre with nightly entertainment of films and dancing. There is a 'nature track' amongst the trees on one side of the site. A nearby sailing centre has windsurfing boards and boats for hire. Trips are organised to famous towns and nearby beauty spots. Much of the site is devoted to bungalows and tour operators, but there are plenty of attractive pitches for touring units. The picturesque old fishing port of Porto Garibaldi is well worth a visit.

Facilities

Two of the main toilet blocks have been refurbished to a very high standard and all are kept very clean. Facilities for disabled visitors. Washing machines. Motorcaravan services. Supermarket, greengrocer, ice-cream parlour, tobacconist and newsagent. Bar, restaurant, pizzeria and snack bar by pool. Swimming pool (23/5-20/9). Play area. Minigolf. Jogging track. Bicycle hire. Canoe and pedalo hire. Entertainment and excursions (high season). WiFi over part of site (charged). Off site: Golf 2 km. Fishing 4 km. Riding 5 km.

Open: 23 April - 20 September.

Directions

From SS309 Ravenna-Venice road, look for signs for Porto Garibaldi, Lido degli Scacchi and Lido di Pomposa. Follow the coast road northbound, and site is well signed. GPS: 44.72527, 12.23605

Charges guide

Per unit incl. 2 persons	
and electricity	€ 24.00 - € 56.60
extra person	€ 6.00 - € 11.30
child (3-9 yrs)	free - € 7.30
dog	free - € 5.00

Lido di Pomposa
International Camping Tre Moschettieri

Via Capanno Garibaldi 22, I-44020 Lido di Pomposa (Emilia-Romagna) T: 53 338 0376.
E: info@tremoschettieri.com **alanrogers.com/IT60760**

Tre Moschettieri (Three Musketeers) is a compact, attractive site alongside the sea at Lido di Pomposa. The sandy beach, all decked out with its colourful umbrellas, is delightful. The gently shelving beach is ideal for swimming and having fun with the family. The site is in a garden setting and has many trees providing excellent shade for the 418 grass pitches (70-80 sq.m, 4/8A chargeable electricity). The roads are tarmac to reduce the dust and there are many water points around the site. The friendly management take care that campers are informed of programmed events and are eager to please. There is an amazing range of entertainment on offer. The pools, bar, entertainment area and restaurant are of a uniformly high standard. This is an ideal site for excursions to places of interest in the area. In our opinion, this is one of the most attractive sites on the Adriatic coast, offering just about everything you could need for a great family holiday in an authentic Italian atmosphere.

Facilities

Eleven refurbished toilet blocks placed around site. Facilities for disabled visitors (check first). Washing machines and dryers. Bar, restaurant/pizzeria and takeaway with terrace. Swimming pools on elevated section with a hoist for disabled access (June-Sept). Tennis. Gym. Giant chess. Play areas. Entertainment programme in season. Excellent miniclub. Windsurfing school. Beach bar. ATM. Disco. Bicycle hire. Dogs are not allowed on the beach or in the pool area. WiFi over part of site (charged). Off site: Excursions.

Open: 20 April - 16 September.

Directions

Site is east of Ferrara. Take the road to the coast and Comaccio, then the SS309 north to Lido de Pomposa. Site is well signed. GPS: 44.71666, 12.23333

Charges guide

Per unit incl. 2 persons	
and electricity	€ 23.00 - € 41.50
extra person	€ 6.00 - € 11.50
child (2-8 yrs)	€ 2.00 - € 7.00
dog	€ 4.00 - € 4.50

For latest campsite news, availability and prices visit
alanrogers.com

Lido di Spina

Spina Camping Village

Via del Campeggio 99, I-44024 Lido di Spina (Emilia-Romagna) T: 0533 330 179.
E: info@spinacampingvillage.com **alanrogers.com/IT60780**

This new camping venture in the Adriatic Riviera is a real treat. Upon arrival it is clear that whilst much of the site is devoted to seasonal units and tour operators, every effort is made to meet the needs of touring units. There are lots of choices here – the splendid, private beach or on-site pool, beach sports or games in the superb sports areas. Pitches vary in size, services and setting, from park-like, open areas with rows of trees to heavily shaded pinewoods. The different types of rental units are thoughtfully nestled within the site to provide a pleasing mix in an informal layout.

Facilities

The three toilet blocks have been refurbished to a very high standard. Excellent facilities for disabled visitors. Bright and cheerful baby rooms. Washing machines. Motorcaravan services. Supermarket. Bakery. Bar with modern restaurant. Miniclub. Play areas. Swimming pools (15/5-end Aug. with lifeguard, caps required). Beach and pool bars with entertainment programmes in both areas. Watersports. ATM. Torches and long electricity leads useful. Excursions. TV room. WiFi (charged).

Open: 17 April - 19 September.

Directions

Site is north of Ravenna and east of Ferrara. Take road from Ferrara to the coast at Comacchio, then SS309 south to Lido di Spina. Site is signed from here. GPS: 44.627721, 12.255061

Charges guide

Per unit incl. 2 persons	
and electricity	€ 15.00 - € 38.00
extra person	€ 3.50 - € 10.50
dog	free - € 9.00

Marina di Ravenna

Piomboni Camping Village

Viale della Pace 421, I-48122 Marina di Ravenna (Emilia-Romagna) T: 054 453 0230.
E: info@campingpiomboni.it **alanrogers.com/IT60730**

The pine forest which is home to Piomboni forms part of the Po Delta National Forest and has been spared the frantic commercial development of other parts of the Adriatic coast. The site, still family owned and run, maintains a totally natural feel with pitches located between the ancient, tall pines and younger, dividing trees. There are 376 pitches for tiny tents and motorcaravans up to eight metres, all with 4-10A electricity. Access to the beach is just 100 metres from the site gate and there are large, free public areas. Road noise is negligible and our night here was peaceful.

Facilities

Seven toilet blocks, two with hot and cold showers. Baby rooms. Facilities for disabled visitors. Washing machines and dryer. Dog bath. Well stocked shop. Bar, restaurant and takeaway (22/4-12/9). Dancing and entertainments area. TV room with library. Games and play area with boules pitch. Children's activities programme. Archery. Bicycle hire. Free WiFi. Excursions. Off site: Sandy beach across the road. Restaurants within a short distance.

Open: 22 April - 12 September.

Directions

Heading north from Ravenna, take beach road from Punta Marina Terme towards Marina di Ravenna. The site is on the left, but not signed. Coming south from Marina di Ravenna, the site is well signed and is on the right. GPS: 44.466414, 12.284989

Charges guide

Per unit incl. 2 persons	
and electricity	€ 20.30 - € 33.20

No credit cards.

Montecreto

Campeggio Parco dei Castagni

Via del Parco 5, I-41025 Montecreto (Emilia-Romagna) T: 0536 635 95. E: camping@parcodeicastagni.it
alanrogers.com/IT60980

This lovely little mountain site is well situated on the edge of a small village and is open all year round. It takes its name from the magnificent, centuries old chestnut trees. The owners here have completely cleared a former campsite and started afresh. The sanitary facilities are of top quality, the pool, bar and small restaurant are also very good. The pretty Swiss-style rental chalets and the pitches are on terraced ground and all 15 touring pitches have access to 3A electricity. The amenities here promise to make this site extremely popular with people looking for a quiet site with some dramatic scenery.

Facilities

The new, purpose built toilet block is heated, clean and provides very good facilities. Facilities for disabled visitors. Washing machines and dryers. Restaurant/bar (all year). Swimming pool (1/6-30/9). Play area. Bicycle hire. Barbecues are not permitted. Off site: Chairlift 50 m. Village with shops and restaurants 300 m. Fishing, golf and riding 6 km.

Open: All year.

Directions

Site is clearly signed from the centre of Montecreto which is near Sestola on SS324. Best approached from Modena as southern approach, from Pistioa or Lucca via Abetone, involves steep climbs and numerous hairpins. GPS: 44.24667, 10.71194

Charges guide

Per unit incl. 2 persons	
and electricity	€ 23.00 - € 29.00
extra person	€ 7.00 - € 8.00

For latest campsite news, availability and prices visit
alanrogers.com

Montese
Camping Eco-chiocciola

Via Testa 80, Fraz. Maserno, I-41055 Montese (Emilia-Romagna) T: 0599 800 65. E: info@ecochiocciola.com

alanrogers.com/IT66030

Tucked away in the Apennines, in a small village, this interesting little campsite has many surprises. Eco-chiocciola (named after the snail wearing his house on his back) is being developed by the owner Ottavio Mazzanti as a place to enjoy the natural geographic, geological, botanical and zoological features of the area. Comforts such as the swimming pool are designed to offer relaxation when not exploring. The 40 small touring pitches, all with 6A electrical connections, are on level or gently sloping ground with some terraces, many enjoying superb views. Ottavio speaks excellent English and there are mementos of his extensive travels in the reasonably priced restaurant, which serves international dishes as well as traditional local Italian. This is a peaceful site with a distinctly rustic feel for people who enjoy natural settings. It is best suited to tent campers and small motorcaravans.

Facilities

Two refurbished sanitary blocks have some British style WCs and hot showers (a reader reports they do not always work well in high season). Solar panels have been installed. Facilities for disabled campers. Washing machine. Motorcaravan services. Restaurant. Bar. Large multipurpose room for entertainment. Swimming pool open afternoons and weekend mornings (23/6-3/9). Tennis and volleyball area as well as a tree house. Bicycle hire. Torches necessary. Off site: No shop on the site but the village is 300 m. Local bus stop in village. Riding 3 km. Hotel Belvedere for gastronomic meals. Riding trails, guided tours and mountain biking.

Open: 4 April - 2 December, 19 December - 6 January.

Directions

From the A1 take Modena South exit through Vignola, Montese, Sesta la Fanano, to Maserno di Montese. Site is 200 m. from the village, well signed. GPS: 44.25575, 10.93274

Charges guide

Per unit incl. 2 persons	
and electricity	€ 23.00 - € 39.00
extra person	€ 5.00 - € 8.00
child (2-8 yrs)	€ 4.00 - € 6.00
dog	€ 3.00 - € 5.00

Show this guide and stay for 3 days, pay for 2. Also 7 days for 4 (low season).

Pinarella di Cervia
Camping Adriatico

Via Pinarella 90, I-48015 Pinarella di Cervia (Emilia-Romagna) T: 0544 715 37. E: info@campingadriatico.net

alanrogers.com/IT60220

Adriatico, on the Italian Riviera, is a busy seaside-style site popular with Italians. It is well run, kept in good order and all of the facilities are clean. As you would expect, there is occasional noise from the local resort (nearest disco is 200 m), and on the western side you will be serenaded by the voluble frogs in the adjacent allotment. The 210 level touring pitches (with 6A electricity) vary in size and are well shaded. The swimming pool and paddling pool are very well looked after and carefully supervised. A new restaurant and bar offer a variety of Italian fish and meat dishes and pizzas at very reasonable prices. In a pleasant situation and a short walk (600 m) from the busy Adriatic beach, this site would be good for families who enjoy traditional Italian seaside sites.

Facilities

Four very clean sanitary blocks, two large two small, have some British style WCs, individual washbasins and free hot showers. Baby rooms. Facilities for disabled campers. Washing machines and a dryer. Motorcaravan services. TV in bar. Small shop. Restaurant/bar, snack bar and takeaway. Large swimming pool and paddling pool (15/5-13/9). Bicycle hire. Market. Play area. Excursions and tourist literature. WiFi on part of site (charged). Off site: Fishing and boat launching within 1 km. Riding 3 km. Golf 4 km. Excursions. Aquatic parks. Spa treatments.

Open: 14 April - 19 September.

Directions

From A14 take Cesena or Ravenna exit and head for Cervia on SS16. Site is south of Cervia, well signed. Drive along the seafront and signs are between the 167/169 markers. GPS: 44.24763, 12.35910

Charges guide

Per unit incl. 2 persons	
and electricity	€ 20.40 - € 36.90
extra person	€ 6.10 - € 10.20
child (2-10 yrs)	€ 3.90 - € 6.70
dog	€ 3.80 - € 6.00

For latest campsite news, availability and prices visit
alanrogers.com

Punta Marina Terme
Adriano Camping Village

Via dei Campeggi 7, I-48100 Punta Marina Terme (Emilia-Romagna) T: 0544 437 230.
E: info@adrianocampingvillage.com **alanrogers.com/IT60620**

Adriano has to be one of the very best campsites in a region renowned for its sightseeing and exploring opportunities. Even so, there is so much to see and do on site that it would be quite believable if visitors remained on site for the whole duration of their holiday. There are 370 touring pitches, some fully serviced, and most shaded by the tall pines. The superb toilet facilities are well maintained and easily accessed and include wet rooms for disabled visitors. There are swimming pools, a sailing centre, bar, restaurants, shops, minigolf, an amusement arcade, bicycle hire and many sports facilities. Built and run by an engineering consortium, the site is professionally managed by a permanent team under the guidance of Guiliani Drudi.

Facilities

Two first class toilet blocks are fully equipped, one heated with British and Turkish style toilets. Each has facilities for disabled visitors. Drinks and snacks machines. Shop. Bar. Restaurant and takeaway. Swimming pools. Sailing. Sports facilities. Bicycle hire. Amusements. WiFi over part of site (charged). Torches and long EHU leads may be useful. Off site: Close by are the monuments of Ravenna, the Mirabilandia Park and the Po Delta Regional Park. Beach 500 m. Fishing 1 km. Golf and riding 4 km.

Open: 19 April - 16 September.

Directions

Site is well signed from autostrada A14 (toll bridge). GPS: 44.43361, 12.29722

Charges guide

Per unit incl. 2 persons and electricity	€ 22.50 - € 60.00
extra person	€ 6.50 - € 13.50
child (4-10 yrs)	free - € 11.00
dog	€ 5.00 - € 7.00

Riccione
Camping Alberello

Viale Torino 80, I-47838 Riccione (Emilia-Romagna) T: 0541 615 402. E: direzione@alberello.it
alanrogers.com/IT60640

Camping Alberello is a busy holiday site on the Adriatic coast with direct access to the beach via a short underpass below the promenade. The beach is wide with fine sand sloping gently into the sea. The friendly owners of Alberello have designed it with campers in the centre and sports facilities plus entertainment to the rear. The bar, restaurant and reception are at the front. This ensures that campers have the pitches with least road and rail noise. The 100 level, grass pitches are small and well shaded with tarmac access roads and regular water points. If you would like to be close to the sea and enjoy the vibrant atmosphere of the Adriatic Riviera where the Italians love to holiday, this lively, family-style campsite has a lot to offer.

Facilities

Three traditional toilet blocks are brightly painted and kept very clean. British and Turkish style WCs. Facilities for disabled visitors. Washing machines. Supermarket. Bazaar. Bar, large restaurant with terrace. Pizzeria. TV room. Very large play area. Limited entertainment programme in season. Miniclub. Watersports. ATM. Free WiFi over site. Dogs are not accepted. Torches useful. Off site: Boat launching 4 km. Excursions arranged. Local bus rides to Riccione and Cattolica.

Open: 5 April - 24 September.

Directions

Site is south east of Rimini. From A14 take Riccione exit and follow S16 towards town. Site is well signed and is on the beach road. GPS: 43.98622, 12.68753

Charges guide

Per unit incl. 2 persons and electricity	€ 24.10 - € 44.40
extra person	€ 5.00 - € 10.90
child (3-8 yrs)	€ 4.00 - € 8.50

For latest campsite news, availability and prices visit
alanrogers.com

Savignano Mare

Camping Villaggio Rubicone

Via Matrice Destra 1, I-47039 Savignano Mare (Emilia-Romagna) T: 0541 346 377.
E: info@campingrubicone.com **alanrogers.com/IT66240**

This is a sophisticated, professionally run site where the friendly owners, Sandra and Paolo Grotto are keen to fulfil your every need. Rubicone covers over 30 acres of thoughtfully landscaped, level ground and has direct access to the beach. The 446 touring pitches (6/10A electricity), are in neat, shaded rows and vary in size (up to 100 sq.m). Of these, 150 also have water and drainage and 20 have private sanitary facilities. There are plenty of places to enjoy a drink; from beach bars to nightclub bars, and the restaurant offers excellent food and efficient service at very reasonable prices. Entertainment for all ages takes place in a circular, terraced area near the main bar.

Facilities

Modern heated toilet blocks have hot water for showers and washbasins (half in private cabins), mainly British style toilets, baby rooms and two excellent units for disabled visitors. Washing machines. Motorcaravan services. Shop, bazaar and bars. Restaurant and snack bar (26/5-9/9). Pizzeria. Swimming pools (caps mandatory). Games room. Golf (lessons available). Tennis. Archery. Canoeing. Solarium. Jacuzzi. Beach with lifeguard. Fishing. Sailing and windsurfing schools. Dance lessons. Miniclub. Bicycle hire. No dogs. WiFi (charged). Booking for day trips.

Open: 21 May - 20 September.

Directions

From Bologna (autostrada A14) take exit for Rimini Nord. Continue on SS16 Adriatica towards Ravenna, then exit for Savignano Mare. At roundabout go straight on to San Mauro Mare and turn left just after the railway. GPS: 44.16475, 12.441117

Charges guide

Per unit incl. 2 persons	
and electricity	€ 24.20 - € 46.80
extra person	€ 5.60 - € 11.50
child (2-8 yrs)	€ 4.20 - € 8.90

Tabiano di Salsomaggiore Terme

Camping Arizona

Via Tabiano 42/A, I-43039 Tabiano di Salsomaggiore Terme (Emilia-Romagna) T: 0524 565 648.
E: info@camping-arizona.it **alanrogers.com/IT60900**

Camping Arizona is a green site with a zero carbon rating, set on steep slopes, and 500 m. from the pretty town of Tabiano with its thermal springs dating back to the Roman era. The focus on water is continued within this pleasant, family run site by a complex of four large pools, long water slides into a plunge pool, a jacuzzi and play area, all set in open landscaped grounds with superb views (open to the public). There are 300 level pitches with electricity (3A solar-generated on site) which vary in size from 60 90 sq.m. Those on terraced pitches enjoy shade from mature trees, others have no shade. Cars must be parked in the large adjacent car park under a solar panel array. Trolleys are provided. Sport facilities include the water park area, tennis, volleyball and basketball courts and a five-a-side football pitch. Younger children can be entertained by the large, supervised play centre and indoor and outdoor games.

Facilities

Two modern toilet blocks provide good facilities including some for disabled visitors. Solar-heated water. Washing machines and dryers. Small shop, bar/restaurant with patio (all 1/4-6/10). Swimming pools, slides and jacuzzi (16/5-15/9, also open to the public but free for campers). Tennis. Boules. Large play centre. WiFi throughout (charged). Off site: Pizza restaurant at gate.

Open: 1 April - 15 October.

Directions

From autostrada A1 take exit for Fidenza and follow signs for Tabiano. Site is well marked on left 500 m. after Tabiano town centre. GPS: 44.80621, 10.0098

Charges guide

Per unit incl. 2 persons	
and electricity	€ 20.00 - € 34.00
extra person	€ 6.00 - € 9.50
No credit cards.	

For latest campsite news, availability and prices visit
alanrogers.com

TUSCANY COMPRISES THE FOLLOWING PROVINCES: AREZZO, FLORENCE, GROSSETO, LIVORNO, LUCCA, MASSA CARRARA, PISA, PISTOIA, PRATO AND SIENA

Tuscany probably represents the most commonly perceived image of Italy, with its classic rolling green countryside, lush vineyards and olive groves with a backdrop of medieval hilltowns and historical cities, where Renaissance art and churches abound.

One of the most beautiful cities in Italy, much of Florence was rebuilt during the Renaissance, although there are parts which still retain a distinctly medieval feel. The city boasts a wealth of historical and cultural sights, including the Cathedral, the Baptistry, the Campanile, and the church of Santa Croce, to name but a few. It is also home to the Uffizi Gallery which holds Italy's greatest art collection. Siena is another popular draw. At the heart of the city is the Piazza del Campo, one of the loveliest Italian squares, which plays host to the famous Palio, a bareback horse race which takes place twice a year in summer. Overlooking the piazza is the Gothic town hall of Palazzo Pubblico and bell tower, which is the second highest medieval tower ever built in Italy. Elsewhere in Tuscany, medieval San Gimignano is famed for its thirteen towers built during the 12th and 13th centuries, which dominate the landscape. Lucca's old town is set inside a ring of Renaissance walls fronted by gardens. Another medieval hill town, Monteriggioni also has beautifully preserved walls, while Volterra is dramatically sited on a high plateau, which offers fine views over the hills. And Pisa with its famous leaning tower needs no introduction.

Places of interest

Alpi Apuan Nature Park: protected area with hiking trails through wooded valleys.

Arezzo: 13th-century San Francesco church houses famous frescoes by Piero della Francesca.

Bagni di Lucca: spa town.

Cortono: oldest hilltown in Tuscany with maze of old streets and medieval buildings.

Elba: largest island off Tuscan coast with white sandy beaches and woodlands, good for walking.

Fiesole: idyllic hilltop town offering superb views of Florence.

Viareggio: coastal town boasting Art Nouveau architecture.

Vinci: birthplace of Leonardo da Vinci, with a museum celebrating his works.

Cuisine of the region

Soups are very popular, particularly *ribollita* (stew of vegetables, beans and chunks of bread) and the best place to try *cacciucco* (spiced fish and seafood soup) is in Livorno, the town of its birth. Meat is often grilled and kept plain. Local cheeses include *pecorino*, made with sheep's milk, and *marzolino* from the Chianti region, which is also renowned for producing some of the best wines in Italy. Tuscan desserts include *panforte* (a dense cake full of nuts and fruit) and *cantuccini* (hard almond-flavoured biscuits), which are often served together with Vinsato, a traditional dessert wine.

Bistecca alla Fiorentina: rare chargrilled steak.

Pollo alla diavola: marinated chicken, grilled with herbs.

Scottiglia di Cinghiale: wild boar chops.

Torta di Riso: rice cake with fruit.

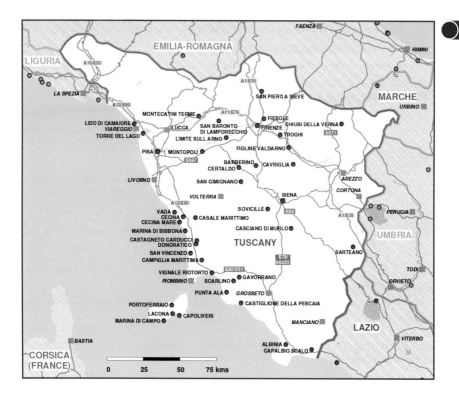

Albinia

Camping Marina Chiara

SS Aurelia km 153, I-58010 Albinia (Tuscany) T: 0564 870304. E: info@marinachiara.it

alanrogers.com/IT66087

Marina Chiara is alongside and twinned with Camping Voltoncino (IT66800) and all facilities are shared. This is a traditional Italian beach site with pitches mainly positioned under a cool canopy of pine trees. There are 133 flat pitches with 3A electricity, of a variety of sizes. They are close to the sea but none have beach views. The bar/restaurant/pizzeria and an attached shop looked very smart when we visited. They overlook a grassy entertainment area. The combination of amenities at the two sites gives a very large choice of activities and services. The beach is of fine dark sand and covers the length of the two campsites. Day trips to local attractions are a feature, along with visits to the Parco Natural Della Marenna and various Etruscan and Roman sites close by. The Argentario peninsula is attractive and a ferry will transport you to the offshore island of del Giglio. There are thermal baths at Saturnia which are fun to visit. These family owned sites have delighted Italian camping families for years and the friendly atmosphere is great to share.

Facilities

Two well positioned sanitary blocks provide some cabins with shower, toilet (mixed styles) and washbasins. Showers are of a very high standard (on payment by token). Cold water only at washbasins, sinks and for laundry. Rooms for children. Facilities for disabled campers. Washing machines. Well stocked shop. Bar and restaurant/pizzeria. Entertainment area. Amenities at the sister site. WiFi over part of site (charged). Dogs are not accepted. Off site: Bus service 2 km. Bicycle hire 2 km. Riding 10 km.

Open: 1 April - 30 September.

Directions

Site is south of Grossetto, north east of Ortobello. From the SS1 (Aurelia) leave at the 153 km. marker towards Albinia. Site is well signed from here and is on a slip road amongst several other sites. GPS: 42.52458, 11.18909

Charges guide

Per unit incl. 2 persons and electricity	€ 17.00 - € 37.00
extra person	€ 5.00 - € 11.00
child (1-7 yrs)	€ 3.00 - € 5.00

For latest campsite news, availability and prices visit

alanrogers.com

Albinia

Camping International Argentario

Localitá Torre Saline, I-58010 Albinia (Tuscany) T: 0564 870 302. E: info@argentariocampingvillage.com
alanrogers.com/IT66710

Argentario is split into three areas. One is a huge, brick built apartment and bungalow complex; the second is a large, flat, shaded area for motorcaravans and large caravans (4-6A electricity); the third is a separate shaded beach camping area with direct access to the dark sand. The 800 pitches and additional accommodation share facilities so they can be very busy in high season and involve some walking. There is daily organised entertainment with something for everyone. We see this site more for short stays than extended holidays and unsuitable for disabled visitors.

Facilities	Directions
Three mature blocks have mostly Turkish style toilets, a few cramped showers with hot water, and cold water at the sinks (showers are very busy at peak periods). Facilities for disabled campers but the sand surface and remoteness of some facilities are unsuitable. Washing machines. Motorcaravan services. Shop. Restaurant, bar and takeaway. Swimming pools. Tennis. Boat hire. Minigolf. ATM. Free WiFi. Cars are parked in a separate car park in high season. Torches very useful. Dogs are not accepted. Off site: Bar and restaurant on the beach.	Site is south of Grosseto, off the SS1 at the 150 km. mark, signed Porto San Stefano. Ignore the first 'combined' campsite sign and proceed 300 m. to the main entrance. GPS: 42.49623, 11.19413

Open: 1 April - 30 September.

Charges guide

Per unit incl. 2 persons	
and electricity	€ 24.00 - € 44.00
extra person	€ 8.00 - € 14.20
child (1-6 yrs)	€ 4.00 - € 7.00

Albinia

Camping Voltoncino

SS1 Aurelia km 153, I-58010 Albinia (Tuscany) T: 0564 870 158. E: info@voltoncino.it
alanrogers.com/IT66800

Voltoncino has been formally combined with the site next door, Marina Chiara, and now has a long beach of soft, grey sand, with a wide choice of high grade restaurants, sport and entertainment. Voltoncino has 284 flat, shaded pitches, all with 3A electricity, while the area adjacent has 133. Some motorcaravan pitches are set outside the canopy of pines and there is some traffic noise. The touring pitches enjoy direct access to the long, narrow beach with gently shelving, soft sand and pleasant views. Much time and money has been spent on improving these sites and the results are excellent.

Facilities	Directions
Two modern, clean toilet blocks at each end of the site, with mainly British style WCs, lovely family rooms for children and a bright baby room. Showers are pushbutton (on payment). Facilities for disabled visitors. Washing machines. Motorcaravan services. Shop. Restaurant, pizzeria and bar. Play area. Tennis. Shared entertainment programme. Miniclub (1-8 yrs). Fishing. Barbecues only allowed on communal area. WiFi (charged). Dogs are not accepted. Off site: Bicycle hire 2 km. Riding 10 km.	Site is south of Grosseto, north east of Ortobello. From the SS1 (Aurelia) leave at 153 km. marker towards Albinia. Site is well signed from here. GPS: 42.51666, 11.18333

Open: 1 April - 20 September.

Charges guide

Per unit incl. 2 persons	
and electricity	€ 17.00 - € 37.00
extra person	€ 5.00 - € 11.00
child (1-8 yrs)	€ 3.00 - € 5.00

Barberino

Camping Semifonte

Via Ugo Foscolo 4, I-50021 Barberino (Tuscany) T: 0558 075 454. E: semifonte@semifonte.it
alanrogers.com/IT66630

Barberino lies in the heart of Tuscany between Florence and Siena. It is an area rich in history and known for that special Italian wine, Chianti. Camping Semifonte is a small, uncomplicated site with fine views over the surrounding, vine-clad hills, but with limited facilities. The 60 shaded pitches, all with 4/6A electricity, are on steep terraces. Some are small and tight for manoeuvring. Each terrace has a tap for water. There is a very small shop selling basics. This site is difficult for disabled campers and infirm visitors. The site facilities are all at the bottom of the site.

Facilities	Directions
Two small sanitary blocks have a mixture of British and Turkish toilets, showers and washbasins. Motorcaravan services. Shop selling basics, plus local oil and wines. Swimming pools. Supported paddling pool for children with no safety fence – next to small play area. WiFi (charged). Off site: Regular bus route to/from Florence and Siena. Restaurant 500 m. Bicycle hire 500 m.	From Florence-Siena autostrada take Tavarnelle exit to Barberino Val Elsa. Take first left on entering village. Site is signed, 500 m. at end of cul-de-sac. Park outside to check in. GPS: 43.54655, 11.17852

Open: Easter - 10 October.

Charges guide

Per unit incl. 2 persons	
and electricity	€ 22.00 - € 30.00
extra person	€ 7.50 - € 8.50

For latest campsite news, availability and prices visit
alanrogers.com

Campiglia Marittima
Blucamp

Via Tuttiventi, 18, I-57021 Campiglia Marittima (Tuscany) T: 056 583 8553. E: info@blucamp.it
alanrogers.com/IT66410

Blucamp is an attractive site in a tranquil setting with fabulous views, near the pretty village of Campiglia Marittima. The islands of Elba and Capraia can be sighted as you check in at reception. The 113 touring pitches (50-80 sq.m) are terraced, all have 4A electricity (14 are fully serviced) and trees provide shade. One area is set aside for tents only and cars are parked off the pitches in numbered bays. This is a very peaceful site with attentive owners and would suit those who prefer not to holiday on the more lively and larger coastal sites. The site is entirely for tourers.

Facilities

Two fully modernised and one new toilet block have mostly British and some Turkish style WCs and solar heated water. Six private sanitary units on pitches for hire. Washing machine. Delightful restaurant/bar with terrace is run by a separate family and offers good Tuscan food. Bread and milk available daily. Small swimming pool. Free WiFi on part of site. Barbecues are not permitted. Off site: Bus 200 m. Supermarket 400 m. Riding 2 km. Bicycle hire 5 km. Fishing and beach 8 km.

Open: 21 May - 11 September.

Directions

Site is north east of Piombino. Take exit for San Vincenzo Sud off the main S1 road (Livorno to Follonica). Follow signs for Campiglia Marittima then camping signs from town. Site is well signed 1 km. from town. GPS: 43.05735, 10.60801

Charges guide

Per unit incl. 2 persons and electricity	€ 23.65 - € 37.45
extra person	€ 6.75 - € 9.70

Capalbio Scalo
Camping Capalbio

Strada Litoranea del Chiarone, località Graticciaia, I-58010 Chiarone Scalo bei Capálbio (Tuscany)
T: 0564 890 101. E: mauro.ricci@ilcampeggiodicapalbio.it **alanrogers.com/IT66810**

Camping Capalbio is a simple coastal site with a wide, grey sand beach and will appeal to those keen on 'back to nature' experiences. The 175 pitches set in the dunes are charmingly private with tall hedges, 3A electricity, and many have artificial shade. Some are alongside the beach and very secluded. The low key restaurant and bar have a fair choice of food and drinks at reasonable prices. Do not expect too much by way of entertainment here but you will get peace by the bucketful.

Facilities

Three blocks have basic but clean services, but only the central block has hot showers (tokens) and it is some distance from peripheral pitches. Baby facilities in restaurant toilet area. Motorcaravan services. Supermarket. Bar. Restaurant. Beach bar (high season). Takeaway. Live musical entertainment in peak season. Direct access to beach. Basic play area. Tennis. Bicycle hire. WiFi in bar area (charged). Mobile homes and chalets for rent. Off site: Riding 10 km. Capalbio 12 km.

Open: 1 April - 22 September.

Directions

Head south from Livorno and Pisa on the SS1 (Via Aurelia). Shortly after passing the Lago di Burano, ignore sign to Capalbio to the left, but take the next road to the right (signed Chiarone Scalo). Site is well signed from here. GPS: 42.381027, 11.446606

Charges guide

Per unit incl. 2 persons and electricity	€ 24.00 - € 44.00
extra person	€ 8.00 - € 14.00

Capoliveri
Camping Stella Mare

Via del Moletto 426 c, Lacona, I-57037 Capoliveri (Tuscany) T: 0565 964 007. E: info@stellamare.it
alanrogers.com/IT66094

Camping Stella Mare is located on the shores of the Gulf of Lacona, on the island of Elba. Some of the 127 touring pitches (3A electricity) are on high terraces with excellent sea views. There are many delightfully private, informal pitches, which will suit many campers. Two beaches can be accessed from the site, one in a private cove, the other is the public beach. The small but busy snack bar/takeaway and bar/restaurant complex is at the bottom of the site and enjoys some views of the spectacular sunsets over the lowest row of pitches.

Facilities

Three sanitary blocks. Shop. Bar/snack bar and restaurant. Small swimming pool and children's pool. Spas. Play areas. Limited entertainment and activity programme, mainly for children. WiFi over part of site (charged). Apartments and chalets for rent. Direct beach access. Off site: Snorkelling. Scuba diving. Windsurfing. Bicycle and boat hire 1 km. Fishing. Trekking through the chestnut forests. Organised boat tours. Tennis. Golf 5 km.

Open: 26 April - 19 October.

Directions

From the ferry follow signs for 'tutte le direzioni' then 'Porto Azzurro' continue on to Porto Azzurro turning right to Lacona. In Lacona follow signs for site. If using GPS, avoid port area on beach road as this is impassable for larger units. Go around the town. GPS: 42.75752, 10.31363

Charges guide

Per unit incl. 2 persons and electricity	€ 32.00 - € 52.00
extra person	€ 9.50 - € 14.50

For latest campsite news, availability and prices visit
alanrogers.com

Capoliveri
Camping Laconella

Localitá Lacona Via Laconella 431, Isola d'Elba, I-57031 Capoliveri (Tuscany) T: 0565 964 228.
E: info@campinglaconella.it **alanrogers.com/IT66098**

Camping Laconella is a delightful site on the attractive Mediterranean island of Elba and has been owned by the Rotellini family for 50 years. There are 125 pitches here, all for touring, with 3A electricity. They are randomly positioned on pleasant terraces and some have the benefit of great sea views. There is direct access to two quite different beaches – one is quiet and natural, the other is of a typical Mediterranean style. There are brilliant views from the on-site bar and restaurant where locally caught fish is a speciality. Other on-site amenities include free bicycle hire and a small shop selling essentials and souvenirs. The main beach is just 10 m. from the campsite gate.

Facilities	Directions
Two traditional style sanitary blocks have been refurbished to a good standard. Basic cold water laundry facilities. Motorcaravan services. Small shop. Restaurant/pizzeria. Bar. Sports and games facilities including table tennis and football. Playground. Children's club. Free bicycle hire. WiFi on 70% of site (charged). Communal barbecues and picnic areas. Off site: Lively village of Lacona with shops, restaurants and outdoor markets (Thurs. and Sun) 1 km.	Take the ferry from Piombino (it is recommended to let the site book your ferry when making your site reservation). From Portoferraio to Lacona is approximately 5 miles, and the site is signed from the village outskirts. GPS: 42.758866, 10.297105

Charges guide

Per unit incl. 2 persons and electricity	€ 25.00 - € 46.00
extra person	€ 6.50 - € 12.50

Open: 15 March - 31 October.

Capoliveri
Camping Lacona Pineta

Localitá Lacona, Capoliveri, I-57031 Isola d'Elba (Tuscany) T: 0565 964 322.
E: info@campinglaconapineta.com **alanrogers.com/IT66860**

Camping Lacona Pineta is a neat and very tidy site with an excellent, large, heated swimming pool complex. The 179 well shaded pitches (150 for touring units with 6A electricity) are well kept. The soft sand beach is just 50 m. away, so it is easy to stay cool here. The site has a great restaurant with a pizzeria and snack bar, plus a pleasant bar with entertainment in high season. This would make a good base for exploring the natural beauty of this sub-tropical paradise or for a beach holiday relaxing by the turquoise bay. Cars are parked separately in designated areas.

Facilities	Directions
Basic sanitary facilities have mainly Turkish style toilets and free hot water. Laundry with iron and ironing board. Well stocked shop. Bar, pizzeria and excellent restaurant. Large, heated swimming pool. Play area. Entertainment and activities for adults and children in high season. Diving school. Bicycle hire. Only charcoal barbecues provided by site are allowed. Infirmary. WiFi over site (charged).	From the port at Portoferraio follow the site signs. GPS: 42.75978, 10.3133

Charges guide

Per unit incl. 2 persons and electricity	€ 21.00 - € 58.80
extra person	€ 7.00 - € 15.50
child (3-10 yrs)	€ 4.40 - € 9.30

Open: 1 April - 30 October.

Casale Marittimo
Camping Valle Gaia

Via Cecinese 87, I-56040 Casale Marittimo (Tuscany) T: 0586 681 236. E: info@vallegaia.it
alanrogers.com/IT66320

Valle Gaia is a delightful family site with a friendly, laid back atmosphere, which is in marked contrast to some of the busy sites on the coast. Just 9 km. from the sandy beaches at Cecina, this pretty site has two enticing pool complexes with a great lagoon pool, children's pools and sunbathing terraces. One is for campers, the other is in the higher accommodation area. The 220 pitches are of a reasonable size (80-120 sq.m), some are shaded by pine or cypress trees and surrounded by oleanders. All have 6A electrical connections and 58 are fully serviced. The bar/pizzeria are both popular.

Facilities	Directions
Three spotless toilet blocks of modern construction are maintained to a high standard with mainly British style toilets and provision for disabled visitors. Some washbasins in cubicles. Excellent facilities for children and babies. Washing machines. Bar. Restaurant. Pizzeria/snack bar/pool bar. Well stocked shop. Swimming pools. Tennis. Games room. Bicycle hire. Satellite TV. WiFi over site (charged). Daily entertainment. No charcoal barbecues (communal provided).	From A12 take Rosignano Marittimo exit, follow SS1 signs towards Roma then take Cecina Centro exit and follow signs to Casale Marittimo. Site is clearly signed from here. GPS: 43.30054, 10.58149

Charges guide

Per unit incl. 2 persons and electricity	€ 18.70 - € 34.20
extra person	€ 5.10 - € 9.25
No credit cards.	

Open: 12 April - 4 October.

For latest campsite news, availability and prices visit
alanrogers.com

Casciano di Murlo
Camping le Soline

Via delle Soline 51, I-53016 Casciano di Murlo (Tuscany) T: 0577 817 410. E: camping@lesoline.it
alanrogers.com/IT66650

Le Soline is a country hillside site with wonderful views of the beautiful Tuscan landscape from its steep slopes, and has a very pleasant atmosphere. Just 20 km. south of Siena and 1 km. from the village of Casciano, it has 154 neat, terraced pitches for large units and tents, all with 6A electricity and Europlugs, water and waste water. Olive trees provide shade. The kind and attentive Broggini family spare no efforts in making your stay a pleasant memory and are extremely hard working to this end. The site offers real value for money and we spoke to many contented visitors.

Facilities

A high quality, heated sanitary block is on the third terrace, providing mixed British and Turkish style WCs and generous hot showers on payment. Facilities for children and disabled visitors. Family room. Motorcaravan services. Gas supplies. Laundry. Freezer. Restaurant, bar and pizzeria (20/3-31/10). Shop (20/3 -31/10). Swimming pools (solar heated, 20/3-31/10). 12-person heated whirlpool (can be covered). Excursions (June-Aug). Riding. Volleyball. Communal barbecue. Playground. WiFi over site (free). Mobile homes and bungalows for rent.

Open: All year.

Directions

From Siena, turn off SS223 (Siena-Grosseto) left to Fontazzi (20 km) and keep right for Casciano, following signs. Alternatively, from Via Cassia SS2 turn at Lucignano d'Arbia for Murlo.
GPS: 43.1552, 11.3323

Charges guide

Per unit incl. 2 persons	
and electricity	€ 26.50
extra person	€ 8.50
child (2-12 yrs)	€ 5.00

Castagneto Carducci
Camping le Pianacce

Via Bolgherese, I-57022 Castagneto Carducci (Tuscany) T: 0565 763 667. E: info@campinglepianacce.it
alanrogers.com/IT66350

In a quiet situation in the Tuscan hills, six kilometres from the sea at Donoratico, this high quality site has a busy and attractive medium sized pool, overlooked by a pleasant restaurant/bar. The terrace has commanding views over the area and the sea and sunsets are spectacular. The site is set on steeply rising ground and has 213 pitches; 101 shaded pitches are for touring units, all with 3/10A electricity. They are in tiered rows on fairly narrow terraces. Although busy in high season, it remains peaceful at night. There is a large nature reserve adjacent and a free bus to the 20 km. long sandy beach.

Facilities

Three toilet blocks have British style WCs, individual washbasins with hot water throughout and free hot showers. Baby room. Washing machines. Gas supplies. Motorcaravan services. Shop. Restaurant/bar/takeaway. Swimming pools with water games. Archery. Tennis. Football. Beach volleyball. Minigolf. Bicycle hire. Playground. Entertainment in season. Communal barbecue area only. WiFi. ATM. Free bus to beach. Torches required in some areas. Dog area outside gate. Off site: Bus 1.5 km. Beach and riding 6 km.

Open: 19 April - 27 September.

Directions

Site is south of Livorno. Turn off main S1 just north of Donoratico in hamlet of Il Bambolo to Castagneto Carducci. After 3 km. turn left at signs to Bolgheri and site. Follow signs on fairly long, single track final approach. GPS: 43.16589, 10.6149

Charges guide

Per person	€ 5.50 - € 11.30
child (1-10 yrs)	€ 3.50 - € 8.30
pitch incl. electricity	€ 6.50 - € 25.00
dog	€ 1.00 - € 7.50

Castiglione della Pescaia
Campeggio Stella del Mare

Locailtá le Rocchette, I-58043 Castiglione della Pescaia (Tuscany) T: 0586 696 855.
E: info@stelladelmarecamping.it **alanrogers.com/IT66108**

This is a traditional campsite with 128 generous, flat and well shaded pitches for touring, with 3A electricity. A main feature of the site is the large and very pleasant swimming pool area where three pools are looped together. The site's busy centrepiece includes the bar, restaurant and takeaway with various terraces. The large shop provides for most campers' needs, including cooked meats and cheeses. Unfortunately, the beach is mainly taken up by expensive sun loungers and parasols hired out by private companies. It is possible to hire fully equipped bungalow tents.

Facilities

Five toilet blocks. Washing machines. Bar, restaurant and takeaway. Large shop with fresh bread. Swimming pools and children's pool (caps required). Play area. Tennis. Football. WiFi over part of site (charged). Bungalow tents for hire. Off site: Beach 300 m. Tuscany countryside and historic sites. Castiglione della Pescaia 5 km.

Open: 12 April - 19 October.

Directions

Site is on the SS322 18 km. to the west of Grossetto Tuscany. Well signed.
GPS: 42.776924, 10.792994

Charges guide

Per unit incl. 2 persons	
and electricity	€ 28.00 - € 55.00

For latest campsite news, availability and prices visit
alanrogers.com

Castiglione della Pescaia
Camping Maremma Sans Souci

Localitá Casa Mora, I-58043 Castiglione della Pescaia (Tuscany) T: 056 493 3765.
E: info@maremmasanssouci.it **alanrogers.com/IT66600**

This delightful seaside site has been open since 1965 and sits in natural woodland on the coast road between Follonica and Grosseto. The minimum amount of undergrowth has been cleared to provide 370 individually marked and hedged, flat touring pitches with considerable privacy. All have 6A electrical connections and 40 have a satellite TV point. Cars are parked away from pitches. There is a wide road for motorcaravans but other roads are narrow. Access to some parts is difficult so each pitch is earmarked either for touring units or for tents. An excellent sandy beach is less than 100 m. from one end of the site (400 m. from the other) and is used only by campers.

Facilities

Five small, very clean, older style toilet blocks are well situated around the site. Free hot showers. Three blocks have private cabins each with WC, basin and shower. Motorcaravan services. Laundry. Shop. Excellent restaurant and pizzeria. Bar with snacks. ATM. Bicycle hire. Diving school. Excursions organised. WiFi (free). Torches required in some areas. Direct beach access. Off site: Sailing school 300 m. Riding 5 km. Golf 8 km.

Open: 26 March - 2 November.

Directions

Site is 2.5 km. north west of Castiglione on road to Follonica on the S322. GPS: 42.77343, 10.84392

Charges guide

Per unit incl. 2 persons	
and electricity	€ 24.00 - € 47.00
extra person	€ 8.00 - € 14.00
child (3-5 yrs)	€ 6.00 - € 8.00
dog	€ 3.00 - € 4.00

Castiglione della Pescaia
Camping Village Santapomata

Strada Provinciale delle Rocchette snc, I-58043 Castiglione della Pescaia (Tuscany) T: 056 494 1037.
E: info@campingsantapomata.it **alanrogers.com/IT66605**

Camping Village Santapomata is a traditional type of campsite with direct access to a sandy beach. There are 362 pitches with just 2A electricity, shaded by tall pines. Pitches vary from roomy to rather tight, some are close to the beach and have privacy. The whole site appears a little dated but is popular with some regular visitors and prices are reasonable compared to some in the area. A short walk takes you to the first section of beach where you are required to pay for sun loungers and umbrellas, filling the beach in unbroken rows. The area beyond this is free. Off-pitch parking is compulsory.

Facilities

Two clean but dated sanitary blocks are equipped with a mixture of Turkish and British style WCs, showers and washbasins. Facilities for disabled visitors. Laundry. Shop. Bar with TV. Restaurant/pizzeria. Takeaway. Play area. Miniclub (July/Aug). Pedalo and canoe hire. WiFi (free). Private beach. Off site: Bicycle hire 1 km. Golf 5 km. Castiglione della Pescaia 7 km. Windsurfing school and riding 7 km.

Open: 24 March - 22 October.

Directions

From the SS1 motorway and the north, exit at Follonica north. Take SP322 Delle Collacchie via Castiglione della Pescaia. Then take the SP62 for Rochette and look for site signs in 1.5 km. GPS: 42.77000, 10.80989

Charges guide

Per unit incl. 2 persons	
and electricity	€ 26.00 - € 45.00
extra person	€ 8.00 - € 14.00

Castiglione della Pescaia
Camping Village Baia Azzurra

Via Le Rocchette, I-58043 Castiglione della Pescaia (Tuscany) T: 0564 941092. E: info@baiaazzurra.it
alanrogers.com/IT66690

Encircled by hills, Baia Azzurra is a cool green site with lots of trees. There are 260 pitches with 180 average sized, grassy pitches for touring units. These are flat, shaded by tall trees and some have artificial shade. All have 3A electricity and eight also have water and drainage. This is a neat site with a regular layout and amenities are away from the pitches. The focal point of the site is the lagoon-shaped pool with bridge, modern restaurant and entertainment complex. There is direct access, across a minor road and a 150 m. walk, to the gently sloping sandy beach with plenty of loungers and umbrellas. This beach may be difficult for disabled guests.

Facilities

Two refurbished sanitary blocks and one brand new (2015) with an excellent nursery and baby room, one unit for disabled visitors. Hot showers. Laundry facilities. Market/bazaar, bar and restaurant/pizzeria. Swimming pools. Paddling pool. Play area. Football and volleyball fields. Entertainment and miniclub (June-Aug). Bicycle hire. WiFi (one hour free on arrival, then charged). ATM.

Open: 25 March - 15 October.

Directions

From SS1 Livorna-Roma road take Grosseto exit on SS322. Follow SS322 north from Castiglione della Pescaia and turn left for Rocchette. Site is 3 km. on the right. GPS: 42.7778, 10.79392

Charges guide

Per unit incl. 2 persons	
and electricity	€ 26.00 - € 58.00
extra person	€ 8.00 - € 16.50

Castiglione della Pescaia
Camping Village Rocchette

Strada Provinciale 62 delle Rocchette, snc, I-58043 Castiglione della Pescaia (Tuscany) T: 056 494 1123.
E: booking@rocchette.com **alanrogers.com/IT66760**

Camping Village Rocchette can be found at the heart of the Maremma woods, 6 km. to the north of Castiglione della Pescaia. This well maintained site includes 105 modern bungalows grouped around the high quality facilities. The 150 flat, shady touring pitches with 6A electricity are in a separate area, further away from the facilities. A 300 m. walk will take you to the beach but the on-site pool complex here is stunning with several pools to choose from to suit all ages. Excursions are organised by the campsite and, during the high season, there is a lively entertainment programme.

Facilities

Sanitary facilities include private cubicles and facilities for disabled visitors. Laundry facilities. Supermarket and other shops, bar, restaurant and takeaway. Swimming pool with whirlpools (from 20/4). Pool bar. Two children's pools. Tennis. Sports field. Play area. Bicycle hire. Free WiFi over part of site. Miniclub (14/5-2/9). Entertainment and activities (28/5-2/9). Direct but awkward access to beach 300 m. Bungalows and new safari tents for rent. Off site: Fishing and beach 300 m. Castiglione 6 km.

Open: 24 March - 22 October.

Directions

Approaching from the north, take the Follonica Nord exit from the E80/S1 superstrada and head south to Castiglione on the S322. Before reaching Castiglione, turn right (Roccamare and Rocchette). Site is well signed. GPS: 42.77926, 10.801234

Charges guide

Per unit incl. 2 persons	
and electricity	€ 20.00 - € 55.00
extra person	€ 5.00 - € 15.00

Cavriglia
Camping Village Orlando

Localitá Cafaggiolo, 170, I-52022 Cavriglia (Tuscany) T: 0559 674 22.
alanrogers.com/IT66121

Perched on a very high ridgeline called Piana di Orlanda, and with superb views, expect a warm welcome at Orlando. Its 180 pitches, 70 for tourers, are all equipped with 6/16A electricity. They are clean, level and some are on terraces in a shady pine forest, and so have restricted views, but can be enjoyed from installed seats placed on the site's eastern side. The facilities are all set in an attractive central area, including the heated pool complex with its soft slides and cascades. There are views over the pools from the terraces of the busy restaurant. Lovely safe play areas are provided for children.

Facilities

One clean and smart sanitary block with British style toilets, hot showers and cold water at the basins. Facilities for disabled campers. Motorcaravan services. Shop. Bar. Restaurant. Pizzeria. Gelateria. Floodlit, heated swimming pools. Aquagym. Outdoor fitness facilities. Excellent play area. Mini-disco. Ponies for children to ride and groom. 5-a-side football. Children's club. Full entertainment programme. Tours arranged. Bicycle hire. WiFi over site (free). Torches required. Accommodation for rent.

Open: 12 April - 19 October.

Directions

From A1 Florence/Rome take Incisa exit (not Valdaro). Take R60 (San Giovanni Valdarno). At Restone take P14 to Badiacchia a Montemuro for the site (signed from a great distance out). It is a long winding climb. GPS: 43.53829, 11.41101

Charges guide

Per unit incl. 2 persons	
and electricity	€ 17.00 - € 43.00
extra person	€ 5.00 - € 11.00

Cecina
Villaggio Club Cecina

Via F. D. Guerrazzi, 15, localitá le Gorette, I-57023 San Pietro in Palazzi (Tuscany) T: 0586 620 583.
E: info@villaggioclubcecina.it **alanrogers.com/IT66315**

Villaggio Club Cecina is a pine-covered holiday centre located near the attractive Etruscan resort of Cecina (3 km), and with direct access to a superb sandy beach to one side. Please note that there are no touring pitches at this site. Accommodation is provided in 50 mobile homes or chalets. Amenities include two restaurants offering local cuisine with a choice of buffet-style downstairs or waiter service upstairs where there are excellent sea views. Numerous activities are organised in high season, including ambitious entertainment with discos and live music plus a full sports programme.

Facilities

Shop. Bar/restaurants/snack bar. Basketball. Archery. Volleyball. Canoeing. Windsurfing. Play area. Gym. Aqua gym. Entertainment and activities. Fishing. Mountain bike, hiking and day trip excursions. Mobile homes and chalets for rent. Bicycle hire. Direct beach access. Torches useful. Barbecues are not permitted. Only small dogs accepted. WiFi around reception area (charged). Off site: Riding 2 km. Cecina 3 km. Volterra and Pisa 40 km.

Open: 2 June - 8 September.

Directions

Approaching from the north (A12), take the exit at Rosignano Marittimo, follow directions towards Rome, and take SS1 express road. Take Cecina Nord exit and follow signs to Cecina and site. GPS: 43.30835, 10.48539

Charges guide

Contact the site for details.

(111)

For latest campsite news, availability and prices visit
alanrogers.com

Cecina Mare
Camping le Tamerici
Via della Cecinella 5, I-57023 Cecina Mare (Tuscany) T: 0586 620 629. E: info@letamerici.it
alanrogers.com/IT66091

Camping Le Tamerici is on the Etruscan coast, only 600 m. from the beach and surrounded by beautiful Tuscan countryside. All 100 touring pitches (50-80 sq.m) are separated and shaded by trees and have access to electricity (6A). A separate camper van area, close to sanitary facilities and with electricity, is available for short stays of up to seven days. The swimming pool and bar complex has a family area for sunbathing and relaxation. Le Tamerici is an ideal location from which to explore the area's historic, cultural and natural environment.

Facilities

Sanitary facilities include provision for disabled visitors. Laundry. Bazaar/newsagent. Pool bar (breakfast and snacks), restaurant, pizzeria, mini market (all 1/5-30/9). Swimming pool and paddling pool (10/5-30/9). Hairdresser. Arcade games room. Sports area (beach volleyball, football, tennis). Playground. Miniclub. Entertainment (high season). ATM. Barbecue area. Bicycle hire. Free WiFi. Mobile homes and tents to rent.

Open: 1 May - 30 September.

Directions

From the north take A12 exit Rosignano Marittimo, then E80/SS1 (Grosseto). Exit Cecina Centro and follow signs for Marina di Cecina. Take Viale della Repubblica, then Via Ferrucci and Viale Galliano to Via della Cecinella. GPS: 43.637222, 10.3675

Charges guide

Per unit incl. 2 persons and electricity	€ 17.00 - € 39.00
extra person	€ 5.00 - € 11.00

Cecina Mare
Camping Village Mareblu
Via dei Campilunghi, I-57023 Cecina Mare (Tuscany) T: 0586 629 191. E: info@campingmareblu.com
alanrogers.com/IT66310

Mareblu is a well equipped family site with an impressive range of amenities, including a large swimming pool with an attractive terraced surround and a comprehensive shopping complex. The warm welcome you receive on arrival at reception is replicated throughout the site. A 350 m. walk through a pine forest leads to a soft, sandy beach. The 360 level touring pitches have a spacious feel, are well shaded and all have 6A electrical connections. Parking for all cars is in a dedicated area at the front of the site. A number of mobile homes and chalets are available for hire. A good, value-for-money site.

Facilities

Five modern toilet blocks include facilities for disabled visitors. Shopping centre. Bar, restaurant and pizzeria and takeaway. Swimming and paddling pools (April-Oct). Play area. Games field. Boules. Bicycle hire. Miniclub. Entertainment. Direct access to beach via a 350 m. track. Windsurfing and sub-aqua diving organised. Dedicated areas for barbecues. WiFi over site (charged). Dogs are not accepted in July/Aug. Off site: Beach 350 m.

Open: 28 March - 17 October.

Directions

Site is south of Livorno. From north, take A12 to Rosignano and then join the E80 to Vada, then to La Mazzanta. From here site is well signed. GPS: 43.31848, 10.47407

Charges guide

Per unit incl. 2 persons and electricity	€ 17.50 - € 38.00
extra person	€ 5.00 - € 9.50
child (1-7 yrs)	€ 3.50 - € 7.50

Certaldo
Camping Panorama del Chianti
Via Marcialla 349, localitá Marcialla, I-50020 Marcialla (Certaldo) (Tuscany) T: 057 166 9334.
E: info@campingchianti.it alanrogers.com/IT66640

Formerly named Toscana Colliverdi, this site is slowly developing. A small country hillside site in Tuscany, it has space for 60 large units on deep terraces and two areas for tents. All the terrace pitches have 3/5A electricity. There are panoramic views of the surrounding countryside. If you are content to be self-supporting and wish to explore Tuscany with the advantage of reasonable campsite fees, then this could be for you. A small bar with a tiny terrace offers welcoming cool drinks, excellent coffee, aperitif with local products, fresh bread and good breakfast in the mornings.

Facilities

A small, clean toilet block is on the second terrace with British style toilets, showers and washbasins, plus dishwashing and laundry sinks, all with hot water. No facilities for disabled campers. Washing machine. Motorcaravan services. Small bar and terrace (basic supplies on sale). Communal barbecue. Good size above ground pool (15/5-15/9). Play area. WiFi over part of site. Off site: Restaurant, shop, butcher, greengrocer, post office 1 km. Fishing 5 km. Riding and bicycle hire 7 km.

Open: 24 March - 31 October.

Directions

From A1 Florence-Siena autostrada take exit for Tavarnelle and head for Tavarnelle. At the village follow signs for Marcialla. Site entrance is on the left 700 m. after village of Marcialla. GPS: 43.58235, 11.13828

Charges guide

Per unit incl. 2 persons and electricity	€ 31.00 - € 38.00
extra person	€ 8.00 - € 9.50
No credit cards.	

Chiusi della Verna
Camping la Verna

Localitá Vezzano, I-52010 Chiusi della Verna (Tuscany) T: 0575 532 121. E: info@campinglaverna.it
alanrogers.com/IT66130

Camping la Verna is a small, country campsite, 850 m. above sea level, on the edge of the Casentino National Forest and close to the beautiful historic village of Chiusi della Verna, which is widely known as an area of religious retreat and pilgrimage. There are 90 pitches of varying sizes on terraces and set amongst tall trees. They are mostly level, on grass and sand and all have 10A electricity. The limited facilities at Camping la Verna include a small pool, a bar and a restaurant/pizzeria. This is a peaceful and remote site suitable for campers who enjoy simple pleasures. There are medieval hamlets and other sites of interest in the area, including the sanctuary of San Francesco. This village is known for its association with Francis of Assisi and as the birthplace of Michelangelo.

Facilities

The sanitary block offers British style WCs and pushbutton showers. No facilities for disabled visitors. Washing machines. Bar, restaurant and pizzeria with small terrace. Communal barbecues only. Torches very useful. Small, outdoor pool (15/6-15/9). Excellent adventure style play area. Charcoal barbecues are not permitted. WiFi over part of site (charged). Off site: Riding and ATM 1 km. Exploration of world famous religious/commercial centre.

Open: Three weeks before Easter - 30 September.

Directions

Site is in village of Chiusi della Verna, north of Arezzo. From E45 go to Pieve Sto Stefano. From here take P208 to Chiusi della Verna. Site is well signed in the village. From the west on the P208 involves a very long winding drive – great views but hard driving. GPS: 43.69780, 11.92351

Charges guide

Per unit incl. 2 persons	
and electricity	€ 19.00 - € 30.00
extra person	€ 6.50 - € 10.00
child (3-9 yrs)	€ 5.00 - € 7.00
dog	free

Donoratico
International Camping Etruria

Via della Pineta snc, Marina di Castagneto Carducci, I-57027 Donoratico (Tuscany) T: 0565 744 254.
E: info@campingetruria.it **alanrogers.com/IT66052**

In the heart of the Maremma, on the Etruscan Coast south of Livorno, International Camping Etruria is an ideal place for a peaceful, healthy and enjoyable holiday with family and friends. It is a large, well equipped site with 600 impressive pitches, all with 6A electricity connections and with direct access to a fine sandy beach. Here, there is a popular brasserie, open in the evenings and serving good food. Unlike many pine-dominated sites, there is an attractive open canopy with clever landscaping. The main services are centrally located and are all of a high standard. The staff are friendly and speak English, Dutch and German. A swimming pool complex is planned for the 2016 season and the owners have ambitious plans for further improvements. A range of mobile homes, bungalows and glamping-style tents are available for hire.

Facilities

Sanitary facilities with hot showers. Motorcaravan services. Supermarket, bar, restaurant, pizzeria and takeaway. Brasserie on beach and lifeguard. Beach chairs, umbrellas and gazebos can be rented at the beach, which has wheelchair access. Cold showers on beach. Water aerobics, beach volleyball, towing boats, pedal boat and canoe rental. Swimming pool complex planned. Playground. Communal barbecue area. Entertainment and activities for children and families. WiFi throughout (charged). Off site: Riding 150 m. Beach bars and restaurants nearby. Shops, bars and restaurants in Donoratico 4 km.

Open: 24 April - 11 October.

Directions

Marina di Castagneto Carducci is 55 km. south of Livorno via E80 motorway. Take exit for Donoratico. At the roundabout take the third exit onto SP17 towards Marina di Donoratico. Turn right at next roundabout and follow signs to campsite. GPS: 43.18812, 10.53974

Charges guide

Per unit incl. 2 persons	
and electricity	€ 21.00 - € 56.00
extra person (1-10 yrs)	€ 5.00 - € 13.00
child	€ 3.00 - € 9.00
dog	€ 4.00 - € 14.00

For latest campsite news, availability and prices visit
alanrogers.com

Fiesole

Camping Village Panoramico Fiesole

Via Peramonda 1, I-50014 Fiesole (Tuscany) T: 055 599 069. E: panoramico@florencevillage.com

alanrogers.com/IT66100

This is a mature but pleasant site in a superb hilltop situation offering wonderful views over Florence. The 120 pitches, all with 5A electricity, are on terraces and steep walks to and from the various facilities could cause problems for guests with mobility problems. There is shade in many parts. The pool is on the upper level along with the restaurant/bar, and the views are really stunning. Some evenings you can hear music from the nearby Roman amphitheatre famous for its classical entertainment in summer. Pitches are separated; motorcaravans and caravans in the upper area and tents on the lower terraces. A shuttle bus service operates one way from the site to the centre of town to connect with the service to Florence (tickets from site office). However, it is an extremely long uphill walk back to the campsite from the town and thus the local bus (to within 300 m) or a taxi may be useful.

Facilities

Two tastefully refurbished toilet blocks have mainly British style WCs, free hot water in washbasins and good showers. Washing machines and dryers. Fridges, freezer, microwaves, irons and little cookers for campers' use. Shop (1/4-31/10). Bar and restaurant (1/4-31/10). Swimming pool (1/6-30/9). Play area. Nursery. Torches required in some parts. English is spoken. Free shuttle service to Fiesole. WiFi on part of site (charged). Off site: Riding 9 km. Golf 20 km. Florence with leather markets, Pitti Palace, Uffizi museum and much more.

Open: 19 March - 3 November.

Directions

From A1 take Firenze-Sud exit and follow signs to Fiesole. From Fiesole centre follow SP54 and camping signs which should keep you out of the town centre as its roads are very narrow for large units. Take care on the last part of your journey up a steep access road to the site. Do not use sat nav. GPS: 43.8065, 11.3051

Charges guide

Per unit incl. 2 persons and electricity	€ 26.00 - € 42.00
extra person	€ 7.00 - € 13.00
child (3-12 yrs)	free - € 6.00

Figline Valdarno

Camping Norcenni Girasole Club

Via Norcenni 7, I-50063 Figline Valdarno (Tuscany) T: 0559 151 41. E: girasole@ecvacanze.it

alanrogers.com/IT66120

The Norcenni Girasole Club is a brilliant, busy and well run resort style site in a picturesque, secluded location with great views of Tuscan landscapes, 19 km. south of Florence. Owned by the dynamic Cardini-Vannucchi family, great care has been taken in its development and the buildings and infrastructure are most attractive and in sympathy with the area. Of the 850 pitches, there are 148 roomy pitches for touring units, 107 with 10A electricity and 41 fully serviced with 16A electricity. Most are shaded by well tended trees. A considerable number of mobile homes and other types of accommodation are available for rent. Families will enjoy this site as there really is something for everyone. In the huge, resort style pool complex there is a superb choice, with pools for children of all ages plus free water flumes. Everything is available and to hand and a road train service operates between its two sections. You will only need to leave to visit and enjoy the many local attractions.

Facilities

Sanitary facilities are excellent with British WCs. Some hot water is available. Family bathrooms for rent (book in advance). Facilities for disabled visitors. Laundry facilities. Motorcaravan services. Supermarkets and gift shops. Bars and three restaurants. Pizzerias. Gelaterias. Two resort style pool complexes. Pool bar/snacks. Small health complex with saunas, jacuzzi, steam bath, fitness centre and massage at extra cost. Tree walk. Zip wire. Games area. Soundproofed disco. Two floodlit tennis courts. Riding. Minigolf. Bicycle hire. Scooter hire. WiFi (charged but free for gold pitches). ATM. Entertainment. Excursions. Information point. Customer service desk. Off site: Daily bus to Florence and shuttle buses to local railway station. Riding 3 km. Fishing 5 km. Golf 20 km.

Open: 28 March - 10 October.

Directions

From Florence take Rome Al/E35 autostrada and take Incisa exit. Turn south on route 69 towards Arezzo. In Figline turn right for Greve and watch for Girasole signs. Site is 4 km. up a twisting, climbing road. GPS: 43.61333, 11.44944

Charges guide

Per unit incl. 2 persons and electricity	€ 25.00 - € 61.00
extra person	€ 7.50 - € 14.90
child (3-11 yrs)	€ 5.90 - € 8.90
dog	free

Firenze

Camping Internazionale

Via San Cristofano 2, Bottai, I-50029 Firenze (Tuscany) T: 0552 374 704.
E: internazionale@florencevillage.com **alanrogers.com/IT66090**

Camping Internazionale is set in the hills about 5 km. south of Florence. This is a well shaded, terraced site with 240 informal touring pitches set around the top of a hill. Although it is a very green site, the camping area is somewhat more open with two electricity pylons at the top of the hill and some noise from the busy motorway which is below and next to the site. It is often lively at night with many young people from tour groups. There is a small restaurant half way up the slope of the site with a resonable menu. A well located site for visiting Florence rather than for extended stays.

Facilities

Two traditional toilet blocks include free hot showers. Laundry. Some kitchen facilities. Motorcaravan services. Shop. New bar and restaurant at the lower level. Evening entertainment. Two swimming pools. Playground. WiFi over part of site (charged). Gas and electric barbecues only. Off site: 800 m. walk to bus stop. Florence 5 km. Golf 5 km. Riding and bicycle hire 10 km.

Open: 15 March - 3 November.

Directions

From A1 take Firenza Certosa exit (Florence). Just outside Bottai turn left to site (if you reach Galluzzo you have gone too far). From Florence take Via Senese (S2) through Galluzzo, turn right at site sign (just before Bottai). GPS: 43.72187, 11.22058

Charges guide

Per unit incl. 2 persons	
and electricity	€ 28.00 - € 39.00
extra person	€ 7.50 - € 12.00

Gavorrano

Camping la Finoria

Via Monticello 66, I-58023 Gavorrano (Tuscany) T: 0566 844 381. E: info@campeggiolafinoria.it
alanrogers.com/IT66670

An unusual site, la Finoria is primarily set up for school groups and tents, hence the short season. Set high in the mountains with incredible views, it is a rugged site with a focus on nature. Italian school children attend education programmes here. Three motorcaravan pitches are at the top of the site for those who enjoy a challenge, with a dozen caravan pitches on lower terraces accessed by a very steep gravel track. Under huge chestnut trees there is a very pretty terraced area for tents. Electricity (3A) is available to all pitches, although long leads may be needed.

Facilities

Two mature blocks provide British and Turkish style toilets, hot showers and cold water at washbasins and sinks. Facilities for disabled campers. Washing machines and dryer. Quaint, small shop. Good restaurant and bar. Swimming pool. Tennis. Lessons on the environment. Excursions. Torches essential. Gas barbecues only. WiFi over part of site. Off site: Riding 2 km. Village 3 km. Bicycle hire 6 km. Golf 8 km. Site's private beach 12 km.

Open: 23 June - 15 September.

Directions

From SS1 (Follonica-Grosseto) take Gavorrano exit, then Finoria road. This is a steady, steep climb for some 10 minutes. Start to descend and at junction (the only one), look left (difficult turn) downhill for a large white sign to site. Access to this site is only possible for small units. GPS: 42.9225, 10.91233

Charges guide

Per unit incl. 2 persons	
and electricity	€ 16.00 - € 29.00
extra person	€ 5.50 - € 8.00

Lacona

Camping Valle Santa Maria

Viale dei Golfi, Lacona, I-57031 Isola d'Elba (Tuscany) T: 0565 964 188. E: info@vsmaria.it
alanrogers.com/IT66920

This small family site has smart, paved roads and neat, clipped hedges and is proudly run by the experienced Rotellini family. Reception is a short walk from the road entrance. There is a small bar. Some of the 100 regularly sized pitches (with 4A electricity) are shaded by mature gum trees, some by shade screens. Cars are parked in a separate area. There are a few pitches on the sea boundary giving great views over the soft sand beach. This is a very pleasant site, popular with windsurfers and German campers. With its easy beach access the site is ideal for campers with mobility problems.

Facilities

One very smart, modern, centrally located toilet block has excellent fittings. Mixed Turkish and British style WCs. Facilities for children and disabled visitors. Laundry facilities. Motorcaravan services. Shop. Bar and beach restaurant. TV room. Play areas. Tennis. Entertainment in season and miniclub. Massage (charged). Watersports on beach. WiFi over site (free with stays of 1 week). Off site: Public transport 100 m. Bicycle hire 300 m.

Open: 15 March - 1 November.

Directions

Site is on the south side of the island, in Lacona. From Portoferraio take the Lacona road and site is well signed as you approach the village. Do not take the first right turn signed to Lacona as this takes you across country. GPS: 42.7608, 10.30221

Charges guide

Per unit incl. 2 persons	
and electricity	€ 27.00 - € 53.00
extra person	€ 7.00 - € 13.00

For latest campsite news, availability and prices visit
alanrogers.com

Lacona

Camping Tallinucci

Lacona, I-57031 Isola d'Elba (Tuscany) T: 0565 964 069. E: info@campingtallinucci.it

alanrogers.com/IT66940

Camping Tallinucci is a small family site operated by the same family for over 40 years. It has a clean and pleasant feel with lots of green hedges. The roads are all paved and access is very easy (particularly for disabled campers) to the 100 touring pitches, all with 4A electricity. A few pitches are directly alongside the beach and have pleasant views over the pretty bay. A shop is very close to the site entrance, and the self-service restaurant and bar on the beach serves very attractive food. This small site would be good for families who just wish to relax or enjoy beach sports. Cars are parked off the pitches in a separate area. This peaceful site in the Tuscany Archipelago National Park is well managed.

Facilities

One excellent, solar heated (water and underfloor) toilet block has washbasins in cubicles and family shower rooms. Children's facilities and baby baths. Washing machines and dryers. Motorcaravan services. Shop. Bar and restaurant/pizzeria on the beach. Tennis. Games room. Play areas. Organised activity weeks. Massage. Boat tours. Guided walks in Spring and Autumn. WiFi over site (charged). Off site: Watersports on beach.

Open: Easter - 31 October.

Directions

Site is on south side of the island in Lacona. From Portoferraio take the Lacona road. Site is well signed approaching the village. GPS: 42.76125, 10.30035

Charges guide

Per unit incl. 2 persons	
and electricity	€ 29.00 - € 57.80
extra person	€ 7.00 - € 13.00
child (1-8 yrs)	€ 5.00 - € 9.50

Lido di Camaiore

Camping Versilia Mare

Via Trieste, 175, I-55043 Lido di Camaiore (Tuscany) T: 0584 619 862. E: info@campingversiliamare.com

alanrogers.com/IT66073

Upon entrance to Camping Versilia Mare you will drive between chalets set out in neat rows to get to the touring pitches at the far end. These flat pitches, 96 in total, have 6A electricity and some shade. The site amenities are housed in a large round building through which you will gain access to a pleasant pool, paddling pool and the sports facilities. On Saturday evenings a typical Italian meal is served beside the pool, ending with dancing and a floodlit midnight swim. The site is situated between two roads so there is some road noise particularly alongside the pool area.

Facilities

Five smallish sanitary blocks (older in style but clean), one of which is for disabled visitors. A mixture of Turkish and British style toilets, open washbasins with cold water only and preset showers. Washing machines. Small shop in bar, restaurant/snack bar (all April-Sept). Outdoor swimming pool (April-Sept, lifeguard, hats compulsory). Play area. Children's club (July/Aug). Entertainment. Children's football camp. Tennis. Torches useful.

Open: All year.

Directions

Site is between La Spezia and Viareggio. Leave the A12 at the Viareggio exit and head for Lido di Camaiore. On entering town look for yellow camping signs onto a major road (Via Triest). Site is number 175 on this long road. GPS: 43.90752, 10.22405

Charges guide

Per unit incl. 2 persons	
and electricity	€ 24.00 - € 54.00
extra person	€ 7.00 - € 10.00

Limite Sull'Arno

Camping Village San Giusto

Via Castra, 71, I-50050 Capraia e Limite (Tuscany) T: 0558 712 304. E: info@campingsangiusto.it

alanrogers.com/IT66075

Camping San Giusto is a friendly, family run site in an unspoilt, typically Tuscan setting within the Montalbano National Park. There are 100 terraced touring pitches, the lower ones with 6A electricity and well shaded. Some of these pitches have superb views over the Tuscan countryside, while almost all of the upper pitches enjoy spectacular views. Amenities include a restaurant specialising in wonderful Tuscan food. San Giusto will suit those looking for the peace and quiet of a traditional campsite in a natural setting. At busy times vehicles are parked in a large car park at the front of the site.

Facilities

Four sanitary blocks provide a variety of services. Most toilets are Turkish style. The small upper block is more modern. Washing machines. Bar and snack bar. Excellent restaurant. Shop. Swimming and paddling pools. Playground. Games room. WiFi (free). Communal barbecue area. Shuttle bus service. Mobile homes and chalets for rent. Off site: ATM 5 km. Bicycle hire 10 km. Walking and cycling. Florence, Siena, Vinci and Volterra.

Open: 15 March - 5 November.

Directions

From A1 Milan-Rome autostrada take Firenze exit, then the Firenze, Pisa, Livorno road towards Empoli and Pisa. Leave at Montelupo and head towards Limite Sull'Arno and on to Castra. Site is signed on the left after Castra. GPS: 43.783251, 10.988329

Charges guide

Per unit incl. 2 persons	
and electricity	€ 22.50 - € 38.00
extra person	€ 7.00 - € 9.00

For latest campsite news, availability and prices visit

alanrogers.com

Marina di Bibbona
Camping Free Time

Via dei Cipressi, I-57020 Marina di Bibbona (Tuscany) T: 0586 600 934. E: info@freetimecamping.it

alanrogers.com/IT66330

Camping Free Time is 700 m. from the beach (by road train) and 500 m. from the little resort of Marina di Bibbona. The sister site to IT66356 nearby, it is attractively landscaped with flowers and trees provide welcome shade to most of the 111 level grass pitches, all with 10A electricity. Forty-four have great, thatched private facilities with toilet and shower, outside kitchen and patio. The bar/restaurant/pizzeria complex overlooks the lagoon-style pool and paddling pool and offers a reasonably priced and varied menu. There is also a superb thatched open-air gym and sauna alongside the fishing lakes.

Facilities

Modern, clean toilet blocks are well maintained. Facilities for disabled visitors. Some pitches have private sanitary facilities (extra charge). Excellent room for babies and children. Motorcaravan services. Shop. Bazaar. Bar and restaurant/pizzeria. Fishing (charged). Play areas. Lively entertainment programme in peak season. Sauna. Gym. Bicycle hire. WiFi in restaurant area (charged). Road train to beach. Off site: Beach and fishing 700 m. Watersports.

Open: 12 April - 19 October.

Directions

Site is south of Livorno. From Livorno-Civitavecchia road (autostrada) take La California exit and follow signs to Marina di Bibbona. Site is well signed. GPS: 43.25235, 10.5309

Charges guide

Per unit incl. 2 persons	
and electricity	€ 26.50 - € 53.00
extra person	€ 7.50 - € 16.00
child (1-9 yrs)	€ 5.00 - € 10.00

Marina di Bibbona
Camping Free Beach

Via Cavalleggeri Nord 88, I-57020 Marina di Bibbona (Tuscany) T: 0586 696 855.
E: info@campingfreebeach.it **alanrogers.com/IT66335**

Camping Free Beach is 350 metres from the Mediterranean beaches, which can be reached by road train through the shady pine trees. There are 450 shady and level pitches, 150 for touring, all with 3A electricity. A variety of mobile homes and fully equipped bungalow tents are for hire. The swimming pools, play area and comprehensive entertainment programme make this a sound site for families. Visitors may also make use of the leisure facilities at the sister site, IT66330. Discerning adults will appreciate the fine dining restaurant; an alternative is the self-service takeaway/pizzeria.

Facilities

Four sanitary blocks have clean, modern facilities with British style toilets and hot water throughout. Washing machines and dryers. Shop and bazaar. Bar. Restaurant. Self-service, takeaway and pizzeria. Swimming pool and children's pool. Play area. Games arcade. Bicycle hire. Accommodation for rent. Road train to beach. WiFi in bar and reception. Off site: The Mediterranean beaches. Pisa. Elba. Local market towns. Riding. Cycling. Excursions.

Open: 12 April - 22 September.

Directions

Site is south of Livorno. From Livorno-Civitavecchia road (autostrada) take La California exit and follow signs to Marina di Bibbona. Site is well signed. GPS: 43.251481, 10.52803

Charges guide

Per unit incl. 2 persons	
and electricity	€ 26.50 - € 50.00
extra person	€ 7.50 - € 15.00
child (2-12 yrs)	€ 5.00 - € 10.00

Marina di Bibbona
Camping Il Capannino

Via Cavalleggeri Sud 26, I-57020 Marina di Bibbona (Tuscany) T: 0586 696 855. E: capannino@capannino.it

alanrogers.com/IT66365

Wonderfully situated on the Etruscan coast of Tuscany, Il Capannino is a small, traditional campsite which has been part modernised. It is twinned with Free Time (IT66330) some two kilometres away, where visitors must go for many of the facilities. There are 200 pitches in total, providing a mix of bungalows for rent, touring and tent pitches. Electricity (3A) is available. Most of the shaded tent pitches are mixed in with the rental accommodation. The sandy/pebble beach with safe bathing can be accessed from the site. This is a relatively unsophisticated site benefiting from direct beach access.

Facilities

One modern toilet block with hot water throughout, controllable showers and facilities for disabled visitors, plus three older blocks requiring updating. Laundry facilities. Well stocked shop. Bar/takeaway. Small play area. Two small fishing lakes. Children's club (1/6-1/9). WiFi in bar area (charged). Off site: Sports facilities, swimming pool and entertainment at Camping Free Time 2 km. Bicycle hire and boat launching 500 m. Riding 10 km. Ferries from Piombina to Elba (40 mins).

Open: 12 April - 22 September.

Directions

Leave A12 motorway at Rosignano Marittimo, go on to SS1 Aurelia and head for Marina di Bibbona. Exit at La California-Bibbona-Marina di Bibbona, and after 4 km. turn left at roundabout and 2 km. further turn right to site. GPS: 43.237224, 10.532034

Charges guide

Per unit incl. 2 persons	
and electricity	€ 26.50 - € 50.00
extra person	€ 7.50 - € 15.00

For latest campsite news, availability and prices visit
alanrogers.com

Marina di Campo
Camping la Foce

Localitá la Foce, I-57034 Marina di Campo (Tuscany) T: 0565 976 456. E: info@campinglafoce.com

alanrogers.com/IT66056

Located on the isle of Elba, la Foce was opened in 1954 by the Frassinetti family. The beautiful sandy beach, which can be seen from the main gate, is just 10 m. away across a narrow road. The site has 100 fairly compact touring pitches with 4A electricity, in the shade of pine and eucalyptus trees. Some require interesting manoeuvring to gain access. A separate bar and restaurant with a terrace overlooking the sea are just outside the entrance. There is a range of accommodation to rent, including bungalows and mini apartments. The family take great pride in their campsite which is close to many facilities. Guests may use the tennis and football facilities of the adjacent hotel. There are diving centres, windsurfing and sailing schools, boat, dinghy, car, motorbike and bicycle hire nearby.

Facilities

The single toilet block has showers and washbasins with hot water, hairdryers and a mixture of British and Turkish style toilets. Facilities for children and disabled visitors. Washing machines, dryers and ironing board. Well stocked mini-market/bazaar. Free WiFi over site. Electric barbecues are not permitted (if gas, must be before 22.30). Accommodation for hire. Off site: Beach 10 m. Restaurants 50 m. Bars, pubs and nightclubs within 1 km. The Church of San Giovanni. The Roman columns in Seccheto. Monte Cocchero. Pianosa National Park.

Open: All year.

Directions

From the ferry in Portoferraio, follow signs for Procchio, then for Marina di Campo. After Procchio, at junction for airport, turn left and follow signs for La Foce-Marina di Campo. After 1 km. at roundabout follow signs for site. After 800 m. at end of pine wood next to beach, turn right and site is at end of cul-de-sac road. GPS: 42.74971, 10.24554

Charges guide

Per unit incl. 2 persons	
and electricity	€ 22.00 - € 48.00
extra person	€ 6.50 - € 14.50
child (3-10 yrs)	€ 2.50 - € 9.50
dog	free - € 5.00

Marina di Campo
Camping Ville degli Ulivi

Via della Foce 89, Marina di Campo, I-57034 Isola d'Elba (Tuscany) T: 0565 976 098. E: info@villedegliulivi.it

alanrogers.com/IT66680

Camping Ville degli Ulivi is an impressive site with many quality activities for families and a great atmosphere. In a pleasant setting amongst pines and olives, it has access through a rear gate to a pretty sandy bay with a safe beach and all manner of watersports. Of the 285 pitches, 200 are available for touring units. There is a very large contingent of tour operators and some bungalow and apartment accommodation. The good quality touring pitches are of a reasonable size, flat and most have natural shade. All have 6A electricity. Cars are not allowed to stay on the site. There is some aircraft noise from a local airport. Watch for the extras. The bar/restaurant, takeaway and pizzeria with terraces overlook the pool and entertainment takes place alongside at designated times. Below the pool there is a luxurious wellness centre should you wish to pamper yourself. This is a splendid site where you can either relax or become fully involved with the comprehensive programme of events and entertainment.

Facilities

Toilet facilities are good with hot showers, baby rooms and facilities for disabled visitors. Laundry facilities. Bar/restaurant. Pizzeria. Takeaway. Shop. Swimming pool. Play area. Bicycle and scooter hire. Diving centre. Multisports pitch. Amusement arcade. TV. Entertainment programme (May-Sept). Aquagym. Miniclub. Excursions. Internet access. No charcoal barbecues. WiFi throughout. Off site: Local markets. Watersports on the beach. Village 1 km. Riding 3 km. Golf 8 km.

Open: 17 April - 17 October.

Directions

From Portoferraio ferry port follow signs for Procchio, then Marina di Campo. Before Marina di Campo village, turn left towards La Foce-Lacona. In 800 m. turn right to site. GPS: 42.7519, 10.24502

Charges guide

Per unit incl. 2 persons	
and electricity	€ 22.50 - € 53.50
extra person	€ 7.00 - € 15.50
child (0-4 yrs)	€ 3.00 - € 10.00
dog	free - € 6.00

Montecatini Terme
Camping Belsito

Via delle Vigne, localitá Vico, I-51016 Montecatini Terme (Tuscany) T: 0572 673 73.
E: info@campingbelsito.it **alanrogers.com/IT66010**

The owners of this site wish it to be for families and thus the emphasis is on peace and tranquillity. Whilst the towns below are blisteringly hot, the cool breezes here do make it as the name says, Belsito – a beautiful place. There are now 200 pitches of varying size, all with electricity (6-8A) and some with shade. It is very much a touring site with no permanent occupants and only six bungalows for hire. There are 64 pitches with a private sanitary unit for hire on the pitch. The views are excellent from most pitches, and from an amazing new swimming pool on the upper terrace.

Facilities

Two sanitary blocks (one new) plus 64 private units for hire. Hot water is provided throughout. Facilities for disabled visitors. Washing machines. Good shop, bar/restaurant, snack bar with takeaway (all April-Sept). New swimming pool. Play area. Book exchange. Communal freezer and barbecue area. Satellite TV. WiFi throughout (charged). Off site: Bus 100 m. from gate to railway station. Collodi – Pinocchio's town!

Open: 1 April - 30 September.

Directions

From A11 Firenze-Mare autostrada take exit for Montecatini Terme. Follow brown signs for site and take Montecatini Alto road (do not use sat nav as you may end up in a very narrow village street). Site is on the left in 3 km. GPS: 43.90480, 10.78783

Charges guide

Per unit incl. 2 persons	
and electricity	€ 23.00 - € 40.00
extra person	€ 6.00 - € 10.00

Montopoli
Camping Toscana Village

Via Fornoli 9, I-56020 Montopoli (Tuscany) T: 0571 449 032. E: info@toscanavillage.com
alanrogers.com/IT66610

This area was once a forest surrounding the attractive medieval Tuscan village of Montopoli. Toscana Village has been thoughtfully carved out of the hillside under mature pines and it is ideal for a sightseeing holiday in this central and peaceful area. The 135 level pitches (some large) are on shaded terraces and are carefully maintained. All pitches have 6A electricity. The amenities are centrally located close to the top of the hill in a pleasant modern building. English is spoken by the helpful reception staff who also organise a programme of visits and events.

Facilities

Two modern and clean blocks have quality facilities including British style toilets, hot water at all sinks, private cabins plus two large en-suite cubicles. Facilities for disabled visitors. Laundry facilities. Motorcaravan services. Shop (bread to order), restaurant, pizzeria/barbecue (grill night on Saturdays), takeaway (all 15/4-15/10). Swimming pool (June-Sept). Play area. Bicycle hire. Organised activities and tours. Torches useful. WiFi over site (charged). Off site: Montopoli village 1 km. Fishing 6 km.

Open: All year.

Directions

From A12 (Genova-Florence) take Pisa Centro exit. Take F1,P1,L1 and then Montopoli exit. Follow signs to Montopoli. Look for cemetery on right. Opposite is Via Masoria leading to Via Fornoli and site. Follow brown signs to site (ignore sat nav directions through a prohibited area). GPS: 43.67611, 10.75277

Charges guide

Per unit incl. 2 persons	
and electricity	€ 26.00 - € 34.00
extra person	€ 6.00 - € 8.50

Pisa
Camping Torre Pendente

Viale delle Cascine 86, I-56122 Pisa (Tuscany) T: 0505 617 04. E: info@campingtorrependente.com
alanrogers.com/IT66080

Torre Pendente is a most friendly site, efficiently run by the Signorini family who speak good English and make everyone feel welcome. It is amazingly close to the famous leaning tower of Pisa and therefore busy throughout the main season. It is a medium sized site with 220 touring pitches, all with 5A electricity, on level, grassy ground with some shade from trees and lots of artificial shade. Fifty bungalows are also available for hire. The excellent site facilities are near the entrance including a most pleasant restaurant, swimming pool complex with pool bar and a large terrace.

Facilities

Three toilet blocks are very clean and smart with British style toilets and good facilities for disabled campers. Private cabins for hire. Hot water at sinks. Washing machines. Motorcaravan services. Supermarket. Restaurant, bar and takeaway. Swimming pool with pool bar, paddling pool and spa. Playground. Boules. Entertainment in high season. WiFi over site (charged). Bungalows for hire. Off site: Bicycle hire. Bus 100 m.

Open: 1 April - 15 October.

Directions

From A12, exit at Pisa Nord and follow for 5 km. to Pisa. Do not take first sign to town centre. Site is well signed at a later left turn (Viale delle Cascine). GPS: 43.7252, 10.3819

Charges guide

Per unit incl. 2 persons	
and electricity	€ 29.50 - € 35.00
extra person	€ 8.00 - € 10.00

For latest campsite news, availability and prices visit
alanrogers.com

Pisa

Camping Village International Saint Michael

Via della Bigattiera lato mare, 24 -Tirrenia, I-56128 Pisa (Tuscany) T: 050 330 41.

E: info@campingstmichael.it **alanrogers.com/IT66085**

Camping Saint Michael is a pleasant, family owned site and is quietly situated close to the Migliarino National Park and around 600 m. from a sandy beach. Beneath the site's trees there are 150 level pitches, 30 of which are occupied by seasonal units, all with 4A electrical connections. Around the perimeter there are 30 mobile homes for rent. This site is mainly used by Italian holiday makers and there is plenty to do here in high season with much activity focused on the beach although a great new pool has been added. Tirrenia and Marina di Pisa are 2.5 km. away.

Facilities	Directions
The modernised facilities are well placed with British style WCs, open washbasins with cold water and controllable showers (charged). Facilities for children and disabled visitors. Laundry facilities. Small shop for basics, bar, restaurant and pizzeria. Takeaway. Outdoor swimming pool. Play area. Multisports court. Children's club. Free WiFi. Dogs are not accepted. Off site: Beach, fishing, sailing and watersports 600 m. Golf 2 km. Riding 4 km.	Tirrenia is 12 km. north of Livorno. From the south, take SS224 to Tirrenia and continue towards Marina di Pisa. Site is 2 km. further north and is well signed. GPS: 43.64694, 10.295

Open: 14 May - 11 September.

Charges guide

Per unit incl. 2 persons and electricity	€ 25.00 - € 31.00
extra person	€ 7.00 - € 8.00
child (3-12 yrs)	€ 5.00 - € 6.50

Portoferraio

Camping La Sorgente

Localitá La Sorgente, Acquaviva, I-57037 Portoferraio (Tuscany) T: 0565 917 139.

E: info@campinglasorgente.it **alanrogers.com/IT66072**

Set on a terraced hillside overlooking the sea on the north east coast of Elba, La Sorgente is a compact, pine-clad campsite offering peace and tranquillity in natural surroundings. The views from much of the site are stunning. There are 70 pitches available for touring with 4A electricity and a small number of bungalows to rent. There is direct, fairly steep access down to two pebble beaches, popular for snorkelling and scuba diving. Larger units may find access and manoeuvring a challenge. Units over 7 m. are not accepted. The site is just 6 km. from the island's capital, Portoferraio.

Facilities	Directions
Sanitary facilities include controllable hot showers and mostly British WCs. Good area for babies. Facilities for disabled visitors. Laundry area. Well stocked shop (from May). Small bar/restaurant. Some takeaway. Playground (no ball games on site). Communal barbecue area with picnic tables. Bicycles to use free of charge. Fridges to rent. Safety deposit boxes. Direct beach access. Torches useful. Free WiFi over site. Off site: Sandy beaches.	From the port of Portoferraio, follow the signs 'tutti direzione' and then 'Enfola – Viticcio' for approximately 6 km. La Sorgente is clearly signed. GPS: 42.821903, 10.280218

Open: 1 April - 30 October.

Charges guide

Per unit incl. 2 persons and electricity	€ 24.50 - € 52.50
extra person	€ 6.50 - € 15.50

No credit cards.

Portoferraio

Camping Acquaviva

Spiaggia dell'Acquaviva, Acquaviva, I-57037 Portoferraio (Tuscany) T: 0565 919 103.

E: campingacquaviva@elbalink.it **alanrogers.com/IT66074**

Camping Acquaviva lies on the rocky north coast of Elba, just 8 km. from Portoferraio – the port and principal town. One side of the site is set along the pebble beach with a boat launching point. There are 110 pitches here, 70 for touring with 3A electricity and high oleander hedges. Some are in premium spots overlooking the beach and others are very privately tucked away. A few are scattered amongst a busy terraced bungalow area (40 for hire) opposite the main touring pitches. A small canvas-covered restaurant offers a limited menu and some entertainment is provided in high season.

Facilities	Directions
One central and clean toilet block with washbasins and controllable showers. Laundry facilities. Basic shop. Small bar and restaurant. Takeaway. Small elevated children's pool. Play area. Miniclub. Animation in high season. Safety deposit boxes. No electric barbecues on pitches. Communal barbecue area. Special rates at local diving school. Boat launching. Torches useful. Free WiFi throughout. Off site: Buses to Portoferraio and other parts of Elba. A choice of 100 beaches.	From the port of Portoferraio, follow the signs 'tutti direzione' and then 'Enfola – Viticcio' for approximately 6 km. Camping Acquaviva is clearly signed. GPS: 42.8221, 10.2863

Open: April - October.

Charges guide

Per unit incl. 2 persons and electricity	€ 22.50 - € 55.40
extra person	€ 6.50 - € 15.30
child (3-10 yrs. acc. to age)	€ 3.00 - € 11.00

For latest campsite news, availability and prices visit

alanrogers.com

Portoferraio
Camping Scaglieri
Locailtá Scaglieri, Portoferraio, I-57037 Isola d'Elba (Tuscany) T: 0565 969 940. E: info@campingscaglieri.it
alanrogers.com/IT66850

Camping Scaglieri is a small coastal site on a steep slope with a steep entrance and relatively high prices. A small pool is directly alongside reception at the top of the site, as is the restaurant and bar. The 55 touring pitches are of varying sizes, all on terraces with 3A electricity and views over the bay, but the slopes are interesting! Some pitches have shade from trees. The campsite is part of a group with two hotels and the facilities there may be used by camping guests. Due to the steep slopes this site is not recommended for disabled or infirm campers and there is a maximum van length of 7.5 m.

Facilities

One central toilet block is kept very clean with good fittings. WCs are mostly British style. Baby room. Washing machines. Motorcaravan services. Fridge hire. Bar, restaurant and takeaway. Gelateria and small shop. Swimming pool. Play areas. Entertainment in season. No barbecues allowed on pitches (communal area). Car hire. Torches very useful. Internet access. WiFi throughout (charged). Off site: Golf 200 m. Sailing, windsurfing school and watersports 500 m. Beach 200 m. Riding 5 km.

Open: 20 April - 21 October.

Directions

Site is west of Portoferraio on the coast. From Portoferraio ferry take the Procchio road. After 5 km. and on a hilltop turn right towards Biodola and Scaglieri. Site entrance is on the right after 2 km. GPS: 42.80349, 10.27072

Charges guide

Per unit incl. 2 persons	
and electricity	€ 28.00 - € 65.00
extra person	€ 7.50 - € 15.50

Portoferraio
Camping Rosselba le Palme
Localitá Ottone 3, Portoferraio, I-57037 Isola d'Elba (Tuscany) T: 0565 933 101. E: info@rosselbalepalme.it
alanrogers.com/IT66880

Rosselba le Palme is a fabulous, large resort style campsite with a tropical feel, set beneath a towering medieval castle on a cliff top. Of the 280 steeply terraced pitches, 150 are available for touring, all with electricity (1.5-3A). The large pool complex has slides, jacuzzi and a great children's pool feature. There is also a terraced poolside bar and entertainment area here. The range of sporting facilities is diverse and children can enjoy the kids' club with its young explorers course. There is a superb restaurant specialising in fish dishes with a terrace leading into the botanical gardens.

Facilities

Eight modern and clean toilet blocks are spread over the site, but the steep terrain may be difficult for those with mobility problems. Laundry facilities. Supermarket, restaurant, pizzeria, pool bar and café/bar (21/4-30/9). Pool complex with swimming courses and aquarobics (15/5-30/9). Tennis with coaching. Volleyball. Archery. Five-a-side football. Basketball. Trampolines. Bicycle track. Bicycle and motorcycle rental. Secure car park. Botanical gardens. WiFi (charged).

Open: 21 April - 5 October.

Directions

From ferry at Portoferraio follow signs for Porto Azzurro to begin. Then turn left towards Bagnaia and follow campsite signs, on the right, just after a fork to the left. GPS: 42.80146, 10.36488

Charges guide

Per unit incl. 2 persons	
and electricity	€ 13.70 - € 52.60
extra person	€ 5.00 - € 15.20
child (3-8 yrs)	free - € 11.70

Punta Ala
Camping Baia Verde
Via delle Collacchie, I-58043 Punta Ala (Tuscany) T: 0564 922 298. E: info@baiaverde.com
alanrogers.com/IT66078

This typically Italian beach site on Tuscany's popular coast and is ideally situated for trips to Pisa in one direction and Florence in the other. Baia Verde is a well equipped site with a good bar/restaurant, amongst other amenities. The 1,150 touring pitches, with 3A electricity, are all under shady pines and are marked. The amenities are a distance from some of the pitches. The site has direct access to a sandy beach, a focal point for many games and activities, and a great spot to enjoy the glorious sunsets for which the region is celebrated. There is an attractive beach bar serving food at set times.

Facilities

Sanitary blocks with hot showers and facilities for disabled visitors. Washing machine. Motorcaravan services. Supermarket, bakery, greengrocer, butcher, tobacconist and newsagent. Bar/restaurant/pizzeria. Takeaway. Bazaar. Games room. Tennis. Evening shows and dancing. Children's clubs. Hairdresser. Riding. Bicycle hire. Torches useful. No dogs (22/6-23/8). Off site: Shops, cafés and restaurants in Punta Ala.

Open: 23 April - 16 October.

Directions

From Florence, head south for Siena, then exit at Colle Val d'Elsa Nord. Pass through Massa Maritima, Scarlino and Castigliani before arriving at Punta Ala, where the site is signposted. GPS: 42.834, 10.779333

Charges guide

Per unit incl. 2 persons	
and electricity	€ 22.00 - € 50.00
extra person	€ 7.00 - € 15.00

For latest campsite news, availability and prices visit
alanrogers.com

Punta Ala
PuntAla Camping Resort

Locatitá Punta Ala, Castiglione della Pescala, I-58043 Punta Ala (Tuscany) T: 0564 922 294.
E: info@campingpuntala.it **alanrogers.com/IT66730**

This very large site was established some 35 years ago but almost all of the infrastructure has been rebuilt and is superb. The touring unit/tent pitches are shaded, secluded and vary tremendously in size. They are on flat sand (with 3/6A electricity, 67 also have water and drainage). There is something for everyone here, with a very busy entertainment programme in high season. The beach is safe and of soft sand, with easy access for disabled campers. A lively, green and friendly site which will suit families.

Facilities

Eight blocks are modern and the ninth requires updating. Facilities are clean with private cabins to hire. Excellent units for disabled campers. Washing machines and dryer. Motorcaravan services. Bars, restaurants and takeaway. Shop. Bazaar. Entertainment. Play areas. Free WiFi over site. Bicycle hire. Tennis. Beach with watersports. ATM. Communal barbecue areas – no barbecues allowed on pitches. Excursions. Dogs are not accepted. Torches essential. Off site: Golf and riding 3 km. Town 6 km.

Open: Easter - 15 October.

Directions

From E80/S1/Aurelia superstrada take Follonica Nord exit onto S322 for Punta Ala and Castiglione della Pescaia. Watch for district of Pian d'Alma on maps. Site is now signed to the right along a narrow road. GPS: 42.84143, 10.7796

Charges guide

Per unit incl. 2 persons and electricity	€ 31.50 - € 67.60
extra person	€ 1.70 - € 4.00
child (2-17 yrs)	€ 1.10 - € 4.00

Punta Ala
Baia Verde International Camping

Via delle Collacchie, I-58040 Punta Ala (Tuscany) T: 0564 922 298. E: info@baiaverde.com
alanrogers.com/IT66740

Baia Verde is a large, mature, sprawling family site with direct access to a narrow sandy beach. The 1138 level, dusty pitches (with 3A electricity) are totally shaded by very large pines and vary in size. When we visited in June, the cicadas were in full throat! The site has an impressive range of amenities, including a busy shopping and restaurant complex. This is a huge site, very popular with Italians in peak season, with an entertainment programme primarily aimed at youngsters. The programme includes a beach gym, various sports tournaments and loud evening discos.

Facilities

Nine mature but clean sanitary blocks provide a mixture of British and Turkish style toilets and unisex showers (stretched in peak season). Laundry. Motorcaravan services. Shopping centre. Bazaar. Bar/restaurant. Pizzeria with terraces. Takeaway. Picnic area. Hairdresser. Beach bar. Play area. Games room. Bicycle hire. Boat and canoe hire. Direct access to beach. Evening entertainment in high season. No dogs (20/6-31/8). Mobile homes for rent. WiFi on part of site (charged).

Open: 24 April - 13 October.

Directions

From the north, take E80 to Rosignano and join Via Aurelia (SS1) leaving at Follonica Sud exit. Follow signs to Punta Ala and site is well signed from here. GPS: 42.83446, 10.77988

Charges guide

Per unit incl. 2 persons and electricity	€ 21.00 - € 50.00
extra person	€ 6.50 - € 15.00
child (3-9 yrs)	€ 4.00 - € 9.00
dog	€ 4.00

San Baronto di Lamporecchio
Camping Barco Reale

Via Nardini 11/13, I-51035 San Baronto di Lamporecchio (Tuscany) T: 0573 883 32. E: info@barcoreale.com
alanrogers.com/IT66000

Just forty minutes from Florence and an hour from Pisa, this site is beautifully situated high in the Tuscan hills close to the fascinating town of Pistoia. Part of an old walled estate, there are impressive views of the surrounding countryside. It is a quiet site of 15 hectares and the 265 terraced pitches enjoy shade from mature pines and oaks. Some pitches are huge with great views and others are very private. Most are for touring units, although some have difficult access (the site provides tractor assistance). All 187 touring pitches have electricity and 40 are fully serviced. A member of Leading Campings group.

Facilities

Three modern sanitary blocks are well positioned and kept very clean. Good facilities for disabled visitors (dedicated pitches close by). Baby room. Laundry facilities. Motorcaravan services. Shop, restaurant and bar. Supervised swimming pools (10.00-18.00, caps required). Ice cream shop. Playgrounds. Bowls. Riding. Disco. Entertainment. Tuscan-style cooking lessons. Bicycle hire. WiFi over part of site. Off site: Village 1 km.

Open: 1 April - 30 September.

Directions

From Pistoia take Vinci-Empoli-Lamporecchio signs to San Baronto. From Empoli signs to Vinci and San Baronto. Final approach involves a sharp bend and a steep slope. GPS: 43.84190, 10.91130

Charges guide

Per unit incl. 2 persons and electricity	€ 26.60 - € 50.50
extra person	€ 7.30 - € 12.80
child (3-11 yrs)	€ 4.50 - € 8.30

San Gimignano
Camping Boschetto di Piemma

Localitá Santa Lucia 38/C, I-53037 San Gimignano (Tuscany) T: 0577 907 134. E: info@boschettodipiemma.it
alanrogers.com/IT66270

The medieval Manhattan of San Gimignano is one of Tuscany's most popular sites and this new campsite lies just 2 km. from the town. There are 100 small pitches here, all with 6A electrical connections and some with shade from mature trees. The site is in woodland surrounded by olive groves and vineyards and has been developed with much care for the environment, using rain water for irrigation and with many solar panels. Located with a sports centre, the site has use of many of the sporting amenities (tennis carries an extra charge). The swimming pool alongside the site is shared with the public, but site security is good. An hourly bus service connects the site with the town.

Facilities

Excellent sanitary block includes facilities for disabled visitors. Cool room with fridge and freezer for campers. Shop (specialising in local produce), restaurant/pizzeria and bar (all 1/4-30/10). Heated outdoor swimming pool (1/6-15/9, small charge). Tennis (charged, lessons available). Sports centre. Playground. Entertainment and activity programme in high season. WiFi (charged). Apartments for rent. Off site: San Gimignano 2 km.

Open: All year.

Directions

From the Florence-Siena superstrada take exit for Poggibonsi Nord and follow signs to San Gimignano. At first roundabout follow signs to Volterra, then take first road to the left (Santa Lucia). Site is well signed close to the sports area. GPS: 43.4533, 11.0536

Charges guide

Per unit incl. 2 persons	
and electricity	€ 25.00 - € 31.00
extra person	€ 8.50 - € 11.00

San Piero a Sieve
Camping Village Mugello Verde

Via Massorondinaio 39, I-50038 Scarperia e San Piero (Tuscany) T: 055 848 511.
E: mugelloverde@florencevillage.com **alanrogers.com/IT66050**

Mugello Verde is a country, hillside site with 200 good sized pitches for motorcaravans and caravans and smaller pitches for tents. All have 6A electricity. Some are on flat ground, others are on steep terraces where mature trees provide shade. The big attraction here is the site's proximity to the Mugello racing track, just 5 km. away. It is used by Ferrari for practice runs and is also an international car and motorcycling track. The site has a pleasant, open feel and English is spoken at reception.

Facilities

Two toilet blocks are well positioned and the facilities are clean with mixed British and Turkish style WCs. Facilities for disabled visitors. Laundry facilities. Shop. Restaurant/bar and pizzeria. Swimming pool (28/5-11/9; no paddling pool). Play area. Tennis. WiFi on part of site (first hour free). Off site: Riding, golf and fishing 5 km.

Open: 11 March - 1 November.

Directions

From A1 autostrada take Barberino del Mugello exit and follow SS65 towards San Piero a Sieve and before town, turn left and just past Tamoil garage turn right to site. GPS: 43.96148, 11.31030

Charges guide

Per unit incl. 2 persons	
and electricity	€ 25.00 - € 33.00
extra person	€ 8.00 - € 10.00

San Vincenzo
Camping Park Albatros

Pineta di Torre Nuova, I-57027 San Vincenzo (Tuscany) T: 0565 701 018. E: parkalbatros@ecvacanze.it
alanrogers.com/IT66380

Camping Albatros is situated on the historic Costa Degli Etruschi and is a huge site with something for everyone. Of the 1,000 shaded pitches (6/10A electricity), the 300 for touring are in a separate area on flat ground. All have water and drainage. The top quality facilities and entertainment here are so good that you need not leave the site during your holiday. The extensive pools and water features are outstanding and the wide range of recreational facilities are superb. This is a great site for family holidays if you do not mind a few queues and several thousand people holidaying around you.

Facilities

Two superb circular toilet blocks with brilliant rooms for children, hot showers and facilities for disabled visitors. Washing machines. Huge air-conditioned supermarket. Bazaar. Beauty salon. Lagoon complex with five amazing pools (one covered and heated). Central area includes two bars, two restaurants and pizzeria with large terrace and waiter service. Takeaway. Daily entertainment in season. Disco. Miniclub (4-12 yrs). Minigolf. Play areas. Diving organised. Bicycle hire. No barbecues allowed. WiFi over site (charged). Train around site in high season.

Open: 18 April - 21 September.

Directions

Site is north west of Grossetto and south of Livorno on the coast. From the SS1 take San Vincenzo exit. Site signed in San Vincenzo and is 6 km. south of village along beach road. GPS: 43.04972, 10.55861

Charges guide

Per unit incl. 2 persons	
and electricity	€ 26.50 - € 58.10
extra person	€ 7.50 - € 16.30
child (3-11 yrs)	free - € 11.90
dog	free

For latest campsite news, availability and prices visit
alanrogers.com

Sarteano
Parco delle Piscine

Via del Bagno Santo 29, I-53047 Sarteano (Tuscany) T: 0578 269 71. E: info@parcodellepiscine.it
alanrogers.com/IT66450

Sarteano is an ancient spa town and this large, smart site utilises that spa in its very open environs. This site is well run with an excellent infrastructure, if a little expensive. There is a friendly welcome from the English speaking staff. The 500 individual, flat pitches, (389 for touring) are all 100-150 sq.m. in size with high, neat hedges giving real privacy. Electricity (6A) is available. The three unique swimming pools fed by the natural thermo-mineral springs are a novel feature here. These springs have been known since antiquity as Del Bagno Santo (Holy Bath) and flow at a constant temperature of 24 degrees. Two of these pools (the largest is superb with water cascade and hydro-massage, and the other large shallow pool is just for children) are set in a huge park-like ground with many picnic tables. A third excellent pool is on the campsite itself and is opened in the main season for the exclusive use of campers.

Facilities

Two heated toilet blocks are of high quality with mainly British style WCs, many cubicles also with bidet. Gas supplies. Motorcaravan services. Restaurant/pizzeria with bar. Takeaway. Coffee bar. Swimming pools (one all season). Excellent play area for children. TV room and mini-cinema with 100 seats and very large screen. Tennis. Exchange facilities. Free cookery lessons and art classes in high season. Free guided cultural tours. Internet. Free WiFi over site. Dogs are not accepted. Off site: The site is in the town. Old city 100 m. Bicycle hire 100 m. Riding 3 km.

Open: 1 April - 30 September.

Directions

From autostrada A1 take Chiusi/Chianciano exit, from where Sarteano is well signed (6 km). In Sarteano follow camping/piscine signs to site (entrance sign reads Piscine di Sarteano). GPS: 42.9885, 11.8639

Charges guide

Per unit incl. 2 persons	
and electricity	€ 35.00 - € 62.00
extra person	€ 10.00 - € 17.00
child (3-10 yrs)	€ 9.00 - € 13.00

No credit cards.

Scarlino
Camping Village Il Fontino

Localitá Il Fontino, Maremma Toscana, I-58020 Scarlino (Tuscany) T: 0566 370 29. E: info@fontino.it
alanrogers.com/IT66720

The name means Little Fountain as springs provide all the drinking water here. The Maurizio family have worked hard to provide a most pleasant site for campers. There are 60 terraced pitches for touring units on a sloping site, all with 3/6A electricity and shade from mature olives. Once settled on the pitch, cars are parked separately. The 25 m. pool with its separate paddling pool is the site's strength – it is stunning, safe and free. As you swim you can enjoy the views over the town of Follonica below you, whilst in turn the village of Scarlino sits hundreds of metres above on the cliff top. A large, very attractive building in the centre of the site, restored in traditional style, houses the restaurant/pizzeria, shop and bar with a rooftop terrace. A few bungalows are placed at irregular intervals around the site. The beach is 4 km. away and a free shuttle bus is provided in high season.

Facilities

Two dated sanitary blocks provide hot showers (2.5 minute timer). Mostly Turkish style toilets, cold water at washbasins. Single facility for disabled visitors. Washing machines and dryer. Bar/restaurant and takeaway. Shop. Swimming and paddling pools. Entertainment programme and miniclub (high season). Play area. Bicycle hire. WiFi over part of site (charged). Free bus in high season to beach with watersports. Off site: Tennis 200 m. Town 2 km. Golf, riding, beach and boat launching 4 km.

Open: 24 April - 30 September.

Directions

From E80/S1 autostrada take Scarlino exit. Head for the hills and Scarlino. On approach to town look for site signs to right (towards Grosseto). Site is 1.4 km. on the left. GPS: 42.91101, 10.84347

Charges guide

Per unit incl. 2 persons	
and electricity	€ 21.50 - € 36.00
extra person	€ 6.00 - € 10.00
child (3-12 yrs)	€ 4.50 - € 7.50
dog	€ 3.50

No credit cards.

For latest campsite news, availability and prices visit

alanrogers.com

Scarlino
Camping Butteri

I-58020 Scarlino (Tuscany) T: 0566 959 958. E: camping@rivadeibutteri.info

alanrogers.com/IT66780

This is a sister site of Camping Baia dei Gabbiani (IT66770) and is closer to Follonica. The site is just 100 m. from the public beach and 15 minutes walk from the town centre. The 150 marked pitches are located beneath low trees and most have 3A electricity connections. The site has a good range of leisure amenities including a restaurant, bar and supermarket. A varied activity and entertainment programme is organised in peak season, including activities for children. This is a suitable site for a reasonable overnight stay whilst travelling in the low season. Follonica is a major resort with shops, restaurants and nightclubs, as well as a race course and water park. It is also a centre for various watersports including windsurfing and sailing.

Facilities

Sanitary facilities include hot showers (payment by token) and provision for visitors with disabilities. Laundry facilities. Motorcaravan services. Shop and newsagent, restaurant, bar and takeaway (all open as site). Playground. Mountain bike hire. Entertainment and activity programme in high season. Miniclub. Security wristbands are used. Dogs not accepted 6/8-19/8. Chalets for rent. Off site: Nearest beach 100 m. Follonica 3 km. Siena, Florence and Pisa are all within 2 hours drive.

Open: 24 April - 12 September.

Directions

From Livorno take southbound Via Aurelia (S1). Leave at Follonica Nord exit. Head initially towards Follonica and then towards Grosseto. Site is signed to left just as you leave Follonica.
GPS: 42.9111, 10.7736

Charges guide

Per unit incl. 2 persons	
and electricity	€ 27.20 - € 43.10
extra person	€ 8.30 - € 13.20
child (3-7 yrs)	€ 6.10 - € 8.40
dog (excl. 6/8-19/8)	€ 3.50 - € 5.00
No credit cards.	

Siena
Camping Colleverde

Strada Scacciapensieri 47, I-53100 Siena (Tuscany) T: 057 733 2545. E: info@sienacamping.com

alanrogers.com/IT66245

Camping Colleverde enjoys a panoramic setting overlooking the beautiful Tuscan city of Siena and the surrounding Chianti hills. The proprietor Andrea Sassolini and his family are on hand to ensure you have an enjoyable stay. Open for a long season, this is a great base for visiting Siena and the Chianti region. A bus stop is just 30 m. away and the railway station is 1.5 km. There are 221 touring pitches, 97 of which have 10A electricity and hardstandings and some are shaded. Smart on-site facilities include a swimming pool, a pizzeria/restaurant, bar and a shop. There are 25 mobile homes which can be reserved for short stays. Siena needs little introduction and is undeniably one of Tuscany's finest medieval cities, famous for its Palio horse race and its fine cathedral.

Facilities

Three new top quality sanitary facilities include provision for disabled visitors. Laundry. Motorcaravan services. Shop, bar, restaurant/pizzeria (all March-Oct). Swimming and paddling pools (June-Sept). Play area. WiFi over site (charged). Mobile homes for rent. Bicycle hire. Dog exercise area. Bus tours to major attractions arranged. Off site: Railway station 1.5 km. City centre 2 km. Bicycle hire 3 km. Riding 10 km. Chianti countryside. Cycle and walking tracks.

Open: 1 March - 31 December.

Directions

Site is north of the city. Approaching from the north, leave RA3 superstrada (Florence-Siena) at Siena Nord exit. Turn right and follow signs for Hospital (Ospedale) and Camping. Site is 1 km. from the hospital, well signed, and is the only campsite here, so all signs refer to Colleverde.
GPS: 43.33771, 11.33048

Charges guide

Per unit incl. 2 persons	
and electricity	€ 32.50 - € 37.00
extra person	€ 9.50 - € 11.00
child (3-11 yrs)	€ 5.00 - € 6.00

For latest campsite news, availability and prices visit
alanrogers.com

Sovicille
Camping la Montagnola

Strada della Montagnola, I-53018 Sovicille (Tuscany) T: 0577 314 473. E: montagnolacamping@libero.it
alanrogers.com/IT66250

An agreeable, reasonably priced alternative to sites closer to the centre of Siena, la Montagnola is set in secluded woodland to the north of the village of Sovicille. The owners have worked hard to provide a good basic standard of amenities. The 52 pitches are 60-80 sq.m. in size and some offer privacy. Clearly marked and with shade, all are suitable for caravans and motorcaravans, all having electricity connections (some need long leads). However, there are just three water points on the site. There is a large wooded area and an overflow field for tents with no electricity and another field has a play area.

Facilities

A single toilet block provides free hot showers and mainly British style toilets – not luxurious, but adequate and clean. Small, well stocked shop and bar. Play area. Torches definitely required in tent areas. WiFi throughout (charged). Off site: Small supermarket in Sovicille 2 km. Large supermarket in San Rocco a Pilli and Rosia 6 km. Two restaurants in the village. Bus service to Siena. Golf 10 km.

Open: Easter - 30 September.

Directions

From north on Firenze-Siena motorway take exit for Siena Ouest. Turn left on SS73 and at Malignano turn right towards Sovicille. Turn left just before mini roundabout. Site is 2 km. on the right. From south (Grosseto) take SS223 turn at crossroads to Rosia from where site is signed. GPS: 43.2811, 11.2199

Charges guide

Per unit incl. 2 persons and electricity	€ 25.00
extra person	€ 8.00

Torre del Lago
Camping Europa

Viale dei Tigli, I-55049 Torre del Lago Puccini (Tuscany) T: 0584 350 707. E: info@europacamp.it
alanrogers.com/IT66060

Europa is a large, flat, rectangular site directly off the beach road. Inside the gate you will pass 400 permanent pitches in 17 long rows, before reaching the 200 touring pitches which occupy six rows at the far end of the site. These are flat, very sandy and close together (55-70 sq.m) with some shade from trees or artificial cover and 6A electricity. The site's facilities include a bar, mini-market, bazaar, air-conditioned restaurant and a pleasant, secluded swimming pool and jacuzzi. The site has been owned by the Morescalchi family since 1967 and they are very keen that you have an enjoyable stay.

Facilities

Two clean sanitary blocks provide hot and cold showers (€ 0.50 token from reception). Toilets are mixed Turkish and British style. Facilities for disabled visitors. Laundry facilities. Motorcaravan services outside gate. Small shop. Bar/restaurant and takeaway. Swimming pool (1/5-23/9, caps required). Large play area. Entertainment. Miniclub. Bicycle hire. Satellite TV. Internet access. No dogs (3/8-23/8). Torches useful. WiFi over part of site (charged).

Open: 2 April - 2 October.

Directions

From A11-12 to Pisa Nord take Marina di Torre del Lago exit following the sign 'mare' towards the sea for Marina di Torre Lago Puccini. Follow clear signs for site. GPS: 43.83115, 10.27073

Charges guide

Per unit incl. 2 persons and electricity	€ 18.00 - € 41.00
extra person	€ 4.50 - € 9.50

Torre del Lago
Camping Italia

Viale del Tigli 52, I-55048 Torre del Lago (Tuscany) T: 0584 359 828. E: info@campingitalia.net
alanrogers.com/IT66260

This is a large and cheerful site split by the beach road. There are 100 flat pitches for touring units which are set apart from 340 permanent units across the road. The touring pitches have 6A electricity and enjoy shade from mature trees. Owned by the Forti family since 1969, the site has undergone a transformation over the last few years and has much to offer families for an enjoyable stay. Facilities include a restaurant with terraces, a secluded swimming pool and comprehensive entertainment. Free buses will take you to the beach 1 km. away. A lake is just 450 m. and is a pleasant walk.

Facilities

One older style but very clean unisex toilet block. Additional toilets in the new amenity block. WCs are British/Turkish style, showers are pushbutton (50c token). Facilities for disabled visitors. Baby bath. Laundry facilities. Motorcaravan services. Supermarket. Bar, restaurant and pizzeria/takeaway. Swimming pool and paddling pool (1/6-31/8; charged). Play area. TV in bar. Entertainment. Bicycle hire. Bungalows to rent. No dogs in high season. Torches useful. WiFi on part of site (charged).

Open: 20 April - 30 September.

Directions

Torre del Lago is on the west coast 15 km. north of Pisa. From A8 northbound leave at Viareggio exit, when heading south use Pisa North exit. Then take the S1 heading for Pisa. Continue towards Torre del Lago (site signed). GPS: 43.82965, 10.27339

Charges guide

Per unit incl. 2 persons and electricity	€ 18.50 - € 30.50
extra person	€ 4.50 - € 9.50

For latest campsite news, availability and prices visit
alanrogers.com

Troghi
Camping Village Il Poggetto

Via Il Poggetto 143, Strada Provinciale Aretina per San Donato, I-50067 Troghi-Firenze (Tuscany)
T: 055 830 7323. E: info@campingilpoggetto.com **alanrogers.com/IT66110**

This superb site has a lot to offer. It benefits from a wonderful panorama of the Colli Fiorentini hills with acres of the Zecchi family vineyards to the east adding to its appeal and is just 15 km. from Florence. The charming and hard working owners, Marcello and Daniella, have a wine producing background and you can purchase their fine wines at the site's shop. Their aim is to provide an enjoyable and peaceful atmosphere for families. All 106 touring pitches are of a good size, kept neat and tidy and have 6A electricity. On arrival you are given a joining pack and escorted to view available pitches.

Facilities

Two spotless sanitary blocks with piped music offer British style WCs. Three private sanitary units for hire. Five very well equipped units for disabled visitors. Separate facilities for children and baby room. Laundry facilities. Motorcaravan services. Gas supplies. Shop. Bar. Restaurant. Swimming pools and jacuzzi (1/5-30/9). Fitness room. Bicycle and scooter hire. Playground and entertainment for children. Excursions and organised trekking. Wine and oil tastings. WiFi throughout (charged). Off site: Tennis 100 m. Riding 500 m. Fishing 2 km.

Open: 9 March - 15 October.

Directions

Exit A1 at Incisa south east of Florence and turn right on the SS69. After 4 km. turn left following signs for Pian dell Isola. At next crossing turn right (Firenze) and follow site signs. Use sat nav with caution on final approach here as you may be taken into the steep, narrow streets of the nearby village. Follow campsite signs. GPS: 43.701415, 11.405262

Charges guide

Per unit incl. 2 persons and electricity	€ 29.50 - € 35.00
extra person	€ 8.00 - € 10.00

Vada
Camping Baia del Marinaio

Via Cavalleggeri 177, I-57018 Vada (Tuscany) T: 0586 770 164. E: info@baiadelmarinaio.it
alanrogers.com/IT66280

This well run, family owned site provides an inclusive quality holiday experience where all of your requirements are catered for without needing to set foot outside the campsite. Facilities here are of a high standard, particularly the magnificent pool complex. The site is split into two sections with the 200 flat and shaded touring pitches on one side of a minor road and 200 bungalows (50 available to rent) on the other. Electricity (6A) is available to all. The two restaurants, bars and pizzerias are all open all season. There is a short walk to the beach and the site is just within walking distance of the town centre.

Facilities

Six toilet blocks, all of a high standard, provide British and Turkish style WCs, hot showers and washbasins. Laundry. Facilities for disabled visitors. Shop. Bakery. Bazaar. Bars, restaurants and pizzeria. Large swimming pool complex with 30 m. water slide. Multisports court. Tennis courts. Bicycle hire. Entertainment and excursions arranged. WiFi over site (charged). Bungalows for rent.

Open: 25 April - 12 October.

Directions

From the S1/E80 take Cecina exit and follow road towards Vada. Site is well signed and is on the left side of the road towards Marina di Cecina. GPS: 43.33512, 10.461114

Charges guide

Per unit incl. 2 persons and electricity	€ 20.00 - € 40.00
extra person	€ 6.00 - € 11.00

Vada
Camping Tripesce

Via Cavalleggeri 88, I-57016 Vada (Tuscany) T: 0586 788 017. E: info@campingtripesce.it
alanrogers.com/IT66290

Neat and tidy, this family owned and run site has the great advantage of direct beach access through electronically controlled gates with CCTV. The beach is of fine sand and shelves gently – super for children with watersports and a lifeguard in season. This great beach makes up for the lack of a pool on the site and the fairly small size of the 230 pitches. All have 4A electricity and 60 are serviced with water and drainage. Some shade is provided by trees and by artificial shading. The site is contained within a rectangle and bungalows for rent are discreetly placed near reception.

Facilities

Three clean, fresh toilet blocks provide hot and cold showers (water is solar heated and free). British and Turkish style toilets. Facility for disabled visitors. Washing machines. Motorcaravan services. Bar/restaurant and takeaway. Shop. Excellent beach. Aquarobics and aerobics (high season). Play area (supervision required). Miniclub (high season). WiFi throughout (free). Fishing. Bicycle hire. No dogs (23/5-4/9). No charcoal barbecues.

Open: 30 March - 16 October.

Directions

From S1 autostrada (free) between Livorno and Grosetto head south and take Vada exit. Site is well signed along with many others as you approach the town. GPS: 43.34301, 10.45825

Charges guide

Per unit incl. 2 persons and electricity	€ 20.00 - € 37.00
extra person	€ 5.00 - € 8.00
No credit cards.	

For latest campsite news, availability and prices visit
alanrogers.com

Vada

Camping Molino a Fuoco

Via Cavalleggeri 32, I-57018 Vada (Tuscany) T: 0586 770 150. E: info@campingmolinoafuoco.com

alanrogers.com/IT66420

This is a peaceful site with an open feel and just a short stroll (80 m) to the beach through towering pines. The 123 touring pitches are light and airy, with natural shade. Motorcaravans are placed in pairs on very large 170 sq.m. shaded plots. Cars are parked away from the pitches in designated areas. Pleasant permanent pitches do not encroach on the touring units. The bar, restaurant and shop complex are centrally placed and will please anyone who enjoys good food and happy company. This family owned site is part of the 'Tuscan For You' group and the Storace family will make you feel very welcome (they speak excellent English). The site is pristine and everything is spotlessly clean. This is a great site for families that value quality combined with peaceful surroundings.

Facilities

Three very clean toilet blocks provide British style WCs and good hot showers. Excellent facilities for disabled visitors. Baby bath and block for children with pretty showers and toilets. Washing machines. Motorcaravan services. Central area includes bar, excellent restaurant and pizzeria (all with terraces). Swimming pool complex (mid May-end Sept). Outdoor fitness area. Play area. Bicycle hire. Watersports. Fishing. Entertainment programme in season. TV room. Miniclub. Weekend entertainment. Communal barbecue area (only gas allowed on pitches). Torches very useful. Dogs are not accepted 28/6-24/8. Bungalows to rent. Free WiFi. Off site: Bus stop at entrance. Riding 2 km. Train 5 km.

Open: 12 April - 18 October.

Directions

Site is south of Livorno and Vada. From the SS1 take Cecina exit and the site is well signed from here towards Marina di Cecina. GPS: 43.33196, 10.45966

Charges guide

Per unit incl. 2 persons and electricity	€ 18.00 - € 46.00
extra person	€ 5.50 - € 10.00
child (0-10 yrs)	€ 3.50 - € 7.00
dog (not accepted 29/6-25/8)	€ 2.00

Vignale Riotorto

Camping Pappasole

Carbonifera 14, I-57025 Vignale Riotorto (Tuscany) T: 0565 204 20. E: info@pappasole.it

alanrogers.com/IT66400

This lively, well ordered and modern site offers an amazing array of services and activities and is located 380 metres from its own sandy beach facing the island of Elba. It is a large site on flat, fairly open ground offering 477 pitches, of which 427 are for touring units. The majority of these (327 pitches) are 90-100 sq.m. and fully serviced (cars must be parked separately from most pitches). They are separated by neatly clipped bushes with shade from mature trees and artificial shade in other areas. The four excellent swimming pools are a strong feature, complete with cascades and hydro-massage sections, in an open garden setting (the children's pool is huge). The central focus of the site is an attractive covered area (a very tall, open marquee-type structure, floodlit at night) for dancing, music and entertainment. This site is a quality site and excellent for families.

Facilities

Four modern sanitary blocks have free hot water for washbasins and showers and British style WCs. Sanitary facilities for children. Laundry facilities. Motorcaravan services. Gas supplies. Fridge hire. Supermarket. Good deli. Wet fish shop in high season. Hairdresser. Restaurant. Snacks. Bar. Swimming pools (23/05-11/10). Play area. Tennis. Bowls. Football. Watersports. Minigolf. Bicycle hire. Fishing. Medical services. Safety deposit boxes. WiFi on part of site (charged). Off site: Beach 380 m. Beach for visitors with dogs 3 km. Riding 5 km. Excursion programme (26/5-8/9).

Open: 23 April - 17 October.

Directions

Site is north of Follonica. From SS1 motorway take Follonica Nord exit onto SS322 and follow signs toward Piombino, not Follonica. After 1 km. turn east towards Torre Mozza. Site is 1.5 km. down this road to the north. GPS: 42.94893, 10.6863

Charges guide

Per unit incl. 2 persons and electricity	€ 24.00 - € 67.00
extra person	€ 6.00 - € 16.00
child (3-9 yrs)	€ 4.00 - € 10.00
dog	€ 3.00 - € 7.00

For latest campsite news, availability and prices visit

alanrogers.com

UMBRIA HAS TWO PROVINCES: PERUGIA AND TERNI

Known as the 'green heart of Italy', Umbria is a beautiful region of rolling hills, woods, streams and valleys that gives way to high mountain wilderness. It is well known for the beauty and profusion of its medieval hilltowns.

Umbria's main attractions are the Vale of Spoleto and the hill towns of Spoleto and Assisi. The birthplace of Saint Francis, Assisi attracts vast numbers of art lovers and pilgrims throughout the year who visit his burial place, the Basilica di San Francesco, built in 1228, two years after his death. With a scenic woodland setting, Spoleto was once an important Roman colony. The town has the remains of a Roman amphitheatre, reputedly where ten thousand Christian martyrs were slaughtered, and a variety of Romanesque churches. It also boasts an impressive 14th-century aqueduct. Near Perugia, the regional capital, is Lake Trasimeno, the fourth largest lake in Italy. It has plenty of opportunities for fishing, swimming and watersports. The lakeside town of Castiglione del Lago is a good place to relax and unwind on the small sandy beaches; from here, boats make regular trips to the Isola Maggiore, one of the lake's three islands. Further north is Gubbio, the most thoroughly medieval of all the Umbrian towns. A charming place full of twisting streets with soft pink stone houses and terracotta tiled rooftops, its beauty is enhanced by the forest-clad Apennine mountains looming up behind.

Places of interest

Deruta: town renowned for its ceramics.

Monte Cucco Regional Park: offers organised trails and outdoor activities.

Monti Sibillini: national park with good walking trails.

Norcia: mountain town, birthplace of St Benedict.

Orvieto: boasts one of the greatest Gothic churches in Italy.

Spello: renowned for frescoes in the 12/13th-century church of Santa Maria Maggiore, Roman ruins.

Todi: striking hilltown, 13th-century church and palaces.

Cuisine of the region

Simple pastas and roast meats are popular, especially pork and *la porchetta* (whole suckling pig stuffed with rosemary or sage, roasted on a spit). Truffles can be found in abundance, particularly in Noria which also produces some of the country's best hams, sausages and salamis. The rivers yield fish such as eel, pike, trout and crayfish. Locally grown vegetables include lentils, beans, celery and cardoons. Good quality olive oil is readily available. Orvieto is a popular Umbrian white wine.

Agnello alla cacciatora: lamb with a sauce of anchovies, garlic and rosemary.

Crescionda: rich traditional cake prepared with almond biscuits, lemon rind and bitter chocolate.

Fichi: candied figs with almonds and cocoa.

Tartufo nero: black truffles.

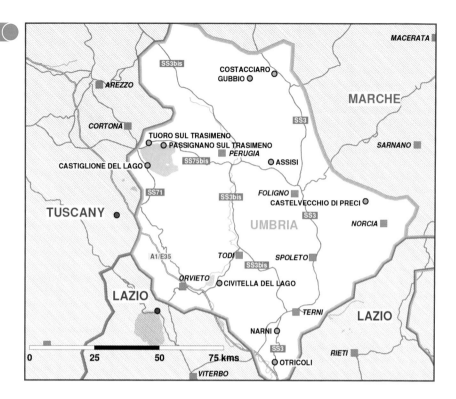

Assisi

Camping Village Assisi

San Giovanni in Campiglione 110, I-06081 Assisi (Umbria) T: 0758 137 10. E: info@campingassisi.it

alanrogers.com/IT66550

Camping Village Assisi is an excellent site situated on the west side of Assisi and provides a good base to visit both Saint Francis' city and nearby Perugia and Lake Trasimeno. The 100 flat pitches, with 6A electricity, vary in size and some are specifically for motorcaravans. It can be very hot in this part of Italy and a welcome relief is the site's pleasant, large pool. The excellent restaurant serves reasonably priced meals, ranging from pizzas to local Umbrian dishes. A large terrace can be completely enclosed. A regular shuttle bus is available to the city which is lit up in the evenings to provide a beautiful backdrop from some areas in the site. Assisi boasts one of the finest cathedrals in Christendom, among many other attractions, and a stay in this area should not be cut too short. The site organises many tours in the area for individuals and groups including artistic, religious, wine, food, archaeological and nature.

Facilities

The neat and clean toilet block is central and provides free hot showers, mainly Turkish style WCs (only four British style in each block) and facilities for disabled visitors. Washing machine. Gas supplies. Motorcaravan services. Campers' kitchen. Restaurant/pizzeria with self-service section. Bar with snacks. Shop. Swimming pool, jacuzzi and circular paddling pool (1/6-5/9, charged, caps mandatory). Bicycle hire. Tennis. Five-a-side. Volleyball. No charcoal barbecues on pitches. Communal barbecue. WiFi throughout (free). Off site: Riding 2 km. Fishing 3 km. Excursions to Assisi centre. Bus service to city four times daily from the site.

Open: 1 April - 31 October.

Directions

From the SS75 take the exit for Ospedalicchio Sud and follow the SS147 towards Assisi for 5 km. The site is well signed on the right. GPS: 43.07510, 12.5744

Charges guide

Per unit incl. 2 persons	
and electricity	€ 26.00 - € 40.00
extra person	€ 8.00 - € 10.00
child (3-9 yrs)	€ 4.00 - € 5.00
dog	free

For latest campsite news, availability and prices visit

alanrogers.com

Castelvecchio di Preci
Camping Il Collaccio
Località Collaccio, I-06047 Castelvecchio di Preci (Umbria) T: 0743 939 005. E: info@ilcollaccio.com
alanrogers.com/IT66560

Castelvecchio di Preci is tucked away in the tranquil heights of the mountainous Umbrian countryside, as is Camping Il Collaccio, which is set on a hillside. The 104 terraced touring pitches, with shade and 6A electricity, have stunning views. The friendly Baldoni family have run the business well for over 30 years. A dip in the pools is wonderfully cooling in summer and an evening meal whilst taking in the views of the lush green vegetation of the surrounding hills, is a must (try the wild boar!). A clean, crisp and tranquil place, with a really pleasant feel – we liked it here!

Facilities

Four modern sanitary blocks spaced through the site have mostly British style WCs, cold water in washbasins and hot, pre-mixed water in showers and sinks. Facilities for disabled visitors. Washing machine. Motorcaravan services. Bar. Happy Pig restaurant and takeaway. Shop (basics, 1/6-20/9). Two swimming pools (20/5-30/9). Play area. Tennis. Boules. Entertainment in high season. Excursions. WiFi over part of site (charged). Bungalows and chalets to rent. Off site: Monti Sibillini National Park is nearby (excursions organised). Walking and cycling opportunities. Fishing and bicycle hire 10 km. Kayaking 20 km. Hang-gliding 25 km.

Open: 1 April - 30 September.

Directions

Approach on A14-E55 down the east coast, then via autoroute approach on SS17 from Civitanova Marche to Polverina, then left on the SS209. Look for Campeggio sign (no site name) 8 km. from Preci. Ensure you leave the site down the hill on the unsigned one way system. GPS: 42.888, 13.01464

Charges guide

Per unit incl. 2 persons	
and electricity	€ 20.50 - € 35.00
extra person	€ 6.00 - € 9.50
child (3-12 yrs)	€ 3.00 - € 6.00

Castiglione del Lago
Camping Listro
Via Lungolago, I-06061 Castiglione del Lago (Umbria) T: 075 951 193. E: listro@listro.it
alanrogers.com/IT66530

This is a simple, pleasant, T-shaped site with the best beach on Lake Trasimeno. Listro has 100 pitches, all with 3A electricity, many of which are on the lakeside giving stunning views out of your windows and shade is available on most. Facilities are fairly limited with a small shop, bar and snack bar, and there is no organised entertainment. English is spoken and British guests are particularly welcome. The campsite's beach is private and the lake has very gradually sloping beaches making it very safe for children to play and swim. A great site for those who enjoy the peace and quiet of simple camping without the comprehensive facilities and busy activities found on many other lakeside sites. This is reflected in the prices which are very reasonable. The lake water is very warm and kept clean as fishing and tourism are the major industries hereabouts. Camping Listro is a few hundred yards north of the historic town of Castiglione which is built into the hillside above the site and has the usual services.

Facilities

Two sanitary blocks are kept clean. One is rustic in style with outside showers. One includes British style WCs. Facilities for disabled visitors. Washing machine. Motorcaravan services. Bar. Shop. Snack bar. Play area. Fishing. Bicycle hire. Private beach. Guided tours. WiFi over part of site (charged). Dogs are not allowed on the beach. Off site: Shops, bars and restaurants nearby. Good swimming pool and tennis courts (discounts using the campsite card). Town 800 m. Excursions.

Open: 1 April - 30 September.

Directions

From A1/E35 Florence-Rome autostrada take Val di Chiana exit and join the Perugia (75 bis) superstrada. After 24 km. take Castiglione exit and follow town signs. Site is clearly signed just before the town. GPS: 43.1341, 12.0448

Charges guide

Per unit incl. 2 persons	
and electricity	€ 17.70 - € 20.20
extra person	€ 4.90 - € 5.90
child	€ 3.90 - € 4.90

Less 10% for stays over 8 days in low season.

CAMPING LISTRO ★★
In a green setting on the shores of Lake Trasimeno • Private beach • Free hot water and electricity • Newly renovated shower and toilet facilities • Shop for essentials • Bar • Play area for children. By the site exit are: Swimming pool, Tennis courts, Athletics track, Football field, Windsurfing, Canoeing, Disco, Restaurant. Only 500 m. from the historic centre of Castiglione del Lago, the site is an ideal base for visits to Rome, Umbria and Tuscany. **GPS: N 43° 8' 5" - E 12° 2' 38"**

I-06061 Castiglione del Lago (PG) · Tel. + Fax 0039/075951193 - www.listro.it

For latest campsite news, availability and prices visit
alanrogers.com

Castiglione del Lago

Camping Badiaccia

Via Pratovecchio 1, I-06061 Castiglione del Lago (Umbria) T: 075 965 9097. E: info@badiaccia.com

alanrogers.com/IT66540

A lakeside site, Camping Badiaccia has excellent views of the surrounding hills and the islands of the lake. Being directly on the lake, with a long sandy beach, gives an almost seaside atmosphere. Unusually, the site uses a birdcage as the post box! The 260 numbered and well tended pitches have electricity (4-12A), vary in size and are shaded and separated by trees and bushes. Badiaccia has a relaxed atmosphere enhanced by a variety of plants and flowers, and English is spoken by the friendly staff. A very pleasant, large pool is by the restaurant and a children's pool is in the beach area.

Facilities	Directions
Three top quality, heated sanitary blocks with sliding doors include hot showers, provision for children and superb units for disabled visitors. Washing machines and dryer. Motorcaravan services. Gas supplies. Restaurant, snack bar and shop. Health and wellness centre. Swimming and paddling pools (15/5-30/9). Play areas. Tennis. Fitness room. Bicycle hire. Boules. Minigolf. Watersports. Fishing. Boat hire. Entertainment and excursions (July/Aug). WiFi (free). Torches handy.	From A1 (Milan-Rome) take Val di Chiana exit and turn east towards Perugia on SS75bis. At Castiglione exit take SS71 towards Castiglione. Site well signed 5 km. north of town. GPS: 43.18103, 12.0163

Open: 1 April - 30 September.

Charges guide

Per unit incl. 2 persons	
and electricity	€ 18.00 - € 27.00
extra person	€ 6.50 - € 8.00
child (2-9 yrs)	€ 4.50 - € 6.00

Civitella del Lago

Camping Il Falcone

Localitá Vallonganino 2/a, I-05023 Civitella del Lago (Umbria) T: 0744 950 249.

E: info@campingilfalcone.com **alanrogers.com/IT66485**

This small and neat, eco-friendly site provides just 36 terraced pitches (half for motorcaravans and caravans) in a steeply sloping olive grove that gives some shade. There are magnificent views across the valley below. The terrace of the small bar is an ideal spot from which to watch the magnificent sunsets over the countryside beyond. A small pool is very welcome when the weather is hot. This is an excellent base from which to explore the Tuscany, Umbria and Lazio regions. The friendly Valeri family will do all they can to make your stay peaceful and enjoyable.

Facilities	Directions
The single, spotless and well maintained sanitary block provides hot water throughout, toilets, washbasins and showers and a separate room with sinks for clothes and dishwashing. Bar with a shop is next to reception. Outdoor swimming pool (1/5-30/9). WiFi (charged). Off site: Fishing 6 km. Orvieto, Civitella del Lago and the Lago di Corbara.	From Orvieto take SR205 then SS448 towards Todi. Just past 4 km. marker on SS448 turn right on S90 up towards the hilltop town of Civitella del Lago. Go past village, 6 km. up the hill, and bear right. Site is 1 km. further on the right. GPS: 42.70762, 12.29127

Open: 1 April - 30 September.

Charges guide

Per unit incl. 2 persons	
and electricity	€ 17.60 - € 27.00
extra person	€ 5.40 - € 8.00

Costacciaro

Camping Rio Verde

SS3 Flaminia km 206.5, I-06021 Costacciaro (Umbria) T: 075 917 0138. E: info@campingrioverde.it

alanrogers.com/IT66470

This is a very peaceful and simple campsite located in a wooded valley with plenty of shade. There are 50 informally arranged pitches with 6A electricity connections. Some pitches are a little uneven and the site slopes in parts. Amenities include a small, fenced swimming pool (with lifeguard) and a restaurant serving simple food from the region. This campsite is ideal for outdoor activity enthusiasts. The area is also excellent for hill walking and mountain biking, with a pleasant excursion possible up Monte Catria where wild horses graze on the lower slopes.

Facilities	Directions
A large, modern toilet block is a short walk. Facilities include British and Turkish style toilets and free showers. Facilities for disabled visitors (key from reception). Small shop. Restaurant. Swimming pool (mid June-Sept, hats compulsory). Play areas. Five-a-side. Riding. Chalets to rent. Communal barbecue. WiFi (free). Off site: Gubbio with old Roman settlement and grottos. Hang-gliding instruction. Trekking in Monte Cucco Natural Park.	From Via Flaminia SS3, follow brown camping signs which can be seen in all surrounding towns. GPS: 43.35076, 12.6845

Open: 1 June - 30 September.

Charges guide

Per unit incl. 2 persons	
and electricity	€ 21.00 - € 25.00
extra person	€ 7.00 - € 9.00
child (3-12 yrs)	€ 4.00 - € 6.00
dog	free

Gubbio
Camping Villa Ortoguidone-Citta di Gubbio
Frazione Cipolleto 49-Ortoguidone, I-06024 Gubbio (Umbria) T: 075 927 2037. E: info@gubbiocamping.com
alanrogers.com/IT66570

This simple site, owned by the same family for 135 years, is situated just 3 km. from the walls of the fabulous old city of Gubbio. It has been constructed on an old farm and the villa is now used for guest accommodation. There are 14 excellent large pitches in the grounds of the villa (book ahead for these) and 100 serviced pitches in a flat area where young trees are beginning to provide some shade. There is a pleasant and peaceful feel here and would suit those who prefer a simple, uncomplicated site with few amenities and nothing in the way of on-site entertainment.

Facilities

Two unusual, prefabricated units provide few British style toilets and dated showers in cubicles. Facilities for disabled campers. Solar heating for water used in some parts (free), gas heated water (charged). Facilities would be stretched during busy periods. Washing machines. Fridge, freezer and good kitchen. Motorcaravan services. Snack bar/bar (plans for a restaurant). Swimming pools (also open to public), paddling pool and spa (July/Aug). Fitness area by the pool. Basic play area. Tennis. Free Internet access. Off site: Restaurants and shops 3 km.

Open: 23 April - 16 September.

Directions

From A1 take Orte exit and the E45 towards Perugia-Cesena, then Bosco Gubbio exit. Take SS298 to Gubbio and look for camping signs at 15 km. marker. GPS: 43.3217, 12.5683

Charges guide

Per unit incl. 2 persons	
and electricity	€ 22.00 - € 29.50
extra person	€ 8.00 - € 9.50
child (2-8 yrs)	€ 5.00 - € 6.50
No credit cards.	

Narni
Camping Monti del Sole
Strada di Borgaria 22, Borgaria, I-05035 Narni (Umbria) T: 0744 796 336. E: info@campingmontidelsole.it
alanrogers.com/IT66480

Monti del Sole is a very friendly site situated in woodland, just 5 km. from the medieval town of Narni. Alfredo Petrini and his delightful daughter, Angela-Rose, will give you a very warm welcome. There are 85 pitches of various sizes, all with 6A electricity and most well shaded and grassy. A small shop sells basics and a bar/restaurant offers pleasant local cuisine. The swimming pools are attractive. Prices here are reasonable but the facilities are fairly limited. This is a quiet, unsophisticated site that will suit those looking for peaceful surroundings.

Facilities

The traditional sanitary block has a mixture of British and Turkish style toilets and hot showers. Motorcaravan services. Good, small bar/restaurant (1/6-30/8). Swimming pool and adjacent paddling pool (1/6-30/8). Play area. Tennis court. Games field. Woodland walks. WiFi (free). Off site: Riding 1 km. Fishing 4 km. Narni 5 km. Marmore falls and Piediluco lake both 20 km.

Open: 1 April - 30 September.

Directions

From A1 (Rome-Florence-Milan) autostrada take Malian Sabina exit. Follow signs to Narni. Site is on Borgaria road, 800 m. off the SS3, and is well signed. GPS: 42.48306, 12.50389

Charges guide

Per unit incl. 2 persons	
and electricity	€ 20.00 - € 31.00
extra person	€ 7.00 - € 10.00

Otricoli
Capitello Camping
Via Flaminia km 68, I-05030 Otricoli (Umbria) T: 040 979 0652. E: infocapitello@gmail.com
alanrogers.com/IT66482

Capitello Camping is an attractive and peaceful family site set near the curving River Tiber. It is efficiently run by the dynamic young owner, Alberto. The 35 slightly sloping pitches (80-120 sq.m) have electricity (5A), water and shade and enjoy great views of the medieval hilltop town of Otricoli. The swimming pool complex is a superb place for all the family with a variety of swimming and paddling pools, large soft slides and an area for relaxation. A fascinating archaeological site is next to the campsite; the ruins of what was once a Roman city. The site is well placed for exploring the surrounding Umbrian countryside and is only an hour's drive from the centre of Rome.

Facilities

Single sanitary block with provision for disabled visitors and babies. Laundry. Bar, restaurant, snack bar, pizzeria and takeaway (all from 1/6). Fresh bread. Swimming pool complex (lifeguard 1/6-15/9). Playground. Sports field. Games room. Table tennis. Beach volleyball. Canoes and kayaks to rent. Organised excursions (1/6-30/8). WiFi zone (free). Off site: Mountain bike trails from site.

Open: 12 March - 27 September.

Directions

From Rome going north take A1/E35/E45 taking Magliano Sabina exit to SS3. Continue to Otricoli and follow signs to site. GPS: 42.40901, 12.46223

Charges guide

Per unit incl. 2 persons	
and electricity	€ 24.00 - € 32.00
extra person	€ 8.00 - € 10.00
child (3-11 yrs)	€ 6.00 - € 7.00

For latest campsite news, availability and prices visit
alanrogers.com

Passignano sul Trasimeno

Camping la Spiaggia

Via Europa 22, I-06065 Passignano sul Trasimeno (Umbria) T: 075 827 246. E: info@campinglaspiaggia.it

alanrogers.com/IT66460

La Spiaggia has its own beach and is pleasantly covered with pine and oak trees providing shade to most pitches. The 50 touring pitches (60-100 sq.m) with 6/10A electricity are clearly defined and some are separated by dwarf hedges. This is an attractive, compact site which is well managed and cared for with attractive pools and a small café/restaurant with terrace overlooking the lake. A small shop provides fresh bread to order. All sorts of activities are possible on the lake including canoeing, sailing and windsurfing and there are numerous opportunities for hiking and mountain biking in the surrounding hills.

Facilities

The toilet block is very clean and modern with free hot water. It includes facilities for disabled visitors and a baby room. Separate laundry room. Small shop for basics, bar/restaurant with terrace (April-October). Takeaway (April-Sept). Lake swimming. Heated swimming pool and paddling pool. Lake swimming. Play area. Bicycle and canoe hire. WiFi throughout (free). Beach for dogs.

Open: 1 April - 1 November.

Directions

From A1 (Firenze-Roma) take Bettolle exit towards Perugia (S326). Follow to Passignano exit (30 km. from A1). Take the exit and go towards town (site signed). GPS: 43.1837, 12.1492

Charges guide

Per unit incl. 2 persons	
and electricity	€ 23.00 - € 29.00
extra person	€ 6.50 - € 8.50
child (3-9 yrs)	€ 5.00 - € 7.00

Passignano sul Trasimeno

Camping Kursaal Hotel

Via Europa 24, I-06065 Passignano sul Trasimeno (Umbria) T: 0758 280 85. E: info@campingkursaal.it

alanrogers.com/IT66500

Opened in 1965, Camping Kursaal is the oldest campsite at Lago Trasimeno and sets a very high standard. Located directly beside the lake, it is a small site with 70 touring pitches. Attractively laid out under tall pines, all pitches have 4/6A electricity and shade from trees and large flowering shrubs. Superb views are enjoyed by the pitches on the lakeside itself whilst others have more limited lake views. The site is in the grounds of an attractive old villa, which is now a good quality hotel. Camping visitors can use the hotel amenities including the bar, lounge and the excellent restaurant. We loved it here.

Facilities

Two spotless toilet blocks have showers and toilets in separate areas and are very well maintained. One is built around an old pine tree to prevent it from being felled. Baby room and facilities for disabled visitors. Motorcaravan services. Shop. Bar. Excellent restaurant. Swimming pool with slide. Paddling pools. Spa. Hydro-massage. Private beach and pier. Play area. WiFi over site (charged). Off site: Passignano 1 km. Riding 3 km. Golf 20 km. Excursions and boat trips.

Open: 1 April - 2 November.

Directions

On the A1 (Firenze-Rome) take exit at Valdichiana-Bettolle. Follow until Passignano Est exit (30 km. from the A1 exit) and turn right and site is 200 m. on the left. GPS: 43.18354, 12.15063

Charges guide

Per unit incl. 2 persons	
and electricity	€ 25.00 - € 33.50
extra person	€ 6.50 - € 9.00
child (3-9 yrs)	€ 5.50 - € 6.50

Tuoro sul Trasimeno

Camping Village Punta Navaccia

Via Navaccia 4, I-06069 Tuoro sul Trasimeno (Umbria) T: 0758 263 57. E: info@puntanavaccia.it

alanrogers.com/IT66490

Situated on the north side of Lake Trasimeno, close to two of the lake's islands, Punta Navaccia is run by the three ebullient Migliorati sisters. It is a large site with 400 flat, shaded touring pitches (with 6A electricity), mostly near the lakeside. The site is adjacent to a soft sand beach and has a dock with facilities for mooring and launching your boat. The hub of the site is bustling with a full animation programme for children and adults. A huge amphitheatre stages entertainment, and is located close to all the other services. This is a great and very Italian site, where families will have fun at reasonable prices.

Facilities

Three sanitary blocks with varied facilities are in the areas for seasonal campers. Sanitary facilities for children. Washing machine and dryer. Motorcaravan services. Heated swimming and paddling pools (1/5-30/9). Shop, bar, restaurant and takeaway (1/4-30/9). Play area. Tennis. Huge covered amphitheatre. Cinema screen. Miniclub. Entertainment in high season. Boat launching. Fitness room. Fishing. Bicycle hire. WiFi (charged).

Open: 15 March - 31 October.

Directions

Going south on the A1 (Florence/Firenze-Rome), take exit for Val di Chiana to Perugia near Bettolle. After 15 km. take Tuoro sul Trasimeno exit. Site is well signed. GPS: 43.19191, 12.07665

Charges guide

Per unit incl. 2 persons	
and electricity	€ 21.50 - € 27.00
extra person	€ 6.50 - € 8.50
child (2-9 yrs)	€ 4.50 - € 6.50

THERE ARE FOUR PROVINCES IN MARCHE: ANCONA, ASCOLI PICENO, MACERATA AND PESARO E URBINO

Lying between the Adriatic Sea and the Apennine mountains, Marche boasts a pretty mixture of woods and remote hills, medieval towns and seaside resorts, sandy beaches and sleepy coves, plus the snow-capped peaks of the Monti Sibillini.

Marche is not as well known or publicised as other regions, but despite that it has plenty to offer. The medieval town of Urbino with its spectacular Renaissance palace is one of the highlights, as is Ascoli Piceno, which also boasts a medieval heritage, various churches and an enchanting town square. The dramatic fortress at San Leo is considered to be one of the best, while nearby San Marino is Europe's oldest republic. A tiny area with no customs regulations, its borders are just seven miles apart at its widest point. The republic has its own mint and army and produces its own postage stamps. South of Ancona, the regional capital, and overlooked by the dramatic white cliffs of Monte Cónero, is the Cónero Riviera, an impressive stretch of coast with small beaches, coves and picturesque little resorts, including Portonovo, Sirolo and Numana. Along the coast is Loreto, one of Italy's most popular pilgrimage destinations, and more beaches can be found at San Benedetto del Tronto. Further inland, near the Verdicchio wine-producing hilltop villages around Jesi, is the Grotte di Frasassi, one of Europe's largest accessible cave networks. And the mountainous region of Monti Sibillini in the south offers good walking trails and stunning views.

Places of interest

Ancona: regional capital and Adriatic's largest port.

Fano: beach resort with old centre and historic monuments.

Jesi: medieval town walls, Renaissance and Baroque palaces.

Macerata: university town surrounded by lovely countryside, famous for its annual outdoor opera and ballet festival.

Numana: seaside resort on Cónero peninsula, boat trips to the offshore islets of Due Sorelle.

Sarnano: spa town.

Urbania: palace with art gallery and museum.

Ussita: winter sports resort.

Cuisine of the region

The food is a mix of seafood along the coastline and country cooking inland, involving locally grown produce – tomatoes, fennel and mushrooms. Typical seafood dishes include *zuppa di pesce* (fish soup with saffron) and *brodetto* (fish broths). Rabbit and lamb are popular plus *porchetta* (roast suckling pig). The region is best known for its Verdicchio wine although it does produce a variety of others.

Coniglio in porchetta: rabbit cooked with fennel.

Cicercchiata: balls of pasta fried and covered in honey.

Olive ascolane: olives stuffed with meat and herbs, served with *crema fritta,* little squares of fried cream.

Vincisgrassi: baked pasta dish with ham and truffles.

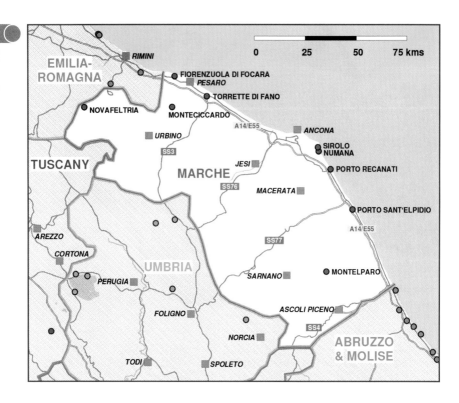

0   25   50   75 kms

RIMINI

EMILIA-
ROMAGNA

FIORENZUOLA DI FOCARA
PESARO

TORRETTE DI FANO

NOVAFELTRIA

MONTECICCARDO

A14/E55

ANCONA

URBINO

SS3

SIROLO
NUMANA

TUSCANY

JESI

MARCHE

PORTO RECANATI

SS76

MACERATA

PORTO SANT'ELPIDIO

A14/E55

AREZZO

SS77

CORTONA

UMBRIA

SARNANO

MONTELPARO

PERUGIA

FOLIGNO

ASCOLI PICENO

SS4

NORCIA

ABRUZZO
& MOLISE

TODI

SPOLETO

Fiorenzuola di Focara

Camping Panorama

Strand Panoramica, Pesaro, I-61121 Fiorenzuola di Focara (Marche) T: 0721 208 145.

E: info@campingpanorama.it **alanrogers.com/IT65070**

Camping Panorama is a peaceful site located on a scenic coastal drive within a small national park (Parco del San Bartolo) and quite close to the delightful town of Pesaro. The site lies 100 metres above the sea and a pleasant path nearby leads to the beach below. There are 120 touring pitches ranging in size from 50-100 sq.m, all have 6A electrical connections and are well shaded. Leisure amenities include a magnificent swimming pool (with smaller children's pool) and a sports court. This is a largely undeveloped area and has many opportunities for walking and mountain biking. Famous local residents include Silvio Berlusconi and formerly Luciano Pavarotti. Pesaro, to the south was formerly the home of Rossini and has a small museum dedicated to him. Other day trips include Urbino and San Marino.

Facilities

Four toilet blocks. Washing machines. Motorcaravan services. Swimming and paddling pools. Bar, pizzeria and shop (all season). TV room. Games room. Play area. Sports court. No gas or electric barbecues. WiFi over part of site. Off site: Nearest village is Fiorenzuola di Focara, perched over the sea with bars, shops and restaurants 2 km. Fishing 3 km. Bicycle hire 6 km. Pesaro 6 km. Golf 8 km. Riding 10 km. Urbino 35 km. San Marino 42 km. Mountain biking and walking.

Open: 15 April - 30 September.

Directions

From A14 (Bologna-Taranto) take Cattolica exit and join SS16 southbound towards Siligata. Here join coast road (Strad Panoramico) towards Fiorenzuola. Site is beyond this town and Fiorenzuola di Focara but before Pesaro. Coming from Pesaro, pass 2 green signs and turn right at next brown sign. GPS: 43.941683, 12.84585

Charges guide

Per unit incl. 2 persons	
and electricity	€ 24.00 - € 37.00
extra person	€ 7.00 - € 10.00
child (under 6 yrs)	€ 4.00 - € 6.00
dog	€ 3.40

No credit cards.

Monteciccardo
Camping Podere Sei Poorte

Via Petricci 14, I-61020 Monteciccardo (Marche) T: 072 191 0286. E: info@podereseipoorte.it
alanrogers.com/IT65080

Podere Sei Poorte is owned and run by Hans and Sietske Poorte, who in just a few years have transformed a derelict farm into a stress-free haven of rustic charm and tranquillity. On arrival you will be welcomed with a smile and a drink. The restaurant offers good, Italian-style food in a convivial setting. The site is laid out on two terraces so everyone has good views. The 130 spacious, grassy pitches (100 for touring units with 6A electricity) are almost flat, and some have shade.

Facilities

One main toilet block near reception, and nine smaller ones around the site, are modern and tiled with free hot water. Facilities for disabled visitors. Motorcaravan services. Shop. Bar and restaurant. Swimming pool with stunning views (8x16 m; all season). Play area. WiFi on part of site (free). Off site: Golf, bicycle hire and sailing 25 km. Beach 25 mins. by car. Medieval town of Fano.

Open: 29 April - 1 October.

Directions

From St Angelo in Lizzola (inland from Pesaro and A14) follow SP26 to Mombaroccio. At Villa Ugolini look for P-6-P campsite sign and turn into Via Petricci and site is 1.4 km. on the right. GPS: 43.8009, 12.82113

Charges guide

Per unit incl. 2 persons and electricity	€ 25.00 - € 40.00
extra person	€ 6.00 - € 10.00

Montelparo
Agricamp Picobello

Ctra Cortaglie 24, I-63853 Montelparo (Marche) T: 073 478 9012. E: info@agricamppicobello.com
alanrogers.com/IT65260

Situated only 28 km. inland from the Adriatic coast at Pedaso, this very small site caters for campers who like to go back to basics. Catering only for tents, the site offers up to 15 pitches, some with shade. There is a hammock house in the central area where campers can rig their hammocks in a shady and peaceful spot. Rob and his partner, Erna, are keen outdoor people and are very enthusiastic about keeping the spirit of true camping aflame. Rob will be your guide for hiking tours to the Sibillini mountains and also organises rock climbing. A relaxing campsite for the purist camper away from the hectic atmosphere of some of the coastal sites.

Facilities

The central toilet block is well maintained and very clean. Facilities for disabled visitors. Small bar. Small kitchen and social area for preparing light meals with fridge and freezer space. Bicycle hire. Undercover playroom and a new climbing wall. WiFi over site (free). No electric barbecues. Dogs are not accepted. Off site: Lively little village with shops, bars, café, supermarket 3.5 km.

Open: 1 April - 15 October.

Directions

From Pedaso on SS16 turn south west onto SP238 towards Comunanza. Just after Oretezzano, turn right following brown signs (PicoBello, not Agriturismo). GPS: 43.02703, 13.55552

Charges guide

Per person	€ 8.50 - € 9.50
pitch	€ 9.00 - € 10.00
Electricity by arrangement (3A).	

Novafeltria
Camping Perticara

Via Serra Masini 10/d, Perticara, I-47863 Novafeltria (Marche) T: 0541 927 602.
E: info@campingperticara.com **alanrogers.com/IT66170**

High in the Marche hills, not far from San Marino, Ravenna and Rimini, is Camping Perticara, a purpose built camping site with glorious views across a valley to the mountains and the nearby traditional village of Perticara. Each of its 80 generous pitches have water and drainage, all arranged on terraces to take advantage of the fabulous scenery. Good sized trees have been planted to provide shade in the future. The shop, bar and restaurant are attractively presented, with a terrace overlooking the swimming pool which shares the incredible vistas.

Facilities

Two immaculate modern units provide really excellent facilities with all the extras. Facilities are all in large luxury cabins with shower, toilet and basin. Washing machine and dryers. Gas. Small shop. Restaurant (limited menu but good value). Snack bar. Swimming and paddling pools. Play areas and field for games. Entertainment (miniclub) in high season. Suggested walking/hiking trails are free from reception. Dogs are not accepted. WiFi throughout (charged). Off site: Fishing 10 km. Golf 25 km.

Open: 15 May - 20 September.

Directions

After Bologna on A1 take A14 (Ancona) and exit for Rimini Nord. After 200 m. turn right (San Leo), over several roundabouts. At traffic lights turn right to Novafeltria (32 km). At Novafeltria, turn right towards Perticara. Climb for 7 km. and at top turn left for Santa Agata Feltria. After 400 m. turn right to site and descend with care. GPS: 43.89609, 12.24293

Charges guide

Per unit incl. 2 persons and electricity	€ 24.00 - € 38.00
extra person	€ 5.50 - € 10.00

For latest campsite news, availability and prices visit
alanrogers.com

Numana

Numana Blu Camping Village

Via Costaverde 37, I-60026 Numana (Marche) T: 0717 390 993. E: info@numanablu.it

alanrogers.com/IT66190

Numana Blu lies on the Cónero Riviera, south of Ancona, just 300 metres from the sea, and close to the town of Marcelli. Beneath the site's 12,000 trees there are 330 shady pitches, most offering electrical connections. Separate areas have a range of rentable accommodation, including chalets and bungalows. There is plenty to do here but the site retains a relaxed atmosphere. In peak season there are several children's clubs catering for different ages. The site also boasts an impressive array of leisure amenities including an excellent swimming pool, a restaurant/pizzeria and a small supermarket.

Facilities

Supermarket, bar, restaurant/pizzeria and takeaway meals (all 28/5-10/9). Swimming pool with a children's section (28/5-10/9). Playground. Bicycle hire. Basketball/volleyball court. Football pitch. Two tennis courts. Games rooms. Children's clubs. Entertainment programme in high season. WiFi over site (charged). Off site: Beach 300 m. Riding 1 km. Golf 6 km. Cónero Riviera, Monte Cónero (at 572 m. the highest peak in the area) and Ancona. Cycling and walking trails.

Open: 24 April - 30 September.

Directions

Take the Loreto Porto Recanati exit from the A14 autostrada and follow signs to Numana. Site is south of Numana, 1.5 km. from the small town of Marcelli. GPS: 43.47641, 13.63381

Charges guide

Per unit incl. 2 persons and electricity	€ 26.10 - € 56.10
extra person	€ 5.40 - € 12.90
child (under 6 yrs)	€ 3.30 - € 8.20

Porto Recanati

Camping Bellamare

Lungomare Scarfiotti 13, I-62017 Porto Recanati (Marche) T: 071 976 628. E: info@bellamare.it

alanrogers.com/IT65180

Situated on the Cónero Riviera, just south of the River Musone, this site is ideal for campers who enjoy a well ordered and efficiently run site. The grounds are maintained to a meticulous standard. Unlike most sites along the Lungomare Adriatico, it does not suffer from either train or motorway noise. There are 355 flat, grassy pitches which are separated by maturing trees offering some shade. Touring pitches are of average size, centrally located and easily accessed. Most beach holiday activities are provided on site or within easy walking distance.

Facilities

Large, very clean central toilet block with two smaller blocks having mainly Turkish style toilets. Free cold showers, hot showers need electronic key supplied on registration. Shop, bar, restaurant, takeaway. Swimming and paddling pools (1/6-1/9). TV/games room. Play areas. Football. Bicycle hire. Organised family activities (high season). WiFi over site (charged). Dogs are not accepted.

Open: 24 April - 30 September.

Directions

From A14 take Porto Recanati exit. Follow beach road (Recanati-P Recanati) towards Numana. Site is signed in both directions. GPS: 43.47095, 13.6412

Charges guide

Per unit incl. 2 persons and electricity	€ 19.00 - € 48.60
extra person	€ 4.50 - € 14.30
child (under 4 yrs)	free

Porto Sant'Elpidio

Villaggio Turistico Le Mimose

Via Faleria 15, I-63821 Porto Sant'Elpidio (Marche) T: 073 490 0604. E: info@villaggiolemimose.it

alanrogers.com/IT65200

Le Mimose is a quiet site away from the town centre, bordering the extensive and well kept shingle beach. There are 65 grassy or sandy pitches, all for touring, with electricity (6A). The touring pitches, scattered among the holiday apartments, are surrounded by hedges and mature trees giving good shade. Space may be a little tight in high season. The short walk to the beach is very pleasant – as is a stroll along the promenade. The site, with its bar and restaurant, are now open all year.

Facilities

Two central toilet blocks with all necessary facilities, including those for campers with disabilities. Shop (1/6-30/9). Bar and restaurant. Takeaway (1/1-30/9). Swimming and paddling pools (1/6-12/9). Wellness centre. Two children's playgrounds. Sports facilities. Bicycle hire. Beach adjacent. ATM in reception. WiFi over site. Off site: Tennis adjacent. Boat launching 1 km. Fishing 3 km. Golf 10 km. Riding 15 km.

Open: All year.

Directions

From SS16 Adriatico in Porto Sant'Elpidio follow well marked signs to site. Access through town difficult for large outfits (4 m. high and 3 m. wide restrictions) and care is needed passing through the gate. GPS: 43.23768, 13.77365

Charges guide

Per person	€ 4.50 - € 9.00
child (2-6 yrs)	€ 2.00 - € 5.00
pitch	€ 7.00 - € 22.00
electricity	€ 3.00

Sirolo
Camping & Club Internazionale

Via San Michele 10, I-60020 Sirolo (Marche) T: 0719 330 884. E: info@campinginternazionale.com

alanrogers.com/IT65150

This is a high quality site with a particularly attractive, cliffside location within the Parco del Cónero. The 230 pitches (110 for touring units, most with 10A electricity) are on terraces shelving down towards two bays. Most pitches have fine sea views and all have shade. The terrain and access are steep, and the pitches small (25-50 sq.m), so large caravans and motorcaravans may find this site unsuitable. It may also prove challenging for those who find hills a problem. However, the site is efficiently run and well maintained with a good range of leisure amenities. The restaurant and bar are very popular, thanks no doubt to their magnificent views and good local cuisine. The adjacent beaches (down steep pathways) are attractive and understandably popular.

Facilities

Two large toilet blocks cater well for this busy site, with adequate hot water to sinks and showers. Facilities for disabled visitors. Small shop with delicatessen. Bar and restaurant/pizzeria, takeaway (all season). Outdoor swimming pool (25/5-10/9). Play area. Children's club (high season). Entertainment programme in high season. WiFi over part of site (charged). Chalets and mobile homes for rent. Dogs are not accepted. Off site: Beach adjacent. Cónero Riviera. Ancona. Urbino. Riding. Cycle and walking trails. Golf.

Open: 10 May - 23 September.

Directions

From the A14 autostrada take Loreto Porto Recanati exit and follow signs to Numana and Sirolo. Follow brown signs, taking care in Sirolo itself where manoeuvring can be tight.
GPS: 43.523706, 13.620472

Charges guide

Per unit incl. 2 persons and electricity	€ 23.00 - € 60.00
extra person	€ 5.00 - € 12.00
child (1-6 yrs)	free - € 7.00

Torrette di Fano
Camping Stella Maris

Via A Cappellini 5, I-61032 Torrette di Fano (Marche) T: 0721 884 231. E: stellamaris@camping.it

alanrogers.com/IT66180

This clean, modern Adriatic coast site is, without doubt, the best in the area. The owner, Francesco Mantoni, is friendly, enthusiastic and proud of his site. There are 161 pitches, 100 for tourers, all with electricity (6A), water and drainage. In an informal setting, touring pitches, permanent sites and cabins are blended together with pleasing results. For swimming and relaxing there is the choice of a clean, long, soft sand beach or an excellent pool complex with loungers, umbrellas, jacuzzi and paddling pool. Alongside the pool is a most attractive restaurant with table service, a varied menu and good selection of wine. English is spoken and the site has a crisp, efficient feel about it. A site for holidays and touring, where a high standard of service is provided in all areas.

Facilities

Clean, modern sanitary blocks are nicely decorated with separate male and female areas and include hairdryers. Facilities for babies and disabled campers. Laundry facilities. Motorcaravan services. Well stocked shop. Restaurant/bar. Snacks. Large swimming pool. Games room. TV room. Hard court with arena style seating used for organised games. Children's activities day and evening in season. Entertainment. Beach. Free WiFi over site. Dogs or other animals are not accepted.

Open: 21 April - 30 September.

Directions

Site is between Fano and Falconara. From autostrada take Pesaro exit and follow signs on the SS16 for Ancona, site is 3 km. past Fano on the inner coast road. Well signed.
GPS: 43.79826, 13.09547

Charges guide

Per person	€ 7.00 - € 11.30
child (2-6 yrs)	€ 4.00 - € 7.50
pitch incl. electricity	€ 12.50 - € 19.00

For latest campsite news, availability and prices visit

alanrogers.com

**LAZIO HAS FIVE PROVINCES: FROSINONE,
LATINA, RIETI, ROMA AND VITERBO**

Lazio lies between the Apennines and the
Tyrrhenian Sea, with the Pontine marshes
in the south and wooded hills in the north.
Home to the historic city of Rome it also has
numerous lakes and coastal resorts which
provide the perfect antidote to the heat of the
city and its crowds.

Rome, the capital city of Italy, is crammed full of
history, boasting a dazzling array of architectural
and artistic masterpieces of the ancient world.
Within Rome lies the Vatican City, the world
capital of Catholicism, ruled by the Pope,
Europe's only absolute monarch. It's also the
world's smallest state, occupying 43 hectares
within high walls watched over by guards. More
historical sites can be found just outside Rome,
including the ruins of Villa Adriana, just outside
the hilltown of Tivoli. Once a favoured resort of
the ancient Romans, the town is also home to
the 16th-century Villa d'Este, renowned for its
beautiful gardens. Nearby Ostia Antica boasts
one of the finest Roman sites. For 600 years it
was the busy, main port of Rome, and the site is
well preserved. Viterbo, in the north, is a medieval
town with grand palaces and churches enclosed
by preserved medieval walls. For recreation, there
are numerous lakes including Lakes Bolsena,
Bracciano, Vico and Albano. These lakes were
created by volcanic activity which also left Lazio
with hot springs, most notably those around Tivoli
and Fiuggi. Popular coastal resorts include
Sperlonga, Anzio and Nettuno, with some of the
best beaches lying between Gaeta and Sabaudia.

Places of interest

Anguillara: pretty medieval lake town on
the shore of Lake Bracciano.

Bolsena: lakeside beach resort on Lake
Bolsena with medieval castle.

Caprarola: medieval village 4 km. from
Lake Vico, with grandiose Renaissance villa.

Fiuggi: spa town.

Rome: Colosseum, Forum, Palatine Hill,
Pantheon, Trevi Fountain, the list is endless.

Sermoneta: pretty hilltown overlooking the
Pontine Plains, with medieval houses,
palaces and churches.

Tarquinia: archaeology museum, frescoed
tombs of the necropolis.

Vatican City: St Peter's church, Sistine
Chapel with famous painted ceiling by
Michelangelo, museums.

Cuisine of the region

Pasta is eaten with a variety of sauces
including *aglio e olio* (garlic and oil), *cacio
e pepe* (percorino cheese and black pepper)
and *alle vongole* (with baby clams). The well
known dish *spaghetti alla carbonara* was
first devised in Rome. Fish and offal are
popular. Mushrooms and, in particular,
artichokes (*carciofi*) are used in a variety of
dishes, and rosemary, sage and garlic are
used frequently for seasoning. Local wines
include Frascati and Torre Ercolana, one of
the few red wines produced in Lazio. Fresh
drinking water is freely available in the
numerous fountains scattered around
Rome.

Risotto alla Romana: rice with sauce of liver,
sweetbreads and Marsala.

Saltimbocca: veal with ham and sage.

Torta di Ricotta: cheesecake made with
ricotta, Marsala and lemon.

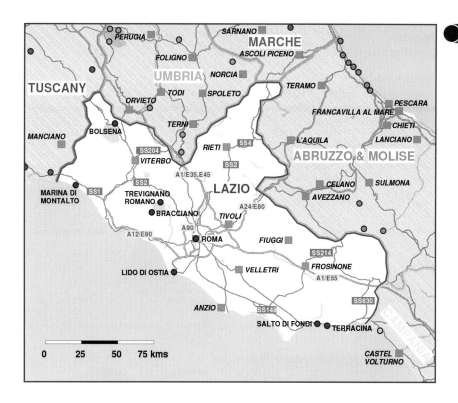

Bolsena

Lido Camping Village

Via Cassia km 111, I-01023 Bolsena (Lazio) T: 076 179 9258. E: info@lidocampingvillage.it

alanrogers.com/IT67680

Lido Camping Village is located on the edge of Lake Bolsena, 1.5 km. south of the fascinating town of Bolsena. This landscaped site has a fine pool (with a high additional charge). There are 600 flat, sandy pitches of an average size with 3A electricity. Some have shade. Sadly all the lakeside pitches are occupied by seasonal or tour operator units. An attractive, modern restaurant, bar, pizzeria and terrace are located on the edge of the lake and have wonderful views over the black sand. Some entertainment is provided. There are a disco, entertainment area and cinema on the site and the site's sporting facilities are of a high standard. Watch for the extra charges here!

Facilities

Modern facilities include showers (charged). Expect all facilities to be under pressure in high season. Supermarket, bar, restaurant and pizzeria (all open all season). Swimming pools (mid June-Aug; high extra charges). Dance area, cinema and music area. Tennis. Windsurfing and water skiing. Lake swimming and boat launching. Playground (but dated equipment needs strict supervision). Limited entertainment in high season. WiFi over site (charged). Dogs are not accepted. Off site: Bolsena 1.5 km. Excursions. Watersports.

Open: 25 April - 30 September.

Directions

Site is by Lake Bolsena south of the town of Bolsena off the S2 (Via Cassia). It is well signed. GPS: 42.62716, 11.99524

Charges guide

Per unit incl. 2 persons	
and electricity	€ 23.00 - € 31.00
extra person	€ 7.00 - € 9.00
child (3-10 yrs)	€ 3.00 - € 5.50

For latest campsite news, availability and prices visit

alanrogers.com

Bolsena

Camping Internazionale Il Lago

Viale Cadorna 6, I-01023 Bolsena (Lazio) T: 076 179 9191. E: anna.bruti@libero.it

alanrogers.com/IT67700

Camping Internazionale Il Lago is enchanting. A tiny and simple, rustic site with only 34 pitches, it is in a peaceful garden setting on the lake shores of Bolsena, only 500 metres from the centre of the town. The flat and grassy pitches, all for touring units, are spread around the lake. Electricity (4A) is available and there is shade from many trees, good hedging and two gravel roads. The same family has owned the campsite for over 50 years and some English is spoken. A small bar and café offers snacks, with four restaurants within 100 metres of the campsite and more in the town. If you enjoy small, uncomplicated and very friendly sites, this is perfect. The history of the area is teamed with the local wine areas in an unpolluted lake setting. Lake Bolsena is the fifth largest lake in Italy and the greatest volcanic lake in Europe. We saw this small site in low season and thought it was perfect at that time for exploring from a quiet but central lakeside position.

Facilities	Directions
The single well cared for sanitary block is clean and has mixed style toilets and good showers. Facilities for disabled visitors. Drinks and snack bar. Fishing. Lake swimming. Boat launching. WiFi over part of site (very small charge). Off site: Restaurants nearby. Bicycle hire 500 m. Riding 3 km. Sailing.	Site is beside Lake Bolsena in the south east area of the town of Bolsena. In town, follow lake and camping signs and site is easy to locate. GPS: 42.63833, 11.98472

Open: 15 April - 30 September.

Charges guide

Per unit incl. 2 persons	
and electricity	€ 19.00 - € 29.00
extra person	€ 5.00 - € 7.00
child (3-6 yrs)	€ 3.50 - € 4.50

No credit cards.

Bracciano

Camping Roma Flash

Via Settevene Palo km 19,800, I-00062 Bracciano (Lazio) T: 0699 805 458. E: info@romaflash.it

alanrogers.com/IT68120

This pleasant site is in a superb location with magnificent views over Lake Bracciano and Castello Odescalchi. Although it was busy when we visited, it was still peaceful and relaxing. There are 175 flat, shaded pitches with 6A electricity (Europlug). A pleasant, covered restaurant offers pizza and a limited menu. Set alongside the lake with its fabulous views, the restaurant complex has a large terrace, as does a smaller indoor area. Elide speaks excellent English and will happily go out of her way to ensure guests enjoy their holiday. Many of the visitors told us that they return year after year and some stay for eight to twelve weeks at a time, enjoying all that the Lazio region has to offer. A campsite booklet full of very useful information is provided, plus a suggested itinerary for visiting Rome, including places to eat. The ancient Etruscan ruins are fairly close by if you wish to visit something even older than Rome itself.

Facilities	Directions
Two large, but tired sanitary blocks (scheduled for refurbishment) have free hot water throughout and fully adjustable showers. Facilities for disabled visitors in one block. Rooms for children. Laundry facilities. Gas supplies. Bar/restaurant/pizzeria, small shop (all open as site). Swimming pool (1/6-31/8). Play area. Watersports. Games room. Entertainment for children in high season. WiFi (charged). Excursions. Private bus to Roma San Pietro and return. Sports area. Off site: Riding 6 km. Golf 22 km. Beach 23 km. Rome (40 minutes).	From A1/E45 north of Roma take exit for Orte and Viterbo (SS675), Vetralla, Sutri (SS2), Trevignano Romano (SP12d) and then towards Bracciano (SP4a). Site is well signed off the lakeside road. GPS: 42.130113, 12.173527

Open: 1 April - 30 September.

Charges guide

Per unit incl. 2 persons	
and electricity	€ 19.00 - € 37.00
extra person	€ 7.00 - € 9.50
child (3-10 yrs)	€ 4.00 - € 6.50
dog	€ 3.50 - € 5.50

Bracciano
Camping Porticciolo

Via Porticciolo, I-00062 Bracciano (Lazio) T: 0699 803 060. E: info@porticciolo.it

alanrogers.com/IT68130

This is a small, family run site. Useful for visiting Rome, it has its own private beach on the lake and is overlooked by the impressive Bracciano Castle. The 170 pitches, some with lake views and 120 having electricity (4-6A), are level, peaceful and shaded by very green trees. The bar/restaurant with takeaway and wood-fired pizzeria has two large terraces. Alessandro and his wife, Alessandra, have worked hard to build up this basic site since 1982. They are charming and speak excellent English.

Facilities

Three sanitary units with children's toilets and showers are showing some signs of wear and tear. Hot showers. Laundry facilities. Motorcaravan services. Gas supplies. Shop (bread and milk to order). Bar. Trattoria/pizzeria and takeaway. Tennis. Play area. Bicycle hire. Fishing. Internet point (€ 3/h) and free WiFi. Torches required in some areas. Excursions. Off site: Bus service from outside the gate runs to central Rome. Air-conditioned train service from Bracciano (1.5 km) into city. Riding 2 km.

Open: 1 April - 30 September.

Directions

From Rome ring road (GRA) north west side take Cassia exit to Bracciano S493. 2 km. before Bracciano village, just after going under a bridge, follow site signs and turn along lake away from Anguillara. Site is 1 km. on the SP1f and has a fairly steep entrance. GPS: 42.10582, 12.18928

Charges guide

Per unit incl. 2 persons and electricity	€ 17.00 - € 29.00
extra person	€ 5.00 - € 8.00

Lido di Ostia
Camping Internazionale Castelfusano

Via Litoranea 132, I-00122 Lido di Ostia (Lazio) T: 0656 233 04. E: info@romacampingcastelfusano.it

alanrogers.com/IT67790

For a beach holiday, this site is ideally situated with easy access across the road to a lovely, long sandy beach. There are a total of 350 pitches, 150 of which are for touring, interspersed on undulating ground among mature trees. Although they offer plenty of shade, there are many low hanging branches (they are protected) and, as a result, some pitches are small and inappropriate for larger units. However, tents and smaller units can tuck themselves away in interesting nooks and crannies. The soil is sandy but the access roads are mostly tarmac and gravel. Most of the pitches have 3A electricity. An access road to the beach provides an area for larger units to park.

Facilities

Three toilet blocks with basic facilities including hot showers (mainly cold water for dishwashing and laundry). Unit for disabled visitors. Washing machine and dryer. Motorcaravan services. Well stocked shop (April-Oct). Bar/restaurant (Feb-Oct) with terrace. Live music (high season). Outdoor pool (June-Sept). Playground. Games area. Entertainment for children twice a week (July/Aug). Internet access and information in reception. Communal barbecue area. Off site: Beach 50 m. Riding 2 km.

Open: All year.

Directions

From GRA exit 26 or 27 (depending on direction) onto Via Cristoforo Colombo towards Flumicino. Continue on this road to end (beach). Keeping in left lane, follow road to right then immediately left and left again in 100 m. Turn right in 150 m. and site is 1.5 km. on right. GPS: 41.706075, 12.340111

Charges guide

Per unit incl. 2 persons and electricity	€ 20.50 - € 36.50
extra person	€ 6.00 - € 11.00

Marina di Montalto
California International Camping Village

SS1 Aurelia km 105,500, I-01014 Marina di Montalto (Lazio) T: 076 680 2848.
E: info@californiacampingvillage.com **alanrogers.com/IT68160**

The first vision of California Camping on the approach is the excellent lagoon-style pool complex with its bridges and large fountain surrounded by palms. All facilities are shared with the very large population of holidaymakers in rental accommodation. A smart bar, pizzeria and restaurant complex are in an octagonal building overlooking the pools. The 420 pitches for touring units (4A electricity) are large, arranged mainly in close, level, shaded rows. Cars are parked separately in high season. The long, grey sand/shingle beach is cleaned daily; it is virtually private and easily accessed.

Facilities

Nine refurbished blocks with varying facilities; some investment will soon be required. These include facilities for disabled campers. Hot water for showers, cold at sinks. Showers are in one block (so a walk for some). Supermarket. Excellent restaurant, bar and takeaway. Large lagoon pool complex. Minigolf. Amphitheatre. Tennis. Discos. Play areas. Entertainment. Miniclub. Boat hire. Fishing. WiFi (charged). Dogs are not accepted.

Open: 1 May - 15 September.

Directions

Site is 100 km. north of Rome off SS1 between Ortobello and Civitavecchia. At Montalto di Castro take minor road to coast and Montalto Marina and look for signs. GPS: 42.3055, 11.62333

Charges guide

Per unit incl. 2 persons and electricity	€ 21.00 - € 41.00
extra person	€ 7.00 - € 13.00

For latest campsite news, availability and prices visit
alanrogers.com

Marina di Montalto

Camping Pionier Etrusco

Via Vulsinia snc, I-01014 Marina di Montalto di Castro (Lazio) T: 076 680 2807. E: info@campingpe.it

alanrogers.com/IT68165

This family run site has 250 pitches (with 3A electricity), just under half of which are used for seasonal units. On sandy ground, all the pitches are under tall pine trees resulting in full shade. Oriented towards families, this site in a small seaside town would make a good base for touring the local Etruscan ruins or perhaps as a transit stop. The beach is about 100 m. away and is of dark volcanic sand. There is a bright new bar, restaurant and café (great crêpes!) here now, and the promenade and beach are just 100 metres away. The delightful town of Montalto di Castro is about 8 km. away near the Via Aurealis (SS1) and offers opportunities for sightseeing and shopping.

Facilities	Directions
Two mature, but well maintained sanitary blocks provide toilets (some Turkish style), washbasins and unisex hot showers. Motorcaravan services. Shop. Bar. Restaurant (self-service), pizzeria and café. Bicycle hire. Dogs are not accepted 1/6-31/8. Bungalows to rent. WiFi over part of site (charged). Off site: Bars, shops, beach and everything you would find at a busy seaside resort. Boat launching 500 m. Golf 6 km. Montalto di Castro 8 km.	Leave the SS1 at exit for Marfina di Montalto di Castro and head towards the coast. At roundabout turn left, then right and at T-junction turn right again. Site is off to the left and is clearly signed. GPS: 42.32706, 11.58155

Open: 1 April - 30 September.

Charges guide

Per unit incl. 2 persons and electricity	€ 20.00 - € 42.00
extra person	€ 8.00 - € 13.00

Roma

Fabulous Camping Village

Via Cristoforo Colombo km 18, I-00125 Roma (Lazio) T: 0652 593 54. E: fabulous@ecvacanze.it

alanrogers.com/IT67780

Fabulous Camping Village is another venture in the Cardini/Vannucchi family group of campsites. Purchased only a few years ago, developments are still in progress to create a superb family campsite on top of a hill, midway between Rome and the sea. The site is attractively located under tall pine trees which give plenty of shade. Pitches are of varying size, all with 6/10A electricity and access is by tarmac and hardcore roads. They are frequently positioned close to the access routes so it can be quite noisy. The pools and tennis courts are at the far end of the site where there are superb views towards Rome.

Facilities	Directions
Two blocks, one in traditional style in the permanent area and one new for the touring units. This block is excellent. Facilities for disabled visitors. Baby rooms. Washing machines. Motorcaravan services. Excellent supermarket. Restaurant/pizzeria and bar. Three swimming pools, one for paddling, with lifeguards. Play area. Tennis. Miniclub (5 yrs plus) and teenage activities. Entertainment for all ages. Bicycle hire. Torches useful. WiFi (charged).	Site is on the GRA (Rome's equivalent of the M25). Take exit 27 or 26 depending on the direction of approach. Continue for 6 km. towards Ostia. At traffic lights turn right. Site on right well before 2.6 m. height restriction. GPS: 41.77743, 12.39594

Open: 1 April - 31 October.

Charges guide

Per unit incl. 2 persons and electricity	€ 27.10 - € 36.40
extra person	€ 8.90 - € 11.60

Roma

Camping Village Roma

Via Aurelia 831, I-00165 Roma (Lazio) T: 0666 230 18. E: campingroma@ecvacanze.it

alanrogers.com/IT67800

Perched high on a hilltop on the edge of Rome, this is another venture by the Cardini/Vanucchi family who have other quality city sites in Italy. The diverse range of facilities are designed in particular to meet the needs of young travellers and the aim here is to provide a friendly helpful service all year round. There are 100 touring pitches of varying sizes on level terraces. Motorcaravans are mostly placed in a separate area where 20 pitches are fully serviced. There is some shade, however a large construction project is underway adjacent to the site, with completion scheduled for 2017.

Facilities	Directions
Two toilet blocks with British style WCs and showers. Good facilities for disabled visitors and children. Baby baths. Washing machines. Motorcaravan services. Well stocked supermarket (closed in winter). Large restaurant and late night bar with DJ plus pizzeria with terrace and poolside bar (high season). Swimming pool and jacuzzi. Huge TV screen. Evening entertainment/disco and regular themed parties. Play area. Free WiFi over site.	From A1 take Roma North exit towards Fuimcino airport. Take GRA and exit 1 'Aurelia' towards Citta del Vaticano-Centro. At 831 km. marker site is well signed. On exit at dual carriageway go straight on to site 50 m. on right. GPS: 41.8877, 12.4042

Open: All year.

Charges guide

Per unit incl. 2 persons and electricity	€ 25.80 - € 38.50
extra person	€ 8.30 - € 12.30

Roma
Camping Tiber

Via Tiberina km 1,400, I-00188 Roma (Lazio) T: 0633 610 733. E: info@campingtiber.com
alanrogers.com/IT68090

An excellent city site with extensive facilities, which also caters for backpackers. Although a lively site, the thoughtful layout and the division of different areas with flowering shrubs makes it surprisingly peaceful. It is ideally located for visiting Rome with a shuttle bus every 30 minutes to the station and then an easy train service to Rome (20 minutes), with trams operating late at night. The 350 touring pitches (with electricity) are mostly shaded under very tall trees and many have very pleasant views over the River Tiber. This mighty river winds around two sides of the site boundary (safely fenced) providing a cooling effect for campers and it is possible to fish for carp. Camping Tiber is extremely well run with friendly and helpful staff and especially good for campers with disabilities.

Facilities

Fully equipped, very smart sanitary facilities include hot water everywhere, private cabins, a baby room and very good facilities for disabled campers. Laundry facilities. Motorcaravan services. Shop. Bar, restaurant, pizzeria and takeaway. Swimming pool (May-end Sept, hat required) and bar. Carp fishing in river. Play area. Shuttle bus (on payment) to the underground station every 15 or 30 minutes according to season. Torches useful. WiFi on part of site (charged). Off site: Local bars, restaurants and shops. Golf 5 km. riding 20 km.

Open: 1 April - 31 October.

Directions

From Florence, exit at Rome Nord Fiano on A1 and turn south onto Via Tiberina and site is signed. From other directions on Rome ring road (GRA) take exit 6 northbound on S3 Via Flaminia following signs to Tiberina. GPS: 42.0095, 12.50233

Charges guide

Per unit incl. 2 persons	
and electricity	€ 29.50 - € 30.00
extra person	€ 9.50 - € 10.50
child (3-12 yrs)	€ 6.50 - € 7.50

Roma
Camping Seven Hills Village

Via Cassia 1216, I-00189 Roma (Lazio) T: 0630 310 826. E: info@sevenhills.it
alanrogers.com/IT68100

Close to Rome, this site has both quiet and lively areas on steep slopes set in a delightful, lush green valley, flanked by two of the seven hills of Rome. The 250 well tended pitches for touring units are on steep terraces, mostly shaded, with 6A electricity. Two fine restaurants and the snack bar/pizzeria/takeaway cater for everyone. The site runs a regular shuttle bus and a daily bus to Rome. The pool (extra charge), also with bar snacks, is great for cooling off and relaxing after a busy day in the city. The site is a profusion of colour with flowering trees and shrubs and a good covering of trees providing shade. English is spoken. All cash transactions on the site are made with a card from reception. This is a bustling site and there can be many touring buses with their occupants on site during high season.

Facilities

Three well constructed sanitary blocks are situated around the site with open washbasins and hot water in the average sized showers. Facilities for disabled campers. Well stocked shop. Bar. Two excellent restaurants with terraces. Money exchange. Swimming pool at the bottom of the site with bar/snack bar and a room where the younger element tends to congregate (separate pool charge). Disco. Excursions. Bungalows and apartments to rent. Free WiFi. Off site: Golf 4 km. Excursions to Tivoli gardens.

Open: All year (on request).

Directions

From autostrada ring road exit 3 take Via Cassia (signed SS2 Viterbo, NOT Via Cassia Bis) and look for site signs. Turn right after 1 km. and follow small road, Via Italo Piccagli, for 1 km. to site. This narrow twisting road is heavily parked on during the day. GPS: 41.993, 12.41685

Charges guide

Per unit incl. 2 persons and car	€ 24.90 - € 32.20
extra person	€ 8.00 - € 9.50
child (5-12 yrs)	€ 6.00 - € 7.50
dog	free

For latest campsite news, availability and prices visit
alanrogers.com

Roma
I Pini Camping

Via delle Sassete 28, Fiano Romano, I-00065 Roma (Lazio) T: 076 545 3349. E: ipini@ecvacanze.it

alanrogers.com/IT68110

I Pini was built a few years ago by a family of experienced campers and is now part of the Elite Club Vacance group. The 117 pitches, with 6-10A electricity, are set on shaded, grassy terraces, some with views of the nearby hills. The beautifully designed restaurant, with a very large terrace, is typical of the thought that has gone into making I Pini a place where you can relax. The pool complex is buzzing with the sound of happy children making use of the novel slides. This tranquil site is 45 minutes from Rome to which buses are available on a daily basis and the site offers plenty of excursions. The staff at reception are most helpful at providing comprehensive information for tours to nearby attractions.

Facilities

The single excellent sanitary block is spotless throughout and hot water is free. Two well equipped units for disabled visitors and a separate child's shower. Washing machines and dryers. Motorcaravan services. Bar. Restaurant with large terrace. Snack bar and pizza oven. Pleasant market. Bazaar. Lagoon style swimming pools (with lifeguard). Pool bar. Tennis. Play area. Entertainment (1/6-30/8). Buffet or traditional dinner and pool party (both weekly). Free WiFi. Torches required in some areas. Excursions organised. Off site: Air-conditioned buses to Rome daily. Fishing 3 km. Golf and riding 20 km.

Open: 18 April - 29 September.

Directions

From Rome ring road (GRA) take A1 exit to Fiano Romano. As you enter the town turn right along via Belvedere opposite an IP petrol station and follow camping signs (there is only the one site). GPS: 42.1558, 12.5732

Charges guide

Per unit incl. 2 persons	
and electricity	€ 19.70 - € 35.50
extra person	€ 5.90 - € 11.30
child (3-11 yrs)	free - € 8.40
dog	free

Roma
Flaminio Village Camping Bungalow Park

Via Flaminia Nuova 821, I-00189 Roma (Lazio) T: 0633 326 04. E: info@villageflaminio.com

alanrogers.com/IT68140

We were impressed with Camping Flaminio. It is a high quality campsite, near Rome, with many flowers, shrubs and trees giving some shade. Being 400 metres from the main road it is protected from traffic noise. Although it is quite a large site, there are only 250 pitches, all with 6A electricity, which are approached by environmentally approved brick access roads. There is reasonable space allocated to touring units and the majority of these pitches in the lower areas are of average size. Pitches are situated away from the main facilities so there is quite a walk between the two. There are 120 well equipped bungalows attractively arranged in a village-style setting on the slopes. The site is ideally situated for visiting the 'Eternal City', being close to a cycle route and with a regular bus/underground service into the centre of Rome from outside the site entrance, which operates until late evening.

Facilities

The sanitary facilities are of a high quality including provision for disabled visitors and a very good baby room. Motorcaravan services. Bar/pizzeria and restaurant. Well stocked shop. Swimming pool (hats required), pool bar and solarium (15/6-5/9). Bicycle hire. Bus service. Torches useful. Pick-up service to and from Ciampino airport. Small electric bus runs between reception and pitches. WiFi throughout (charged). Off site: Shops, service station, bank and access to cycle route alongside river into the city. Buses and trains outside the gate. Fishing 3 km.

Open: All year.

Directions

From ring road north of city take Flaminia exit (towards Rome centre/saxa rubra). After 3-4 km. follow Flaminia signs, bear left where road splits to avoid tunnel and follow signs to Corso di Francia. Warning: site entrance appears suddenly on right as central barrier ends 150 m. after passing tunnel entrance. GPS: 41.95618, 12.4824

Charges guide

Per unit incl. 2 persons	
and electricity	€ 31.00 - € 39.50
extra person	€ 10.00 - € 12.00
child (3-16 yrs)	€ 6.50 - € 10.00
dog	€ 3.50 - € 4.00

For latest campsite news, availability and prices visit
alanrogers.com

Salto di Fondi
Camping Village Bungalow Park Settebello

Via Flacca km 3,6, I-04020 Salto di Fondi (Lazio) T: 077 159 9132. E: settebello@settebellocamping.com
alanrogers.com/IT68190

The SS213 hugs this beautiful coastline for many miles, running between small towns and villages and alongside the pine forests that are directly behind the beach. Camping Settebello, a large, attractive and well managed site, is in a rural area but unfortunately the site straddles this busy road and inevitably there is a great deal of traffic noise. The touring pitches are all on the beach side of the site in a wooded area and all are limited to a 3A electricity supply. The ground rises before the beach and this is where many of the bungalows for rent have been built. With a total of 500 pitches, about 260 are available for touring units. There is direct access to the beach which also has a fine restaurant overlooking the sea.

Facilities

Five toilet blocks include showers, WCs (Turkish and some British style) and washbasins. Facilities for disabled visitors. Motorcaravan services. Well stocked shop, fruit and vegetable shop, bar and restaurant/takeaway (1/6-31/8). Swimming pool and children's pool (at extra cost 51/5-31/9). Skating. Tennis. Minigolf. Miniclub. Disco. Amphitheatre and cinema. WiFi. Pets by prior arrangement. Accommodation to rent. Bicycle hire.

Open: 1 April - 30 September.

Directions

The Via Flacca is a comparatively short stretch of the SS213 between Sperlonga and Terracina. The site straddles this road at km. 3.6 which is close to Terracina. Turn towards the beach to find reception. GPS: 41.29028, 13.33111

Charges guide

Per unit incl. 2 persons	€ 38.00 - € 88.00
extra person	€ 8.00 - € 14.00
child (3-12 yrs)	€ 5.00 - € 10.00

Terracina
Camping Romantico

Via Flacca km 0,45, I-04019 Terracina (Lazio) T: 077 372 7620. E: info@campingvillaggioromantico.com
alanrogers.com/IT68180

This is a pleasant small site of only 70 pitches, half for seasonal units and half for tourers. These are set randomly among the seasonal units and consequently there is a feeling of being part of a typical Italian holiday experience. Although it is near the busy SS213, it is far enough away for traffic noise not to be a problem, and the only noise we did hear was from the occasional small boat going down the river and this was hardly noticeable. The small pitches of about 60 sq.m. are all marked by tidy hedges and are shaded under pine trees. The site enjoys a semi-rural location alongside a private beach which campers may use. Terracina is just 3 km. away and is worth a visit. Rome and Naples are about 100 km. away.

Facilities

One main toilet block includes showers, Turkish and British style WCs and washbasins. Facilities for disabled visitors. Motorcaravan services. Washing machine. Small shop. Bar and restaurant/pizzeria. Children's club and entertainment in high season. Five bungalows and mobile homes to rent. WiFi over site. Off site: Terracina 3 km. Sandy beach with sun beds and shades. Bicycle hire, boat launching and sailing 3 km.

Open: 1 April - 30 September.

Directions

Site is 3 km. south of Terracina on Via Flacca, the small coast road, and is down the road alongside the river just before the estuary. If you come through the Terracina tunnel take first exit and turn back towards the town. GPS: 41.298383, 13.28155

Charges guide

Per unit incl. 2 persons and electricity	€ 20.00 - € 48.00
extra person	€ 6.00 - € 13.00

Trevignano Romano
Camping Internazionale Lago di Bracciano

Via del Pianoro 4, I-00069 Trevignano Romano (Lazio) T: 0699 850 32. E: camping.village@gmail.com
alanrogers.com/IT67850

Lago di Bracciano, just 45 km. north of Rome, is of a size that provides excellent opportunities for watersports and is inevitably very popular with windsurfers. With some pitches alongside a little beach, the site provides 110 pitches of which about 50 are for touring units. Our pitch had a full view of the lake and the gentle breeze made the temperature at the end of June quite bearable. Some shade is provided by large trees. A bar and restaurant near the entrance are behind the site's small swimming pool and play area. The local bus has a regular service to Rome.

Facilities

Two toilet blocks are clean and have open style washbasins, preset showers and facilities for disabled visitors (key). Washing machine. Motorcaravan services. Small shop. Bar and restaurant/pizzeria. Small swimming pool (15/5-15/9). Play area. Beach volleyball court. WiFi and Internet access. Mobile homes and bungalows to rent. Off site: Lago di Bracciano.

Open: 1 April - 30 September.

Directions

From Rome GRA take exit 5 on SS2 for Cassia. Turn left at Trevignano exit (km. 35) and follow SP4a towards the lake. Site is on the left, well signed. The access road is narrow. GPS: 42.14472, 12.26865

Charges guide

Per unit incl. 2 persons and electricity	€ 23.00 - € 30.00
extra person	€ 6.00 - € 8.00

For latest campsite news, availability and prices visit
alanrogers.com

THE REGIONS ARE DIVIDED INTO THE FOLLOWING PROVINCES: ABRUZZO: CHIETI, L'AQUILA, PESCARA AND TERAMO, MOLISE: CAMPOBASSO AND ISERNIA

Until 1963, Abruzzo and Molise were combined in one region known as Abruzzi. With some of the wildest terrain in Italy, Abruzzo is bordered by the Apennine mountain range with vast tracts of forest, while Molise has a gentler countryside with high plains, soft peaks and valleys.

A popular attraction in Abruzzo is the medieval hilltown of Scanno. Surrounded by high peaks looming above, the town hosts a range of activities in the summer including riding, boating and a classical music festival. Close by is Italy's third largest national park. With mountains, rivers, lakes and forests it is an important wildlife refuge, home to bears, wolves and the golden eagle. It also offers good walking, riding, skiing and canoeing. Around Scanno are the historic mountain towns of L'Aquila and Sulmona, and the village of Cocullo, where the bizarre Festival of Snakes takes place in May; a statue of a local saint is draped with live snakes and paraded through the streets. Along the Abruzzo coast is Pescara, the main resort, which has a 16 km. long beach. Ferries to Croatia and the Dalmatian islands depart from here. Nearby are the small hill towns of Atri, Penne and Loreto Apruntino. In Molise, the city of Isernia is where traces of a million-year-old village were unearthed in 1979, the most ancient signs of human life ever found in Europe. And the quiet resort and fishing port of Térmoli, from where Italian and Central European time is set, is a good place to relax.

Places of interest

Alba Adriatica: most northern of Abruzzo's coastal resorts.

Atri: 13th-century cathedral, archaeology and ethnography museums.

Celano: pretty village with turreted castle.

Lanciano: historic town.

Larino: medieval town centre, cathedral, amphitheatre.

Pineto: coastal resort.

Saepinum: ruined Roman town.

Téramo: remains of Roman amphitheatre, theatre and baths.

Cuisine of the region

As sheep farming dominates the regions, lamb is popular: *abbacchio* (roasted baby lamb), and *castrato* (castrated lamb) is used to make *intingolo di castrato*, a casserole prepared with tomatoes, wine, onion and celery. Chilli is another favourite ingredient, known locally as *pepdinie* (*peperoncino* elsewhere in Italy). Abruzzo is famous for *maccheroni all chitarra*, pasta made by pressing sheets over a wooden frame, and other local pastas include *stengozze* and *maltagliati*, usually served with a lamb sauce.

Ceci e Castagne: chickpeas and chestnuts.

Coniglio all zafferano: rabbit with saffron.

Linguine d'Ovidio: pasta with pancetta and truffles.

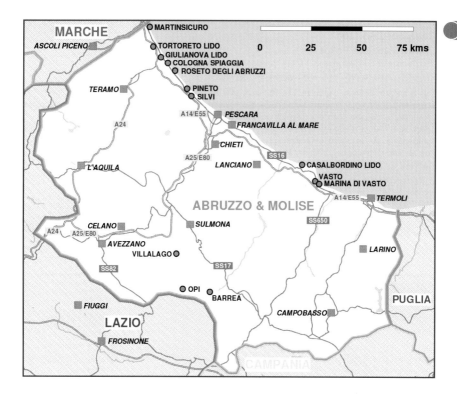

Barrea
Camping la Genziana

SS83 Ctra Tre Croci, Parco Naz. d'Abruzzo, I-67030 Barrea (Abruzzo) T: 086 488 101. E: info@pasetta.it
alanrogers.com/IT68080

This is the place to get away from it all – situated in the middle of Italy, high in the peaceful Abruzzo mountains with magnificent views over the Barrea lakes. The 105 touring pitches (4A electricity) are set on a hillside amongst wild flowers and grasses. The ebullient owner Tommaso Pasetta d'Amico and his family make everyone welcome to this peaceful, natural site. Pasetta is an expert in Alpine walking and a great raconteur. Ask him about 'calling wolves' – he really does and has appeared on BBC World in this role! This uncomplicated site is an hour from Rome and Pescara, and it could be another world in terms of peace and quiet. English is spoken. If mountain walking is for you, Pasetta will give sound advice on the many tracks starting from the site. The site has limited facilities, but swimming, riding and fishing are all possible nearby.

Facilities	Directions
Single clean, modern sanitary block with hot water throughout (honesty payment in high season). Mainly British style toilets. Laundry facilities. Motorcaravan services. Bar, coffee bar and small shop. WiFi (free). Torches are essential. Off site: Village of Barrea and ATM 500 m. Lake beach 3 km. Canoeing, fishing and sailing all within 3 km. Bicycle hire 3 km. Riding 7 km. Trekking and walking information.	From A25 take route 83 from Celano and site is signed 4 km. before Barrea. Alternatively route 17 from Pratola/Sulmona through Castel di Sangro then right to route 83 and site is 1 km. before Barrea. GPS: 41.74267, 13.98867

Open: April - October.

Charges guide

Per unit incl. 2 persons and electricity	€ 23.90 - € 24.90
extra person	€ 8.20
child (under 9 yrs)	€ 4.00
dog	€ 3.00

No credit cards.

For latest campsite news, availability and prices visit
alanrogers.com

Casalbordino Lido
Centro Vacanze Poker

Ctra Termini 27 Lungomare sud, I-66021 Casalbordino Lido (Abruzzo) T: 087 391 8321.
E: info@centrovacanzepoker.it **alanrogers.com/IT67960**

This is an extraordinary campsite. The 15 luxury pitches (6A electricity) are set among attractive palms at one end of the hotel grounds (some rail noise). They are an integral part of a five-star hotel which has beautifully landscaped gardens, cleverly complementing a plush restaurant/bar complex. The adjacent beach is a mixture of sand and small rocks, but fabulous swimming and paddling pools and a jacuzzi compensate. An excellent entertainment team work hard to ensure the children enjoy themselves. Popular and a little pricey, Vacanze Poker is a great family site.

Facilities	Directions
15 medium pitches each with a private bathroom nearby (key entry). Swimming pools and jacuzzi. Restaurant and bar. Ambitious entertainment programme. WiFi over part of site (charged). Off site: Beach adjacent (lifeguard, loungers and toilet facilities). Amenities at Casalbordino Lido. Watersports. **Open:** 1 June - 15 September.	Leave A14 at Torino di Sangro and join SS16 south. In Casalbordino Lido go under railway, continue south along seafront road. Hotel complex is signed at end of the road. GPS: 42.19094, 14.64433

Charges guide

Per unit incl. 2 persons and electricity	€ 49.00 - € 89.00
extra person	€ 12.00 - € 22.00

Cologna Spiaggia
Stork Camping Village

Via del Mare 11, I-64020 Cologna Spiaggia (Abruzzo) T: 085 893 7076. E: info@storkcampingvillage.com
alanrogers.com/IT67860

This is a relaxed site in a 21-acre park with a selection of pitches for larger caravans and motorcaravans, mainly around the perimeter. The 457 touring pitches (all with 6-16A electricity) are well laid out between mature trees that offer good shade. Some pitches are available adjacent to the beach, for a small supplement. There is direct access to the superb sandy beach with a range of amenities on offer, including a beach bar and beach volleyball. A lively entertainment programme is organised in peak season, including a children's club and aquagym. Leisure facilities are extensive and include a large swimming pool and separate children's pool. Visitors with dogs are sited in a designated area.

Facilities	Directions
Two centrally located toilet blocks with a mixture of British and Turkish style WCs, showers and washbasins. Well stocked shop. Bazaar. Bar. Restaurant/pizzeria. Beach bar. Swimming pool. Children's pool (swimming lessons available). Jacuzzi. Tennis. Beach volleyball. Play area. TV room. Bicycle hire. Entertainment and children's activities (July/Aug). WiFi over site (charged). Chalets for rent. Only gas barbecues are permitted. **Open:** 15 May - 15 September.	From A14 (Bologna-Taranto) take Teramo-Giulianova exit and join SS80 towards Giulianova, and then continue towards Cologna Spiaggia. Site is well signed. Please note there are low bridges under the railway. GPS: 42.72119, 13.98901

Charges guide

Per unit incl. 2 persons and electricity	€ 20.00 - € 45.00
extra person	€ 8.00 - € 17.00

Giulianova Lido
Don Antonio Camping Residence

Via Padova s/n, I-64021 Giulianova Lido (Abruzzo) T: 085 800 8928. E: info@campingdonantonio.it
alanrogers.com/IT68020

Set alongside the beautiful Adriatic coast with its long, soft sand beaches, this site has 270 pitches, all with 6A electricity, 200 with water and waste water. The site is aimed at families and the swimming pools, play areas and entertainment programme will keep everyone busy. The atmosphere is lively and the management do their utmost to keep everyone happy. There is a self-service restaurant and a lovely bar/café on the beach, with a gelateria and superb miniclub. A novel feature is the American-style grill bar serving mouth watering food. The friendly staff speak English and are keen to help.

Facilities	Directions
Four traditional units are kept clean and provide a mixture of British and Turkish sanitary facilities. The new units for disabled campers are of a high standard. Washing machine. Motorcaravan services. Snack bar. Beach bar. Swimming pools with slides and whirlpool (caps compulsory). Wheelchair users have special access to the pools and beach. Entertainment for families. Bicycle hire. Torches useful. Dogs are not accepted 1/7-26/8. WiFi (free 2 hours on arrival, then charged). **Open:** 14 May - 11 September.	Leave A14 north of Pescara and take SS80 to Giulianova Lido. Follow site signs on coast road. Take care to find tunnel under railway with a 3.6 m. clearance (north of town). All other bridges have 'car only' 2.3 m. clearance, so do not use sat nav. Site is 400 m. from tunnel. GPS: 42.777322, 13.951178

Charges guide

Per unit incl. 2 persons and electricity	€ 21.00 - € 66.00
extra person	€ 5.00 - € 13.00

Marina di Vasto
Camping & Residence Il Pioppeto

SS16 Sud km 521, I-66055 Marina di Vasto (Abruzzo) T: 087 380 1466. E: infocampeggio@ilpioppeto.it
alanrogers.com/IT67970

Il Pioppeto lies to the south of Pescara and is a clean and friendly family site. It is well maintained and tidy, with 110 level pitches with 5A electricity and plenty of shade. The local food offered in the small, unassuming restaurant is superb and reasonably priced (cash only). Diners can eat inside or enjoy the atmosphere on the terrace, although there is some road noise. The delightful beach just outside the site is long and very wide so there is no difficulty in escaping from the maddening crowd.

Facilities

The four toilet blocks of differing sizes are of a good standard, although some washbasins have only cold water. Excellent motorcaravan services. Supermarket. Bar and snack bar. Restaurant. Play area. Games room. Entertainment and children's club in peak season. Adjacent beach. Chalets for rent. Bicycle hire. WiFi over part of site. Off site: Boat launching 500 m. Riding centre (owned by site) 1 km. Disco. Tennis. Roller skating rink.

Open: 15 May - 15 September.

Directions

From the A14 motorway (Bologna-Taranto) take Vasto exit and join SS16 towards Vasto from where site is well signed. GPS: 42.088, 14.73667

Charges guide

Per unit incl. 2 persons	
and electricity	€ 26.00 - € 36.90
extra person	€ 6.80 - € 9.60

Credit cards accepted during high season.

Martinsicuro
Camping Riva Nuova

Via dei Pioppi 6, I-64014 Martinsicuro (Abruzzo) T: 086 179 7515. E: emanuele.dionisi@rivanuova.it
alanrogers.com/IT67980

Situated at the south end of the small town of Martinsicuro on the Adriatic coast, this excellent site offers a first class camping experience with a great ambience. Set in pleasant, neat, landscaped gardens and obviously well planned, there are 334 pitches for touring units varying in size from 60 to 120 sq.m. There are 140 pitches with water, drainage and electricity and a further 23 with a private bathroom on the pitch. Across a beach road is a long beach of soft sand and a promenade with the usual seaside facilities. This is a great site for low or high season, especially for families with children.

Facilities

An exceptional, central sanitary block provides everything to the highest standard. Ample toilets, showers and washbasins. Children's bathroom. Facilities for disabled visitors. Private bathrooms to rent. Laundry facilities. Bar, restaurant and shop. Swimming pool (extra daily charge) and sunbathing area. Gym. Boules. Tennis. Entertainment in high season. Bicycle hire. Sailing. ATM. WiFi (charged). Dogs are not accepted. Off site: Fishing 100 m.

Open: 1 May - 18 September.

Directions

Leave A14 at San Benedetto and take SS16 to Martinsicuro. Turn onto coast road and go south of town to site in Via dei Pioppi (well signed). Be sure to follow the campsite signs as other roads to beach road are dead ends. GPS: 42.8801, 13.9205

Charges guide

Per unit incl. 2 persons	
and electricity	€ 16.90 - € 45.90
extra person	€ 4.00 - € 11.50

Opi
Camping Il Vecchio Mulino

SS Marsicana 83 km 52, I-67030 Opi (Abruzzo) T: 086 391 2232. E: ilvecchiomulino@tiscali.it
alanrogers.com/IT67920

Il Vecchio Mulino enjoys a fine woodland setting on the slopes of Monte Marsicano, at the heart of the Abruzzo National Park. The site is open all year and is popular for walking and cycling in the summer and is well located for the Pescasseroli and Macchiarvana ski resorts in the winter. The focal point of the site is the old mill and the attractively restored farm buildings housing the restaurant and bed and breakfast accommodation. The restaurant serves local Abruzzese cuisine and is open from May to September. The 70 pitches here are spacious and level and all are equipped with a wooden picnic table and electrical connection. This is a friendly site with traditional facilities showing signs of wear.

Facilities

Centrally located toilet block. Motorcaravan services. Small shop (local produce). Bar/restaurant. Snack bar. Sports field. Play area. Games room. Barbecue area. Fishing. Off site: Village centre 1 km. Bus service from site entrance. Abruzzo National Park. Mountain biking and walking.

Open: All year (but check with site).

Directions

Take Pescina exit from A24/A25 Rome-Pescara and join SS83 through Passo del Diavolo to Pescasseroli from where the site is well signed (1 km. from Opi). GPS: 41.780017, 13.867767

Charges guide

Per unit incl. 2 persons	
and electricity	€ 20.50 - € 25.50
extra person	€ 6.00 - € 7.00
child	free - € 6.50

For latest campsite news, availability and prices visit
alanrogers.com

Pineto
International Camping

Ctra Torre Cerrano, I-64025 Pineto (Abruzzo) T: 085 930 639. E: into@internationalcamping.it
alanrogers.com/IT68060

This small, very Italian, family run site, just north of Pescara and south of Pineto, is situated between the coastal railway line and a superb sandy beach. Inevitably there is some railway noise. The 100 small pitches for touring units (cars parked away from pitches), all have 6A electricity, and are shaded by trees which you will need to watch out for when manoeuvring. It is quieter than the larger sites that are usually found on this coast. During June to August it is very much an Italian family site with entertainment and all sorts of fun and games on the beach. Nearby Pineto is a pleasant, small, seaside town with a small market, good restaurants and cafés and all essential shops.

Facilities

One sanitary block provides ample toilets (British and Turkish style) washbasins and hot showers (token). Children's bathrooms and baby changing room. Good facilities for disabled visitors. Shop (1/5-15/9). Bar, restaurant and takeaway. Direct beach access. Play area. Boules. Entertainment for all (high season). Excursions organised. Mobile homes to rent. WiFi. Dogs are not accepted 1/6-30/9. Off site: Pineto. Riding and bicycle hire 3 km. Golf 15 km. National Park and Cerrano Tower.

Open: 1 May - 23 September.

Directions

On the SS16 at 431.2 km. marker just past the Cerrano Tower, take the turn marked camping and pass under the railway (4 m. bridge). Then turn immediately right to site. GPS: 42.58140, 14.09290

Charges guide

Per unit incl. 2 persons	
and electricity	€ 23.00 - € 48.50
extra person	€ 5.50 - € 13.00
child (3-6 yrs)	free - € 9.50

Roseto degli Abruzzi
Camping Village Eurcamping

Lungomare Trieste Sud, I-64026 Roseto degli Abruzzi (Abruzzo) T: 085 899 3179. E: eurcamping@camping.it
alanrogers.com/IT68040

Eurcamping is about 2 km. south of the small town of Roseto degli Abruzzi. This is a pleasant and relatively quiet site, situated beside the sea, with 265 well defined pitches. All pitches have 6A electricity, some are very large and many have shade. There are good facilities which are grouped around the reception area including a very pleasant swimming pool and an entertainment area is at the far end of the site. Access to the site's beach of soft sand and rugged stone is just 75 m. from the gate.

Facilities

Three sanitary blocks with free hot showers. Facilities for disabled visitors. Baby rooms. Motorcaravan services. Laundry. Bar. Restaurant. Takeaway. Pizzeria. Shop. Swimming pools (hats must be worn) with solarium terrace. Play area. Outdoor fitness area. Tennis. Bowling. Bicycle hire. Artificial turf football ground. Entertainment in high season. Clubs for children and teenagers. WiFi (charged). Pets restricted to assigned pitches. Bungalows to rent. Free shuttle to Roseto beach. Security bracelets compulsory. Off site: Beach. Canoe and pedalo hire.

Open: 1 May - 22 October.

Directions

From north or south on A14 motorway, take exit Roseto degli Abruzzi exit. Turn onto SS150 to Roseto degli Abruzzi. From Rome and L'Aquila on A24 motorway take Villa Vomano-Teramo exit onto SS150 (Roseto degli Abruzzi). NB: there are railway bridges under 5 m. on the SS16 crossings to the coast road. GPS: 42.6577, 14.0353

Charges guide

Per unit incl. 2 persons	
and electricity	€ 19.00 - € 47.00
extra person	€ 5.00 - € 13.00

Silvi
Camping Europe Garden

Ctra Vallescura n. 10, I-64028 Silvi (Abruzzo) T: 085 930 137. E: info@europegarden.it
alanrogers.com/IT68000

This site is 13 kilometres north west of Pescara and lies just back from the coast about 2 km. up a long and very steep hill from where it has great views over the Adriatic sea. The site predominantly consists of bungalows and chalets for hire, with around 40 pitches at the top of the site available for smaller touring units (with 6A electricity). These are mainly on level terraces but access to some may be difficult. If installation of caravans is a problem a tractor is available to help. The site is not suitable for disabled or infirm visitors as the roads are extremely steep.

Facilities

The toilet block provides a mixture of British and Turkish style WCs. Hot showers. Washing machines. Shop, bar, restaurant, takeaway. Swimming pool (May-Sept; caps compulsory), small paddling pool and jacuzzi. Tennis. Playground. Entertainment programme. Free weekly excursions (15/6-8/9). Free shuttle bus service (18/5-7/9) to site's own private beach. Free WiFi. Dogs are not accepted. Barbecues are not allowed on pitches.

Open: 18 May - 14 September.

Directions

Turn inland off SS16 coast road at km. 433 for Silvi Alta and follow site signs. From autostrada A14 take Pineto exit from north or Pescara Nord exit from the south. GPS: 42.56738, 14.09247

Charges guide

Per unit incl. 2 persons	
and electricity	€ 24.50 - € 49.50
extra person	€ 5.00 - € 13.00
child (3-8 yrs)	€ 4.00 - € 10.00

For latest campsite news, availability and prices visit
alanrogers.com

Tortoreto Lido

Camping Village del Salinello

Lungomare Sud, I-64018 Tortoreto Lido (Abruzzo) T: 086 772 31. E: info@salinello.com

alanrogers.com/IT67990

This large, attractive site offers 150 touring pitches with 6A electricity and a further 275 small pitches (60 sq.m) for camping under trees. There is direct access to a sand and stone beach alongside the turquoise Adriatic where various sports are organised. It is a well organised site with something for all the family. Like many Adriatic sites however, it does suffer from some railway noise. The central complex has a vast array of shops, a bar and a restaurant plus a self-service option on the first floor. Use of the pool and the sports facilities are charged as extra.

Facilities

Two large, well maintained sanitary blocks have a mixture of British and Turkish style toilets, showers in cubicles and open plan washbasins. Facilities for disabled visitors. Private bathrooms to rent. Swimming complex (€ 4 adult, € 3.50 child; caps compulsory). Bars. Restaurants. Commercial centre and open-air cinema/theatre. Full programme of entertainment (1/6-31/8). Tennis (€ 6/day). 5-a-side pitches (pitch hire € 30/day). ATM. Bicycle hire. Free WiFi over part of site. Dogs are not accepted.

Open: 15 May - 15 September.

Directions

From A14 join SS16 via either Valvibrata or Teramo exit and head for Tortoreto. In town turn left into Viale Napoli, final turning before site (small sign on main road by junction). Turn south on Lungomare to site. Turn under railway at km. 402, other access is via low bridge (2 m). GPS: 42.784129, 13.952664

Charges guide

Per unit incl. 2 persons and electricity	€ 21.50 - € 43.00
extra person	€ 6.00 - € 12.00

Vasto

Camping Grotta del Saraceno

Via Osca, I-66050 Vasto (Abruzzo) T: 0873 310213. E: info@grottadelsaraceno.it

alanrogers.com/IT67985

Set on a beautiful stretch of the Adriatic Coast, Camping Village Grotta del Saraceno is on a promontory overlooking an attractive bay with stunning views. The site has rows of pitches with 6A electricity, most with artificial shade, others with shade provided by trees. Unfortunately, the few pitches with sea views are occupied by permanent units. The trio of pools, including fountains, is very pleasant and is floodlit at night. There is a choice of restaurants and a pizzeria and plenty of activities on offer especially for children. The soft sand beach is down 100 steps, and halfway down there is a charming 'ristopub' which sits alongside the famous grotto. If you are at all infirm and looking for a beach, this site is not for you.

Facilities

A mix of newer and older style sanitary facilities are clean and well maintained and include both British and Turkish style WCs and showers. Laundry. Motorcaravan services. Bazaar. Bar/snack bar. Ristopub. Central and beach bars. Supermarket. News stand. Greengrocer. Swimming pool complex. Restaurants and pizzeria. Hairdresser. Sports fields. Beach volleyball. Auditorium. Games room. Fitness area. Entertainment. Fishing. Bicycle hire. Torches useful. WiFi on part of site (free). Dogs are not accepted.

Open: 4 June - 18 September.

Directions

Vasto is 62 km. south east of Pescara via the A14/E55. Site is north of town. From north leave at exit for Vasto Nord, to join SS16 (Foggia). In 7 km. turn left to site. From south leave at exit for Vasto Sud, join the SS16 north towards Pescara. In 12 km. turn right to site. GPS: 42.15431, 14.71578

Charges guide

Per unit incl. 2 persons and electricity	€ 21.00 - € 43.00
extra person	€ 5.50 - € 12.00

Villalago

Camping I Lupi

Riviera di Villalago, Lago di Scanno, I-67030 Villalago (Abruzzo) T: 086 474 0625. E: campingilupi@libero.it

alanrogers.com/IT67930

I Lupi is a traditional, friendly and very peaceful site in a beautiful location within the Abruzzo National Park on the banks of the Lago di Scanno. The 170 medium sized pitches (6A electricity) are informal with little shade, but many have fine views of the lake and mountain scenery. There is an attractive bar/restaurant (opening may be limited to July/August). Amenities on site are sometimes limited, but campers have access to the facilities of the nearby Albergo Acquevive Hotel, which is linked to the site.

Facilities

Two well appointed toilet blocks have good facilities with hot water throughout. Motorcaravan services. Communal freezer. Small shop. Bar, snack bar. Bread and milk to order. Supermarket. Play area. Children's club in peak season. Shuttle bus (high season). Games room. Sports field. Direct access to lake. Accommodation for rent. Torches essential. Off site: Riding 20 m. Sailing and fishing 300 m. Boat launching 400 m. Bicycle hire 1 km.

Open: 1 May - 30 September, also Easter and Christmas.

Directions

From A25 (Rome-Pescara) take Cocullo exit and join SP60 towards Anversa Degli Abruzzi. At this town, join SR479 towards Scanno and you will reach the Lago di Scanno and site (well signed) shortly after passing Villalago. GPS: 41.92009, 13.859081

Charges guide

Per unit incl. 2 persons and electricity	€ 19.80 - € 23.60

For latest campsite news, availability and prices visit

alanrogers.com

THE REGION HAS FIVE PROVINCES: AVELLINO, BENEVENTO, CASERTA, NAPOLI AND SALERNO

Campania boasts one of the finest coastlines in Italy, incorporating the dramatic Amalfi Coast, the beautiful Bay of Naples, and the enchanting islands of Capri, Ischia and Prócida. It is also home to some of the best preserved ancient sites, most notably Pompeii, plus the historic city of Naples.

Filled with palaces, churches and convents, the regional capital of Naples also boasts an archaeology museum housing artefacts excavated from the nearby Roman sites of Pompeii and Herculaneum. Situated on the Bay of Naples, these sites were buried after Mount Vesuvius erupted in 79 AD, leaving them frozen in time. Although still active (the only one on mainland Europe) it is possible to scale up the volcano. Not far from Pompeii is the popular holiday destination of Sorrento and off the coast of the bay are the islands of Ischia, Capri and Prócida. The largest is Ischia, which along with Capri, attracts vast numbers of tourists; Prócida is the smallest and least visited. Further south is the Amalfi coast, a spectacular stretch of coastline littered with superb beaches and resorts, including Positano, Amalfi and Ravello. The busy port of Salerno is near to the ancient Greek site of Paestum, with temples dating back to the 6th century BC, and the area known as the Cilento, a mountainous region with a quiet coastline. It has a number of seaside resorts including Agropoli, Acciaroli and Palinuro plus the inland villages of Castelcivita and Pertosa, both of which have cave systems open to the public.

Places of interest

Benevento: once an important Roman settlement, monuments include the Arch of Trajan and the Roman theatre.

Campi Flegri: area known as the Fiery Fields, with volcanic craters and hot springs.

Caserta: opulent royal palace with gardens open to the public.

Ravello: offers best view of the Amalfi Coast.

Salerno: medieval old quarter, 11th-century cathedral, annual fair in May.

San Marco: picturesque fishing village.

Santa Maria Capua Vetere: ruined Roman amphitheatre with a series of tunnels beneath it.

Cuisine of the region

Naples is the home of pizza, pasta and tomato sauce. Aubergines and courgettes are frequently used in pasta sauces. Seafood is widely available along the coast including fresh squid, octopus, clams and mussels. Cilento produces strawberries, artichokes and mozzarella cheese. Made with buffalo milk, mozzarella is usually accompanied by tomatoes.

Calzone: stuffed fried pizza with ham and cheese.

Marinara: pizza topped with tomato, garlic and basil, no cheese.

Sfogliatella: flaky pastry case stuffed with ricotta and candied peel.

Zuppa di cozze: mussels with a hot pepper sauce.

Zuppa Inglese: dessert made with sponge fingers, peaches, custard, brandy and egg whites.

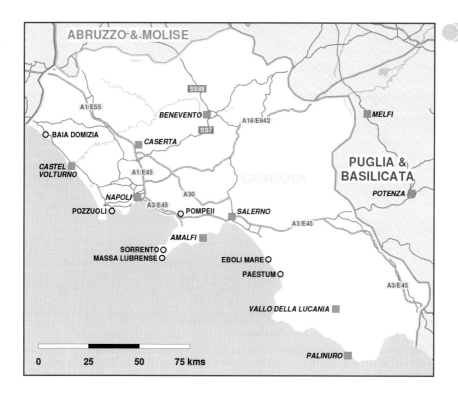

Baia Domizia
Baia Domizia Villaggio Camping

SP Garigliano Monte Massico, I-81030 Baia Domizia (Campania) T: 082 393 0164. E: info@baiadomizia.it
alanrogers.com/IT68200

This large, beautifully maintained seaside site is about 70 kilometres north west of Naples and is within a pine forest, cleverly left in its natural state. Although it does not feel like it, there are 750 touring pitches in clearings, either of grass and sand or on hardstanding, all with electricity; 80 now also have water and waste water. Finding a pitch may take time as there are so many good ones to choose from, but staff will help in season. Most pitches are well shaded, however there are some in the sun for cooler periods. The central complex is superb with well designed buildings providing for all needs (the site is some distance from the town). The site is very well organised with specific regulations (e.g. no dogs or loud noise), so the general atmosphere is relaxing and peaceful. Charges are undeniably high, but this site is well above average and most suitable for families with children.

Facilities

Seven new toilet blocks have hot water in washbasins (many cabins) and showers. Good access and facilities for disabled campers. Washing machines, spin dryers. Motorcaravan services. Gas supplies. Supermarket and general shop. Large bar. Restaurants, pizzeria and takeaway. Ice cream parlour. Swimming pool complex. Playground. Tennis. Windsurfing hire and school. Disco. Cinema. Gym. Excursions. Torches required in some areas. WiFi (charged). Dogs are not accepted.
Off site: Bicycle hire 100 m. Fishing and riding 3 km.

Open: 23 April - 13 September.

Directions

The turn to Baia Domizia leads off the Formia-Naples road 23 km. from Formia. From Rome-Naples autostrada, take Cassino exit to Formia. Site is to the north of Baia Domizia and well signed. Site is off the coastal road that runs parallel to the SS7. GPS: 41.207222, 13.791389

Charges guide

Per unit incl. 2 persons	
and electricity	€ 25.00 - € 48.50
extra person	€ 6.50 - € 12.00
child (1-11 yrs)	free - € 8.00

For latest campsite news, availability and prices visit
alanrogers.com

Eboli Mare
Camping Village Paestum
Litoranea Localitá Foce Sele, I-84025 Eboli Mare (Campania) T: 082 869 1003. E: info@campingpaestum.it
alanrogers.com/IT68410

This large, family owned site is set some way back from the beach near Paestum and the important ancient Greek temples of ancient Poseidon, built by the Greeks in the sixth century BC and taken by the Romans and renamed in 273 BC. Fast becoming a popular tourist resort, the town of Paestum is some way south of the site which enjoys a quiet, rural environment. With 540 level and well defined pitches, it has 200 allocated for international touring units and these are sited in a special area maintained for non-Italian guests on the basis that they prefer more peace and quiet.

Facilities

Five toilet blocks are well finished and provide mainly Turkish style WCs. Free hot showers and hot and cold to washbasins. Facilities for disabled visitors. Motorcaravan services. Washing machines. Small shop. Bar. Restaurant. Swimming pool, children's pool and slide (swimming caps compulsory). Tennis. Entertainment. Miniclub. Disco. Shuttle bus to beach. WiFi (charged). No pets allowed.

Open: 1 May - 30 September.

Directions

From Paestum go north along main coast road. At T-junction turn left and past military zone to site 3 km. on right. From the A3 near Salerno follow signs initially for Pontecagnano, then keep south on coast road (SP175). GPS: 40.491167, 14.944583

Charges guide

Per unit incl. 2 persons and electricity	€ 22.00 - € 37.00

Massa Lubrense
Camping Nettuno
Via A Vespucci 39, Marina del Cantone, I-80061 Massa Lubrense (Campania) T: 081 808 1051.
E: info@villaggionettuno.it alanrogers.com/IT68380

Camping Nettuno is owned and run by the friendly Mauro family, who speak excellent English. Nestled in the bay of Marina del Cantone, it is situated in the protected area of Punta Campanella, away from the busiest tourist spots. As a result the approach roads are difficult and narrow. This tiny campsite of only 42 pitches (with 4A electricity available) is spread over three levels above the pebbly beach. Up several steps and across the road are the amenities, reception, shop and dive centre and then above this is a restaurant with magnificent views over the bay. Pitches are informally arranged, some with a fabulous sea view (extra charge) and most with shade. The site has two pathways to the nearby beach that, unusually for the area, involves little walking or steps.

Facilities

The single central sanitary block includes facilities for disabled campers (and access via a ramp to the beach). Washing machine. Basic motorcaravan service point. Gas supplies. Small shop. Delightful restaurant with sea views. Bar (lively at night). Dive centre. Excursions. TV in bar area. Small play area. Free tennis arranged at court next door. Bicycle hire. Off site: Small beach (pebbles) 5 m. from bottom of site. Excellent restaurant 100 m. Amalfi Coast, Capri, nature parks, walking etc.

Open: 20 March - 2 November.

Directions

From A3 (Naples-Salerno), take C. di Stabia exit onto S145. Pass Castellamare, follow signs to Meta di Sorrento via tunnel and turn off towards Positano in Meta. After 5 km. turn to Sant'Agata dei due Golfi (6.5 km) then Nerano and finally M. del Cantone. Continue 100 m. then turn round to negotiate steep, narrow entrance. GPS: 40.58389, 14.35194

Charges guide

Per unit incl. 2 persons and electricity	€ 23.00 - € 41.50

Paestum
Camping Villaggio Athena
Via Ponte di Ferro, I-84063 Paestum (Campania) T: 082 885 1105. E: vathena@tiscalinet.it
alanrogers.com/IT68530

This is a rather basic site but has the benefit of direct access to the beach. Most of the 120 touring pitches are undefined but are set amongst mature trees that give some good shade. Part of the site is in woodland. The access is easy and the staff are friendly, but little English is spoken. There are a few bungalows available for rent. Limited entertainment is staged in July and August. The management, the Prearo brothers, aim for a pleasant and happy environment and visit most days to keep an eye on things.

Facilities

Toilet facilities in two blocks are basic and have mixed British and Turkish style WCs, washbasins and cold showers. Hot showers are available in the small block adjacent to the beach. Toilets for disabled campers. Small shop (all season). Watersports. WiFi. Dogs are not permitted. Off site: Restaurant/pizzeria close to entrance. Tennis 1 km. Bus service. Greek temples of Paestum.

Open: 1 March - 30 October.

Directions

Take SS18 through Paestum and, at southern end of town before the antiquities, turn right as signed and follow to sea. At crossroads turn left and a little further turn right. Site is well signed, but there are many signs and some are obscured by vegetation, so drive slowly. GPS: 40.42061, 14.99608

Charges guide

Per person	€ 5.00 - € 9.00
pitch incl. electricity	€ 8.50 - € 15.00

For latest campsite news, availability and prices visit
alanrogers.com

Pompeii
Camping Zeus

Via Villa dei Misteri, I-80045 Pompeii (Campania) T: 081 861 5320. E: info@campingzeus.it

alanrogers.com/IT68300

The naming of this site is obvious once you discover it is just 50 metres from the entrance to the fantastic ruins at Pompeii (closer than the car park). It is a reasonably priced, city-type site perfect for visiting the famous Roman archaeological sites here. The site's 100 pitches, all for touring units, are on flat grass under mature trees that give shade. All have access to 10A electricity. Larger units use the tarmac parking area. This site provides a safe central location and is of a high standard for the area, albeit with none of the holidaying trimmings.

Facilities

The single sanitary block is basic but clean and modernised, with British and Turkish style WCs. Showers have hot water with cold water in washbasins. No facilities for disabled campers. Washing machines. Shop. Gas supplies. Bar/restaurant at site entrance with good value daily menu at lunch times (evenings only in high season). WiFi (charged). Accommodation to rent. Off site: Pompeii, Sorrento, Herculaneum, Amalfi Coast.

Open: All year.

Directions

Leave Napoli-Salerno autostrada at the Pompeii Ovest exit. Turn left towards the ruins and go under the autostrada. A further 100 m. turn left towards Pompeii and the site. Site is straight ahead past the railway station. GPS: 40.74958, 14.4724

Charges guide

Per unit incl. 2 persons and electricity	€ 20.00 - € 24.00
extra person	€ 5.00 - € 6.00

Pozzuoli
Camping Il Vulcano Solfatara

Via Solfetara no. 163, I-80078 Pozzuoli (Campania) T: 081 526 7413. E: info@solfatara.it

alanrogers.com/IT68250

This is truly a unique site situated within the crater of an active volcano. Solfatara is one of the many volcanoes that surround Naples, Vesuvius being the most widely known. Here you can camp in a pleasant wooded area with basic but modern facilities, yet be just a couple of minutes from the barren moon-like landscape of the other side of the crater with its steaming fumaroles. There are no designated pitches but there are 100 electricity connections (4A) and you are free to pitch where you like. This is a site (and a sight) not to be missed, but is only for tents and small units, definitely not for any larger units, the problem being the access arch to the site, which is just 2.30 m. wide and is the only way in.

Facilities

The single sanitary block provides toilets (British and Turkish style), hot showers and washbasins. No facilities for disabled visitors. Washing machine. Motorcaravan services. Bar and small shop. Natural sauna and small swimming pool. WiFi (charged). Small volcano museum. Off site: The Solfatara Natural Park and the living, breathing volcano!

Open: All year.

Directions

Take Naples tangenziale from the autostrada and exit at exit N11 (Agnano). Follow signs towards Pozzuoli and turn right at lights at top of hill. Site is 3.5 km. along this road on the right. Local traffic can be a problem. GPS: 40.82858, 14.13583

Charges guide

Per person	€ 8.00 - € 9.90
pitch	€ 4.50 - € 14.50

Sorrento
Village Camping Santa Fortunata

Via Capo 39, I-80067 Sorrento (Campania) T: 081 807 3574. E: info@santafortunata.eu

alanrogers.com/IT68340

Village Camping Santa Fortunata is situated on the hillside just outside Sorrento among olive and lemon groves. There is plenty of shade but low hanging branches make some of the pitches unsuitable for larger units. There is a steep tarmac approach to some but the stunning views over the bay more than compensate. Pitches are of average size with several spaces for larger units and there is a feeling of spaciousness as many are separated by trees and shrubs intersected with wooden constructed walkways. Two small beaches can be reached via long steep inclines. A daily excursion to Capri (well worth taking) departs from one of the beaches.

Facilities

Five older style refurbished sanitary blocks with adjustable hot showers. Hot water for dishwashing but not laundry sinks. Washing machines and dryers. Restaurant/bar. Small well stocked shop. Swimming pool. Disco bar (high season). Mini farm. Boules pitch. Football and basketball court. Excursions. Bicycle and scooter hire. Car hire. WiFi. Off site: Beach 300 m. Boat launching 1 km. Riding 3 km.

Open: 1 April - 25 October.

Directions

From A3 (Naples-Salerno) follow signs to Pensisola Sorrentina. Exit at Castellammare di Stabia and on through Sorrento. Take SS145 towards Massa Lubrense, running along Via Capo. Site is 1.5 km. past Sorrento. GPS: 40.62753, 14.35736

Charges guide

Per unit incl. 2 persons and electricity	€ 22.00 - € 43.00
extra person	€ 6.50 - € 12.50

For latest campsite news, availability and prices visit

alanrogers.com

PUGLIA HAS FIVE PROVINCES: BARI, BRINDISI, FOGGIA, LECCE AND TARANTO

BASILICATA HAS TWO: MATERA AND POTENZA

Puglia is the long strip of land that forms the heel of the Italian 'boot', with the Gargano Peninsula as its spur. Holidaymakers are attracted to its sandy beaches and clean seas. Lying next to it is Basilicata, a remote and wild region that has remained largely unspoilt.

Made into a national park in 1991, the Gargano peninsula in Puglia boasts a diverse landscape of beaches, lagoons, forests and mountains. Up in the hills is the town of Monte Sant'Angelo. Home to one of the earliest Christian shrines in Europe, it attracts pilgrimages from all over the country. Further inland is the Forest of Shadows, an area covering 11,000 hectares with a variety of wildlife, ideal for walking. The seaside towns of Vieste, Rodi Garganico, Péshici and Manfredonia are popular with tourists, as are the Trémiti Islands – including San Nicola, San Domino and Capraia – off the Gargano coast. Heading south is Trani, one of the most important medieval ports with an ornate cathedral, and Bari. Ferries to Greece depart from Bari, as well as from Bríndisi. At the southern tip of Puglia is Lecce, renowned for its Baroque architecture, and the Salentine peninsula. Good beaches can be found along the western coast of the peninsula around Gallipoli. To the west, Basilicata is mostly upland country, scattered with ruins. The brooding town of Melfi has a formidable Norman castle, while nearby Venosa was once the largest Roman colony. The town has an archaeology park with remains of Roman baths and an amphitheatre.

Places of interest

Alberobello: home to white-washed circular buildings with conical roofs known as *trulli*, there are *trulli* restaurants, shops plus a cathedral.

Galatina: important wine-producing town, famous for its *tarantella* dance performed on the feast day of Saints Peter and Paul in June.

Lucera: ruins of Roman amphitheatre, 13th-century castle with fortified walls and towers.

Matera: town perched on edge of a ravine.

Mattinata: popular, small resort in Gargano.

Metaponto: Roman ruins, museums.

Vieste: holiday capital of Puglia with excellent beaches.

Cuisine of the region

Puglia is the main source of Italy's fish. It also produces some of the country's best olives and is famous for its almonds, tomatoes, figs, melons and grapes. Lamb is commonly eaten, often roasted with rosemary and thyme, and as there is little poultry, beef or pork in the region, horsemeat is popular, particularly in the Salento area. Peppers and *zenzero* (ginger) are widely used in dishes throughout Basilicata. Local cheeses include *ricotta*, *mozzarella*, *scamorza*, *burrata* (soft and creamy, made with cow's milk), and *caprini* (small fresh goat's cheese preserved in olive oil).

Braciole di cavallo: horsemeat steaks cooked in a rich tomato sauce.

Latte di mandorla: almond milk.

Panzarotti alla barese: pasta stuffed with meat sauce, egg and cheese, deep fried in olive oil.

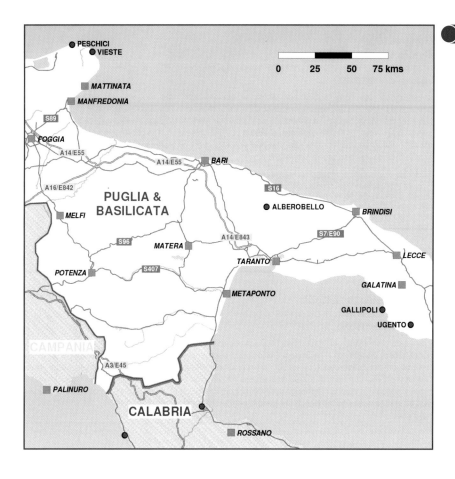

Alberobello
Camping Dei Trulli

Via Castellana, SP113 Monopoli-Alberobello km. 17, I-70011 Alberobello (Puglia) T: 080 432 3699.

E: info@campingdeitrulli.it **alanrogers.com/IT68700**

The UNESCO listed site at Alberobello is just 17 km. inland from the coast and offers the chance to see the unusual trulli properties. It is a dry, almost arid, landscape which is covered with olive groves, orchards, vineyards and the trulli (strange circular buildings with conical roofs and domed within, built from local limestone without mortar). Camping Dei Trulli is a short stay site offering visitors a chance to explore the area. It has 40 touring pitches all with 6A electricity. Bungalows and caravans are available to rent. The grottos of Castellana are not far away. These offer a one- or three-kilometre route through this speleological complex. Alternatively you could visit the Speleological Museum or the astronomical observatory at Sirio which offers the chance to view the sun through a telescope fitted with special filters.

Facilities

The very basic toilet block includes facilities for disabled visitors, but also houses the washing machine and is used for emptying chemical toilets. Small shop. Bar. Swimming pool and children's pool (15/6-30/9). Pool table and electronic games. Indoor disco during the winter months. WiFi over site (free). Off site: Alberobello (trulli properties) 1 km. Grottos of Castellana.

Open: 1 April - 31 October.

Directions

From E55 coast road south of Bari take Alberobello exit (SP113) and bear left then right. Site is 17 km. along this road. At crossroads go straight ahead towards Alberobello and site is on left 1.5 km. before the town. GPS: 40.801283, 17.251217

Charges guide

Per person	€ 0.00 - € 8.00
child (3-8 yrs)	€ 4.00 - € 5.00
pitch	€ 4.00 - € 7.00
electricity	€ 2.50

For latest campsite news, availability and prices visit
alanrogers.com

Gallipoli
Centro Vacanze La Masseria

I-73014 Gallipoli (Puglia) T: 083 320 2296. E: info@lamasseria.net

alanrogers.com/IT68655

Located near the Torre Sabea and within an ancient farm, this site provides 300 pitches under pinewood. During the low seasons most pitches are unmarked in two large areas, but in high season the lines of marked pitches at the end of the site with their high net screens come into use. Gallipoli is just a short ride away and the site operates a shuttle bus in high season. The old town has much to offer and the fish market and restaurants near the port entrance are well worth a visit. The private beach is just across the coastal road at the side of the site.

Facilities

Five sanitary blocks and 36 private bathrooms (to rent) provide ample toilets, showers and washbasins. Washing machines and laundry service. Motorcaravan services. Bar, restaurant and shop. Large swimming pool complex. Entertainment (1/6-15/9). Shuttle bus to Gallipoli in high season. Wine and oil tasting on site. Off site: Gallipoli.

Open: All year.

Directions

From the SS101 (Lecce-Gallipoli) leave at km. 30 towards the Porto. Site is close by and is well signed. Reception is beyond the restaurant and pools. GPS: 40.07417, 18.00889

Charges guide

Per unit incl. 2 persons	€ 20.00 - € 57.00
extra person	€ 6.00 - € 16.00

Gallipoli
Camping Baia di Gallipoli

Litoranea per Santa Maria di Leuca, I-73014 Gallipoli (Puglia) T: 083 327 3210. E: info@baiadigallipoli.com

alanrogers.com/IT68660

The western shoreline of Puglia offers beaches of excellent quality, interspersed with small villages and some holiday complexes. The Baia di Gallipoli campsite is in a quiet rural area to the south west of the town on a minor coast road. It offers 600 pitches, all with 6A electricity, under pine and eucalyptus trees. Cars are parked in a separate area and access for vehicles is strictly controlled, which gives the site a quiet, peaceful ambience. Although it is 800 m. from the beach, it has solved that problem by providing regular shuttle buses to the beach car park in partnership with others.

Facilities

Five clean, modern toilet blocks have been recently refurbished and include facilities for disabled visitors, both on the site and at the beach. Motorcaravan services. Washing machines. Shop. Bar and restaurant. Swimming pool. Tennis. 5-a-side football. Volleyball. Bocce. Fitness trail. Bicycle, car and fridge hire by arrangement. Children's clubs (4-12 yrs, 13-17 yrs). Entertainment. WiFi in bar and pool area (free). Shuttle bus to beach.

Open: 1 April - 15 September.

Directions

The SS101 south of Bari heads first to Lecce, then turns south west towards Gallipoli. Join SS274 towards S. Maria di Leuca and exit at Lido Pizzo. Follow coast road (SP215) towards Gallipoli. Site is 4 km. before Gallipoli. GPS: 39.998317, 18.0265

Charges guide

Per unit incl. 2 persons and electricity	€ 20.00 - € 54.00
extra person	€ 5.00 - € 16.00

Peschici
Centro Turistico San Nicola

Localitá San Nicola, I-71010 Peschici (Puglia) T: 088 496 4024. E: sannicola@sannicola.it

alanrogers.com/IT68450

This large site occupies a hillside position, sloping down to a cove with a 500 metre beach of fine sand – a special feature is an attractive grotto at the eastern end. Hard access roads lead to 800 terraced, sand/grass pitches (5A electricity), some with real shade. Some pitches are on the beach fringes (no extra charge) and there is a separate area for campers with animals. The infrastructure was beginning to look a little tired when we visited. Cars have to be parked away from the pitches in high season. The site is popular with German campers (tannoy announcements and most notices are in German only).

Facilities

Four toilet blocks of variable standards with British and Turkish style toilets, some with hot water in the washbasins and hot showers. One in the beach area had queues for showers when we visited (late June). Laundry facilities. Supermarket. Beach bar and snacks. Large bar/restaurant with terraces and pizzeria. Games room. Multisports area. Tennis. Watersports. Playground. Organised activities and entertainment for children (July/Aug). ATM. Dogs are not accepted in high season. Off site: Peschici town 1 km. Riding 6 km.

Open: 1 April - 15 October.

Directions

Leave A14 at Poggio Imperiale exit, and SS693 towards Peschici and Vieste. It is a winding coast road to Peschici. Follow signs to San Nicola and follow campsite signs. There are two sites very close to each other with virtually the same name. You want the second on the approach. It is 1.5 hours from the motorway. GPS: 41.94291, 16.03493

Charges guide

Per unit incl. 2 persons and electricity	€ 23.80 - € 49.40
extra person	€ 6.80 - € 13.40

Min. 1 week stay in high season.

For latest campsite news, availability and prices visit
alanrogers.com

Ugento
Camping Riva di Ugento

Litoranea Gallipoli, Santa Maria di Leuca, I-73059 Ugento (Puglia) T: 083 393 3600. E: info@rivadiugento.it

alanrogers.com/IT68650

There are some campsites where you can be comfortable, have all the amenities at hand and still feel you are connecting with nature. Under the pine and eucalyptus trees of the Bay of Taranto foreshore is Camping Riva di Ugento. Its 850 pitches nestle in and around the sand dunes and the foreshore area. They have space and trees around them and differ in size since the environment dictates the shape of many. The sea is only a short walk from most pitches and some are at the water's edge. The site buildings resemble huge wooden umbrellas and are in sympathy with the environment.

Facilities	Directions
Twenty toilet blocks with WCs, showers and washbasins (check opening times before pitching). New bathrooms. Supermarket and boutique. Bar. Restaurant. Takeaway. Swimming and paddling pools (10/6-10/9, charged). Tennis. Bicycle hire. Watersports incl. windsurfing school. Cinema. TV in bar. Entertainment for all ages (13/6-5/9). New play area. Beach volleyball. Bicycle hire. ATM. No dogs. WiFi over site (charged). Off site: Fishing. Riding 500 m. Boat launching 4 km. **Open:** 16 May - 11 October.	From Bari take Brindisi road to Lecce, then SS101 to Gallipoli, then SR274 towards Santa Maria di Leuca. Continue to Felline exit, and continue towards Torre San Giovanni, following the signs for Riva di Ugento. Site is well signed, turn right at traffic lights on SS19. GPS: 39.87475, 18.141117

Charges guide

Per unit incl. 2 persons, 1 child and electricity	€ 21.00 - € 47.00
extra person (over 2 yrs)	€ 5.00 - € 12.00

Vieste
Camping le Diomedee

CP289, I-71019 Vieste (Puglia) T: 088 470 6472. E: info@lediomedee.com

alanrogers.com/IT68460

Diomedee is situated at the far end of the Gargano peninsula, close to the Foresta Umbra, and is part of a chain. The site has 170 level touring pitches (6A), Some shade is obtained from mature trees and screens, and there are some flat, beachside pitches. The pleasant beach is of soft sand or you can jump into the swimming pool. The beach-front restaurant/pizzeria offers a value tourist menu and is great for a sunset meal in the cooling summer breezes.

Facilities	Directions
The large, modernised toilet block has hot water throughout, showers, British style WCs and washbasins. Facilities for disabled visitors. Washing machines. Motorcaravan services. Shop and fruit stall. Bar. Restaurant/pizzeria/takeaway. Large swimming pool with loud music. Windsurfing school. Tennis. Beach volleyball. Children's entertainment (high season). Free WiFi in pool area. No charcoal barbecues. Off site: Vieste and the Gargano park area. Excursions. **Open:** 1 May - 22 September.	Site is 5 km. from Vieste on the winding P52 coast road towards Pocchici. Allow extra time for the coast road. GPS: 41.91195, 16.124083

Charges guide

Per unit incl. 2 persons and electricity	€ 22.00 - € 54.00
extra person	€ 6.00 - € 16.00
child (3-12 yrs)	€ 3.00 - € 12.00
dog	free

Vieste
Punta Lunga Camping Village

CP339, localitá Defensola, I-71019 Vieste (Puglia) T: 088 470 6031. E: puntalunga@puntalunga.com

alanrogers.com/IT68480

Punta Lunga is located in the spectacularly beautiful Gargano region, a huge National Park, and nestles in an attractive bay. The 150 medium sized, terraced, sandy pitches (3.5-6A) are flat, mostly set on steep slopes, and some have shade. Camping along the shore is less formal and in some cases less shaded, but some pitches have spectacular views. There is a choice of restaurants. The upper one is finer dining, while the lower one is an informal beach restaurant. The site is well suited for energetic windsurfer types, but not for infirm or disabled campers.

Facilities	Directions
Two toilet blocks, some distance from pitches, have a mixture of unisex showers and dedicated toilets, mostly Turkish. The facilities are clean and fresh. Access difficult for infirm and disabled campers. Laundry facilities. Hairdresser. Small shop. Gas. Excellent restaurant with pleasant views. Beach bar with snacks. Gym. Children's clubs (high season). Small play area. Bicycle hire. Windsurfing school. Excursions. WiFi (charged). Dogs are not accepted. Off site: Restaurants, bars and shops. **Open:** 15 May - 25 September.	From north take A14 exit for Poggio Imperiale, then to Vico Gargano and Vieste. From south take A14 exit Foggia, then towards Manfredonia, Mattinata and Vieste. GPS: 41.89798, 16.15047

Charges guide

Per unit incl. 2 persons and electricity	€ 20.00 - € 49.00
extra person	€ 5.00 - € 14.50
child (3-12 yrs)	€ 3.00 - € 11.00

For latest campsite news, availability and prices visit
alanrogers.com

THERE ARE FIVE PROVINCES IN CALABRIA: CATANZARO, COSENZA, CROTONE, REGGIO DI CALABRIA AND VIBO VALENTIA

The toe of the Italian 'boot', Calabria, like its neighbouring region, is a sparsely populated region with unspoilt countryside. The coastline boasts fine, sandy beaches, while the interior features the rugged Aspromonte and Sila mountains, which dominate the landscape.

One of the main towns in the region is Cosenza, which is completely enclosed by mountains – the Sila to the east, the Catena Costiera to the west, separating it from the sea. The Sila massif is divided into three parts: the Sila Greca, Sila Grande and the Sila Piccola. Lying in the Sila Greca are the villages of Santa Sofia, San Sosmo and Vaccarizzo, which come alive during annual festivals held throughout the year. There are ski slopes in the Sila Grande plus numerous lakes, ideal for fishing. Camigliatello is one of the best known resorts here offering winter sports, riding and hiking. Lastly, Sila Piccola is the region's most densely forested section, which has been designated National Park status. South of Cosenza along the Tyrrhenian coast is Tropea, whose old town clings to the cliffside, offering superb views of the sea and beaches. There are more sandy beaches nearby at Capo Vaticano, while across on the Ionian coast is the popular resort of Rossano Scalo. Just inland from here is the attractive hilltown of Rossano while further south are the vineyards of Cirò. To the north of Rossano is Sibari, home to the world's largest archaeological site, covering 1,000 hectares; excavations have revealed evidence of ancient Greek and Roman civilisations.

Places of interest

Aspromonte: scenic mountainous region in the southernmost tip of Italy's boot.

Capo Colanna: Greek ruins, nearby beaches.

Gerace: impressive cathedral, ruined castle.

Locri: Greek ruins.

Pizzo: picturesque town with small castle and beaches.

Reggio di Calabria: national museum.

Soverato: popular resort with good beaches.

Stilo: home to the 10th-century, five-domed Cattolica.

Cuisine of the region

Food is largely influenced by Greek cuisine – aubergines, swordfish and sweets made with figs, almonds and honey. Many biscuits and cakes are made in honour of a religious festival or saint's day; they can be deep fried in oil, soaked in honey or encrusted with almonds. Pasta is popular as are pork and cheeses such as *mozzarella* and *pecorino*. Locally produced wines include the Greco di Bianco, a sweet white wine, and those from Cirò.

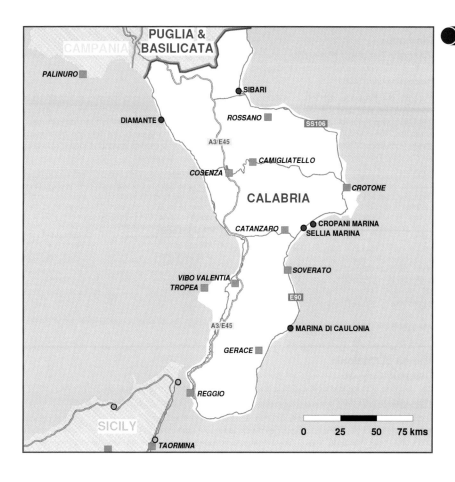

Cropani Marina
Camping Casa Vacanze Lungomare

Viale Venezia 46, I-88050 Cropani Marina (Calabria) T: 096 196 1167. E: info@campinglungomare.com

alanrogers.com/IT68830

Camping Casa Vacanze Lungomare is a small, family run site close to the town of Cropani Marina. There are 100 marked pitches in total and 80 of these are for touring. They are well laid out, all have 3/6A electricity and water points nearby and shade is provided on most by tall pine trees. The site has a private sandy beach which is accessed across a small road, just 20 m. from the pitches. Just outside the site, close to the entrance/reception area there are also a number of mobile homes/chalets available for rent. The friendly and helpful owner is able to arrange excursions to various places of interest. An excellent base for sightseeing with a National Park and waterfalls nearby which are well worth visiting.

Facilities

Two toilet blocks include showers (tokens required), and a mixture of Turkish and British style WCs. Facilities for disabled visitors. Washing machine. Motorcaravan services. Bar and restaurant/pizzeria. All weather tennis court/football pitch. Play area. Entertainment in high season. Accommodation to rent. WiFi on part of site. Off site: Sandy beach and local bars and restaurants. Riding 1 km.

Open: 1 April - 30 September.

Directions

Site is on the main coast road (SS106) south of Crotone on the way to Catanzaro. Just south of the resort of Botricello you come to Cropani Marina. Site is well signed at the junction towards the beach and is 500 m. on the right. GPS: 38.908917, 16.80945

Charges guide

Per unit incl. 2 persons	
and electricity	€ 18.80 - € 31.60
extra person	€ 5.50 - € 9.80
child (3-8 yrs)	€ 3.70 - € 6.80

For latest campsite news, availability and prices visit
alanrogers.com

Diamante
Villaggio Turistico Mare Blu

Cirella di Diamante, I-87020 Diamante (Calabria) T: 098 586 097. E: info@villaggiomareblu.it

alanrogers.com/IT68950

Mare Blu is a large site with lots of watersports activities and an open feel to the site, and is aimed at Italian families spending their holidays by the sea. This is a good site for a short stay to get a taste of the Italian way of camping, or a transit site whilst passing as it is one of the best in the area with many amenities. The 100 touring pitches are flat with some grass, 40 have electricity (3A) and most enjoy shade from trees. There is beach access under the railway line and the fine sand provides a safe area for children. The friendly staff speak a little English and are keen to please.

Facilities

Two units provide a mixture of British and Turkish style toilets. Facilities are in separate blocks – showers are separate from toilets, but are clean with hot water. Unit for disabled campers. Washing machines and dryers. Motorcaravan services. Shop. Self-service restaurant. Bar and terrace with views. Snack bar. Outdoor swimming pool. TV room. Play area. Minigolf. Tennis. Entertainment on the beach. Full evening entertainment programme. Disco. Miniclub. Canoes. Windsurfing. Communal barbecue. Boat, mountain bike and bicycle hire. Off site: Beach 300 m. Riding 2 km. Golf 40 km.

Open: 3 April - 26 September.

Directions

From E45 Salerno-Cosenza road take Cosenza Nord and SS107 to Paola. Then SS585 coast road north to Diamante. Site is well signed before reaching the village of Cirella. GPS: 39.7035, 15.814

Charges guide

Per person	€ 10.00 - € 21.00
child (3-12 yrs)	€ 6.00 - € 12.00

Marina di Caulonia
Camping Calypso

Via Nazionale, I-89040 Marina di Caulonia (Calabria) T: 096 482 028. E: info@calypso.st

alanrogers.com/IT68860

Camping Calypso is a simple family run site, situated beside the Ionian Sea and with direct access to long, sandy beaches. There are 96 pitches available for touring on level hardstandings with 3A electricity and some have wonderful views. Good shade is provided by mature trees. On-site facilities include a traditional and very pleasant bar, a restaurant and pizza takeaway. A large amphitheatre provides a stage for entertainment in high season and Hawaiian nights are organised on the beach. This site is perfectly located for a relaxing holiday with the added advantage of excellent sightseeing if you wish. If you are feeling energetic, there are hiking trails to the waterfalls in Marmarico. Within 20 km. are the Greek excavations at Monasterace.

Facilities

One large, central and clean sanitary block with mostly British style WCs. Coin-operated showers in small cubicles. Cold water only to open style washbasins. Baby room. Laundry facilities. Good motorcaravan services. Pizza takeaway (wood fired oven), traditional bar and restaurant (15/5-5/9). Beach bar. Play area. Entertainment in high season. WiFi throughout. Off site: Sandy beach 50 m. Bicycle hire 100 m. Supermarket 800 m.

Open: 1 April - 1 October.

Directions

From autostrada, exit (Rosarno) and head east towards Siderno. Take SS106 north to Marina di Caulonia. Site clearly signed 1 km. north of town. GPS: 38.354117, 16.484917

Charges guide

Per unit incl. 2 persons and electricity	€ 18.50 - € 39.50
extra person	€ 4.50 - € 10.00
child (2-5 yrs)	€ 3.00 - € 7.00
dog	€ 1.50 - € 3.00

No credit cards.

For latest campsite news, availability and prices visit
alanrogers.com

Sellia Marina
Camping Costa Blu

Localitá Finocchiaro, I-88050 Sellia Marina (Calabria) T: 0449 602 32. E: info@costabluresidence.it
alanrogers.com/IT68850

This tiny campsite of just 50 clean, level pitches has remarkable features for its size plus an attractive Italian ambience. This is a great site if you think small is beautiful and it is a cut above the other sites in this area, with very favourable prices in low season. The generously sized pitches (with 3A electricity) are shaded by pines and eucalyptus. The clean beach is just 30 m. through a secure gate and it is excellent for relaxing and enjoying the tranquil atmosphere, to soak up the sun or swim in the cool Ionian sea. The very attractive pool has a slide and a separate paddling pool and close by there is a small, smart amphitheatre for family entertainment, which again is unusual in a site of this size. First class tennis and 'bocce' courts (artificial surfaces) are near the beach access.

Facilities

One block of sanitary facilities has a mixture of Turkish and British style toilets and unisex coin-operated showers (20c). Washing machine. Motorcaravan services. Bar, restaurant and takeaway. Pleasant small pool complex with a slide. Paddling pool. Play area. Beach volleyball. Small amphitheatre. Entertainment and miniclub. Bicycle hire. WiFi over site (free). Off site: Watersports. Fishing. Restaurants, bars and shops.

Open: 25 May - 14 September.

Directions

Take SS106 Crotone-Reggio road. At km. 199.7 marker in village of Sellia Marina take a turn towards beach with campsite signs. Site well signed over railway line. At tall eucalyptus trees, turn left then left again and right where signed. Narrow turn into site. GPS: 38.8929, 16.7634

Charges guide

Per unit incl. 2 persons	
and electricity	€ 12.00 - € 36.00
extra person (over 3 yrs)	€ 3.00 - € 9.00
dog	€ 1.00 - € 4.00

Sibari
Camping Pineta di Sibari

Ctra da Fuscolara, I-87011 Sibari (Calabria) T: 098 174 135. E: info@pinetadisibari.it
alanrogers.com/IT68600

Calabria was immortalised in the drawings of Edward Lear who, travelling on a donkey in 1847, was transfixed by the landscape. Camping Pineta di Sibari is on the Ionian Sea coast and has 500 touring pitches, all with electricity (4-6A), under pine and eucalyptus trees. Most are of a good size and many have sea views. The large sandy beach stretches for miles in both directions and the backdrop is the mountains of the Pollino National Park. This is a rural area and is away from the industrial areas found further south along this coast. Karin Rudolph runs a happy site where peace and quiet are prime features. This is a good site for a long stay in low season or for family holidays in the summer months, but expect to find the site very busy then as it is very popular with German and Italian campers.

Facilities

Five toilet blocks include showers, WCs (Turkish and British style) and open style washbasins. Facilities for disabled visitors. Motorcaravan services. Bar, restaurant takeaway, bazaar and shop (all 1/6-10/9). Bicycle hire. Tennis. Sandy beach with sunbeds and shades (to rent). Communal barbecue area. Mobile homes to rent. WiFi on part of site (charged). Off site: Ancient Sibari. Pollino National Park. Golf and riding 4 km.

Open: 26 March - 25 September.

Directions

Take SS106 south towards Reggio Calabria. South of Trebisacce take Villapiana Scalo exit (third Villapiana exit). Turn right along coast road (SS106R), then left at sign for site and over level crossing. To avoid narrow tunnel (2.8 m. headroom), after level crossing turn right and go straight on as road bears left. Site is 700 m. GPS: 39.77983, 16.4791

Charges guide

Per unit incl. 2 persons	
and electricity	€ 20.00 - € 38.00
extra person	€ 5.00 - € 9.50
child (3-6 yrs)	free - € 5.00
dog	€ 3.00 - € 5.00

For latest campsite news, availability and prices visit
alanrogers.com

SICILY COMPRISES THE FOLLOWING PROVINCES:
AGRIGENTO, CALTANISSETTA,
CATANIA, ENNA, MESSINA, PALERMO,
RAGUSA, SIRACUSA AND TRAPANI

The largest island in the Mediterranean, Sicily has seen a range of settlers come and go, from the early Greeks and Romans to the Arabs and Normans, French and Spanish. With its beach resorts, volcanic islands, ancient sites and varied cuisine, Sicily is also home to Mount Etna.

The capital of Sicily is the bustling city of Palermo. With its medieval streets and markets, it has the island's greatest concentration of sights and architecture that boasts a range of styles from Arabic to Norman, Baroque and Art Nouveau. Boats depart from here to the tiny volcanic island of Ústica, renowned for its marine life and popular with divers. Along with Milazzo and Messina, the capital also provides connections to the Aeolian Islands, of which Lípari is the most popular. Outside the capital is Monte Pellegrino, which offers superb views of the city, plus the seaside resort of Mondello. Europe's highest volcano, Mount Etna, is situated in the east. Still active, its lower reaches are accessible on foot or by public transport. The closest town to the summit is Randazzo, built entirely of lava, as is Catania, situated further down the Ionian coast. Engulfed by lava in 1669 followed by an earthquake in 1693, Catania has been rebuilt on a grand scale. The coastline also bears traces of ancient Greek cities, most notably at Megara Hyblaea and Siracusa. To the west is Marsala, famous for its fortified wine, and the harbour town of Trápani, a jumping off point for the Egadi Islands.

Places of interest

Acireale: spa centre, hosts one of Sicily's best festivals in February.

Agrigento: nearby archaeological area known as the Valley of the Temples.

Enna: Sicily's highest town.

Erice: medieval town, cathedral.

Marsala: home of the famous wine, in production since the 18th century.

Segesta: ancient temple, nearby ruins of an ancient theatre where summer concerts are held.

Taormina: lively resort with sandy beaches, ancient Greek theatre and 13th-century cathedral.

Vulcano: Aeolian Island, with hot mud baths and fine black beaches.

Cuisine of the region

Given its location, Sicily has attracted an endless list of invaders which has impacted on its food, resulting in one of Italy's most varied cuisines. Fish is abundant, including anchovies, sardines, tuna and swordfish, often teamed with pasta, as in *spaghetti con le sarde*. Sicily is famous for its sweets, in particular *cannoli*, fried pastries stuffed with sweet ricotta. Made from sheep's milk, ricotta is used in a variety of desserts, with *pecorino* and *provolone* cheeses also widely available. Wines include Marsala, Corvo and Regaleali.

Maccheroni con le sarde: sardines cooked with fennel, raisins, pine nuts, breadcrumbs and saffron.

Pesce spada: swordfish steak, grilled or pan-fried with lemon and oregano.

Sicilin cassata: ice-cream made with ricotta, nuts, candied fruit and chocolate in a sponge cake.

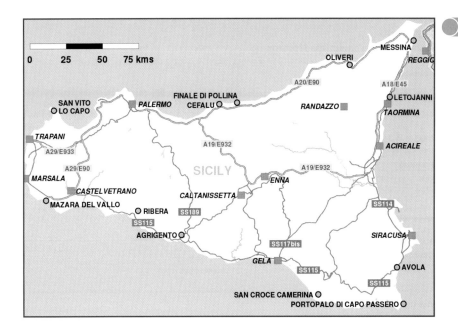

Agrigento
Camping Valle dei Templi

Viale Emporium, I-92100 Agrigento (Sicily) T: 092 241 1115. E: info@campingvalledeitempli.com

alanrogers.com/IT69175

This site shares its name with Sicily's premier attraction, the UNESCO World Heritage-listed complex of temples and old city walls of the ancient town of Akragas, although this is about 2.5 km. to the north. Built as a beacon for homecoming sailors, the five Doric temples built on a ridge are an impressive sight even at a distance. This site is therefore a good base from which to explore these ruins, together with the numerous coach loads of tourists. With 195 unmarked pitches, about half are suitable for caravans and campers. The majority have access to 8A electricity. The site occupies a sloping, suburban location and has a good swimming pool and sun deck (in use during high season). Tents pitch informally around the site. The modern, large town of Agrigento is about 4 km. away and a regular bus service operates from outside the site.

Facilities

The single sanitary block in the centre of the site provides WCs, showers and washbasins. Facilities for disabled visitors. Motorcaravan services. Washing machine. Bar and takeaway service (1/6-30/9). Swimming pool (from 1/6 to end of season). Playground. Free WiFi throughout. Off site: Fishing 1 km. Riding 2 km. Valle dei Templi and Agrigento.

Open: All year.

Directions

From the main SS115 road or the SS640, follow signs to San Leone, just east of Agrigento. Site is on left just as you enter the town, 700 m. before the coast. GPS: 37.26935, 13.5835

Charges guide

Per unit incl. 2 persons and electricity	€ 19.00 - € 27.00
extra person	€ 5.50 - € 7.50
child (4-13 yrs)	€ 4.00 - € 5.50

For latest campsite news, availability and prices visit
alanrogers.com

Agrigento
Camping Internazionale Nettuno

Via Lacco Ameno N3, San Leone, I-92100 Agrigento (Sicily) T: 092 241 6268. E: info@campingnettuno.com

alanrogers.com/IT69180

You will receive a friendly welcome from the helpful owner and staff at Internazionale Nettuno. It is a small site in an excellent location, providing a good place to get an early start to see the amazing ruins before the heat of the day. Alternatively, it would make a quiet place to stay after touring the ruins as it is alongside a beautiful sandy beach. The 50 pitches for touring are on shady level terraces, some with their own beach access. Various games, music and entertainment are provided on site. There is also a restaurant, pizzeria and a bar, all open all year. A small number of mobile homes are available for rent.

Facilities

One large central sanitary block (unisex in low season) provides controllable hot showers and small cabins. Facilities for disabled visitors. Motorcaravan service area. Well stocked shop. Bar. Restaurant and pizzeria. Direct beach access. Fishing. Free WiFi on part of site. Only charcoal barbecues permitted. Off site: Bar, restaurants and excellent white sandy beach nearby.

Open: All year.

Directions

Site is by the beach at San Leone on the south coast of Sicily. From S115 road follow signs to San Leone from where site is well signed some 2 km. east of the town. Access is a steep climb just after road leaves the coast. GPS: 37.24416, 13.61383

Charges guide

Per unit incl. 2 persons	€ 18.00 - € 24.00
extra person	€ 5.00 - € 7.00
No credit cards.	

Avola
Camping Sabbiadoro

Via Chiusa di Carlo, I-96012 Avola (Sicily) T: 093 156 0000. E: info@campeggiosabbiadoro.com

alanrogers.com/IT69215

This is truly one of Sicily's hidden gems and the Alia family will ensure your stay is pleasant and peaceful at this delightful campsite with 100 pitches. These are on terraces down towards the beach and there are stunning sea views. With over 100 different species of trees and flowers around the site, it is awash with colour and has good shade. A small, sandy beach complements the site's natural charm. When we arrived, a party was in progress to celebrate the natural products of the area and a huge copper pot was being used to make ricotta cheese, which within an hour was being distributed around the site, with local bread. It was delicious! Access would be difficult for larger motorcaravans.

Facilities

An ultra modern, brand new toilet block is now open with facilities for disabled visitors. Motorcaravan services (automated and hands-free). Shop and bar (1/5-31/10). Restaurant (15/5-15/9). TV room. Sandy beach. Fishing. Sailing. WiFi over part of site (charged). Off site: Avola with its unusual town planning.

Open: All year.

Directions

On the SS115 north of Avola the site is 400 m. down a narrow twisting lane. GPS: 36.93639, 15.17472

Charges guide

Per unit incl. 2 persons and electricity	€ 35.00 - € 38.00
extra person	€ 10.00
Credit cards over €70 accepted in high season.	

Cefalù
Camping Costa Ponente

Ctra da Ogliastrillo, SS113, I-90015 Cefalù (Sicily) T: 092 142 0085. E: info@hotel-kalura.com

alanrogers.com/IT69360

The pleasant Costa Ponente site, with easy access from the A20 and SS113 roads, is located between the small coastal railway line and the beach. However, its layout does much to minimise the impact of the infrequent trains. There are 170 touring pitches, all with 2A electricity, arranged on terraces, and almost 25% have water and drainage on the pitch. The site has a good ambiance and lovely views. An area for tents near the swimming pools caters for large groups travelling by coach. There is access to the beach, as well as sunbathing areas near the bar and pools.

Facilities

Four sanitary blocks provide good facilities with mainly Turkish style toilets, washbasins and hot showers. Facilities for disabled visitors. Washing machine. Motorcaravan services. Bar (all season). Shop. Snack bar/takeaway (July/Aug). Swimming pools. Tennis. Dogs are not accepted in August. WiFi. Off site: Bicycle hire 1 km. Cefalù 2 km. Riding 3 km.

Open: 1 April - 31 October.

Directions

From the A20 Cefalù exit take the SS113 towards the town. Site is at the 190.2 km. marker on the left down a slope and across a level crossing. GPS: 38.02684, 13.9828

Charges guide

Per unit incl. 2 persons and electricity	€ 24.00 - € 35.00
extra person	€ 6.50 - € 8.50
dog	€ 3.50

For latest campsite news, availability and prices visit
alanrogers.com

Finale di Pollina
Camping Rais Gerbi

Ctra Rais Gerbi, SS113 km. 172.9, I-90010 Finale di Pollina (Sicily) T: 092 142 6570. E: camping@raisgerbi.it
alanrogers.com/IT69350

Rais Gerbi provides very good quality camping with excellent facilities on the beautiful Tyrrhenian coast, not far from Cefalu. This attractive terraced campsite is shaded by well established trees and the 189 good sized touring pitches (6A electricity) vary from informal areas under the trees near the sea, to gravel terraces and hardstandings. Most have stunning views, many with their own sinks and with some artificial shade to supplement the trees. From the mobile homes to the unusual white igloos, everything here is being established to a high quality. The large pool with its entertainment area and the restaurant, like so much of the site, overlook the beautiful rocky coastline and aquamarine sea.

Facilities

Excellent new sanitary blocks with British style toilets, free hot showers in generous cubicles. Small shop, bar, restaurant and takeaway (all 1/4-31/10). Communal barbecue. Entertainment area and pool near the sea. Tennis. High quality accommodation and tents for rent. Rocky beach at site. WiFi over site (charged). Dogs are not accepted in August. Off site: Small village of Finale 500 m. Riding 4 km. Larger historic town of Cefalù 12 km.

Open: All year.

Directions

Site is on SS113 running along the north east coast of the island, km. 172.9, just west of the village of Finale (turn into site is at end of bridge on outskirts of village). It is 12 km. east of Cefalù and 11 km. north of Pollina. GPS: 38.02278, 14.15389

Charges guide

Per unit incl. 2 persons	
and electricity	€ 20.00 - € 46.00
extra person (over 3 yrs)	€ 5.00 - € 10.00

Letojanni
Camping Paradise

SS114 km 41, SS114 km. 41, I-98037 Letojanni (Sicily) T: 094 236 306.
E: campingparadise@campingparadise.it **alanrogers.com/IT69260**

Forty kilometres south of the ferry port at Messina, Camping Paradise is situated on a long narrow strip along the sea with direct beach access. Most of the pitches have views over the crystal clear waters. The 130 level, grass and gravel touring pitches are fairly small with paved access roads and shade from well established, mainly olive trees. This site with a mountain backdrop is very popular so you may need to book ahead in high season. There is some road noise and the local train runs nearby. Close to the town of Letojanni, this is an ideal place to stop and plan sightseeing tours to the ancient amphitheatre, Byzantine tomb or Mount Etna. Some of the antiquities in nearby Taormina date from the third century BC and are Greek in origin.

Facilities

One large centrally located sanitary block has a mixture of Turkish and British style toilets, fully adjustable hot showers and facilities for disabled visitors. Laundry. Motorcaravan services. Small shop for essentials. Large bar/restaurant with views over the sea. Lovely pool. Fitness area. Play area. Tennis. Football. Boules. Video games. WiFi on part of site. Off site: Rich in history, the area has many antiquities. Nearby town Letojanni is a popular seaside resort. Mount Etna within easy reach.

Open: 1 April - 15 October.

Directions

From the A18 motorway between Messina and Catania take Taormina exit and then turn north on S114 towards Letojanni. Site is on this road (S114) at 41 km. marker just north of the village of Letojanni. There is quite a sharp bend on entering the site and a 3.4 m. bridge. GPS: 37.89717, 15.32699

Charges guide

Per unit incl. 2 persons	
and electricity	€ 25.00 - € 40.00
extra person	€ 6.00 - € 10.00

For latest campsite news, availability and prices visit
alanrogers.com

Mazara del Vallo
Sporting Club Village & Camping
Ctra Bocca Arena, I-91026 Mazara del Vallo (Sicily) T: 092 394 7230. E: info@sportingclubvillage.com
alanrogers.com/IT69160

Mazara del Vallo can be found on Sicily's south west coast. As the crow flies, Tunisia is not far, and the town has a distinct Arabic influence in its winding streets. The site is 2.5 km. from Mazara and boasts some good amenities including a large swimming pool, surrounded by tall palm trees. Pitches (250 for touring) are grassy and generally well shaded. This is a lively site in high season with a wide range of activities and a regular entertainment programme. A pre-loaded card system is in operation, available from reception, as the site does not accept cash in the bar/restaurant.

Facilities
Heated sanitary block with small shower cubicles (may be stretched at busy times). Facilities for disabled visitors. Washing machine. Motorcaravan services. Shop (1/6-15/9). Restaurant, bar and large reception/function room. Play area with bouncy castles. Good sports club with swimming pool, floodlit football pitches, tennis and volleyball. Fishing. Bicycle hire. Free WiFi throughout. Charcoal barbecues permitted. Off site: Beach 350 m. Mazara 2.5 km. Various excursions organised by the site.

Open: 1 April - 5 October.

Directions
From the A29 take the Mazara del Vallo exit and head towards the town. Go straight over the first roundabout and after 1.5 km. turn right at the traffic lights toward the beach. At the roundabout exit left and go straight ahead to the site, not over the bridge. GPS: 37.63647, 12.61631

Charges guide
| Per unit incl. 2 persons and electricity | € 19.00 - € 39.80 |
| extra person | € 4.50 - € 8.90 |

Messina
Nuovo Camping Dello Stretto
Via Circuito, Torre Faro, I-98614 Messina (Sicily) T: 090 322 3051. E: info@campingdellostretto.it
alanrogers.com/IT69255

This delightful campsite is just 15 minutes from the port of Messina. With 70 pitches for caravans and motorcaravans to the rear of the site, all with 6A electricity, this offers a peaceful resting place after the long journey south. The site's restaurant and pizzeria, among the best we have seen on our travels, are set alongside the pools in a beautiful garden and are such that you will not want to walk to the other local establishments.

Facilities
The sanitary blocks provide ample toilets, showers and washbasins. Facilities for disabled visitors (plus another in the restaurant). Motorcaravan services. Shop, bar, restaurant and pizzeria (1/6-30/9). Two swimming pools with lifeguard. Miniclub (July/Aug). Bicycle hire. WiFi (charged). Off site: Messina and Taormina.

Open: 1 June - 30 September.

Directions
At Messina Port exit turn right at lights and head north along V. della Liberta, then Consolare Pompea (SS113), through Ganzirri with lake on your right. At first crossroads turn right again alongside the lake and at T-junction turn left. Site is on the left where the road forks. GPS: 38.26167, 15.63333

Charges guide
| Per unit incl. 2 persons and electricity | € 22.00 - € 27.00 |

Oliveri
Camping Villaggio Marinello
Marinello, I-98060 Oliveri (Sicily) T: 094 131 3000. E: marinello@camping.it
alanrogers.com/IT69300

Camping Marinello is located alongside the sea with direct access to a lovely uncrowded sandy beach with an informal marina and natural pool areas. The 220 gravel touring pitches here are shaded by tall trees and hedges. We enjoyed a delicious traditional meal in the excellent terraced restaurant with its lovely sea views. Tours are arranged to major sightseeing destinations such as Mount Etna, Taormina and the nearby Aeolian Islands. The Greco family have been here for over 30 years and work hard to ensure that their guests enjoy a pleasant stay. There is some noise from the coastal rail line which runs along the length of the site.

Facilities
Two adequate sanitary blocks with free hot showers. Washing machines. Bazaar, market and supermarket. Bar with sea views. Restaurant and terraced eating area also with views. Electronic games. Piano bar in high season. Tennis. Basketball. Volleyball. Diving centre and windsurf school. Dogs are not accepted in July/Aug. Free WiFi on part of site. Off site: Seaside resort-style town of Oliveri.

Open: All year.

Directions
From A20 take Falcone exit and follow signs to Oliveri. At the town turn north towards beach (site sign), then turn west along beach and continue 1 km. to site. Make a right turn immediately before a small narrow bridge (2.2 m. high and 2.5 m. wide). GPS: 38.13246, 15.05452

Charges guide
| Per unit incl. 2 persons and electricity | € 27.00 - € 46.00 |

For latest campsite news, availability and prices visit
alanrogers.com

Portopalo di Capo Passero
Camping Residence Capo Passero

Ctra da Vigne Vecchie, I-96010 Portopalo di Capo Passero (Sicily) T: 093 184 2333. E: info@italiaabc.com
alanrogers.com/IT69210

Camping Residence Capo Passero is located on the south east point of Sicily. There are often nice sea breezes at the campsite, which has a clean and well maintained appearance, although when we visited the shade was patchy due to the Italian custom of trimming trees aggressively. The 200 touring pitches are generally level and all have 6A electricity connections. The sandy beach, only 50 m. walk away, is inviting and there is a very good pool area with grassy areas to sunbathe. The nearby village is quite interesting and has a number of restaurants and bars. This is a good site for this region, there is a bar, mini-market, a restaurant with terrace and some sporting facilities. However, typically for Sicily, there are few hot showers and these are only provided during certain time periods so may be difficult to access in peak season. There are some local ruins and a port/marina close by.

Facilities

Three older style toilet blocks, all clean when visited, have washbasins but only cold showers. There are six warm showers near reception (token). Facilities for disabled visitors in 1 block. Shop (1/5-20/9). Attractive restaurant (1/6-25/8) and bar area. Excellent pool with grassy sunbathing area (July/Aug). Good play area. Disco area. Boules. Tennis. Good access to gently shelving sandy beach. WiFi on part of site (free). Off site: Local town with bars, restaurants and marina 1-1.5 km.

Open: 15 May - 15 September.

Directions

From SS115 road follow signs to Pachino, then Portopalo di Capo Passero. Site is located west of the town on the beach and there are some signs from the village. Low bridges may cause problems on some routes. GPS: 36.6775, 15.1208

Charges guide

Per unit incl. 2 persons	
and electricity	€ 27.50 - € 39.50
extra person	€ 7.00 - € 11.00
child (3-10 yrs)	€ 4.00 - € 8.00

Ribera
Camping Kamemi

Localitá Seccágrande, I-92016 Ribera (Sicily) T: 092 569 212. E: info@kamemivillage.com
alanrogers.com/IT69170

Camping Kamemi can be found close to Ribera in Sicily's south west corner, just 300 m. from the sea. There are 250 pitches here (electricity 6A Europlug) – some are shaded, others make use of artificial screening. Thirteen mobile homes are available for rent. There is a typically Sicilian restaurant (with some excellent local fish cuisine) and a pizzeria. A snack bar incorporates an ice cream parlour with typical Sicilian ice creams. Other on-site amenities include two swimming pools, a tennis court and a football pitch. In high season, a lively activity and entertainment programme is on offer, including Latin American music and a summer carnival.

Facilities

Two new blocks have small shower cubicles (token), open style washbasins with cold water, but no toilets – these are in the pool area. En-suite unit for disabled visitors (key). Laundry. Shop (1/5-30/9). Restaurant (1/6-15/9). Outdoor swimming pools (10/5-15/9, hats compulsory). Tennis. Football pitch. Activity and entertainment (July/Aug). Playground. Diving trips arranged. Mobile homes for rent. WiFi (charged). Off site: Beach and fishing 1 km. Riding 10 km. Ribera 7 km. Agrigento.

Open: All year.

Directions

From Agrigento, head up the coast towards Ribera on SS115. Before reaching Ribera, turn off to Secca Grande, and then follow signs to the site. GPS: 37.438304, 13.245145

Charges guide

Per unit incl. 2 persons	
and electricity	€ 11.00 - € 35.00

For latest campsite news, availability and prices visit
alanrogers.com

San Croce Camerina

Camping Scarabeo

Punta Bracecetto, Santa, I-97017 San Croce Camerina (Sicily) T: 093 291 8096. E: info@scarabeocamping.it
alanrogers.com/IT69190

Camping Scarabeo is a beautiful site located in Punta Braccetto, a little fishing port in Sicily's south east corner. It is a perfect location with exceptional facilities to match. Split into two separate sites (just 50 m. apart) with a total of 70 pitches, it is being constantly improved with care by Angela di Modica. All pitches are well shaded, some naturally and others with an artificial cane roof and have 3/6A electricity. Scarabeo lies adjacent to a sandy beach and the little village is close by. The site layout resembles a Sicilian farm courtyard and is divided into four principal areas. The ancient Greek ruins of Kamerina and Caucana are just a few kilometres from the site and their ruins can be reached by bicycle. The Riserva Naturale at the mouth of the River Irminio is also a popular excursion.

Facilities

Exceptional sanitary blocks provide personal WC compartments (personal key access). Ample hot showers (free low season). Facilities for disabled visitors. Washing machine. Excellent motorcaravan service point. Takeaway. Herb garden for campers. Direct access to beach. Playground. Entertainment programme in high season. Dog washing area. Excursions arranged all year. WiFi over site (charged). Mobile homes for rent. No gas or electric barbecues. Off site: Restaurant/café 500 m. Riding 3 km. Supermarket 4 km. Golf 6 km. Cycling and walking trails.

Open: All year.

Directions

Site is 20 km. south west of Ragusa. From Catania, take S194 towards Ragusa and, at Comiso, follow signs to San Croce Camerina, then Punta Braccetto, from where site is well signed. Use second entrance for reception. GPS: 36.81645, 14.46964

Charges guide

Per unit incl. 2 persons and electricity	€ 14.00 - € 36.50
child (3-7 yrs)	€ 2.00 - € 7.50

Excellent long term discounts in low season.

San Vito Lo Capo

El Bahira Camping Village

Ctra da Makari-Localitá Salinella, I-91010 San Vito Lo Capo (Sicily) T: 092 397 2577. E: info@elbahira.it
alanrogers.com/IT69140

El Bahira is a popular site in quite a remote area overlooking the Gulf of Makari toward Monte Cofano. The views are outstanding and the location is good as it is near the sea, nature reserves and ancient cities such as Segtesta and Selinunte with their awe inspiring antiquities. Partners Maurizio, Maceri, Sugameli and Michele, who speak good English, have chosen this area to develop a campsite of a high standard. The 200 fairly small pitches are on sloping gravel (chocks required), most are shady and all have electricity. There are also numerous statics which unfortunately rather spoil the look of the site. There is a separate area for tents.

Facilities

Three well placed sanitary blocks, showers are by token (€ 4 for 8 showers), these are unisex, in tiny cabins. Motorcaravan services. Supermarket. Restaurant and pizzeria. Swimming pool, children's pool and beach bar. Two entertainment areas. Tennis. Football/volleyball pitch. Sub-aqua facilities. Boat launching at rocky beach on site. Free WiFi on part of site. Off site: Popular resort village of San Vito Lo Capo 3 km. Riding and bicycle hire 4 km.

Open: 1 April - 4 October.

Directions

From the east follow the A19 motorway and take Castellammare del Golfo exit then follow the S187 towards Trapani. After 16 km. turn right and follow signs to San Vito Lo Capo and site is well signed off the road approaching the town. GPS: 38.150707, 12.73191

Charges guide

Per unit incl. 2 persons and electricity	€ 24.90 - € 37.60
child (0-3 yrs)	€ 3.00

For latest campsite news, availability and prices visit
alanrogers.com

**SARDINIA HAS FOUR PROVINCES: CAGLIARI,
NUORO, ORISTANO AND SASSARI**

With dramatic, rolling uplands covered with grassland, and a beautiful coastline boasting isolated coves, long sandy beaches and hidden caves, Sardinia offers more than just sunshine and clear waters: littered around the island are thousands of prehistoric nuraghic remains.

The busy port of Cágliari is the island's capital. Attractions include the city walls, archaeology museum and cathedral plus an impressive Roman amphitheatre. More ruins can be found just outside the city at Nora, while some 7,000 or so nuraghi are dotted all around the island. Unique to Sardinia, these stone-built constructions are remnants of Sardinia's only significant native culture. The most famous of them is at Su Nuraxi, the oldest and largest nuraghic complex, dating from around 1500 BC. The island's second city, Sássari, is known for its spectacular Cavalcata festival on Ascension Day; festivities include traditional singing and dancing plus a horse race. Not far from Sássari is Alghero, a major fishing port and the island's oldest resort. Surrounded by walls and defensive towers, the old town is full of narrow, cobbled streets with flamboyant churches and brightly coloured houses. Boat or car trips can also be made to Neptune's Grotto, a spectacular, deep marine cave, around the point of Capo Caccia. Sardinia's best known resort is the Costa Smeralda, one of the Mediterranean's loveliest stretches of coast, a 10 km. strip between the gulfs of Cugnana and Arzachena. Beaches can be found at Capriccioli, Rena Bianca and Liscia Ruia.

Places of interest

Bosa: small, picturesque seaside town.

Cala Gonone: bustling seaside resort and fishing port, with good beaches, isolated coves and natural caves including the famous Grotta del Bue Marino.

Carloforte: an attractive town on the island of San Pietro.

Dorgali: in the wine-growing region of Cannonau.

Maddalena Islands: popular tourist attraction, sandy and rocky beaches.

Oristano: nearby lagoon is home to one of the island's largest populations of flamingo.

Cuisine of the region

Fresh ingredients are widely used to create simple dishes: seafood, especially lobster, is grilled over open fires, as is suckling pig. Fish stews and pasta are popular. The island also produces a variety of breads. Cheeses tend to be made from ewe's milk, including *pecorino Sardo*. Nougat is a sweet Sardinian speciality and pastries are often flavoured with almonds, lemons or oranges. Vernaccia is the island's most famous wine.

Agnello arrosto: roast lamb, roasted on a spit or in casseroles with rosemary and thyme.

Bottarga: a version of caviar made with mullet eggs.

Culigiones: massive ravioli stuffed with cheese and egg.

Maloreddus: saffron flavoured pasta.

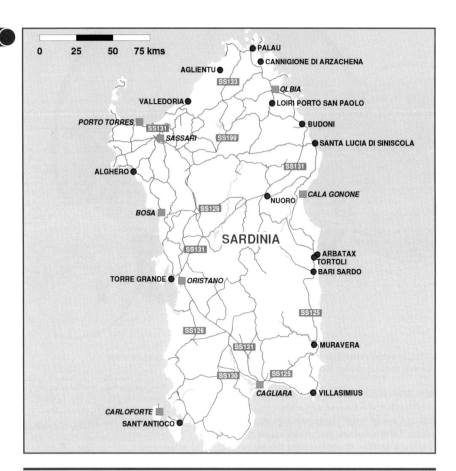

Aglientu

Camping Baia Blu la Tortuga

Pineta di Vignola Mare, I-07020 Aglientu (Sardinia) T: 079 602 200. E: info@campinglatortuga.com

alanrogers.com/IT69550

Tortuga is named after the giant turtle-like rock off the site's beautiful sandy beach, and is a large, professionally run campsite. The 450 sizeable touring pitches (all with 3/10A electricity) are on grass and coarse-grained sand, and mostly shaded by tall pines with banks of colourful oleanders and superb wide paved boulevards providing easy access. This is a busy, bustling site with plenty to do, with its attractive bars and restaurants close to the beach. The excellent play areas are cleverly placed to allow parents a break whilst enjoying lunch and dinner, but there are no pools here. The site's full entertainment programme, based in a pleasant auditorium, is first class. Overall, we were impressed by this quality family site. Tortuga is used by many tour operators, but there is little interference with the touring pitches. A member of Leading Campings group.

Facilities	Directions
Four excellent, clean sanitary blocks (most with solar panels for hot water) with free hot showers, WCs, bidets and washbasins. Facilities for disabled campers. Quality private cabins for rent. Washing machines and dryers. Motorcaravan services. Supermarket. Bazaar. Bars. Restaurant and self-service restaurant, snack bar and takeaway. Gas. Gym. Massage (July/Aug, charged). Hairdresser. Doctor's surgery. Playground. Tennis. Games and TV rooms. Windsurfing, kite surfing and diving schools. Internet point and WiFi area (charged). Entertainment and sports activities (mid May-Sept). Excursions. Barbecue area (not permitted on pitches). Two specially adapted mobile homes are available for family members with disabilities. Off site: Disco 50 m.	Site is on the north coast road (SP 90) between the towns of Costa Paradiso and Santa Teresa di Gallura (18 km) at Pineta di Vignola Mare and is well signed around the 47 km. marker. GPS: 41.12436, 9.067594

Open: 28 March - 14 October.

Charges guide

Per unit incl. 2 persons,	
water and electricity	€ 20.00 - € 43.00
extra person	€ 6.50 - € 14.50
dog	€ 3.50 - € 8.00

Alghero
Camping Torre del Porticciolo

Localitá Porticciolo, Sede lagale via G Ferret 17, I-07041 Alghero (Sardinia) T: 079 919 010.
E: info@torredelporticciolo.it **alanrogers.com/IT69950**

Torre del Porticciolo is set high on a peninsula with fabulous views from some parts of the site over the sea and old fortifications. It is family owned with striking traditional old buildings, attractive landscaping and a large pool and paddling pool. Spread over a large area, the site is mostly under the shade of pine trees. A few pitches enjoy limited sea views through the trees. The attractive beach is accessed down a steep slope. The amenities are all by the entrance, with the restaurant and pool both very popular. We did notice a large number of intrusive stray cats on our visit.

Facilities

The two mature sanitary blocks have exclusively Turkish style toilets. The few British style toilets are in locked cabins with a key on request. Hot showers are free. Washing machines. Motorcaravan services. Supermarket. Restaurant. Good supervised pool and paddling pool. Aerobics. Fitness centre. Play areas. Bicycle hire. Miniclub. Entertainment (July/Aug). Excursion service. Beach 100 m. down very steep slope. Excellent diving. WiFi in restaurant (charged). Off site: Fishing. Sailing.

Open: 15 May - 10 October.

Directions

Take SS291 Sassari-Alghero road east, then the SS55 to Capo Caccia. Turn to Porticciolo town where site is well signed. GPS: 40.6423, 8.1906

Charges guide

Per unit incl. 2 persons and electricity	€ 26.00 - € 52.00
extra person	€ 7.00 - € 15.00
junior (3-12) or senior (over 60 yrs)	€ 4.00 - € 12.00
dog	€ 2.00 - € 8.00

Alghero
Camping Village Laguna Blu

SS 127 bis, Fertilia, I-07041 Alghero (Sardinia) T: 079 930 111. E: info@campeggiocalik.it
alanrogers.com/IT69970

Camping Village Laguna Blu is a large site, pleasantly placed between the sea and a huge lagoon, the beach being directly across the road from the site. Most of the 600 pitches (450 for touring units) have 6A electricity and are shaded with pine and eucalyptus trees. Some pitches are in the trees, others are on level ground in long rows, the end ones enjoying lagoon-side positions. A considerable number are fully serviced. On-site amenities are close to the entrance and include a novel white, canvas-roofed restaurant/pizzeria plus a self-service restaurant.

Facilities

Four renovated sanitary blocks provide a high standard of facilities. Units for disabled campers. Restaurant/pizzeria. Self-service restaurant. Takeaway. Supermarket. Play area. Activity and entertainment programme. Bicycle hire. Boat launching. WiFi (charged). Watersports. Sea fishing. Mobile homes and chalets to rent. Off site: Alghero town. Outdoor swimming pool, golf and riding 2 km.

Open: 1 April - 31 October.

Directions

The site is to the north of Alghero on the north west coast of Sardinia. It is close to the 41 km. marker on the coast road (SS127) near Fertilia. The site is well signed. GPS: 40.594571, 8.29152

Charges guide

Per unit incl. 2 persons and electricity	€ 18.50 - € 44.00
extra person	€ 5.50 - € 12.00
child (3-9 yrs)	€ 3.40 - € 8.50

Arbatax
Camping Telis

Baia di Porto Frailis, I-08048 Arbatax (Sardinia) T: 0782 667 140. E: info@campingtelis.com
alanrogers.com/IT69695

Camping Telis has been cleverly carved out of a steep and rocky hillside above the bay of Port Frailis. The 130 fairly level pitches (with 6A electricity) are mostly well shaded and have absolutely superb views over the bay. There is direct but deeply stepped access to two small private beaches, one sandy, the other a little rugged. The lovely restaurant and bar have very long terraces and are perfect for a relaxing evening whilst enjoying the fabulous views. Two saltwater swimming pools and an impressive wellness centre are new additions to this quality site. The site is not suitable for disabled visitors.

Facilities

Very modern sanitary blocks. Motorcaravan services. Shop, bar/restaurant and terrace, pizzeria (1/8-20/10). Swimming pools (15/4-15/11). Wellness centre. Play area. Private beaches. Limited entertainment in high season. Communal barbecues. Accommodation for hire. WiFi over site (free). Off site: Excursions organised. Roman and Neolithic remains. Bicycle/scooter hire 1 km. Riding 3 km. Golf. Watersports. Boat trips. Wine tasting.

Open: All year.

Directions

Camping Telis is on eastern side of Sardinia off SS131, 1 km. from Arbatax at the bay of Porto Frailis. Site is well signed. GPS: 39.925, 9.7069

Charges guide

Per unit incl. 2 persons and electricity	€ 28.00 - € 52.00
extra person	€ 8.00 - € 15.00
child (3-0 yrs)	€ 5.00 - € 8.00
dog	free - € 5.00

For latest campsite news, availability and prices visit
alanrogers.com

Bari Sardo
Camping La Pineta
Localitá Planargia, I-08042 Bari Sardo (Sardinia) T: 078 229 372. E: info@campingbungalowlapineta.it
alanrogers.com/IT69715

Camping La Pineta is a lovely small campsite run by the delightful couple, Tziania and Guliano Carraeoi, who live on site. The touring pitches are level and clean, equipped with 6A electricity connections, and are shaded by pine and eucalyptus trees. The beautiful beach is a 400 m. walk alongside a safe river complete with waterbirds. The pretty restaurant, bar/café, pizzeria and mini market offer a great choice of fare. La Pineta gives excellent value for money, and if you enjoy cosy sites where you are treated as a friend, this will be a little piece of heaven for you. We loved it! In a quiet, rural location, this would make a good base for exploring the varied coastline and Saracen towers. Many places can be reached by foot, by mountain bike or even on horseback. The nearby little green steam train will take you through some stunning scenery.

Facilities
One spotlessly clean sanitary block with a mixture of British and Turkish style toilets, hot showers, baby room and facilities for disabled campers. Laundry. Motorcaravan services. Shop. Bar. Café/bar. Restaurant and pizzeria. Play area. Kayaking. Barbecue. Diving organised. Dog beach. Activities for children (July/Aug). Accommodation to rent. Bicycle hire. WiFi in bar. Torches useful. Off site: Riding 100 m. Boat trips and hire. Fishing. Steam train. Archaeological sites.

Open: 3 April - 31 October.

Directions
Camping La Pineta is 80 km. north east of Cagliari. From Cagliari take SS125 towards Olbia. Just after Tertenia follow signs to Bari Sardo. On entering Bari Sardo follow signs on right to site in 3 km. GPS: 39.82028, 9.67032

Charges guide
Per unit incl. 2 persons and electricity	€ 15.50 - € 32.00
extra person	€ 4.50 - € 9.50
child (3-10 yrs)	€ 3.00 - € 6.00
dog	free

Bari Sardo
Camping l'Ultima Spiaggia
Localitá Planargia, I-08042 Bari Sardo (Sardinia) T: 078 229 363. E: info@campingultimaspiaggia.it
alanrogers.com/IT69720

L'Ultima Spiaggia (the ultimate beach) is an apt name as the beach really is extremely pleasant, although coarse grained. There are four superb interlinked paddling and swimming pools, and the facilities have a bright, colourful décor. The 252 pitches all have 3/6A electricity, are terraced on sand and some enjoy limited sea views. The entertainment programme can be enjoyed from the terrace of the bar. The restaurant offers a variety of good food, including local seafood specialities. Half of the pitches are occupied by mobile homes but these are kept separate at the top area of the site. Access to the beach (with lifeguard) and a variety of watersports is gained through a security gate. A sound, but rather expensive site.

Facilities
Two toilet units include facilities for babies and disabled campers, but are some way from the lower pitches. Washing machines and dryers. Motorcaravan services. Small supermarket. Restaurant and snack bar. Play areas. Domestic animal area with donkeys. Windsurfing, diving and sailing. Aerobics. Riding. Tennis. Minigolf. Canoeing. Bicycle hire. Miniclub. Multisports area. Entertainment (mostly in Italian). WiFi (charged). Excursions. Torches essential. Off site: Restaurants, bars and shops. Fishing. Boat launching. Kite surfing. Free-climbing.

Open: 20 April - 30 September.

Directions
Site is on east coast of Sardinia, well signed from the main coast road, the SS125 in the village of Bari Sardo. Continue to Torre di Bari and look for signs which direct you along the seafront to the site. GPS: 39.819003, 9.670484

Charges guide
Per unit incl. 2 persons and electricity	€ 26.00 - € 55.50
extra person	€ 7.00 - € 16.00
child (1-12 yrs. acc. to age)	€ 4.50 - € 8.50
dog	€ 4.50 - € 6.50

For latest campsite news, availability and prices visit
alanrogers.com

Budoni
Camping Pedra & Cupa
Via Nazionale, I-08020 Budoni (Sardinia) T: 078 484 4004. E: info@pedraecupa-camping.com
alanrogers.com/IT69650

This small and attractive site has had much thought put into its planning and construction. Modern bungalows (for rent) screen the camping area from the coastal road. It is close to the white sands of the lovely beach and enjoys the shade of eucalyptus and pine trees along the coast. The 55 level, grassy pitches have 6A electricity and some have artificial shade. The pleasant restaurant/bar complex offers a variety of good food, along with entertainment in high season on a stage close to the terraces. The site is divided by a shallow river, which is safely fenced.

Facilities

Twin mature sanitary blocks provide toilets (mainly Turkish style), open style washbasins and ample hot showers (€ 0.50/3 minutes). Motorcaravan services. Shop. Restaurant. Pizzeria. Bar. Takeaway (all 15/6-15/9). Swimming pool and sunbathing terrace (little shade). Tennis. Football. Entertainment (July/Aug). WiFi (charged).

Open: 1 May - 30 September.

Directions

Site is at the southern end of Budoni town and well signed. GPS: 40.700315, 9.71395

Charges guide

Per unit incl. 2 persons	
and electricity	€ 19.00 - € 46.50
extra person	€ 5.50 - € 15.00
child (2-12 yrs)	€ 3.00 - € 9.00

Cannigione di Arzachena
Isuledda Holiday Centre
Localitá Laconia, I-07021 Cannigione di Arzachena (Sardinia) T: 078 986 003. E: info@isuledda.it
alanrogers.com/IT69630

This large, high quality, natural campsite is part of the Baia group and has something for everyone, with an amazing choice of activities and entertainment. Some of the 600 good sized, gravel pitches (with 4A electricity) have magnificent views over the Archena Gulf. We loved the outstanding pitches perched directly over the sea and the many beaches. Other pitches enjoy shade from eucalyptus trees and are flat. Cars must be parked outside the entrance. The central area buzzes with activity, although it is possible to find a quiet area to relax. A very high standard of camping is provided here and when we visited, everything was just right.

Facilities

Five sanitary blocks include British and Turkish style toilets and facilities for disabled visitors. Another block has been upgraded to a very high standard with family rooms for hire. Showers. Washing machines. Motorcaravan services (charged). Large supermarket. Restaurant, pizzeria and snack bar. Aerobics. Gym with bar. Play areas. Boat, car, bicycle and scooter hire. Windsurfing. Sailing. Sub-aqua. Marina. Miniclub. Entertainment. Excursions. Disco and beer bar (can be noisy until late). WiFi (charged). Dogs are accepted in one area. Off site: Riding 10 km. Golf 15 km.

Open: 1 April - 30 October.

Directions

Site is on the Costa Smeralda in the north east of Sardinia. From SS125 Olbia-Cannigione road, south of Arzachena, take road north towards Baia Sardinia. Then follow road north to Cannigione, go through town and further north for 2 km. where the site is well signed. GPS: 41.1302, 9.4387

Charges guide

Per unit incl. 2 persons	
and electricity	€ 21.00 - € 48.00
extra person	€ 7.00 - € 15.50

Loiri Porto San Paolo
Camping Tavolara
Località Porto Taverna, I-07020 Loiri Porto San Paolo (Sardinia) T: 078 940 166.
E: info@camping-tavolara.it **alanrogers.com/IT69640**

This smallish site has just 200 pitches (with 3/10A electricity), which are flat and well shaded, with a garden atmosphere created by flowers and hedging. South of Olbia and just 30 minutes from the ferry port and airport, it is a quiet and pleasant site. It is 500 m. from the beach (shuttle bus provided). This is a great location opposite Isola Tavolara, literally a mountain rising from the sea. It is famous for the legendary 'goats with golden teeth', a phenomenon caused by the grass they eat. The restaurant and bar with their terraces are very welcome in the cool evenings. We like the atmosphere at this typical Sardinian site, which would be enjoyed by mature campers.

Facilities

Three mature sanitary blocks provide toilets (mainly Turkish style), washbasins and showers (torch required). Private facilities for hire. Facilities for disabled campers. Motorcaravan services. Restaurant and bar. Pizzeria. Shop (all facilities open Easter-Sept). Diving school. Archery. Bocce. Football. Tennis. Excursions and entertainment (high season). Free WiFi. Train to beach.

Open: 1 April - 30 October.

Directions

Site is at 300 km. marker on SS125 south of Olbia. From port follow signs for Aeroporto and pass the airport heading for San Teodoro. Site is on left just past Porto San Paolo. GPS: 40.858612, 9.642753

Charges guide

Per unit incl. 2 persons	
and electricity	€ 24.00 - € 49.00
extra person	€ 9.00 - € 11.00
child (3-11 yrs)	€ 4.50 - € 7.00

For latest campsite news, availability and prices visit
alanrogers.com

Muravera
Camping Torre Salinas

Torre Salinas, I-09043 Muravera (Sardinia) T: 0709 990 32. E: info@camping-torre-salinas.de

alanrogers.com/IT69735

This is a small, uncomplicated site which will suit the pockets of some campers. The site is on a slope with some terraced pitches. On sand and grass, most are shaded and all have 4A electricity. Access is good on the site and it is very peaceful. All the facilities are at the entrance and a small friendly bar is faced across the main site road by a little restaurant/pizzeria which serves good food at sensible prices. English is spoken and the staff are all very friendly. There is little sophistication at Torre Salinas but everything is clean and neat. There is no traditional 'animation', so the site welcomes parents who enjoy spending time with their children. The beach is 300 m. away.

Facilities	Directions
The single central sanitary block has been thoughtfully constructed, but is a little tired. Clean throughout, it supplies hot water (solar) and facilities for children and disabled campers. Bar. Pizzeria/restaurant. Bicycle hire. Barbecues and picnic tables. Off site: Beach and fishing 300 m. Boat launching and sailing 1 km. Riding 3 km.	Site is on the south east coast of Sardinia, south of the town of Muravera. From the SS125 head for the town and the site is well signed from there off the coastal SS125 road. GPS: 39.36696, 9.596322
Open: 1 April - 31 October.	**Charges guide**

Per unit incl. 2 persons and electricity	€ 22.80 - € 44.00
extra person	€ 5.50 - € 12.50

Muravera
Camping le Dune

Localitá Piscina Rei, I-09043 Muravera (Sardinia) T: 0709 919 057. E: info@campingledune.it

alanrogers.com/IT69740

The Costa Rei in south east Sardinia is a popular seaside resort. Camping le Dune offers 100 pitches for touring units on sand, some under shade and all with 3/6A electricity. Whilst some of the pitches involve a walk to the beach access, others are positioned nearby and from these you can watch the flamingos. The swimming pool is a pleasant alternative to the salty sea water and the tidy facilities are a pleasure to use. It is very lively here in high season and would particularly suit younger campers. The site staff are most helpful and English is spoken.

Facilities	Directions
Three sanitary blocks provide a mixture of British and Turkish style toilets, washbasins (open style) and showers. Washing machines. Restaurant. Bar. Shop. Swimming pool. Tennis and football. Sailing and boat launching. Entertainment (high season). WiFi (charged). Off site: Costa Rei town. Diving. Riding 1 km.	Site is in south east corner of Sardinia in the north of the Costa Rei. From SS125 go towards Villaggio Capo Ferrato and then Costa Rei. Site is well signed in the village. GPS: 39.2767, 9.5821
Open: 10 April - 30 September.	**Charges guide**

Per unit incl. 2 persons and electricity	€ 20.50 - € 48.50
extra person	€ 7.00 - € 19.00

Muravera
Tiliguerta Camping Village

S.P. 97 km 6 - Loc. Capo Ferrato, I-09043 Muravera (Sardinia) T: 0709 914 37. E: info@tiliguerta.com

alanrogers.com/IT69750

This family site situated at Capo Ferrato has been owned by the same family for a quarter of a century and improvements are made every year, in sympathy with the environment. The 186 reasonably sized pitches are on sand and have 3A electricity. Some have shade and views of the superb, sandy beach and the sea beyond. The very attractive traditional site buildings are centrally located and contain a good quality restaurant and bar. These have a charming ambience with its high arched ceilings. Shaded terraces allow comfortable viewing of the ambitious entertainment programme. Cars must be parked away from pitches. The staff are cheerful and English is spoken.

Facilities	Directions
Three renovated sanitary blocks. One has private bathrooms and facilities for children and disabled visitors. Toilets are a mixture of Turkish and British style. Laundry facilities. Motorcaravan services (extra charge). Shop, restaurant and snack bar/takeaway (10/5-30/9). Play area. Live music concerts. Dog beach. Miniclub and entertainment in high season. Tennis. Water aerobics. Sailing. Sub-aqua diving. Windsurfing school. Riding. Torches essential. Bicycle hire. WiFi over site (charged).	Site is in south east corner of Sardinia in the north of the Costa Rei. From coast road SS125 or the SP97 at km. 6, take the turn to Villaggio Capo Ferrato. Site is well signed from here. GPS: 39.2923, 9.5987
Open: 1 May - 12 October.	**Charges guide**

Per unit incl. 2 persons and electricity	€ 18.00 - € 49.00
extra person	€ 5.00 - € 15.50
child (1-11 yrs. acc. to age)	€ 2.00 - € 11.50

For latest campsite news, availability and prices visit
alanrogers.com

Muravera
Camping Capo Ferrato

Localitá Costa Rei, Via delle Ginestre, I-09040 Castiadas (Sardinia) T: 0709 910 12.
E: info@campingcapoferrato.it **alanrogers.com/IT69770**

Situated at the southern end of the magnificent Costa Rei, this small, very friendly and well managed site has 83 touring pitches, many in great positions on the superb white sand beachfront. All pitches have 3/6A electricity, are of generous proportions and the whole site enjoys absolute tranquillity. The charming restaurant holds it own against the village competition and special evenings are often held when the local wines are matched to the food served. This site is brilliant for beach lovers and there are many watersports on offer. It is reasonably priced and we thoroughly enjoyed the extremely happy, small site atmosphere.

Facilities

Two good sanitary blocks (one top quality) with WCs, washbasins and free hot showers. No facilities for disabled visitors. Washing machine and dryer. Baby room. Motorcaravan services. Bar. Restaurant serving local dishes. Pizzeria. Well stocked shop. TV room. Bicycle hire. Tennis. Football and basketball pitch. Good play area. Entertainment (high season). Tours and visits organised. Wine/food evenings. Bicycle tours. WiFi (charged). Dogs are not accepted in July/Aug. Bungalows to rent. Direct beach access and beach bar.

Open: 1 April - 2 November.

Directions

Camping Capo Ferrato is in the south east of Sardinia and can be reached via the coast road towards Villasimius (SP17 or SS125) then take Costa Rei signs and the site is well signed on southern edge of village. Please note the site is in Costa Rei (Via delle Ginestre) and not on the promontory of Capo Ferrato. GPS: 39.24297, 9.56941

Charges guide

Per unit incl. 2 persons and electricity	€ 21.20 - € 49.80
extra person	€ 5.60 - € 13.40

Nuoro
Camping Agriturismo Costiolou

SS389, I-08100 Nuoro (Sardinia) T: 078 426 0088. E: info@agriturismocostiolou.com
alanrogers.com/IT69670

Costiolou is a wonderful 100-hectare, organic farm high in the hills above Nuoro, with fantastic views in almost every direction. This is a most unusual campsite, located on the working farm run by Giovanni di Costa, cheese maker, winemaker, farmer, gardener and host. Prepare to be amazed by the courtyard with covered terrace, cellars, traditional kitchens and other charming Sardinian features. The site has just ten pitches on a flat and level area behind the farmhouse. Eagles circle overhead and many animals can be seen, including horses and pigs, which are bred here (and horses are available to ride). We loved it and it was an amazing experience! Dogs are not accepted.

Facilities

Toilets and showers are provided in a restored farm building alongside the pitches, including facilities for disabled visitors. Bar. Restaurant (by arrangement, offering very traditional meals). Barbecues. Rooms to rent (full or half board, B&B). Riding. Dogs are not accepted. Off site: Wild Sardinian countryside for walking and wildlife.

Open: All year.

Directions

The site is at the 90 km. marker on the SS389 Nuoro to Bitti road. It is well signed, but there is a 9 km. long roughish track to the farm. GPS: 40.3674, 9.29658

Charges guide

Per unit incl. 2 persons and electricity	€ 22.00 - € 30.00
extra person	€ 7.00 - € 10.00
Cash only.	

Palau
Camping Capo d'Orso

Localitá Saline, I-07020 Palau (Sardinia) T: 078 970 2007. E: info@capodorso.it
alanrogers.com/IT69600

Capo d'Orso is a large, attractive, terraced site with views of the Maddalena Archipelago. Set into a hillside that slopes down to the sea, the 350 terraced pitches (40-80 sq.m) are of gravel, grass and sand, some with views over the sea and some others set alongside the beach. All have 3A electricity. Access to the pitches is good despite the rocky terrain. Cars are parked away from the pitches in high season. The very Italian restaurant at the top of the amenities building serves delicious meals and has a covered terrace giving excellent sea views. This site is suitable for families.

Facilities

Three toilet blocks are being renovated and will provide ample facilities including hot showers, and mainly Turkish style WCs. Motorcaravan services. Shop. Bazaar. Bar/restaurant. Pizzeria. Takeaway. Scuba diving, windsurfing, sailing school, boat excursions, boat hire and moorings. Tennis. Entertainment. Free WiFi.

Open: 15 May - 30 September.

Directions

Site is 5 km. from Palau, in north east of Sardinia. On SS133 Porto Pozzo-Cannigione road. It is well signed towards the beach. GPS: 41.16117, 9.403

Charges guide

Per unit incl. 2 persons and electricity	€ 21.50 - € 50.00

For latest campsite news, availability and prices visit
alanrogers.com

Sant'Antioco
Camping Tonnara
Localitá Alasapone, I-09017 Sant'Antioco (Sardinia) T: 078 180 9058. E: tonnaracamping@tiscalinet.it
alanrogers.com/IT69860

A small, attractive campsite, Tonnara is on the west side of Sant'Antioco island in the south west corner of Sardinia. Access to the island is via a causeway and Tonnara is in the pretty Cala Sapone inlet with its delightful private sandy beach and rocky outcrops. The 150 sandy pitches (with 6A electricity) are terraced down to the sea with small trees and some artificial shade. Some are very close to the beach and most enjoy fabulous views of the inlet. The local seafood is good and cooked to perfection in the small restaurant where you can sit out on the terrace and watch the sunsets.

Facilities

Two modern sanitary blocks have both Turkish and British style toilets, washbasins (cold water only) and great hot showers. Facilities for disabled campers. Superb facilities for children. Baby bathing area. Washing machine. Motorcaravan services. Neat little shop. Restaurant and snack bar (all season). Swimming pool (caps compulsory). Two well equipped play areas. Bicycle hire. Tennis. Bocce. Beach. Beach volleyball. Sub-aqua arranged. Excursions. WiFi (charged). Torches essential.

Open: 20 April - 30 October.

Directions

Site is on island of Sant'Antioco on south west coast of Sardinia. Go over the causeway and immediately at the end, turn left and left again at T-junction towards Cala Sapone (site is well signed). GPS: 39.0053, 8.3873

Charges guide

Per unit incl. 2 persons and electricity	€ 15.00 - € 53.00
extra person	€ 5.00 - € 15.00
child (3-13 yrs)	free - € 10.00

Santa Lucia di Siniscola
Selema Camping
Thiria Soliana, I-08029 Santa Lucia di Siniscola (Sardinia) T: 079 953 761. E: info@selemacamping.com
alanrogers.com/IT69660

Selema is a pretty site with a tropical feel and direct beach access. There is considerable shade from pine and eucalyptus, although access to many pitches is restricted by tall, bending trees. Flowers and cacti have been used to provide landscaping features and unusually there are well watered, grassy areas. There are 200 large pitches of grass and sand, well shaded with shallow terracing. The site runs along the Pineta coast with its long white sandy beaches and vibrant blue water and has a wide river flowing along the other side. Some pitches are near the path to the beach and a few have views of the distant mountains. Staff speak English and are very helpful.

Facilities

Four sanitary blocks provide a mixture of British and Turkish style toilets, good hot showers and facilities for disabled visitors. Washing machine. Motorcaravan services. Pleasant shop. Restaurant and snack bar. Swimming pool (hats required). Paddling pool. Play areas. Tennis. Bocce. Large screen TV. Electronic games. Bicycle hire. Windsurfing. Small boat launching.

Open: 1 April - 31 October.

Directions

Site is on SS125, 30 km. north of Orosei. Turn towards the coast, near 254 km. marker to Santa Lucia. Site is well signed. GPS: 40.5785, 9.7730

Charges guide

Per unit incl. 2 persons and electricity	€ 27.00 - € 51.00
extra person	€ 7.50 - € 14.00

Torre Grande
Camping Village Spinnaker
Strada Provinciale, Oristano, I-09170 Torre Grande (Sardinia) T: 078 322 074. E: info@spinnakervacanze.com
alanrogers.com/IT69900

Set on the undulating foreshore under tall pines, with a superb beach frontage to the camping area, Spinnaker Village is a smart, purpose built, modern beach site. The 143 pitches are level and sandy, with 90 for touring. All have 6A electricity and there are plenty of water taps. Cars must be parked in a car park outside the site. There are many neat, white buildings on site – the restaurant, a café and the swimming pool with loungers are cleverly set around a large square, where entertainment for families takes place. This is a clean, crisp, well run site where English is spoken.

Facilities

Toilet blocks are modern and very clean with British style toilets and facilities for disabled campers. Showers are transponder operated (€ 0.50 per shower). Washing machine. Motorcaravan services. Small shop. Restaurant and small snack bar. Swimming pool and pool bar. Play area. Bicycle hire. Miniclub and entertainment in high season. Excursions. Torches essential. WiFi throughout. Off site: Riding 2 km. Golf 23 km.

Open: 1 April - 30 September.

Directions

Take SS131 Cagliari-Oristano road then minor road to Cabras and Torre Grande. Just before Torre Grande village by large water tower take angled left turn back on yourself to site (well signed). GPS: 39.903, 8.5301

Charges guide

Per unit incl. 2 persons and electricity	€ 23.00 - € 44.00
extra person	€ 8.00 - € 18.00

For latest campsite news, availability and prices visit
alanrogers.com

Tortoli
Camping Cigno Bianco
Lido di Orri, I-08048 Tortoli (Sardinia) T: 078 262 4927. E: info@cignobianco.it
alanrogers.com/IT69700

The very friendly Pinna family work extremely hard to ensure you have an enjoyable holiday on their campsite with direct access to a superb beach and the sea with crystal clear water. The 100 unmarked pitches, all with 6A electricity, are shaded by tall eucalyptus and pine trees. The smart restaurant serves some quality Sardinian food and pizza. Animation is provided in July and August. Everything here is spotlessly clean and well maintained and it is very reasonably priced. Arbatax is worthy of a visit just to see or maybe catch the Trenino Verdi, a narrow gauge railway that runs south to Cagliari. The trip takes several hours and you will enjoy the magnificent scenery.

Facilities	Directions
Two spotless and well placed sanitary blocks provide toilets (some Turkish style), washbasins and showers. Facilities for disabled visitors. Motorcaravan services. Washing machines. Restaurant, bar and small shop. Tennis court and multisport pitch. Beach volleyball. Bicycle hire. WiFi. Dogs are not accepted in July/Aug. Flats and mobile homes to rent.	Site is just off the SS125, south of Tortoli. Look for and follow the large blue signs for Lido d'Orri towards the sea, and then the campsite signs. GPS: 39.9076, 9.6824

Open: 1 May - 30 September.

Charges guide

Per unit incl. 2 persons	
and electricity	€ 26.50 - € 39.50
extra person	€ 8.00 - € 13.00

Valledoria
Camping la Foce
Via Ampurias no. 110, I-07039 Valledoria (Sardinia) T: 079 582 109. E: info@foce.it
alanrogers.com/IT69500

Enthusiastic Matteo Lampati and his wife, Ivona, run la Foce, an attractive, sprawling site in the Golfo del Asinara. A novel feature is the motorbarge to ferry campers to a secluded area of the sea coast on the other side of the river, which flows alongside the site. Here they can enjoy the golden sand dunes and have a refreshing swim away from other beach-goers. The 300 sandy pitches (with 4/6A electricity) vary in size and are informally arranged under tall shady eucalyptus trees stretching along the length of the site, some close to the river. There is a full entertainment programme in high season. We found this site to be of a much higher standard than most on this coastline.

Facilities	Directions
Three sanitary blocks (renovated in 2015) house good facilities with British and Turkish style toilets. Excellent facilities for disabled visitors. Washing machine. Motorcaravan services. Supermarket, bar, restaurant and snack bar. Two pools and sun deck. Massage (charged). Play areas. Tennis. Bocce. Beach volleyball. Excursions. Beaches – ferry by free motorbarge. Sailing. Windsurfing. Canoeing. Sub-aqua diving. WiFi (part site, free).	From Sassari take coast road east to Castelsardo and Valledoria. As you arrive at the village watch for campsite signs towards beach and site. GPS: 40.9335, 8.8174

Open: 25 April - 30 September.

Charges guide

Per unit incl. 2 persons	
and electricity	€ 19.00 - € 36.00
extra person	€ 5.00 - € 9.00
child (3-10 yrs)	€ 4.00 - € 8.00

Villasimius
Villaggio Spiaggia del Riso
Campulongu, I-09049 Villasimius (Sardinia) T: 0707 910 52. E: campriso@tiscali.it
alanrogers.com/IT69780

This spacious site is well kept and professionally run. It is split by a public road, but there is an underpass for campers. Pitches on both sides of the site are mostly flat, some are shaded and all have 3A electricity. The area beside the beach has open pitches for caravans and motorcaravans with sea views, but with a low artificially shaded area alongside. The well designed restaurant is fabulous with lots of local fare, and waiters will fillet local fish at your table. Entertainment is provided for children and adults and a range of sports activities is on offer.

Facilities	Directions
Four modern sanitary blocks provide both British and Turkish style toilets. Only cold water at washbasins. €0.50 tokens (July/Aug). Pristine locked facilities for disabled campers. Washing machines and dryers. Motorcaravan services. Shop. Cafeteria. Restaurant and bar. Pizzeria/snack bar. Archery. 5-a-side football. Bicycle hire. Entertainment (high season). Communal barbecue area only. WiFi over part of site (charged). Torches useful.	Site is in the bottom south east corner of Sardinia, south of the village of Villasimius. From the SS125 take the road to Villasimius where the site is well signed. It is 2 km. towards the sea. GPS: 39.123202, 9.512658

Open: 25 April - 30 October.

Charges guide

Per unit incl. 2 persons	
and electricity	€ 25.00 - € 44.00
extra person	€ 9.00 - € 16.00

For latest campsite news, availability and prices visit
alanrogers.com

What Slovenia lacks in size it makes up for in exceptional beauty. Situated between Italy, Austria, Hungary and Croatia, it has a diverse landscape with stunning Alps, rivers, forests and the warm Adriatic coast.

With its snow-capped Julian Alps and the picturesque Triglav National Park that includes the beautiful lakes of Bled and Bohinj, and the peaceful Soca River, it is no wonder that the north west region of Slovenia is so popular. Stretching from the Alps down to the Adriatic coast is the picturesque Karst region, with pretty olive groves and thousands of spectacular underground caves. The world famous Postojna and Skocjan caves are well worth a visit. Guided tours by special cave trains take you through extensive and marvellous rock formations. Although small, the Adriatic coast has several bustling beach towns such as the Italianised Koper resort and the historic port of Piran, with many opportunities for watersports and sunbathing. The capital, Ljubljana, is centrally located; with Renaissance, Baroque and Art Nouveau architecture, you will find most points of interest are along the Ljubljana river. Heading eastwards the landscape becomes gently rolling hills, and is largely given over to vines (home of Lutomer Riesling). Savinja with its spectacular Alps is the main area for producing wine.

Population
2 million

Capital
Ljubljana

Climate
Warm summers, cold winters with snow in the Alps.

Language
Slovene, with German often spoken in the north and Italian in the west.

Telephone
The country code is 00 386.

Currency
The Euro (€).

Banks
Mon-Fri 08.30-16.30 with a lunch break 12.30-14.00, plus Saturday mornings 08.30-11.30.

Shops
Shops usually open by 08.00, sometimes 07.00. Closing times vary widely.

Public Holidays

New Year 1, 2 Jan; Preseren Day 8 Feb;
Easter Monday; Resistance Day 27 Apr;
Labour Day 1-2 May; National Day 25 Jun;
Assumption; Reformation Day 31 Oct; All Saints Day;
Christmas Day; Independence Day 26 Dec.

Motoring

A small, but expanding network of motorways radiates
from Ljubljana. A 'vignette' system for motorway travel
is in place. The cost is around € 35 (for a six-month
vignette) and they can be purchased at petrol stations
and DARS offices in Slovenia and neighbouring
countries near the border. Failure to display a vignette
will lead to fines of up to € 300. Winter driving
equipment (winter tyres or snow chains) is mandatory
between 15 Nov and 15 March. By law, you must
have your headlights on **at all times**, while driving in
Slovenia. You are also required to carry a reflective
jacket, a warning triangle and a first aid kit in the
vehicle. Do not drink and drive – any trace of alcohol
in your system will lead to prosecution.

Tourist Office

Slovenian Tourist Board Office
10 Little College Street
London SW1P 3SH
Tel: 0870 225 5305
E-mail: london@slovenia.info
Internet: www.slovenia.info

British Embassy

4th Floor Trg Republike 3
1000 Ljubljana
Tel: (386) (1) 200 3910

Places of interest

Adriatic Coast: Venetian Gothic
architecture can be found at Piran, the
best beach along the coast is at Fiesa.

Julian Alps: Mt Triglav is the country's
highest peak, Bled Castle, Bled Island
has a 15th-century belfry with a 'bell of
wishes', Lake Bohinij.

Ljubljana: Municipal Museum, National
Museum, Museum of Modern Art
all along the banks of the Ljubljana
River, Tivoli Park with bowling alleys,
tennis courts, swimming pools and
a roller-skating rink.

Skocjan Caves: filled with stalactites
and stalagmites and housing 250 plant
varieties and five types of bat.

Cuisine of the region

Traditionally the cuisine mainly consists
of venison and fish, but there are
Austrian, Italian and Hungarian influences.

Dunajski zrezek: wiener schnitzel

Golaz: goulash

Klobasa: sausage

Njoki: potato dumplings

Paprikas: chicken or beef stew

Struklji: cheese dumplings

Zavitek: strudel

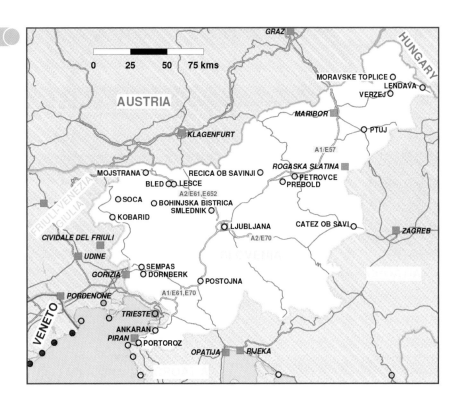

Ankaran

Camping Adria

Jadranska Cesta 25, SLO-6280 Ankaran (Slovenia) T: 056 637 350. E: camp@adrina-ankaran.si

alanrogers.com/SV4310

Camping Adria is on the south side of the Milje/Muggia peninsula, right on the shore of the Adriatic Sea and just beyond the port. It has a concrete promenade with access to the sea, complemented by an Olympic size pool (June-September) with children's pool, both filled with seawater. The site has 450 pitches (300 for tourers), all with 10A electricity, set up on one side of the site close to the sea. Pitches are off tarmac access roads, running down to the sea and most are between 80 and 90 sq.m, and six are fully serviced. Although the port facilities are visible from part of the site, this does not detract from its attractiveness. A quick stop facility is open to tourers in winter when the main site is closed.

Facilities

Five modern toilet blocks with British and Turkish style toilets, open style washbasins. Free hot and cold water, controllable showers. Facilities for disabled visitors. Laundry room. Fridge box hire. Supermarket. Beach shop. Newspaper kiosk. Bar/restaurant with terrace. Swimming pool (40x15 m) with large slide. Wellness centre. Riding (July/Aug). Playground on gravel. Playing field. Tennis. Beach ball. Volleyball. Basketball. Minigolf. Fishing. Jetty for mooring boats. Boat launching. Bowling club. WiFi (charged). Off site: Historic towns of Koper, Izola, Piran and Portoroz are nearby.

Open: 10 April - 15 October.

Directions

From Koper drive north to Ankaran. The site is immediately on the left at roundabout after entering Ankaran. Do not try to enter from Trieste/Muggia using sat nav from autobahn.
GPS: 45.57797, 13.73633

Charges guide

Per person	€ 11.00 - € 13.50
child (2-9 yrs)	€ 5.50 - € 6.75
electricity	€ 4.00
dog	€ 4.00

For latest campsite news, availability and prices visit
alanrogers.com

Bled

Camping Bled

Kidriceva 10c SI, SLO-4260 Bled (Slovenia) T: 045 752 000. E: info@camping-bled.com

alanrogers.com/SV4200

Camping Bled is situated on the western tip of Lake Bled. The waterfront here has a small public beach, immediately behind which runs a gently sloping narrow wooded valley. There are wonderful views across the lake towards its famous island. Pitches at the front, used mainly for overnighters, are now marked, separated by trees and enlarged, bringing the total number to 280. All are on gravel/grass with 16A electricity. A railway line passes close by but it is only a local line with few trains and they do not disturb the peacefulness of the site.

Facilities

Toilet facilities in five blocks are of a high standard (with free hot showers). Three blocks are heated. Private bathrooms for rent. Solar energy used. Washing machines and dryers. Motorcaravan services. Gas supplies. Fridge hire. Supermarket. Restaurant. Play area and children's zoo. Games area. Trampolines. Organised activities in July/Aug including children's club, excursions and sporting activities. Live entertainment. Mountain bike tours. Fishing. Bicycle hire. Free WiFi over site.

Open: 1 April - 15 October.

Directions

From town of Bled drive along south shore of lake keeping to right, to its western extremity (2 km) and the site (well signed). GPS: 46.36155, 14.08075

Charges guide

Per unit incl. 2 persons and electricity	€ 22.30 - € 30.30
extra person	€ 9.40 - € 13.40
child (7-13 yrs)	€ 6.58 - € 9.38
dog	€ 3.00

Bohinjska Bistrica

Camping Danica Bohinj

Triglavska 60, SLO-4264 Bohinjska Bistrica (Slovenia) T: 045 721 702. E: info@camp-danica.si

alanrogers.com/SV4250

For those wishing to visit the famous Bohinj valley, which stretches like a fjord right into the heart of the Julian Alps, Danica Bohinj is an ideal site lying in the valley 3 km. downstream of Lake Bohinjsko. It is spacious, stretching from the main road to the banks of the Sava river, on a flat meadow set in natural woodland. This excellent site has 165 pitches, 145 for touring units (all with 16A electricity), and forms an ideal base for the many sporting activities the area has to offer. Reception is well supplied with maps and tourist information as well as helpful advice as to the state of the various mountain trails.

Facilities

Three good toilet blocks with open plan washbasins and hot showers. Facilities for disabled visitors. Laundry facilities. Motorcaravan services. Bar. Café. Fresh bread (July/Aug). Tennis. Badminton. Volleyball. Cross-country skiing from site. Fishing. Bicycle hire. Free WiFi over site. Excursions in the Triglavski National Park. Off site: Shop (5 mins. walk). Four ski resorts. Riding 6 km. Canoeing, kayaking, rafting, walking and mountain bike trails.

Open: All year.

Directions

Driving from Bled to Bohinj, in Bohinjska Bistrica stay on main road (it goes to the right). Site is 200 m. on the right-hand (north) side of the road. GPS: 46.27335, 13.94868

Charges guide

Per unit incl. 2 persons and electricity	€ 21.00 - € 29.20
extra person	€ 8.50 - € 12.60
child (7-14 yrs)	€ 6.40 - € 9.50

Catez ob Savi

Camping Terme Catez

Topliska cesta 35, SLO-8251 Catez ob Savi (Slovenia) T: 074 936 700. E: info@terme-catez.si

alanrogers.com/SV4415

Terme Catez is part of the modern Catez thermal spa, which includes very large and attractive indoor (31°C) and outdoor swimming complexes, both with large slides and waves. The site has 490 pitches, with 250 places for tourers, arranged on one large, open field with some young trees (a real sun trap) and provides level, grass pitches, which are numbered by markings on the tarmac access roads. All have 10A electricity connections. Although the site is ideally placed for an overnight stop when travelling on the E70, it is well worthwhile planning to spend some time here to take advantage of the excellent facilities that are included in the overnight camping charges.

Facilities

Two modern toilet blocks with washbasins in cabins, large and controllable hot showers. Washbasins for children. Facilities for disabled visitors. Laundry. Motorcaravan services. Supermarket. Kiosks for fruit, newspapers, souvenirs and tobacco. Attractive restaurant with buffet. Bar with terrace. Large indoor and outdoor (20/4-15/10) swimming complexes. Sauna. Solarium. Fishing. Golf. Riding. Organised activities. Bicycle hire. WiFi (free).

Open: All year.

Directions

Site is signed from the Ljubljana-Zagreb motorway (E70) 6 km. west of the Slovenia/Croatia border, close to Brezice. GPS: 45.89137, 15.62598

Charges guide

Per unit incl. 2 persons and electricity	€ 41.50 - € 53.10
extra person	€ 18.50 - € 24.30
child (5-11 yrs)	€ 9.25 - € 12.15
dog	€ 4.00

For latest campsite news, availability and prices visit
alanrogers.com

Dornberk
Camping Saksida

Zalosce 12 a, SLO-5294 Dornberk (Slovenia) T: 053 017 853. E: info@vinasaksida.com

alanrogers.com/SV4320

Camping Saksida is a very small campsite, open all year in a rural setting in the Vipava Valley. It is set in the grounds of a restaurant which has its own vineyard and it is surrounded by vineyards and orchards. There are 25 pitches for all units, including 12 hardstandings, most with electricity (10A, Europlug). There is a large covered picnic area and a communal area for barbecues. The price of one night's stay includes wine tasting from three local wines. There is a small, heated swimming pool where one can relax and the campsite restaurant offers an extensive menu of genuine Vipava dishes.

Facilities

Heated sanitary facilities. Motorcaravan service point. Restaurant. Heated outdoor swimming pool (15/5 30/9). Large covered picnic area. Communal barbecue area. WiFi throughout (free). Off site: Nearest store 1 km. Bus and railway station 1 km. Many marked walks and cycle tracks. Fishing 3 km. Riding 10 km.

Open: All year.

Directions

Site is 13 km. from the western border with Italy. From there leave H4 expressway after 1.8 km. onto road 103 then first exit at roundabout towards Koper/Sezana. At Dornberk left onto 611 for 900 m. then left and second right to site. GPS: 45.88994, 13.74745

Charges guide

Per unit incl. 2 persons and electricity	€ 20.00
extra person	€ 10.00

Kobarid
Lazar Kamp

Gregorciceva, SLO-5222 Kobarid (Slovenia) T: 053 885 333. E: edi.lazar@siol.net

alanrogers.com/SV4265

Lazar Kamp is a fairly open site with a relaxed atmosphere from where there are good views of the surrounding mountains. Located in the countryside 40 m. above the Soca river, which is popular with wild watersport fans, there are plenty of walking and mountain biking opportunities directly from the site in this attractive region of Slovenia. The site has 50 open plan grassy pitches, all with 10A electricity, arranged in large sections divided by low openwork wooden fences. The friendly, informal bar/restaurant (08.00-22.00) serves English breakfast and, in the evenings, traditional Slovenian dishes including those cooked on a large grill.

Facilities

The sanitary block is of a very good standard and includes facilities for disabled visitors. Washing machine. Fridge. Bar. Crêperie and grill with terrace area. Internet corner. WiFi. Ranch-style clubroom. Excursions and lots of local sporting activities. Off site: Kozjak Waterfall. Mountain biking. Walking. Paragliding. Touring. Rafting. Kayaking. Canoeing.

Open: 1 April - 31 October.

Directions

From Tolmin on 102 just before Kobarid turn right on 203 towards Bovec. After 100 m. take descending slip road to right, keeping straight on to Napoléon's bridge (about 500 m), then straight on down gravel road 700 m. to site (road is unsuitable for larger units). GPS: 46.25513, 13.58626

Charges guide

Per unit incl. 2 persons and electricity	€ 24.00
extra person	€ 12.00

Kobarid
Kamp Koren Kobarid

Ladra 1b, SLO-5222 Kobarid (Slovenia) T: 53 891 311. E: info@kamp-koren.si

alanrogers.com/SV4270

Kamp Koren, Slovenia's first ecological site, is in a quiet location above the Soca river gorge, within easy walking distance of Kobarid. The site has 50 slightly sloping pitches, all with 6/16A electricity and ample tree shade. It is deservedly very popular with those interested in outdoor sports, be it on the water, in the mountains or in the air. At the same time, its peaceful situation makes it an ideal choice for those seeking a relaxing break. There are six well equipped chalets and a shady area mainly for tents was opened in 2014 at the top of the site.

Facilities

Two attractive and well maintained log-built toilet blocks, both recently renovated. Facilities for disabled visitors. Laundry. Motorcaravan services. Shop (March-Nov). Café serves light meals, snacks and drinks apparently with flexible closing hours. Play area. Volleyball. Table tennis. Bowling. Fishing. Bicycle hire. Canoe hire. Climbing walls. Adventure park. Communal barbecue. WiFi. Off site: Town within walking distance. Riding 5 km.

Open: All year.

Directions

From Tolmin on 102, just before Kobarid turn right on 203 towards Bovec and after 100 m. take descending slip road to right and keep more or less straight on to Napoléon's bridge (about 500 m). Cross bridge and site is on left in 100 m. GPS: 46.25075, 13.58658

Charges guide

Per unit incl. 2 persons and electricity	€ 26.00 - € 29.00

For latest campsite news, availability and prices visit
alanrogers.com

Lendava
Camping Terme Lendava
Tomsiceva ulica 2a, SLO-9220 Lendava (Slovenia) T: 025 774 400. E: info@terme-lendava.si
alanrogers.com/SV4455

Camping Terme Lendava forms part of an important thermal resort holiday complex, located at the meeting point of Slovenia, Hungary and Croatia. This is an all-year site with 80 grassy pitches, most with electricity connections, and eight hardstandings. Lendava is an open site with views over the vineyards, although some pitches around the edge have shade from mature trees. Campers have access to a large swimming pool complex as well as the resort's various thermal facilities, including bathing in water with paraffin content, considered to be an effective treatment for rheumatic disorders. There are several good restaurants within the complex. Special facilities are also available for naturist bathers.

Facilities

Two toilet blocks, one older and the other a modern, prefabricated unit, have open washbasins, controllable showers and communal changing. Laundry available in hotel. Shop, bar and restaurant in hotel. Swimming pool. Thermal complex with indoor and outdoor pools. Paddling pool. Play area. Entertainment. WiFi (charged). Off site: Shops and restaurants. Fishing 200 m. Golf.

Open: All year.

Directions

Approaching from the west (Maribor) on A5 motorway, take the exit to Lendava and follow signs to the site. GPS: 46.55167, 16.45842

Charges guide

Per person	€ 25.50 - € 28.50
child (7-13 yrs)	€ 17.85 - € 19.95

Lesce
Camping Sobec
Sobceva cesta 25, SLO-4248 Lesce (Slovenia) T: 045 353 700. E: sobec@siol.net
alanrogers.com/SV4210

Sobec is situated in a valley between the Julian Alps and the Karavanke Mountains, in a pine grove between the Sava Dolinka river and a small lake. It is only 3 km. from Bled and 20 km. from the Karavanke Tunnel. There are 500 unmarked pitches on level, grassy fields off tarmac access roads (450 for touring units), all with 16A electricity. Shade is provided by mature pine trees and younger trees separate some pitches. Camping Sobec is surrounded by water – the Sava river borders it on three sides and on the fourth is a small, artificial lake with grassy fields for sunbathing.

Facilities

Three traditional style toilet blocks (all now refurbished) with mainly British style toilets, washbasins in cabins and controllable hot showers. Child size toilets and washbasins. Well equipped baby room. Facilities for disabled visitors. Laundry facilities. Motorcaravan services. Supermarket, bar/restaurant with stage for performances. Playgrounds. Rafting, canyoning and kayaking organised. Miniclub. Tours to Bled and National Park. WiFi over site.

Open: 14 April - 30 September.

Directions

Leave A2 autobahn at exit 3 and follow signs for Lesce-Bled. Straight ahead at roundabout and site is signed to left. GPS: 46.35607, 14.14992

Charges guide

Per unit incl. 2 persons and electricity	€ 26.70 - € 32.90
extra person	€ 11.40 - € 14.50
child (7-14 yrs)	€ 8.50 - € 10.70
dog	€ 3.70

Ljubljana
Camping Ljubljana Resort
Dunajska Cesta 270, SLO-1000 Ljubljana (Slovenia) T: 015 890 130. E: resort@gpl.si
alanrogers.com/SV4340

Located only five kilometres north of central Ljubljana, on the relatively quiet bank of the River Sava, Ljubljana Resort is an ideal city campsite. This relaxed site is attached to, but effectively separated from, the sparklingly modern Laguna swimming pool complex. This is open between mid June and the beginning of September and a small, discounted charge is made in order for campers to gain access. The site has 177 pitches, largely situated between mature trees and all with 16A electricity connections (16A). The main building and the pool complex provide several bars, restaurants and takeaways to cater for the campsite guests and day visitors.

Facilities

The modern toilet block includes facilities for disabled campers, a baby room and children's toilet and shower. Motorcaravan services. Laundry room. Restaurant and bar with terrace. Spa and outdoor swimming pool (13/6-31/8). Play area. Entertainment for children (July/Aug). TV room. Barbecue area. Fitness centre. Beach volleyball. Bicycle hire. Airport transfer service. WiFi over site (free in reception). Off site: Train station 800 m. Ljubljana 5 km.

Open: All year.

Directions

From either direction on the northern city ring road, take exit no. 3 for Ljubljana-Jezica north towards Crnuce for a little over 1 km. Site is signed (blue sign) on the right just before railway crossing and bridge over the river. GPS: 46.09752, 14.5187

Charges guide

Per unit incl. 2 persons and electricity	€ 23.10 - € 31.10
extra person	€ 9.30 - € 13.30

For latest campsite news, availability and prices visit
alanrogers.com

Mojstrana
Camping Kamne
Dovje 9, SLO-4281 Mojstrana (Slovenia) T: 045 891 105. E: campingkamne@telemach.net
alanrogers.com/SV4150

Easily accessed from the A2/E61 autobahn, this small, terraced, south facing site offers striking views of Slovenia's highest mountains which form part of the adjoining Triglav National Park. Camping Kamne has a total of 60 grass pitches for touring, 40 of which have 6/10A electrical connections. Site roads are gravel and tarmac and plenty of trees provide good shade. Ana Voga, the owner, speaks excellent English. The area is a haven for walking and mountain biking with trails of all grades against a backdrop of waterfalls, fast-flowing mountain streams and forests.

Facilities

The small excellent sanitary block is of a high quality and well maintained. New facilities for babies and disabled visitors. Motorcaravan service point. Reception/bar with TV. Small shop for essentials (25/6-10/9). Playground. Two tennis courts. Mountain bike hire. Chalets and bungalows to rent. WiFi throughout (free). Max. 2 dogs. Off site: Walking and mountain bike trails. Rock climbing. Fishing nearby (licence from reception). Riding 5 km.

Open: All year.

Directions

Site is 5.5 km. north west of the southern exit of the Karawanken tunnel joining Villach in Austria with Slovenia. A few hundred meters from the tunnel's southern end, take exit for Kranjska Gora and at the end of the slip road left towards Kranjska Gora. After 5.5 km. at the western village sign for Dovje, site is 100 m. to the right. GPS: 46.46435, 13.95738

Charges guide

Per unit incl. 2 persons and electricity	€ 19.20 - € 25.00

Moravske Toplice
Camping Terme 3000
Kranjceva ulica 12, SLO-9226 Moravske Toplice (Slovenia) T: 025 121 200.
E: recepcija.camp2@terme3000.si **alanrogers.com/SV4410**

Camping Terme 3000 is a large site with 490 pitches; 300 are for touring units (all with 16A electricity, 30 with hardstanding), the remaining pitches being taken by seasonal campers. On a grass and gravel surface (hard tent pegs may be needed), the level, numbered pitches are of 50-100 sq.m. The site is part of an enormous thermal spa and fun pool complex (free entry to campers) under the same name. There are over 5,000 sq.m. of water activities – swimming, jet streams, waterfalls, water massages, four water slides (the longest is 170 m) and thermal baths.

Facilities

Modern and clean toilet facilities provide British style toilets, open washbasins and controllable, free hot showers. Laundry facilities. Football field. Tennis. Water gymnastics. Daily activity programme for children. Golf. WiFi (charged).

Open: All year.

Directions

From Maribor, go east to Murska Sobota, then north towards Martjanci and then east towards Moravske Toplice. Access to the site is on the right before the bridge. Then go through a park for a further 500 m. GPS: 46.67888, 16.22165

Charges guide

Per unit incl. 2 persons and electricity	€ 46.00 - € 48.50

Petrovce
Camp NaturPlac
Primoû pri Ljubnem 22, SLO-3333 Ljubno ob Savinji (Slovenia) T: 051 235 215. E: info@naturavantura.com
alanrogers.com/SV4460

Camping NaturPlac is a small, quiet and peaceful rustic campsite located beside the River Savinja close to the Logar Valley. The site is run by a group of very friendly enthusiasts who will advise you about many organised trips on land or water. This is a great place for the more active families who enjoy nature and who are seeking a quiet site where they can entertain themselves. The site caters for those with their own tents, though small tents in ten wooden shelters are available to rent. Guests have access to a kitchen, a shared dining area and an outside fire pit, very popular for evening meals and social events such as sampling the local specialities.

Facilities

Simple heated toilet block with hot showers. Some meals. Badminton and beach volleyball. Kitchen and shared dining area. Play area. Library under the trees. Bicycle hire. Themed workshops for adults and children. Hammocks and sleeping bags for hire. Communal barbecue. River swimming. WiFi thoughout (free). Off site: Restaurant and bar 1 km. Bus station 4 km. Canyoning, kayaking, rafting, climbing and slackline.

Open: 25 April - 1 October.

Directions

From Ljubljana take the A1 motorway north east for 55.4 km. then take the Sentrupert exit onto road 225 north and continue in the direction of Mozirje - Logarska Dolina. When you reach Ljubno, follow the NaturPlac signs. GPS: 46.35336, 14.81555

Charges guide

Tent pitch per person	€ 10.00 - € 12.00
child (5-13 yrs)	€ 6.00 - € 8.00

For latest campsite news, availability and prices visit
alanrogers.com

Portoroz

Camp Lucija

Seca 204, SLO-6320 Portoroz (Slovenia) T: 056 90 60 00. E: camp.lucija@bernardingroup.si

alanrogers.com/SV4315

This is a long narrow site that enjoys attactive views over the bay at the western end. This part of the site is very popular and becomes quite crowded, while in the bar/restaurant area there is music playing for most of the day. The site is popular with families with young children and a much used public cycle/pedestrian path, formally a railway line linking Triest with Porec, runs through it. There are 550 reasonably level pitches (300 for tourers) on grass/gravel and around half have 6A electricity. There is a separate terrace for tents. There is some aircraft noise. The site is ideally placed for coastal walks. Just 300 m. from the campsite there is a good sports centre with a range of amenities including football, tennis and minigolf. Further afield, day trips to Trieste and the Slovenian coastal towns are possible, while Venice is a longer day out. In addition, Lucija's close proximity to the Croatian border makes touring into Istria easy.

Facilities	Directions
Five sanitary blocks (one heated) have hot showers. Facilities for disabled visitors. Washing machine. Motorcaravan services. Shop. Bar/snack bar and restaurant. Playground. Fishing. Bicycle hire. Free WiFi. Off site: Walk to Secovlje salt pans from site. Sports centre 300 m. Shops, restaurants and cafés in Portoroz. Walking and cycling routes. Watersports.	Approaching from the north (Koper), head south on road 111 beyond Portoroz and continue to Lucija. At bottom of hill, at traffic lights, turn right and follow camping signs. GPS: 45.501506, 13.593905

Open: 15 April - 31 October.

Charges guide

Per unit incl. 2 persons and electricity	€ 27.50 - € 38.50
extra person	€ 12.00 - € 17.00
child (7-14 yrs)	€ 4.00 - € 6.00
dog	€ 3.00

BERNARDIN GROUP
RESORTS & HOTELS

camp LUCIJA ★★★ PORTOROŽ

Camp Lucija, Seča 204, Portorož, Slovenia
T +386 5 690 6000   GPS: 45 30' 6"N, 13 16' 2"E
camp.lucija@bernardingroup.si   **www.camp-lucija.si**

Postojna

Camping Pivka Jama

Veliki Otok 50, SLO-6230 Postojna (Slovenia) T: 057 203 993. E: avtokamp.pivka.jama@siol.net

alanrogers.com/SV4330

Postojna is renowned for its extraordinary limestone caves which form one of Slovenia's prime tourist attractions. Pivka Jama is a most convenient site for the visitor, being midway between Ljubljana and Piran and only about an hour's pleasant drive from either. The 300 pitches are not clustered together but nicely segregated under trees and in small clearings, all connected by a neat network of paths and slip roads. Some level, gravel hardstandings are provided. The facilities are both excellent and extensive and run with obvious pride by enthusiastic staff.

Facilities	Directions
Two toilet blocks with very good facilities. Washing machines. Motorcaravan services. Campers' kitchen with hobs. Supermarket (1/6-15/9). Bar/restaurant. Swimming and paddling pools (15/6-10/9). Tennis. Bicycle hire. Day trips to Postojna Caves and other excursions organised. WiFi. Off site: Fishing 5 km. Riding and skiing 10 km. Riding and golf 30 km.	Site is 5 km. north of Postojna. Leave A1/E61 at Postojna exit. In Postojna follow signs to Postojna Caves (Postojnska Jama) continue for 4 km. where site is signed to right. Follow road through forest 2 km. to site. GPS: 45.79068, 14.19092

Open: 15 April - 31 October.

Charges guide

Per person	€ 9.90 - € 11.90
child (7-14 yrs)	€ 7.90 - € 8.90
electricity	€ 3.90

For latest campsite news, availability and prices visit
alanrogers.com

Prebold
Camp Dolina Prebold

Vozlic Tomaz Dolenja vas 147, SLO-3312 Prebold (Slovenia) T: 035 724 378. E: camp@dolina.si

alanrogers.com/SV4400

Prebold is a quiet village about 15 kilometres west of the large historic town of Celje. It is only a few kilometres from the remarkable Roman necropolis at Sempeter. Dolina is an exceptional little site where reception and the bar are housed in the beautifully converted 150-year-old stable, taking 50 touring units, all with 16A electricity. It belongs to Tomaz and Manja Vozlic who look after the site and its guests with loving care. It has been in existence since 1960 and was one of the first private enterprises in the former Yugoslavia.

Facilities

The small, heated toilet block is immaculately maintained. Washing machine and dryer. Fridge. Coffee machine. Bar. Fresh bread delivered daily. Small swimming pool (heated 30-33ºC, 1/6-30/9). Play area with trampoline. Large wood-fired oven for traditional cooking. Bicycle hire. WiFi (free). Off site: Good supermarket and restaurant 200 m. Tennis and indoor pool within 1 km. Fishing 1.5 km.

Open: All year.

Directions

Leave E57 at Sempeter/Prebold exit. Head south, after 100 m, right at roundabout, over bridge. Follow site signs to the left after 150 m. Upon reaching Prebold, site is signed to the right down a small side street. GPS: 46.24392, 15.09108

Charges guide

Per unit incl. 2 persons and electricity	€ 15.83
extra person	€ 6.25

No credit cards.

Prebold
Camping Park

Latkova vas 227, SLO-3312 Prebold (Slovenia) T: 0599 25 306. E: info@campingpark.si

alanrogers.com/SV4402

Camping Park is set on a grassy field close to the E57, directly beside the Savinja river. It provides 30 pitches (all for tourers, with 10A electricity) and is attractively landscaped with flowers and young trees. Pitching is on one large field with some shade provided by mature trees and the high hedge surrounding the site. Pitches are not separated, but when it is quiet you can take as much space as you need. It is possible to fish and swim in the river.

Facilities

One traditional style toilet block with modern fittings has toilets, open plan washbasins and controllable hot showers. Laundry facilities. Fridge boxes (free). River fishing and bathing. Large barbecue area. Bicycle hire. WiFi (free). Torch useful. Off site: Riding and tennis 1 km. Outdoor pool 2 km. Golf 20 km.

Open: 1 April - 30 October.

Directions

Leave the E57 motorway at the Sempeter/Prebold exit. Head south. At the roundabout just south of the motorway, turn right. Site is 250 m. on left. GPS: 46.25588, 15.09917

Charges guide

Per unit incl. 2 persons and electricity	€ 20.50
extra person	€ 8.50
dog	€ 2.00

Ptuj
Camping Terme Ptuj

Pot v toplice 9, SLO-2251 Ptuj (Slovenia) T: 027 494 100. E: info@terme-ptuj.si

alanrogers.com/SV4440

Camping Terme Ptuj is close to the river, just outside the interesting town of Ptuj. It is a small site with 100 level pitches, all for tourers and all with 10A electricity. In two areas, the pitches to the left are on part grass and part gravel hardstanding and are mainly used for motorcaravans. The pitches on the right-hand side are on grass under mature trees, off a circular, gravel access road. The main attraction of this site is clearly the adjacent thermal spa and fun pool complex that also attracts many local visitors. There is some road noise.

Facilities

Modern toilet block with British style toilets, open washbasins and controllable, hot showers (free). En-suite facilities for disabled visitors with toilet and basin. Two washing machines. Football field. Torch useful. Off site: Bar/restaurant and snack bar and large thermal spa 100 m. Bicycle hire 300 m. Golf 700 m. Riding 1 km.

Open: All year.

Directions

From Maribor go south east towards Ptuj or exit the A4 motorway at exit for Ptuj. Follow Golf/Therm signs, drive past spa/therm complex, camping is a further 100 m. GPS: 46.422683, 15.85495

Charges guide

Per person	€ 29.50 - € 31.50
child (7-13 yrs)	€ 17.85 - € 19.95

For latest campsite news, availability and prices visit
alanrogers.com

Recica ob Savinji
Camping Menina

Varpolje 105, SLO-3332 Recica ob Savinji (Slovenia) T: 035 835 027. E: info@campingmenina.com
alanrogers.com/SV4405

Camping Menina is in the heart of the 35 km. long Upper Savinja Valley, surrounded by 2,500 m. high mountains and unspoilt nature. It is being improved every year by the young, enthusiastic owner, Jurij Kolenc, and has 200 pitches, all for touring units, on grassy fields under mature trees and with access from gravel roads. All have 10A electricity. The Savinja river runs along one side of the site, but if the water is too cold, the site also has a lake which can be used for swimming. This site is a perfect base for walking or mountain biking in the mountains.

Facilities	Directions
Four sanitary blocks have modern fittings with toilets, open plan washbasins and controllable hot showers. Washing machine. Motorcaravan services. Bar/restaurant with open-air terrace (1/5-31/10) and open-air kitchen. Sauna. Playing field. Play area. Tree-top zip wire. Fishing. Russian bowling. Excursions (52). Live music and gatherings around the camp fire. Hostel. Skiing in winter. Climbing wall. Rafting. Kayaking. Mountain bike hire. Mobile homes to rent. WiFi (free).	From Ljubljana/Celje autobahn A1. Exit at Sentupert and turn north towards Mozirje (14 km). At roundabout just before Mozirje, hard left staying on the 225 for 6 km. to Nizka then just after the circular automatic petrol station, left where site is signed. GPS: 46.31168, 14.90913

Open: All year.

Charges guide

Per unit incl. 2 persons and electricity	€ 21.00 - € 25.00
extra person	€ 9.00 - € 11.00

Sempas
Camp Park Lijak

Ozeljan 6a, SLO-5261 Sempas (Slovenia) T: 053 088 557. E: info@parklijak.com
alanrogers.com/SV4325

Camp Lijak is a small campsite with well maintained facilities and enthusiastic and friendly owners. They are continuously working on projects to improve the site and aim to provide the ultimate holiday experience for campers. There are 60 level pitches spread over one hectare. All have electricity (6A), water, drainage and WiFi access. There are also two bungalows and partially underground hobbit style huts. Camp Lijak is a good base for active outdoor pursuits such as hiking, cycling and paragliding which are actively promoted by the owners. The site has its own landing strip for paragliding and offers a minibus service to suitable launch sites.

Facilities	Directions
One large toilet block with showers and open style vanity basins. Laundry facilities. Motorcaravan services. Fresh bread to order (daily). Freezer box hire. Organised cooking competitions and picnics. Communal barbecue. Transport for outdoor pursuits. Paragliding landing strip. WiFi throughout (charged). Off site: Hiking, cycling, rafting, fishing and paragliding. Caves at Postonja and Skocjan.	From Goriza take the 444 through Ajsevica and continue on to Camp Lijak 2 km. on left. GPS: 45.94179, 13.71748

Open: All year.

Charges guide

Per unit incl. 2 persons and electricity	€ 27.20 - € 30.60
extra person	€ 9.00 - € 10.70

Smlednik
Camp Smlednik

Dragocajna 14a, SLO-1216 Smlednik (Slovenia) T: 013 627 002. E: camp@dm-campsmlednik.si
alanrogers.com/SV4360

Camp Smlednik is relatively close to the capital, Ljubljana, yet within striking distance of Lake Bled, the Karavanke mountains and the Julian Alps. It provides a good touring base, set above the River Sava, and also has a small, separate enclosure for those who enjoy naturism. Situated beside the peaceful tiny village of Dragocajni, in attractive countryside, there are 120 places for tourers each with electricity (6/10A). Although terraced, it is probably better described as a large plateau with tall pines and deciduous trees providing some shade. The naturist area measuring some 30x100 m. accommodates 15 units adjacent to the river (INF card not required).

Facilities	Directions
Three fully equipped sanitary blocks are of varying standards, but with adequate and clean provision. In the main camping area, a solar-powered, two-storey block has free hot showers, the lower half for use within the naturist area. WC for disabled visitors. Laundry facilities. Supermarket at entrance. Bar serves food (1/5-15/10). Two clay tennis courts (charged). Swings for children. River swimming and fishing. WiFi (free).	Travelling on road no.1, both Smlednik and site are well signed. From E61 motorway, Smlednik and site are signed at the Vodiice exit 11. (Watch out for sharp right turn to site on a bend just after camping 1 km. sign). GPS: 46.17425, 14.41628

Open: 1 May - 15 October.

Charges guide

Per unit incl. 2 persons and electricity	€ 17.00 - € 20.00

For latest campsite news, availability and prices visit
alanrogers.com

Soca

Kamp Klin

Lepena 1, SLO-5232 Soca (Slovenia) T: 053 889 513. E: kampklin@siol.net

alanrogers.com/SV4235

With an attractive location surrounded by mountains in the Triglav National Park, Kamp Klin is next to the confluence of the Soca and Lepenca rivers, which makes it an ideal base for fishing, kayaking and rafting. The campsite has 50 pitches, all for tourers; 50 with 7A electricity, on one large, grassy field, connected by a circular, gravel access road. It is attractively landscaped with flowers and young trees, which provide some shade. Some pitches are right on the bank of the river (unfenced) and there are beautiful views of the river and the mountains. Like so many Slovenian sites in this area, this is a good holiday base for the active camper.

Facilities

One modern toilet block with controllable showers. WC only for disabled visitors. Laundry with sinks. Bar/restaurant. Play area. Fishing (permit required). Torch useful. WiFi. Off site: Riding 500 m. Bicycle hire 10 km. Rambling. Rafting. Paragliding.

Open: April - October.

Directions

Site is on main Kranjska Gora-Bovec road and is well signed 3 km. east of Soca. Access involves a sharp right turn from main road and over a small bridge and right again. The road is winding in places with a moderate descent. GPS use co-ordinates. GPS: 46.33007, 13.644

Charges guide

Per unit incl. 2 persons and electricity	€ 23.00 - € 27.00
extra person	€ 11.50 - € 13.50
child (7-12 yrs)	€ 6.00 - € 7.00
dog	free

Verzej

Camping Terme Banovci

Banovci 1A, SLO-9241 Verzej (Slovenia) T: 025 131 400. E: terme@terme-banovci.si

alanrogers.com/SV4445

Terme Banovci is a comfortable, quiet, countryside site with 20 textile touring pitches (set among seasonal and rental units) plus 90 FKK naturist pitches which are located separately. A large, grass area is set aside for tents. The grassed pitches have ample shade, are accessed by gravel roads and all have 10A electricity. Entry to the indoor (35-38°C) and outdoor (25-27°C) pools with a total surface area of 2,000 sq.m. is free to campers. The pools with a large outdoor slide and ample space for sunbathing are all that one expects from a modern, well equipped thermal spa. The comfortable restaurant is built in traditional style and drinks and food are available on the terrace by the pool. The indoor pool contains thermal mineral water which is pumped up from a depth of 1,700 m. In addition, there is a paddling pool and a separate FKK pool.

Facilities

Two well appointed, heated sanitary blocks. Washbasins in cabins. Facilities for disabled visitors. Laundry. Motorcaravan services. Nordic walking. Volleyball. Tennis. Morning gymnastics. Entertainment programme. Wellness centre with three Finnish saunas. Solarium. Turkish bath. Various massage programmes (at extra cost). Off site: Numerous walking and cycling paths.

Open: 1 April - 6 November.

Directions

Site is 38 km. east of Maribor. From A5 take Vucja Vas exit and head south on 230 for 5 km. to Knzevci pri Ljutomeru. Then turn north east on 439 for 1 km. and fork right to Banovci. Site is 400 m. north east of Banovci and signed in village. GPS: 46.573181, 16.171494

Charges guide

Per person	€ 26.55
child (7-13 yrs)	€ 18.55

For latest campsite news, availability and prices visit

alanrogers.com

On the move?
Take your guides

You'll find them here...

Croatia has thrown off old communist attitudes and blossomed into a lively and friendly place to visit. A country steeped in history, it boasts some of the finest Roman ruins in Europe and you'll find plenty of traditional coastal towns, clusters of tiny islands and medieval villages to explore.

With its warm seas, crystal clear waters and over one thousand islands to explore, Croatia is an ideal place to try scuba diving. Diving centres can be found at the larger resorts.

The heart-shaped peninsula of Istria, located in the north, is among the most developed tourist regions in Croatia. Here you can visit the preserved Roman amphitheatre in Pula, the beautiful town of Rovinj with its cobbled streets and wooded hills and the resort of Umag, well known for its recreational activities, most notably tennis. Islands are studded all around the coast, making it ideal for sailing and diving enthusiasts. Istria also has the highest concentration of campsites. Further south, in the province of Dalmatia, Split is the largest city on the Adriatic coast and home to the impressive Diolectian's Palace. From here the islands of Brac, Hvar, Vis and Korcula, renowned for their lively fishing villages and pristine beaches, are easily accessible by ferry. The old walled city of Dubrovnik is 150 km. south. At over 2 km. long and 25 m. high, with 16 towers, a walk along the city walls affords spectacular views.

Population
4.5 million

Capital
Zagreb

Climate
Predominantly warm and hot in summer with temperatures of up to 40°C.

Language
Croatian, but English and German are widely spoken.

Telephone
The country code is 00 385

Currency
Kuna

Banks
Mon-Fri 08.00-19.00

Shops
Mainly Mon-Sat 08.00-20.00, although some close on Monday and Sundays.

Public Holidays

New Year's Day; Epiphany 6 Jan; Good Friday; Easter Monday; Labour Day 1 May; Parliament Day 30 May; Day of Anti-Fascist Victory 22 June; Statehood Day 25 June; Thanksgiving Day 5 Aug; Assumption 15 Aug; Independence Day 8 Oct; All Saints 1 Nov; Christmas 25, 26 Dec.

Motoring

Croatia is proceeding with a vast road improvement programme. There are still some roads which leave a lot to be desired, but things have improved dramatically. Roads along the coast can become heavily congested in summer and queues are possible at border crossings. Drive carefully especially at night – roads are usually unlit and have sharp bends. Tolls: some motorways, bridges and tunnels. Cars towing a caravan or trailer must carry two warning triangles. It is illegal to overtake military convoys.

Remember – if you travel to Croatia via Slovenian motorways, you now require a vignette *(see Slovenia introduction)*.

Tourist Office

Croatian National Tourist Office
2 The Lanchesters
162-164 Fulham Palace Road
London W6 9ER
Tel: 020 8563 7979
Fax: 020 8563 2616
Email: info@cnto.freeserve.co.uk
Internet: www.croatia.hr

British Embassy

Ivana Lucica 4, Zagreb
Tel: (385)(1) 6009 100

Places of interest

Dubrovnik: particularly appealing is the old town Stari Grad, with marble-paved squares and steep, cobbled streets.

Risnjak and Paklencia National Parks: both have excellent areas for hiking, the latter has excellent opportunities for rock climbing.

Rovinj: an active fishing port, an excellent collection of marine life can be found at the aquarium.

Split: Diocletian's Palace, Maritime Museum.

Zagreb: the capital of Croatia, with a whole host of museums.

Cuisine of the region

Brodet: mixed fish stewed with rice

Burek: a layered pie made with meat or cheese

Cesnjovka: garlic sausage

Kulen: paprika-flavoured salami

Manistra od bobica: beans and fresh maize soup

Piroska: cheese doughnut

Struki: baked cheese dumpling

Virtually every region produces its own varieties of wine.

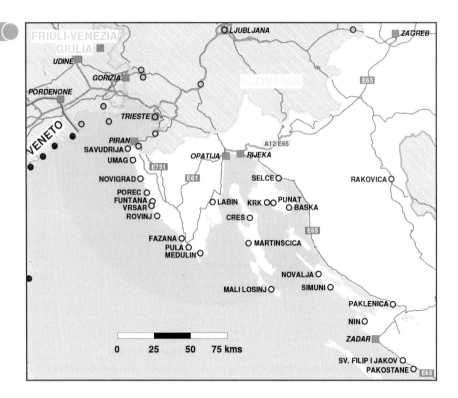

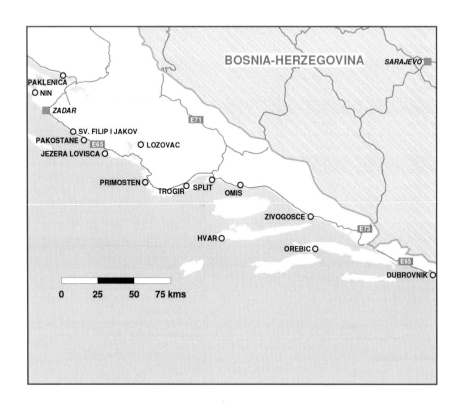

For latest campsite news, availability and prices visit
alanrogers.com

Fazana
Camping Bi-Village

Dragonja 115, HR-52212 Fazana (Istria) T: 052 300 300. E: info@bivillage.com
alanrogers.com/CR6745

Camping Bi-Village is a large holiday village in an attractive location close to the historic town of Pula and opposite the islands of the Brioni National Park. From the beach superb sunsets can be observed as the sun sinks below the sea's horizon. The site is landscaped with many flowers, shrubs and rock walls and offers over 1,000 pitches for touring units (the remainder taken by bungalows and chalets). Pitches are set in long rows accessed by gravel lanes, slightly sloping towards the sea, with only the bottom rows having shade from mature trees and good views over the Adriatic.

Facilities

Four modern toilet blocks with toilets, open plan washbasins and controllable hot showers. Child size washbasins. Baby room. Facilities for disabled visitors. Washing machine. Shopping centre (1/5-11/10). Bars (1/5-30/9) and restaurants. Bazaar. Gelateria. Pâtisserie. Swimming pools. Playground. Trampolines. Motorboat and pedalo hire. Boat launching. Games hall. Sports tournaments. Entertainment. Massage. WiFi areas (charged). Dogs are not allowed on the beach.

Open: 3 April - 30 October.

Directions

Follow no. 2 road south from Rijeka to Pula. In Pula follow site signs. Site is close to Fazana. GPS: 44.91717, 13.81105

Charges guide

Per unit incl. 2 persons	
and electricity	€ 21.00 - € 50.00
extra person	€ 6.00 - € 12.50
dog	€ 3.00 - € 6.00
child (5-12 yrs)	€ 3.50 - € 7.50

Funtana
Naturist Camping Istra

Grgeti 35, HR-52452 Funtana (Istria) T: 052 465 010. E: camping@valamar.com
alanrogers.com/CR6726

Located in the tiny and picturesque village of Funtana, this peaceful naturist site is part of the Camping on the Adriatic group. Istra has a fine array of facilities and, although there is no pool, it is surrounded by sparkling sea on three sides. The formally marked pitches ring the peninsula and some are directly at the water's edge giving great views of the island off to the south (early booking is advised). There are 1,000 pitches on site with 820 for touring, most with ample shade and varying in size from about 90 sq.m. All have 10A electricity and water points are scattered around the site.

Facilities

New and refurbished sanitary blocks provide toilets, washbasins, showers, hairdryers and good facilities for disabled visitors. Laundry facilities. Small supermarket. Restaurant and bars. Play areas. Entertainment for children (from May). Organised sports. Minigolf. Tennis. Massage. Dogs are allowed in some areas. WiFi near reception (free). Off site: Shops and restaurants in Funtana, a short walk from the gate. Riding 1 km. Porec 6 km. with regular bus service from the village.

Open: April - October.

Directions

Site is signed off Porec-Vrsar road 6 km. south of Porec in Funtana. Access for large units could be difficult turning off main road from Porec. If so, go past signed turning and turn around in night club car park a few metres further on. It is easier approaching from Vrsar. GPS: 45.17464, 13.59869

Charges guide

Per unit incl. 2 persons	
and electricity	€ 17.90 - € 33.70
extra person	€ 4.30 - € 8.20

Labin
Camping Marina

Sveta Marina bb, HR-52220 Labin (Istria) T: 052 879 058. E: camping@valamar.com
alanrogers.com/CR6747

Camping Marina is a very quiet site with a somewhat steep approach. It is overlooked by high, tree clad hills and is adjacent to a small bay. The 267 touring pitches, all with electricity, are either centred around the site's facilities or set on a new level terrace on the cliff top. Many have superb views over the sea and to the island of Cres. The site has a new café and a sunbathing area from where you can relax and enjoy the views. A stairway leads down to the crystal clear water's edge, an ideal place for snorkelling and a haven for divers.

Facilities

One well maintained toilet block has free controllable showers and washbasins. Facilities for children and disabled visitors. Washing machine. Motorcaravan services and points for washing diving/snorkelling equipment. Restaurant/bar. Church. Play area. Dog shower and garden. WiFi on part of site. Off site: Well stocked supermarket at start of the entrance road to site.

Open: 12 April - 1 November.

Directions

From E751/21 Pula-Opatija road turn off to Labin and follow signs for Rabac. On outskirts of Labin, site is signed sharp right and up a climbing cobbled road. Turn off country road for site and Marina SV is well signed to left. GPS: 45.033391, 14.157976

Charges guide

Per unit incl. 2 persons	
and electricity	€ 24.30 - € 34.00

For latest campsite news, availability and prices visit
alanrogers.com

Medulin
Camping Village Medulin
Osipovica 30, HR-52203 Medulin (Istria) T: 052 572 801. E: marina@arenaturist.hr

alanrogers.com/CR6734

Medulin is part of the Arenaturist group and it has a fabulous setting near Pula on the tip of the Istrian peninsula, enjoying great views of the offshore island and the town's twin church towers. Consisting of a peninsula about 1.5 km. long and a small island accessed by a road bridge, the site is thickly wooded with mature pine trees producing a carpet of needles. Pitches are marked and separated into three sizes. The land is undulating but there is no shortage of level areas. There are 950 touring pitches, all with 10/16A electricity and some mobile homes which are not intrusive.

Facilities

The sanitary blocks are kept very clean. Washbasins and showers are a mixture of outdoors and under cover. Shop, market and produce stalls. Motorcaravan service area. Seven restaurants or snack bars provide a large range of fare. Cocktail bar. Ice for sale. Fridge rental. Play area. Watersports. Barbecues are not permitted on pitches. Free WiFi. Off site: Golf, fishing (permit) and riding nearby. Restaurants and bars in Medulin village or in Pula.

Open: 27 March - 17 October.

Directions

Approaching from the north (Koper, Rovinj), on outskirts of Pula turn to follow signs for Medulin and site. Site is at far end of village and is well signed. GPS: 44.81466, 13.9316

Charges guide

Per unit incl. 2 persons	
and electricity	€ 16.60 - € 35.30
extra person	€ 5.20 - € 8.40

Prices for pitches by the sea are higher.

Medulin
Arenaturist Camping Kazela
Kapovica 350, HR-52203 Medulin (Istria) T: 052 577 277. E: ackazela@arenaturist.hr

alanrogers.com/CR6735

Camp Kazela is partly naturist and is situated close to Medulin, formerly a fishing port and now a busy tourist town. The site has 965 touring units with electricity connections (12A) and 100 pitches with electricity, water and drainage. The remaining pitches are used for chalets, seasonal guests and tour operators. The site is open with young trees and some pitches have pleasant views over the sea. Some clusters of mature trees provide a little shade, but generally this site is something of a sun trap. The beach which borders part of the site is mainly of sharp rocks and therefore not suitable for paddling.

Facilities

Six adequate toilet blocks have British and Turkish style toilets, open washbasins with cold water only and controllable hot showers. Motorcaravan services. Shopping centre with supermarket and restaurants. Two aqua parks (one FKK). Sailing and diving schools. Water skiing. Parasailing. Trampolines. Entertainment. Games hall. Disco. Live music. WiFi. Communal barbecue. Off site: Historic towns of Medulin 2 km. and Pula 10 km.

Open: 30 March - 4 November.

Directions

Follow the road south from Pula to Medulin. At Medulin, follow the signs for the hotels and the site is 1 km. after the hotels. GPS: 44.80540, 13.95550

Charges guide

Per unit incl. 2 persons	
and electricity	€ 16.60 - € 32.10
extra person	€ 4.60 - € 7.80
child (4-12 yrs)	€ 2.60 - € 4.90

Novigrad
Camping Mareda
Mareda, HR-52466 Novigrad (Istria) T: 052 858 680. E: camping@laguna-novigrad.hr

alanrogers.com/CR6713

Backed by oak woods and acres of vineyards, Camping Mareda is in a quiet coastal location 4 km. north of the small picturesque town of Novigrad. The site slopes down to a half bay and has 600 touring pitches, all with 16A electricity, either set on shallow terraces or slightly sloping gravel/grass. Mature trees provide shade and many pitches have views over the sea; 95 pitches are fully serviced. The site has an attractive, rocky sea frontage with areas for sunbathing, a good size swimming pool, a restaurant bar and a café, all with sea views.

Facilities

Five modern toilet blocks, one excellent one refurbished in 2013, have British and Turkish style toilets, washbasins in cabins and hot showers. Family shower room. Child size toilets and washbasins. Laundry with sinks and washing machine. Motorcaravan services. Supermarket. Beach restaurant, coffee bar and bar with terrace. Seawater swimming pool. Play area. Tennis. Fishing. Boats, kayaks, canoes and pedaloes for hire. Bicycle hire. Games hall with video games. Organised entertainment. Free WiFi.

Open: 1 May - 30 September.

Directions

From Novigrad travel north towards Umag. In 4 km. site is signed to left. GPS: 45.34363, 13.54815

Charges guide

Per unit incl. 2 persons	
and electricity	€ 17.50 - € 42.50
extra person	€ 5.00 - € 8.50
child (5-9 yrs)	€ 3.00 - € 4.50
dog	€ 3.50 - € 5.50

For latest campsite news, availability and prices visit
alanrogers.com

Porec
Camping Lanterna

Lanterna 1, Tar-Vabriga, HR-52465 Porec (Istria) T: 052 465 010. E: camping@valamar.com
alanrogers.com/CR6716

This is a well organised site and one of the largest in Croatia with high standards and an amazing selection of activities, and is part of the Camping Adriatic by Valamar group. Set in 80 hectares with over 3 km. of beach, there are 3000 pitches, of which 1,886 are for touring units. All have 16A electricity and fresh water, and 255 also have waste water drainage. Pitches are 60-120 sq.m. with some superb locations right on the sea, although these tend to be taken first so it is advisable to book ahead. There are wonderful coastal views from the new glamping area with seven luxury tents and private infinity pool. A member of Leading Campings group.

Facilities

The sixteen sanitary blocks are clean and good quality. Facilities for children and baby care areas, some Turkish style WCs, hot showers, with some blocks providing facilities for disabled visitors. Laundry service. Three supermarkets sell most everyday requirements. Fresh fish shop. Four restaurants, bars and snack bars and fast food outlets. Swimming pool and paddling pools. Sandpit and play areas, with entertainment for all in high season. Tennis. Bicycle hire. Watersports. Boat hire. Minigolf. Riding. Internet café. Jetty and ramp for boats. WiFi (free). Impressive new glamping area. Dogs are accepted in certain areas. Off site: Hourly bus service from the reception area. Riding 500 m. Golf 10 km. Nearest large supermarket in Novigrad 9 km.

Open: 3 April - 3 October.

Directions

The turn to Lanterna is well signed off the Novigrad to Porec road 8 km. south of Novigrad. Continue for 2 km. along the turn off road towards the coast and the campsite is on the right hand side.
GPS: 45.29672, 13.59442

Charges guide

Per unit incl. 2 persons and electricity	€ 19.30 - € 38.30
extra person	€ 5.00 - € 9.90
child (5-12 yrs)	free - € 6.50

Prices for pitches by the sea are higher.

Porec
Naturist Resort Solaris

Lanterna bb, HR-52465 Porec (Istria) T: 052 465 010. E: camping@valamar.com
alanrogers.com/CR6718

This naturist site is part of the Camping Adriatic by Valamar group and has a most pleasant atmosphere. When we visited in high season there were lots of happy people having fun. A pretty cove and lots of beach frontage with cool pitches under trees makes the site very attractive. Of the 1,455 pitches, 550 are available for touring, with 400 long stay units. There are 156 fully serviced pitches (100 sq.m) available on a 'first come, first served' basis, with an ample supply of electricity hook-ups (10/16A) and plentiful water points. As this is a naturist site, there are certain rules that must be followed. For those who embrace the naturist regime or want to give it a try, this is a pleasant, quiet site with above average facilities in an Area of Outstanding Natural Beauty.

Facilities

Eleven excellent, fully equipped toilet blocks provide toilets, washbasins and showers. Some have facilities for disabled visitors. Washing machines and ironing facilities. Restaurants, grills and fast food, and supermarkets. Swimming pool. Massage. Beauty and hairdressing salons. Tennis. Minigolf. Bicycle hire. Play areas. Boat launching. Car wash. Entertainment. WiFi on 70% of site (free). Dogs are allowed in certain areas of the site and beach. Off site: Excursions. Riding 1 km.

Open: May - October.

Directions

Site is 12 km. south of Novigrad on the Novigrad-Porec road. Turn towards the coast signed Lanterna. Continue straight on down this road and after passing the security barrier, turn left to Solaris.
GPS: 45.29126, 13.5848

Charges guide

Per unit incl. 2 persons and electricity	€ 19.30 - € 38.30
extra person	€ 5.00 - € 9.90
child (4-12 yrs)	free - € 6.50
dog	€ 4.00 - € 6.50

Prices for pitches by the sea are higher.

For latest campsite news, availability and prices visit
alanrogers.com

Porec
Camping Puntica

Rade Koncara 12, Funtana, HR-52449 Porec (Istria) T: 052 445 720. E: ac.puntica@plavalaguna.hr
alanrogers.com/CR6719

Puntica is a small, unassuming and old-fashioned campsite. Everything is modest here and if small is your thing, you will love it. There are 240 pitches with 130 for touring units. Some of the flat, variably sized pitches (80-120 sq.m) are shaded amongst trees which could test larger units. The waterside pitches are lovely but many of these are occupied by permanent units. Electricity box positioning may warrant long leads in some areas (up to 10A). The marina alongside is very active and there are views from the terraces of the rustic restaurant and bar. There is a paved area around the tip of the site for sunbathing and ladders give access to deeper water.

Facilities	Directions
One main sanitary block and other smaller blocks are kept clean and provide good facilities. British and Turkish style toilets with one unit for disabled visitors. Washing machines and dryers operated by the 'laundry lady'. Small shop. Restaurant and bar. Motorcaravan services. Fishing. Playground. Gas barbecues permitted. Fridge box hire. Off site: Funta town. Bicycle hire and riding 500 m.	Site is on main road between Porec and Vrsar, near the village of Funtana, 7 km. south of Porec. Just watch for camping signs. GPS: 45.1774, 13.6033

Open: 23 April - 1 October.

Charges guide

Per unit incl. 2 persons and electricity	€ 14.50 - € 29.90
extra person	€ 3.40 - € 6.60
child (4-10 yrs)	free - € 3.80

Porec
Naturist Centre Ulika

Cervar, HR-52440 Porec (Istria) T: 052 436 325. E: reservations@plavalaguna.hr
alanrogers.com/CR6720

This naturist site is well located, occupying a small peninsula of some 15 hectares. This means that there is only a short walk to the sea from anywhere on the site. The ground is mostly gently sloping with a covering of rough grass and there are 1,000 pitches with 6A electricity connections, 420 also have water and drainage. One side of the site is shaded with mature trees, while the other side is less shady. There are many activities on site and an excellent swimming pool. The reception office opens 24 hours for help and information. Single men are not accepted. This is a pleasant, uncomplicated site which is well situated, well managed and peaceful.

Facilities	Directions
Six toilet blocks provide mostly British style WCs, washbasins (half with hot water) and showers (a third with controllable hot water). Facilities for disabled visitors. Laundry. Motorcaravan services. Supermarket. Restaurant, pizzeria and snacks. Swimming pool. Massage. Tennis. Minigolf. Watersports. Boating and sailing (marina). Off site: Riding 3 km. Bicycle hire 6 km.	Site is 3 km. off the main Novigrad-Porec road, signed in village of Cevar. GPS: 45.25676, 13.58317

Open: One week before Easter - 10 October.

Charges guide

Per unit incl. 2 persons and electricity	Kn 142 - 267
extra person	Kn 33 - 64
child (4-10 yrs)	free - Kn 43

Porec
Autokamp Zelena Laguna

HR-52440 Porec (Istria) T: 052 410 101. E: mail@plavalaguna.hr
alanrogers.com/CR6722

Zelena Laguna (green lagoon) is a well run and long established site with 540 touring pitches, all with 10A electricity, 42 being fully serviced. Access to the pitches is by hard surfaced roads with gravel side roads. There are many mature trees providing plenty of shade and hedges separate most pitches. Part of the site is on a peninsula with terraced pitches and the remainder are either on level or slightly sloping ground. A path circles the peninsula below which are paved waterside sunbathing areas. Those to the right of the site are within easy reach of the cocktail bar. Further to the right is a small harbour, attractive restaurant and swimming pool. Part of the beach, which has Blue Flag status, is reserved for naturists.

Facilities	Directions
Six modern and well maintained sanitary blocks. The washbasins have hot water and there are free controllable showers. Toilets are mostly British style and there are facilities for disabled visitors. Supermarket and shop. Several restaurants and snack bars. Swimming pool. Tennis (instruction available). Bicycle hire. Boat hire (motor and sailing). Boat launching. Entertainment for the family. Riding. WiFi throughout (free).	Site entrance is 2 km. south of Porec on Vrsar-Porec coastal road. It is well signed and part of a large multiple hotel complex. GPS: 45.19529, 13.58927

Open: One week before Easter - 7 October.

Charges guide

Per unit incl. 2 persons and electricity	€ 19.00 - € 37.60
extra person	€ 4.40 - € 8.70
child (4-10 yrs)	free - € 6.20
dog	€ 3.20 - € 6.70

For latest campsite news, availability and prices visit
alanrogers.com

Porec
Camping Bijela Uvala
Bijela Uvala, Zelena Laguna, HR-52440 Porec (Istria) T: 052 410 551. E: reservations@lagunaporec.com
alanrogers.com/CR6724

Bijela Uvala is a large friendly campsite with an attractive waterside location and an extensive range of facilities. The direct sea access makes the site very popular in high season. The 2,500 pitches, 1,476 for touring, are compact and due to the terrain some have excellent sea views and breezes, however as usual these are the most sought after, so book early. They range from 60-120 sq.m. and all have electricity and water connections. Some are formal with hedging, some are terraced and most have good shade from established trees or wooded areas. There are also very informal areas where unmarked pitches are on generally uneven ground.

Facilities

Eight sanitary blocks are clean and well equipped with mainly British style WCs. Free hot showers. Washing machines. Facilities for disabled visitors. Motorcaravan services. Gas. Fridge boxes. Shop. Large supermarket. Restaurants, fast food cafés, bars and a bakery. Large supermarket and a shop. Two swimming pool complexes, one with a medium size pool, the other larger and lagoon-style with fountains. Tennis. Playground. Entertainment for children. TV room. WiFi (charged).

Open: 19 March - 7 October.

Directions

The site adjoins Zelena Laguna. From the main Porec to Vrsar coast road turn off towards coast and the town of Zelena Laguna 4 km. south of Porec and follow campsite signs. GPS: 45.19149, 13.59686

Charges guide

Per unit incl. 2 persons and electricity	€ 19.00 - € 37.60
extra person	€ 4.40 - € 8.70
child (4-10 yrs)	free - € 6.20
dog	€ 3.20 - € 6.70

Pula
Arenaturist Camping Stupice
Premantura, HR-52100 Pula (Istria) T: 052 575 101. E: marketing@arenaturist.hr
alanrogers.com/CR6737

This quiet site, which offers superb views over the sea to the nearby islands, is situated on a delightful strip of coast on the Istrian peninsula, near the small village of Premantura. Most of the site is covered with undulating, dense pinewood providing ample shade and a carpet of pine needles. There are 588 touring pitches (1,000 in total) in three sizes (ranging from 60-120 sq.m). They are mostly sloping and about a fifth have sea views. Access roads are bitumen or gravel. A narrow pebble beach and low rocks separate the sea from the site and provide a perfect place to relax and enjoy the view.

Facilities

The six toilet blocks, although old, were immaculately clean when we visited. Toilets are a mixture of Turkish and British style. Showers and free hot water. Washing machines. Good supermarket. Kiosk and several good small bars and grills. Some live entertainment at the restaurant in high season. Aquapark. Minigolf. Modern playground. Children's activities. Pebble beach. Marina, boat launching, jetty and scuba diving. Bicycle and beach buggy hire. Free WiFi over 80% of site.

Open: Easter - 25 October.

Directions

Site is 11 km. south east of Pula. Follow signs to Premantura from Pula where there are site signs. GPS: 44.7978, 13.91366

Charges guide

Per unit incl. 2 persons and electricity	€ 17.10 - € 33.00
extra person	€ 4.60 - € 8.00
child (4-12 yrs)	€ 2.60 - € 5.00

Prices for pitches by the sea are higher.

Pula
Arenaturist Camping Indije
Banjole, HR-52100 Pula (Istria) T: 052 573 066. E: acindije@arenaturist.hr
alanrogers.com/CR6739

Camping Indije is on the beautiful Adriatic coast in Banjole (Medulin), only a few kilometres from the historic centre of Pula. This is a very attractive hilly site with many pitches on terraces together with a double row on level ground along the water's edge. All 450 grass and gravel pitches (50-120 sq.m) are for touring units and most are well shaded. All have 10A electricity and 16 are fully serviced. From many pitches there are wonderful open views over the sea to the islands. The layout of the site gives a pleasant, shady atmosphere.

Facilities

Four comfortable toilet blocks have open plan washbasins and showers. Washing machine. Motorcaravan service point. Supermarket and newspaper stand. Bar and restaurant. Miniclub. Live music. Rock plateau beach. Diving centre. Boat mooring. Fishing (with permit). Boat launching. WiFi on part of site. Off site: Historic towns of Pula and Rovinj are close. Riding 10 km. Golf 15 km.

Open: 30 March - 23 September.

Directions

From Pula follow signs for Premantura and Banjole southwards. From Banjole follow site signs. GPS: 44.82382, 13.85078

Charges guide

Per unit incl. 2 persons and electricity	€ 16.60 - € 30.40
extra person	€ 4.60 - € 7.30
child (4-12 yrs)	€ 2.70 - € 5.00

For latest campsite news, availability and prices visit
alanrogers.com

Pula

Arenaturist Camping Stoja

Stoja 37, HR-52100 Pula (Istria) T: 052 387 144. E: acstoja@arenaturist.hr

alanrogers.com/CR6742

Camping Stoja in Pula is an attractive and well maintained site on a small peninsula and therefore almost completely surrounded by the waters of the clear Adriatic. In the centre of the site is the old Fort Stoja, built in 1884 for coastal defence. Some of its buildings are now used as a toilet block and laundry and its courtyard is used by the entertainment team. The 708 touring pitches here vary greatly in size (50-120 sq.m) and are marked by round, concrete, numbered blocks, separated by young trees. About half have shade from mature trees and all are slightly sloping on grass and gravel. Pitches close to the pebble and rock beach have beautiful views of the sea and Pula. This site is an ideal base for visiting Pula, considered to be the capital of Istrian tourism and full of history, tradition and natural beauty, including a spectacular Roman amphitheatre.

Facilities

Four toilet blocks with British style toilets, open plan washbasins with cold water only and controllable hot showers. Child size washbasins. Facilities for disabled visitors. Laundry and ironing service. Fridge box hire. Motorcaravan service point. Supermarket. Bar/restaurant. Miniclub and teen club. Bicycle hire. Water skiing. Boat hire. Boat launching. Surfboard and pedalo hire. Fishing (with permit). Island excursions. Free WiFi throughout. No barbecues on pitches, communal areas provided. Off site: Pula (walking distance). Riding 8 km. Golf 10 km.

Open: 30 March - 4 November.

Directions

Site is on peninsula 2 km. west of Pula. Well signed from Pula. GPS: 44.85972, 13.81450

Charges guide

Per unit incl. 2 persons and electricity	€ 19.90 - € 33.70
extra person	€ 5.20 - € 8.10
child (4-12 yrs)	€ 3.20 - € 5.70
dog	€ 3.10 - € 5.60

Pula

Camping Brioni

Puntizela 155, HR-52100 Pula (Istria) T: 052 517 490. E: camping@valamar.com

alanrogers.com/CR6744

Situated on a small peninsula overlooking the Brioni archipelago (a National Park comprising 14 islands) and within easy reach of Pula, Camping Brioni is a quiet and useful base from which to tour in a scenically attractive and historically interesting region. The site has 420 touring pitches under ample shade, all with 10A electricity and 272 with fresh water taps. On mainly level grass and gravel, the pitches are numbered with some terracing. Part of the site is devoted to a youth hostel which shares the site facilities. This ten-hectare site has a long sea frontage and there are ample places to sit and enjoy the sun and the sea views.

Facilities

Three sanitary blocks, one with facilities for disabled visitors. Cleaning and maintenance needed some attention when we visited. Baby room. Laundry room. Small supermarket and kiosk selling fruit, vegetables and bread (10/5-15/9). Restaurant. Beachside snack bar. Play area. Boat rental. Internet access. Off site: Pula, Brioni National Park.

Open: All year.

Directions

Site is 7 km. north west of Pula. Heading north on the road running alongside the harbour in Pula (Trscanska ulinka) turn left at the roundabout towards Rijeka. After 800 m. site is signed to the left (west). GPS: 44.89812, 13.80833

Charges guide

Per unit incl. 2 persons and electricity	€ 15.70 - € 38.30
extra person	€ 3.75 - € 6.80
child (4-10 yrs)	free - € 4.00
dog	€ 1.35 - € 3.00
No credit cards.	

For latest campsite news, availability and prices visit
alanrogers.com

Rovinj
Camping Amarin
Monsena bb, HR-52210 Rovinj (Istria) T: 052 802 000. E: info@maistra.hr
alanrogers.com/CR6730

Situated 4 km. from the centre of the lovely old port town of Rovinj, this site has much to offer. The complex is part of the Maistra group. It has 12.6 hectares of land and is adjacent to the Amarin bungalow complex. Campers can take advantage of the facilities afforded by both areas. There are 650 pitches for touring units on various types of ground, all between 70-100 sq.m. Most are separated by foliage and 10A electricity is available. A rocky beach backed by a grassy sunbathing area is very popular, but the site has its own superb, supervised round pool with corkscrew slide plus a splash pool for children. Boat owners have a mooring area and launching ramp and a breakwater is popular with sunbathers. The port of Rovinj contains many delights, particularly if you are able to contend with the hundreds of steps which lead to the church above the town from where the views are well worth the climb.

Facilities

Thirteen respectable toilet blocks have a mixture of British and Turkish toilets. Half the washbasins have hot water. Some showers have hot water, the rest have cold and are outside. Some blocks have a unit for disabled visitors. Fridge box hire. Laundry service. Motorcaravan services. Supermarket. Small market. Two restaurants, taverna, pizzeria and terrace grill. Swimming pool. Flume and splash pool. Watersports. Bicycle hire. Fishing (permit). Daily entertainment. Hairdresser. Massage. WiFi (free).

Open: 22 April - 25 September.

Directions

Site is 2 km. north of Rovinj. Follow signs for campsite from main road. GPS: 45.10876, 13.61988

Charges guide

Per unit incl. 2 persons	
and electricity	€ 16.00 - € 39.00
extra person	€ 4.50 - € 9.70
child (5-11 yrs)	€ 3.70 - € 6.30
dog	€ 4.00 - € 7.00

For stays less than 3 nights in high season add 10%.

Camping Amarin . Rovinj

The unique natural environment here is only one small piece of the larger picture for a summer holiday filled with magical experiences.

ONLINE BOOKING

Rich entertainment programs!
Amazing Kids club!
New swiming pool!

tel: +385 (0)52 800 200
e-mail: ac-amarin@maistra.hr
www.CampingRovinjVrsar.com

Istria CROATIA

Rovinj
Naturist FKK Camping Valalta
226

Cesta za Valaltu - Lim 7, HR-52210 Rovinj (Istria) T: 052 804 800. E: valalta@valalta.hr
alanrogers.com/CR6731

This is a most impressive site for up to 6,000 naturist campers, which has a pleasant, open feel. The passage through reception is efficient and this feeling is maintained around the well organised site. Valalta is a family oriented campsite and a friendly, family atmosphere is to be found here. All of the 1,083 touring pitches are the same price and have 10/16A electricity, although they vary in size and surroundings. The variations include shade, views, sand, grass, sea frontage, level ground, slopes and terracing. It is not possible to reserve a particular pitch and campers do move pitches at will. The impressive pool is in lagoon-style with water features and cascades.

Facilities

Twenty very high quality new or refurbished sanitary blocks. Hot showers. Facilities for disabled campers. Washing machines. Supermarket. Four restaurants (one specialising in seafood). Pizzeria. Two bars (own brewery). Large lagoon-style outdoor pool complex (15/5-15/9). Indoor heated pool (29/4-3/10). Beauty salon. Fitness club. Massage. Minigolf. Tennis. Sailing. Play area. Bicycle hire. Beach volleyball. Marina with full services. Internet. Entertainment. Kindergarten. Medical clinic. Special textile area for children. WiFi over site (charged). No dogs.

Open: 29 April - 3 October.

Directions

Site is on coast 7 km. north of Rovinj. If approaching from north turn inland (follow signs to Rovinj) to drive around the Limski Kanal. Then follow signs towards Valalta 2 km. east of Rovinj. Site is at end of road and is well signed. GPS: 45.12235, 13.632083

Charges guide

Per unit incl. 2 persons	
and electricity	€ 24.00 - € 51.00
extra person	€ 5.50 - € 11.50
child (6-11 yrs)	€ 4.70 - € 5.70

For latest campsite news, availability and prices visit
alanrogers.com

Rovinj
Camping Polari

Polari bb, HR-52210 Rovinj (Istria) T: 052 801 501. E: polari@maistra.hr

alanrogers.com/CR6732

This 60-hectare site has excellent facilities for both textile and naturist campers, the latter in an area of 12 hectares to the left of the main site. Most parts of the site have good shade cover provided by mature trees. There are 1,806 level pitches for touring units on grass/gravel, terraced in places; many have open views over the sea to the islands. All have access to 10A electricity. An impressive swimming pool complex is child friendly with large paddling areas and there is an aquapark. The ancient town of Rovinj is well worth a visit and is best reached via the 4.5 km. coastal cycle path or by bus from the campsite. Part of the Maistra group, a massive improvement programme has been undertaken and the result makes it a very attractive site. Enjoy a meal in one of the two restaurants with panoramic sea views.

Facilities

The sanitary facilities are well maintained with plenty of hot water. Washing machines and dryers. Motorcaravan services. Bar/snack bar. Takeaway food. Pool bar. Two restaurants. Aquapark with slide (15/5-15/9). Tennis. Minigolf. Children's entertainment with all major European languages spoken. Bicycle hire. Watersports. Windsurfing school. Trampoline. Miniclub. Games room. Live music (June-Sept). WiFi on part of site (free). Off site: Riding 1 km. Rovinj 3 km. (buses 15/6-15/9).

Open: 22 April - 2 October.

Directions

From any access road to Rovinj look for blue signs to AC Polari (amongst other destinations). The site is 3 km. south of Rovinj. GPS: 45.06286, 13.67489

Charges guide

Per unit incl. 2 persons	
and electricity	€ 18.00 - € 59.80
extra person (18-64 yrs)	€ 5.50 - € 11.40
child (5-17 yrs)	free - € 9.50
dog	€ 3.10 - € 8.00

For stays less than 3 nights in high season add 20%.

Camping Polari . Rovinj

A picturesque cove, ideal for all those who relish the pleasant shade of olive trees and the cleanest sea in the Mediterranean.

ONLINE BOOKING

Mobile homes with a whirlpool! Children's clubs and playgrounds! Pitch with water supply and drain! Wi-Fi!

tel: +385 (0)52 800 200
e-mail: polari@maistra.hr
www.CampingRovinjVrsar.com

Istria CROATIA

Rovinj
Camping San Polo & Colone

Predio Longher bb, HR-52211 Bale (Istria) T: 052 824 338. E: reservations@camping-monperin.hr

alanrogers.com/CR6740

San Polo and Colone are two sister campsites with a number of shared amenities, including reception. They are midway between Pula and Rovinj and have direct access to the sea. There are 800 pitches, many close to the sea, including 500 for touring, well shaded and of a good size (100-120 sq.m), most with 16A electrical connections. Sixty mobile homes and chalets are available for rent. The beach here is long and pebbly with a degree of natural shade. At Colone, a restaurant with a terrace serves delicious pizzas and other dishes prepared over a wood-fired grill. A great site, popular with families with young children and equally suitable for those seeking a relaxing beachside holiday.

Facilities

Eight, well maintained, prefabricated sanitary blocks provide free hot showers and open style washbasins. A new block will include facilities for disabled visitors. Laundry facilities. Mini market with fruit and vegetables. Three restaurants. Bar. Beach bar. Takeaway meals. Aquapark. Sports area. Playground. Volleyball. Direct beach access. Boat hire. Communal barbecue. WiFi on part of site (free). Off site: Walking and mountain bike trails. Bale town. Pula, Rovinj and Brijuni National Park.

Open: 27 March - 12 October.

Directions

Site is on the coast 18 km. south of Rovinj and is well signed on the Rovinj-Pula road at Bale. GPS: 45.01986, 13.72275

Charges guide

Per unit incl. 2 persons	
and electricity	€ 17.20 - € 34.70
extra person	€ 4.40 - € 8.00
child (5-11 yrs)	free - € 4.30
dog	€ 2.60 - € 4.70

For latest campsite news, availability and prices visit
alanrogers.com

Rovinj
Camping Vestar

Vestar bb, HR-52210 Rovinj (Istria) T: 052 803 700. E: info@maistra.hr

alanrogers.com/CR6733

Camping Vestar is a quiet site just 5 km. from the historic harbour town of Rovinj and is one of the rare sites in Croatia with a partly sandy beach. Right behind the beach is a large area, attractively landscaped with young trees and shrubs, with grass for sunbathing. The site has 650 large pitches, of which 500 are for touring units, all with 6/10A electricity (the rest being taken by seasonal units and 60 pitches for tour operators). It is largely wooded with good shade and from the bottom row of pitches there are views of the sea. Pitching is on two separate fields, one for free camping, the other with numbered pitches. The pitches at the beach are in a half circle around the shallow bay, making it safe for children to swim. Vestar has a small marina and a jetty for mooring small boats and excursions to the islands are arranged. There is a miniclub and live music with dancing at one of the bars/restaurants in the evenings. The restaurants all have open-air terraces, one covered with vines to protect you from the hot sun.

Facilities	Directions
Six modern and one refurbished toilet blocks with British style toilets, open washbasins and controllable hot showers. Child size facilities. Baby rooms. Family bathroom. Facilities for disabled visitors. Laundry service. Fridge box hire. Motorcaravan services. Shop. Three bars. Two restaurants. Large swimming pool. Playground. Fishing. Boat and pedalo hire. Miniclub (5-11 yrs). Excursions. Internet access in reception. WiFi (free). Off site: Riding 2 km. Rovinj 5 km.	Site is on the coast 4 km. south east of Rovinj. From Rovinj travel south towards Pula. After 4 km. turn right following campsite signs. GPS: 45.05432, 13.68568

Open: 22 April - 25 September.

Charges guide

Per person	€ 5.00 - € 11.20
child (5-18 yrs)	€ 4.50 - € 9.50
pitch incl. electricity	€ 7.00 - € 33.00
dog	€ 3.10 - € 7.20

Camping Veštar . Rovinj

This campsite has a special charm – a warm welcome is guaranteed, in a stunning beachside setting.

ONLINE BOOKING

Modern sanitary facilities! Pitch with water supply and drain! Amazing Kids club! Wi-Fi!

tel: +385 (0)52 800 200
e-mail: vestar@maistra.hr
www.CampingRovinjVrsar.com

Istria

Rovinj
Camping Val Saline

Cesta Za Valaltu - Lim 7, HR-52210 Rovinj (Istria) T: 052 804 850. E: camp@valsaline.hr

alanrogers.com/CR6741

This brand new campsite will open on 1 May 2016. It is located some seven kilometres north west of Rovinj on a bay close to the Lim Fjord. It is a 12-hectare site, flat or part terraced and the majority of the 259 touring pitches are close to the waterfront, although those further away have good sea views. They are of a good size (100-140 sq.m), all have 10-16A electricity and around half have water connections. The site's own 700 m. long beach slopes gently down to the crystal clear water and there is a jetty for mooring small boats. Val Saline lies adjacent to its sister site, the Valalta Naturist Camp.

Facilities	Directions
Modern sanitary blocks with hot showers, private cubicles, facilities for children and disabled visitors. Washing machines. Motorcaravan services. Shop (15/5-15/9). Bar (15/5-15/9). Internet café. Restaurant and takeaway (1/5-3/10). Outdoor swimming pool (15/5-15/9). Outdoor fitness. Playgrounds. Beach volleyball. Minigolf. Entertainment programme (July/Aug). Bicycle hire. Currency exchange. WiFi. Off site: Riding 2 km.	Site is on coast 7 km. north west of Rovinj in the direction of Val Saline. From north turn inland (follow signs for Rovinj) to drive around the Limski Kanal. Then follow signs for Valalta 2 km. east of Rovinj. Entrance is 1.5 km. from naturist site. GPS: 45.11495, 13.62855

Open: 1 May - 3 October.

Charges guide

Per unit incl. 2 persons and electricity	€ 45.00
extra person	€ 10.00
child (6-11 yrs)	€ 5.00

For latest campsite news, availability and prices visit
alanrogers.com

Savudrija
CampingIN Pineta Umag

Istarska bb, HR-52475 Savudrija (Istria) T: 052 709 550. E: camp.pineta@istraturist.hr

alanrogers.com/CR6711

This pleasant, quiet site is set under tall pines and has direct access to the sea over fairly level rocks. It is of medium size (17 hectares) and gets its name from its setting amongst a forest of fully mature pine trees around two sides of a coastal bay. There are 458 pitches of which 160 are occupied on a long stay basis. Pitches are numbered and are 50-120 sq.m, all with access to electricity (10A). This is a site for those who prefer cooler situations as the dense pines provide abundant shade. Those who like the peaceful life will enjoy it here with sea bathing on the 'doorstep' and sunbathing areas on the rocks the whole length of the site.

Facilities

Five good sanitary blocks provide showers (plus showers for dogs), mostly British style WCs and a few Turkish style and an area for children and babies. Excellent facilities for disabled campers. Fresh water at toilet blocks only. Motorcaravan services. Supermarket. Six bars, three restaurants and snack bar. Tennis. Fishing (permit). Bicycle hire. Boat launching. Activities centre. Evening music. WiFi in some areas (charged). Off site: Gas is available in local garage 500 m. from the site entrance. Riding 6 km. Sailing 9 km. Golf 12 km.

Open: 22 April - 25 September.

Directions

Site is 6 km. north of Umag. From Umag travel north following signs for Savundrija signs. In the village of Basanija, at the tourist office, turn left. Reception is 500 m. on the left. GPS: 45.48674, 13.49246

Charges guide

Per unit incl. 2 persons and electricity	€ 15.70 - € 32.60
extra person	€ 3.80 - € 7.80
child (5-12 yrs)	€ 2.30 - € 4.70
dog	€ 2.30 - € 3.80

For stays less than 3 nights in high season add 10%.

Umag
CampingIN Naturist Kanegra Umag

Kanegra, HR-52470 Umag (Istria) T: 052 709 000. E: camp.kanegra@istraturist.hr

alanrogers.com/CR6710

Situated almost on the Slovenian border, this could be said to be the first and last campsite in Croatia. Part of the Istraturist group, the smart air-conditioned reception sets the tone for this very pleasant naturist site. It is located alongside the large Kanegra bungalow complex and campers are able to share its comprehensive facilities. There are 193 level pitches here on sandy soil with sparse grass (90 are seasonal). They vary in size (60-100 sq.m), are marked and numbered and all have 16A electricity, however 156 also provide water and drainage. The site has an open aspect with very little shade and sparkling clear waters off the rocky beach which runs its total length. An area is roped off for swimmers.

Facilities

Two well equipped toilet blocks are kept very clean. Washing machine. Beach showers. No facilities for disabled campers. Motorcaravan services. Supermarket. Two bars, three snack bars and two restaurants, all open until late. Nightly disco in the adjacent bungalow complex but reportedly not disturbing the campsite. Playground. Use of all sporting facilities in the bungalow park. Many watersports. Miniclub (5-12 yrs). WiFi in reception (charged). Electric barbecues only. Off site: Bicycle hire and boat launching 200 m. Golf 3 km. Riding 7 km. Fishing. Tennis in Kanegra.

Open: 23 April - 25 September.

Directions

From Koper in the north just over the Italian border, follow signs to Umag, but turn north towards Kanegra 5 km. before Umag. If approaching from south, after Umag follow main coast road north towards Savudrija (do not turn off towards this town) and then Kanegra. GPS: 45.480017, 13.570717

Charges guide

Per unit incl. 2 persons and electricity	€ 15.70 - € 32.60
extra person	€ 3.80 - € 7.80
child (5-12 yrs)	€ 2.30 - € 4.70
dog	€ 2.20 - € 3.80

For stays less than 3 nights in high season add 10%.

Umag
CampingIN Stella Maris Umag

Savudrijska cesta bb, HR-52470 Umag (Istria) T: 052 710 900. E: camp.stella.maris@istraturist.hr
alanrogers.com/CR6712

This extremely large, sprawling site of 4.5 hectares is split by the Umag - Savudrija road. The camping site and reception is to the east of the road and the amazing Sol Stella Maris leisure complex, where the Croatian open tennis tournament is held (amongst other competitions), is to the west and borders the sea. Located some 2 km. from the centre of Umag, the site comprises some 575 pitches of which 60 are seasonal and 20 are for tour operators. They are arranged in rows on gently sloping ground, some are shaded. The pitches all have 10A electricity. The site's real strength is its attachment to the leisure complex, with numerous facilities available to campers.

Facilities

Three sanitary blocks of a very high standard. Hot water throughout. Excellent facilities for disabled visitors. Laundry facilities. Large supermarket. Huge range of restaurants, bars and snack bars. International tennis centre with pools and beach area. Watersports. Fishing (permit required from Umag). Entertainment programme and clubs for children of all ages. Communal barbecue areas. Excursions organised. Off site: Land train every 15 minutes into Umag and a local bus service to towns further along the coast. Riding 500 m. Golf 1 km.

Open: 23 April - 26 September.

Directions

Site is 2.5 km. north of Umag. On entering Umag look for signs on the main coast road to all campsites and follow the Stella Maris signs. GPS: 45.450417, 13.5222

Charges guide

Per unit incl. 2 persons	
and electricity	€ 15.50 - € 31.90
extra person	€ 3.80 - € 7.80
child (5-12 yrs)	€ 2.30 - € 4.70
dog	€ 2.30 - € 3.80

For stays less than 3 nights in high season add 10%.

Umag
CampingIN Finida Umag

Krizine 55a, HR-52470 Umag (Istria) T: 052 725 950. E: camp.finida@istraturist.hr
alanrogers.com/CR6714

Finida is a small, fairly quiet and friendly site with good sanitary facilities and with easy access from the Umag-Novigrad road. The sea runs the length of the site and offers places to swim, either from a concrete jetty or from a small beach. The site is heavily wooded affording abundant shade and from the terrace of the bar/restaurant there are views over the sea. There are 285 marked pitches (80-100 sq.m), all with 10A electricity, 103 also have water and TV connection. Finida will appeal to those who prefer the cosiness of a smaller, friendly site.

Facilities

Three new toilet blocks contain mostly British style WCs and a few Turkish style with all modern facilities. Facilities for disabled campers. Washing machines. Motorcaravan services (a bit tight to drive onto). Small but well stocked supermarket. Bar, snack bar and restaurant. Minigolf. Fishing (permit). Boats may be moored off the beach. Bicycle, pedalo and canoe hire. Communal barbecues. WiFi in some areas (charged). Off site: Five buses per day into Umag and Novigrad. Riding 3 km. Golf 10 km.

Open: 23 April - 26 September.

Directions

Site is on the right off the Umag-Novigrad road, 4 km. south of Umag. GPS: 45.39263, 13.54196

Charges guide

Per unit incl. 2 persons	
and electricity	€ 15.70 - € 32.40
extra person	€ 3.70 - € 7.80
child (5-12 yrs)	€ 2.30 - € 4.70
dog	€ 2.30 - € 3.80

For latest campsite news, availability and prices visit
alanrogers.com

Umag
CampingIN Park Umag

Karigador bb, HR-52470 Umag (Istria) T: 052 725 040. E: camp.park.umag@istraturist.hr

alanrogers.com/CR6715

This extremely large site is very well planned in that just 60% of the 127 hectares is used for the pitches, resulting in lots of open space around the pitch area. It is the largest of the Istraturist group of sites. Of the 2,180 pitches, 1,747 are for touring units, all with 10A electricity. Some pitches have shade. There are also 433 mobile homes, some of which are available for rent. Some noise is transmitted from the road alongside the site. The site is very popular with Dutch campers and a friendly and happy atmosphere prevails, even during the busiest times. The very long curved beach is of rock and shingle with grassy sunbathing areas. There are many watersports on offer and a swimming pool complex.

Facilities

Ten toilet blocks (some newly renovated) include two bathrooms with deep tubs. Two blocks have children's WCs. Facilities for disabled visitors. Fresh water and waste water points only at toilet blocks. Motorcaravan services. Shops and supermarket. Bars, snack bars and restaurant (musical entertainment some evenings; one open until the small hours). Swimming pool complex. Tennis. Fishing (permit). Minigolf. Watersports. Massage. Entertainment and miniclubs. WiFi (free in some areas).

Open: 23 April - 26 September.

Directions

Site is on Umag-Novigrad road 6 km. south of Umag. Look for large signs. GPS: 45.36707, 13.54716

Charges guide

Per unit incl. 2 persons	
and electricity	€ 19.00 - € 39.20
extra person	€ 4.50 - € 9.10
child (5-12 yrs)	€ 2.80 - € 5.60

For stays less than 5 nights in high season add 20%.

Vrsar
Camping Porto Sole

Petalon 1, HR-52450 Vrsar (Istria) T: 052 426 500. E: info@maistra.hr

alanrogers.com/CR6725

Located near the pretty town of Vrsar and its charming marina, Porto Sole is a spacious and comfortable campsite with a long water frontage and two tiny bays that provide rocky swimming areas. The site has good facilities, including a large and attractive first floor swimming pool and sunbathing area above the shopping arcade, restaurant, pizzeria and pub. There are 730 grassy touring pitches, most in front of the reception area. They are reasonably level and fairly open with 6-10A electricity, but have hardly any views of the sea. In a separate area, there are a few pitches for tourers set on terraces looking out over a small bay. In peak season the site is buzzing with activity and the hub of the site is the pool and shopping arcade area where there are formal and informal eating areas. The food available is varied but simple, with a tiny terrace restaurant by the water.

Facilities

The five toilet blocks (one refurbished in 2014) have mostly British style WCs and are very clean and well maintained. Facilities for children and disabled visitors. Washing machines and dryers. Large well stocked supermarket (1/5-15/9). Small shopping centre. Pub. Pizzeria. Formal and informal restaurants. Swimming pools (1/5-29/9). Massage. Miniclub. Play area. Boules. Tennis. Minigolf. Entertainment in season. Scuba diving courses. Boat launching. WiFi throughout (free).

Open: All year.

Directions

Site is on the coast 500 m. south of Vrsar. From main road take turning for Koversada then follow site signs. GPS: 45.142117, 13.602267

Charges guide

Per unit incl. 2 persons	
and electricity	€ 17.90 - € 52.60
extra person	€ 5.20 - € 10.30
child (5-12 yrs)	€ 4.20 - € 6.70
dog	€ 3.10 - € 6.50

Vrsar
Camping Valkanela

Valkanela, HR-52450 Vrsar (Istria) T: 052 406 640. E: valkanela@maistra.hr
alanrogers.com/CR6727

Camping Valkanela is located in a beautiful green bay, right on the Adriatic Sea, between the villages of Vrsar and Funtana. It offers 1,771 touring pitches, all have 10A electricity. Pitches near the beach are numbered, have shade from mature trees and are slightly sloping towards the sea. Those towards the back of the site are on open fields without much shade and are not marked or numbered. Unfortunately, the number of pitches has increased dramatically over the years, many are occupied by seasonal campers and statics of every description, and these parts of the site are not very attractive. Most numbered pitches have water points close by, but the back pitches have to go to the toilet blocks for water. Access roads are gravel. For those who like activity, Valkanela has four gravel tennis courts, beach volleyball and opportunities for diving, water skiing and boat rental. There is a little marina for mooring small boats and a long rock and pebble private beach with some grass lawns for sunbathing. It is a short stroll to the surrounding villages with their bars, restaurants and shops. There may be some noise nuisance from the disco by the entrance and in high season the site can become very crowded.

Facilities

Fifteen toilet blocks of varying ages provide open style washbasins and controllable hot showers. Child size facilities. Bathroom (free). Facilities for disabled visitors. Laundry. Dog showers. Two supermarkets. Fish market (08.00-14.00). Souvenir shops and newspaper kiosk. Bars and restaurants with dance floor and stage. Pâtisserie. Tennis. Minigolf. Fishing (permit). Bicycle hire. Games room. Marina. Boat and pedalo hire. Disco by entrance. Daily entertainment (to 12 yrs). Excursions. WiFi (free).

Open: 22 April - 2 October.

Directions

Site is 2 km. north of Vrsar. Follow campsite signs from Vrsar. GPS: 45.16522, 13.60723

Charges guide

Per unit incl. 2 persons	
and electricity	€ 15.50 - € 49.70
extra person	€ 4.50 - € 10.60
child (5-11 yrs)	free - € 5.70
dog	€ 2.50 - € 6.50

Camping Valkanela . Funtana

The deep blue sea and the vibrant colours of Mediterranean vegetation offer a real treat for those who seek to spend their summer surrounded by nature.

ONLINE BOOKING

Mobile homes with a whirlpool/private pool/family(max 8)! Seaside lots! Rich entertainment programs!

tel: +385 (0)52 800 200
e-mail: valkanela@maistra.hr
www.CampingRovinjVrsar.com

Vrsar
Camping Orsera

Sv Martin 2/1, HR-52450 Vrsar (Istria) T: 052 465 010. E: camping@valamar.com
alanrogers.com/CR6728

This is a very attractive site with a 900 m. shoreline from which there are stunning views over the sea to the islands and very often there are spectacular sunsets. This 30-hectare site with direct access to the old fishing port of Vrsar has 535 pitches of which 433 are available to touring units. Marked and numbered, the pitches vary in size with 90 sq.m. being the average. There is some terracing but the pitches to the north of the site are on level ground and offer better views. Ample shade is provided by mature pines and oak trees. All pitches have 10/16A electricity.

Facilities

The modern and well maintained sanitary blocks have mainly British style WCs. Free showers and hot and cold water to washbasins. Some have facilities for disabled visitors. Facilities for babies and children. Motorcaravan services. Laundry. Supermarket (1/5-15/9). Bar/restaurant and takeaway (1/5-15/9). Sports centre. Cinema. Bicycle hire. Fishing. Watersports (no jet skis). Only electric barbecues are permitted. WiFi throughout (free).

Open: 1 April - 8 October.

Directions

Site is on the main Porec (7 km) to Vrsar (1 km) road, well signed. GPS: 45.15548, 13.61032

Charges guide

Per unit incl. 2 persons	
and electricity	€ 18.90 - € 36.40
extra person	€ 4.60 - € 9.00
child (4-10 yrs)	free - € 6.30

Prices for pitches by the sea are higher.

For latest campsite news, availability and prices visit
alanrogers.com

Vrsar

Naturist Kamp Koversada

Koversada, HR-52450 Vrsar (Istria) T: 052 441 378. E: info@maistra.hr

alanrogers.com/CR6729

According to history, the first naturist on Koversada was the famous adventurer Casanova. Today, Koversada is a first class enclosed naturist camping holiday park with bungalows. There are some 1,700 pitches (all with 10A electricity), a shopping centre and its own island, which is reached by a narrow bridge; the island is suitable only for tents and has a restaurant and two toilet blocks. Between the island and the mainland is an enclosed, shallow section of water for swimming. The site is surrounded by a long beach, part sand, part paved. The pitches are of average size on grass and gravel ground and slightly sloping. Pitches on the mainland are numbered and partly terraced beneath mature pine and olive trees. Pitches on the island are unmarked and have shade from mature trees. The bottom row of pitches on the mainland enjoys views over the island and the sea.

Facilities

Seventeen toilet blocks provide British and Turkish style toilets, washbasins and controllable hot showers. Facilities for children and disabled visitors. Laundry service. Motorcaravan services. Supermarket. Kiosks with newspapers and tobacco. Several bars and restaurants. Tennis. Minigolf. Surf boards, canoes and kayaks for hire. Tweety Club for children. Live music. Sports tournaments. Internet in reception and WiFi over site.

Open: 22 April - 25 September.

Directions

Site is just south of Vrsar. From Vrsar, follow site signs. GPS: 45.14288, 13.60527

Charges guide

Per unit incl. 2 persons and electricity	€ 19.50 - € 43.30
extra person	€ 5.50 - € 10.90
child (5-17 yrs. acc. to age)	€ 4.50 - € 7.30
dog	€ 3.20 - € 6.60

Baska

Naturist Camping Bunculuka

Baska, HR-51523 Krk (Kvarner) T: 051 856 806. E: lolic@hotelibaska.hr

alanrogers.com/CR6760

Naturist Camping Bunculuka is on the opposite side of the former fishing village of Baska from its sister site, Camping Zablace. It is situated in an attractive and very private, enclosed environment in a steeply sloping valley bordered by trees on one side and the sea on the other. It has 400 pitches in two separate areas. The 200 plots for touring units are mainly in the open and on ground gently sloping downwards to the sea; the other area, to the rear of the site, is wooded and more hilly and is mainly used for tents. The front row of pitches has beautiful views over the sea and of the private pebble beach. Most pitches are fairly level, although the ground is a little rocky.

Facilities

Three good toilet blocks with open style washbasins and controllable hot showers, plus a small block close to the beach. Supermarket. Lounge bar/restaurant with covered and open-air terrace (Mediterranean and Thai cuisine). Small bakery and the grocery store within the restaurant. Tennis. Minigolf. Kayak rental. Deck chair and parasols rental on the beach. Safety deposit boxes for hire at reception. Electric barbecues only. WiFi throughout (free). Off site: Baska with bars, restaurants and shops 500 m. Walking trails. Fishing.

Open: 17 April - 5 October.

Directions

On Krk follow D102 road south to Baska. Do not turn into Baska centre, continue and site is on left at end of D102. Entrance road is quite steep and may become narrow with parked cars, making site entry difficult. GPS: 44.96923, 14.76702

Charges guide

Per unit incl. 2 persons and electricity	Kn 150 - 349
extra person	Kn 41 - 87
child (5-11 yrs)	Kn 18 - 39
dog	free - Kn 38

For latest campsite news, availability and prices visit
alanrogers.com

Cres

Camping Kovacine

Melin I/20, HR-51557 Cres (Kvarner) T: 051 573 150. E: campkovacine@kovacine.com

alanrogers.com/CR6765

Camping Kovacine is located on a peninsula on the beautiful Kvarner island of Cres, just 2 km. from the town of the same name. The site has just under 1000 pitches for touring units, most with 16A electricity (from renewable sources) and a water supply. On sloping ground, partially shaded by mature olive and pine trees, pitching is on the large, open spaces between the trees. From the waterside pitches there are far reaching views over the sea to the coast beyond. Kovacine is partly an FKK (naturist) site, which is quite common in Croatia, and has a pleasant atmosphere. The site has its own beach (Blue Flag), part concrete, part pebbles, and a jetty for mooring boats and fishing. It is close to the historic town of Cres, the main town on the island, which offers a rich history of fishing, shipyards and authentic Kvarner-style houses. There are also several bars, restaurants and shops.

Facilities

Seven modern, well maintained toilet blocks (water heated by solar power) with open plan washbasins (some cabins for ladies) and free hot showers. Private family bathrooms for hire. Facilities for disabled visitors and children. Laundry sinks and washing machine. Motorcaravan services. Electric car/scooter charging point. Car wash. Supermarket. Bar. Restaurant and pizzeria (May-16/10). Playground. Daily children's club. Evening shows with live music. Mini-marina and boat crane. Boat launching. Fishing. Diving centre. Motorboat hire. WiFi (free). Airport transfers. Off site: Wellness and fitness centre 500 m. Historic town of Cres with bars, restaurants and shops 2 km. Coastal cycle path.

Open: 19 March - 16 October.

Directions

From Rijeka take the coast road E65 towards Senj and Split. After 20 km. follow signs for Krk island (reached over bridge). Continue on the 102 for 20 km. then the 104 to Valbiska-Merag ferry. From Merag drive to the town of Cres where, at the beginning of the town, site is signed to the right. There is a ferry from Brestova to Porozina but the road on to Cres is only suitable for smaller units. GPS: 44.96346, 14.39747

Charges guide

Per unit incl. 2 persons	
and electricity	€ 19.20 - € 41.10
extra person	€ 6.50 - € 13.80
child (3-12 yrs)	€ 3.00 - € 5.50
dog	free - € 3.00

Krk

Camping Jezevac

HR-51500 Krk (Kvarner) T: 051 221 081. E: jezevac@valamar.com

alanrogers.com/CR6757

Camping Jezevac is an excellent and well maintained seaside site, within walking distance of the pretty town of Krk. It is a large site extending to over 11 hectares and is built on a hillside at the western side of the town. The 550 pitches, all for touring, are mainly on level terraces, separated by hedges with some shade and a number enjoy views of the bay below. All have 10A electricity, 120 are fully serviced. Some premium beachside pitches are available with water and electricity. The 800 m. private beach is the focal point and in high season the atmosphere can be very lively. The reception area provides a warm welcome and is well equipped with information about the area. Forty mobile homes are available for rent.

Facilities

Six modern, well maintained toilet blocks with free hot showers. Washing machines. Facilities for disabled visitors and children. Motorcaravan services. Shops (1/4-15/10). Restaurants (1/5-1/10) and bars. Takeaway (1/5-30/9). Tennis. Playground. Activity and entertainment programmes and children's club (May-Sept). Fishing. Bicycle hire. Boat launching and sailing. Max. 1 dog. Communal barbecue area. WiFi over site. Off site: Sports centre 300 m. Shops and restaurants in Krk.

Open: 13 April - 7 October.

Directions

From the toll bridge onto Krk, follow signs to Krk town and the town centre. Take the second right turn and continue ahead for 2.2 km. At the first roundabout take the second exit. Continue for 600 m. following signs to Camp Jezevac. GPS: 45.01964, 14.57072

Charges guide

Per unit incl. 2 persons	
and electricity	€ 25.20 - € 36.30
extra person	€ 5.90 - € 8.80
child (4-10 yrs)	free - € 5.80
dog	€ 3.50 - € 5.50

For latest campsite news, availability and prices visit
alanrogers.com

Krk

Camping Krk

Politin bb, HR-51500 Krk (Kvarner) T: 051 221 351. E: camping@valamar.com

alanrogers.com/CR6758

This is an excellent, attractive and well maintained site in a secluded hillside setting with views over the sea and close to the centre of Krk. On arrival you are assured of a good welcome from the staff, who speak good English. There are 361 clearly defined and well spaced out touring pitches, mostly on level sandy terraces, all with 10A electricity and ranging in size from 70-120 sq.m. Of these, 130 plots are fully serviced and include 96 with satellite TV connection. There are also 55 seasonal pitches that do not impinge on the touring units. A member of Leading Campings group.

Facilities

Two excellent sanitary blocks are clean and well decorated and provide hot showers. Facilities for disabled visitors. Laundry facilities. Restaurant, bar and shop (all 1/5-30/9). Tennis. Playground. Activity programme for children. Fishing. Boat launching. Sailing. New, spacious mobile homes for rent. Payphones at reception. Outdoor pool. Children's pool. Saunas. Free WiFi to most of site. Off site: Fitness centre 1.5 km. Sports centre 2 km. Krk town centre. Buses from Krk to other towns on the island.

Open: April - September.

Directions

Cross toll bridge from mainland to island of Krk, head for island's capital, Krk (28 km). On arrival head to second traffic junction and turn right. After 500 m. turn left (beyond petrol station). Continue for 800 m. to site. GPS: 45.02440, 14.59280

Charges guide

Per unit incl. 2 persons and electricity	€ 23.60 - € 39.50
extra person	€ 5.60 - € 9.00
No credit cards.	

Mali Losinj

Camp Cikat

Cikat 13, HR-51550 Mali Losinj (Kvarner) T: 051 232125. E: info@camp-cikat.com

alanrogers.com/CR6754

Camp Cikat is a very attractive site which has been carefully planned using natural materials, colourful shrubs and flowers and enjoys direct access to the sea. It offers 1000 pitches for touring, all with 10A electricity and water. These are either set on terraces at the front of the site with excellent sea views or to the rear under the shade of mature trees. On-site amenities include a top quality restaurant, a bar overlooking the sea and a well stocked supermarket. At the water's edge there is ample space for sunbathing on the rocks or on paved terraces.

Facilities

Seven excellent sanitary blocks with washbasins in cabins and free showers. Facilities for babies, children and disabled visitors. Family bathrooms to rent. Laundry facilities. Motorcaravan service point. Supermarket. Bar. Restaurant. Play area. Bicycle hire. Massage (high season). Entertainment and activity programme. Mobile homes, chalets and tents for rent. Direct sea access. No charcoal barbecues. WiFi over site.

Open: All year.

Directions

Upon arrival on the island of Cres, head south on road 100 crossing onto the island of Losinj and continue to Mali Losinj. From here follow signs to Cikat, then the site. GPS: 44.53596, 14.4509

Charges guide

Per unit incl. 2 persons and electricity	€ 20.50 - € 46.60
extra person	€ 7.00 - € 10.80
child (3-6 yrs)	€ 2.50 - € 3.70

Mali Losinj

Camping Poljana

Rujnica 9/a, HR-51550 Mali Losinj (Kvarner) T: 051 231 726. E: info@poljana.hr

alanrogers.com/CR6772

Autocamp Poljana lies on the narrow strip of land in the southern part of Losinj island, just north of the pleasant town of Mali Losinj. With 780 pitches (500 for touring), this site is bigger than it looks. The camping area has been newly laid out with some flat areas and some terraces. The pitches are marked with flowers and shrubs. There are some mature trees for shade and 500 electricity connections. Campers may be able to experience both sunset and sunrise from the same pitch! The toilet facilities are new and well maintained, while a shop and a series of bars and restaurants are available close by.

Facilities

New toilet blocks, including solar panels for hot water, are entirely up to date and adequate. Family room. Facilities for disabled visitors. Baby rooms. Motorcaravan services. Washing machine. Daily entertainment programmes. Bicycle hire. WiFi throughout (charged). Rock beach with cocktail bar. Marina. Off site: Losinj 4 km. Riding and canoeing 6 km. Boat excursions.

Open: 1 April - 21 October.

Directions

About 2 km. north of the town, the site occupies both sides of the road along the waterline and opposite the little marina. Well signed. GPS: 44.55555, 14.44166

Charges guide

Per unit incl. 2 persons and electricity	Kn 121 - 334
extra person	Kn 41 - 91
child (3-12 yrs)	Kn 34 - 83

For latest campsite news, availability and prices visit
alanrogers.com

Martinscica
Camping Slatina

Martinscica, HR-51556 Cres (Kvarner) T: 051 574 127. E: info@camp-slatina.com
alanrogers.com/CR6768

Camping Slatina is a well shaded terraced site, beside the fishing port of Martinscica, on a bay of the Adriatic Sea. It has 1600 pitches for touring units, most with 16A electricity, reached by steep, tarmac access roads, sloping down to the sea. Two small tractors are on hand to help visitors with caravans on and off their pitch. Pitches are large and level on a gravel base and enjoy plenty of shade and privacy from mature laurel trees. The site is tastefully landscaped with plenty of flowers and walkways leading down to the rocky beach and crystal clear waters of the Adriatic.

Facilities

Six excellent, refurbished toilet blocks include washbasins in cabins and controllable hot showers. Facilities for children and disabled visitors. Laundry with sinks and washing machine. Fridge box hire. Car wash. Shop. Bar, restaurant, grill restaurant, pizzeria and fish restaurant. Playground. Minigolf. Fishing. Bicycle hire. Diving centre. Pedalo, canoe and boat hire. Excursions to the Blue Cave. WiFi on part of site (charged). Only gas and electric barbecues permitted. Off site: Boat launching 1 km.

Open: 23 March - 1 October.

Directions

From Rijeka go south and over bridge to island of Krk then to Vabiska. Take ferry to Merag on island of Cres and from town of Cres follow road towards Mali Losinj. In 20 km. turn right to Martinscica where site is signed. GPS: 44.82333, 14.34083

Charges guide

Per unit incl. 2 persons	
and electricity	€ 16.00 - € 26.60
extra person	€ 5.00 - € 8.80

No credit cards.

Punat
Camping Pila

Setaliste Ivana Bruscia 2, Punat, HR-51521 Krk (Kvarner) T: 051 854 020. E: pila@hoteli-punat.hr
alanrogers.com/CR6755

Autocamping Pila is right beside the bustling seaside resort of Punat on the biggest Croatian island of Krk, which is connected to the mainland by a toll bridge. Krk is the first island you reach as you travel south into Croatia and the Romans called it the 'Golden Island'. Autocamp Pila is just 100 m. from the Adriatic and has 390 grass or gravel pitches for touring units. All have 10A electricity, plus 130 premium pitches have electricity, water and drainage. Two hundred and fifty pitches are numbered and many benefit from the shade of mature trees. The remainder are unmarked on a separate field. It can get very busy in high season and pitching can become cramped.

Facilities

Three modern, comfortable toilet blocks with toilets, washbasins and showers. Child size showers and washbasins. Baby room. Facilities for disabled visitors. Campers' kitchen with cooking rings. Motorcaravan services. Small shop. Bar/restaurant. Snack bar. Play area. Minigolf. Aerobics and aquarobics. Video games. Daily evening events for children (July/Aug). WiFi (free).

Open: Easter - 15 October.

Directions

On Krk follow D102 road south towards Baska and take exit for Punat. In Punat site is well signed. GPS: 45.01663, 14.62873

Charges guide

Per unit incl. 2 persons	
and electricity	€ 19.90 - € 39.10
extra person	€ 4.20 - € 7.80
child (7-12 yrs)	€ 1.90 - € 4.80

Punat
Naturist Camping Konobe

Obala 94, Punat, HR-51521 Krk (Kvarner) T: 051 854 036. E: konobe@hoteli-punat.hr
alanrogers.com/CR6756

Naturist Camping Konobe is situated south of the historic fishing port of Punat on the island of Krk in a remote and quiet location. Access is down a long, tarmac road which leads to a landscaped terrain, with terraces built from natural stone. The 400 slightly sloping pitches are in two areas, part open, part wooded, with some shade from mature trees and some have beautiful views over the Adriatic. Unmarked pitches for tents are on small terraces, with pitches for caravans and motorcaravans of 50-80 sq.m. on sandy grass off tarmac access roads. The remote location makes this site ideal for quiet camping among the wild charm of a rocky and still green environment.

Facilities

Three modern, comfortable toilet blocks with toilets, open washbasins and preset showers. Child size washbasins. Facilities for disabled visitors. Campers' kitchen with connections (no rings). Gas. Supermarket. Bar/restaurant. Tennis. Minigolf. Fishing. Pebble beach. Boat launching. Evening entertainment programme for children. Croatian language lessons. No charcoal barbecues. ATM. WiFi.

Open: 1 May - 1 October.

Directions

On Krk follow D102 road to south of the island. Take exit for Punat and follow main road through Punat then follow signs for Stara Baska. After 4 km. site is signed to the right. GPS: 44.99107, 14.63065

Charges guide

Per unit incl. 2 persons	
and electricity	€ 18.90 - € 31.80

No credit cards.

For latest campsite news, availability and prices visit
alanrogers.com

Selce
Autocamp Selce
Jasenova 19, HR-51266 Selce (Kvarner) T: 051 764 038. E: kamp-selce@ri.t-com.hr
alanrogers.com/CR6750

With easy access from the E65/8 road, this terraced site, which leads down to an attractive small harbour, is ideally situated not only as a stocking up point on what must be Europe's most picturesque coastal road, but also as a site to spend some time. Relax on the large paved areas at the water's edge or visit Selce with its supermarket, banks and local market which is only a few minutes walk away along the seaside promenade with its bars and restaurants. The site has 300 level touring pitches, all with electricity, mainly on terraces and many shaded by a mixture of trees.

Facilities

Seven toilet blocks with British and Turkish style toilets, open style washbasins and controllable, hot showers (free). Facilities for disabled visitors. Laundry service. Fridge box hire. Motorcaravan service point. Shop. Bar/restaurant with covered and open-air terrace. Fishing. Diving centre. No charcoal barbecues permitted, communal area also provided. ATM. WiFi on part of site. Off site: Boat rental and water skiing 150 m.

Open: 1 April - 10 October.

Directions

Site is on the coast 40 km. south-south east of Rijeka on the E65/8. It is on the southern edge of Selce and is well signed. GPS: 45.1541, 14.725133

Charges guide

Per unit incl. 2 persons	
and electricity	€ 20.50 - € 33.70
extra person	€ 3.50 - € 6.10
child (7-12 yrs)	free - € 3.50

Dubrovnik
Camping Solitudo
Vatroslava Lisinskog 17, HR-20000 Dubrovnik (Dalmatia) T: 020 448 686.
E: camping-dubrovnik@valamar.com alanrogers.com/CR6890

Solitudo is located on the north side of Dubrovnik. There are 21 mobile homes and 550 pitches for touring units, all with 10-16A electricity and 30 with water, arranged on four large fields that are opened according to demand. Field D is mainly used for tents and pitches here are small. Field A has pitches of up to 120 sq.m. and takes many motorcaravans (long leads required). From some pitches here there are beautiful views of the mountains and the impressive Dr. Franjo Tudman Bridge. All pitches are numbered, some are on terraces and most are shaded by a variety of mature trees.

Facilities

Two attractively decorated, clean and modern sanitary blocks have British style toilets, open washbasins and controllable, hot showers. Good facilities for disabled visitors. Laundry. Motorcaravan services. Shop. Attached restaurant/bar. Snack bar. Tennis. Minigolf. Fishing. Bicycle hire. Beach with pedalo, beach chair, kayak and jet ski hire. Excursions to the Elafiti Islands. WiFi (free). Off site: Outdoor pool, bar, disco and restaurant 500 m.

Open: 3 April - 31 October.

Directions

From Split follow no. 8 road south towards Dubrovnik. Site is very well signed, starting 110 km. before reaching Dubrovnik, and throughout the city. GPS: 42.661883, 18.07135

Charges guide

Per unit incl. 2 persons	
and electricity	€ 33.80 - € 49.50
extra person	€ 8.40 - € 11.50
child (4-9 yrs)	free - € 6.10

Hvar
Camp Vira
Mala Vira, HR-21450 Hvar (Dalmatia) T: 021 741 803. E: info@campvira.com
alanrogers.com/CR6865

Situated at the western end of Hvar, Croatia's longest and reputedly sunniest island, Camp Vira is a quiet site built around a small protected bay with crystal clear water and a 200 m. long, curved, pebble beach - an ideal place for sunbathing and swimming. Bordering the beach are an open plan bar and a restaurant. Most of the 172 pitches, all with 16A electricity, surround the bay and are set on steep terracing under ample pine tree shade. With extensive use of natural stone walling and good plant and tree cover, the site fits in very well on an island renowned for its unspoilt beauty.

Facilities

Three well maintained sanitary blocks. Facilities for disabled visitors. Baby room. Laundry with washing machines and dryers. Dishwashing facilities. Motorcaravan services. Supermarket. Restaurant (from 20/5). Boat launching slip and anchorage. Pedal boats and kayaks to hire. Bicycle and scooter hire. Play area. Dog shower. Entertainment programmes. WiFi (charged). Off site: The island's main town Hvar (bus service from site), Stari grad and Jelsa. Numerous small restaurants. Local wines.

Open: 6 June - 19 September.

Directions

Site is on the island of Hvar 4 km. north west of Hvar town. Take regular ferry service from Split to Hvar, or the ferry from Drvenik to Sucuraj then a 77 km. scenic drive, more suited to smaller units, along a narrow twisting road to Hvar (2.5 hours). From Hvar follow Vira signs. GPS: 43.19087, 16.43032

Charges guide

Per unit incl. 2 persons	
and electricity	Kn 153 - 229
extra person	Kn 38 - 65

For latest campsite news, availability and prices visit
alanrogers.com

Jezera Lovisca

Jezera Village

HR-22242 Jezera Lovisca (Dalmatia) T: 022 439 600. E: marketing@jezeravillage.com

alanrogers.com/CR6840

Jezera Lovisca is a family site of 75 acres with 400 informal pitches and would be a good choice for a relaxing beach holiday as it is on the island of Murter. In high season, the site arranges entertainment for children with games, music, drawing and swimming. For adults there are live musical nights at the bar/restaurant which has a large, welcoming terrace from where there are beautiful views of the lagoon. There are 360 grass and gravel pitches for touring units, all with 10A electricity (long leads may be necessary). They are mostly on level terraces, attractively built with low rock walls in the shade of mature trees. Some have sea views and fronting the site is a pebble beach with a concrete sunbathing area.

Facilities

Four modern and comfortable toilet blocks have British style toilets, open washbasins and controllable, hot showers (free) all of a very high standard. Campers' kitchen. Fridge box hire. Shop. Bar/restaurant and takeaway. Tennis. Minigolf. Entertainment program for children. Internet access. Fishing. Watersports. Diving centre. Boat launching. Bicycle hire. Excursions. Live music nights. Barbecues permitted only in communal area. WiFi throughout (charged). Off site: Harbour town of Jerz 500 m. Buses from gate to local attractions.

Open: 29 April - 1 October.

Directions

From Rijeka take no. 8 coast road south towards Zadar and Split. 58 km. south of Zadar is Pirovac. Turn right 4 km. south of Pirovac towards O Murter and continue through Trisco keeping to coast road. Arriving at Jereza Lovisca, site is well signed and just through the village. GPS: 43.791533, 15.6279

Charges guide

Per unit incl. 2 persons and electricity	Kn 173 - 324
extra person	Kn 37 - 76
child (3-12 yrs)	Kn 21 - 53
dog	Kn 36 - 58

Site does not accept Euros.

Lozovac

Camp Krka

Skocici 2, HR-22221 Lozovac (Dalmatia) T: 022 778 495. E: goran.skocic@si.t-com.hr

alanrogers.com/CR6844

If you wish to experience genuine Croatian hospitality, you cannot afford to miss the opportunity to visit this small, rural site located just 2.5 km. from the entrance to the Krka National Park and about 15 km. from Sibenik. The site is owned and enthusiastically run by the Skocic family and they will do all they can to ensure that your stay with them is enjoyable and memorable. There is space for 30 touring units, all on flat grass. Most have good shade and all have 16A electricity and some tree shade. The small, rustic restaurant and bar at the site entrance provides a good selection of homemade and reasonably priced dishes. Many incorporate fresh ingredients from the family garden, together with homemade cheese, cured ham, fresh bread and the family's own excellent wine.

Facilities

Two small toilet blocks, recently renovated, have good hot showers. No facilities for disabled visitors. Washing machine. No shop but bread and milk available. Bicycle hire. Play area. Restaurant/bar and takeaway. Pétanque area. WiFi throughout (free). Off site: Minibus trips to nearby Krka National Park. Riding 3 km. Sailing 4 km.

Open: 1 March - 30 October.

Directions

From Sibenik follow signs to Krka National Park. Site well signed on road 56, 2.5 km. from entrance to National Park. GPS: 43.800633, 15.9421

Charges guide

Per unit incl. 2 persons and electricity	Kn 125
extra person	Kn 35

For latest campsite news, availability and prices visit
alanrogers.com

Nin
Zaton Holiday Resort

227

Draznikova ulica 76 t, HR-23232 Nin (Dalmatia) T: 023 280 215. E: camping@zaton.hr
alanrogers.com/CR6782

Zaton Holiday Resort is a modern family holiday park with a one and a half kilometre private sandy beach. It is close to the historic town of Nin and just a few kilometres from the ancient city of Zadar. This park itself is more like a large village and has every amenity one can think of for a holiday on the Dalmatian coast. The village is divided into two areas separated by a public area with reception, bakery, shops, restaurant and a large car park, one for campers close to the sea, the other for a complex with holiday apartments. Zaton has 1,030 mostly level pitches for touring units, all with electricity, water and waste water. All numbered pitches have shade from mature trees and some have views over the extensive, 2 km long sandy beach and the sea. Access is off hard access roads. Zaton caters for everybody's needs on site with numerous bars, restaurants, shops and two swimming pools. Excursions are organised to the Krka waterfalls, the Zrmanja Canyon and the Kornati, Paklenica and Plitvice National Parks. A member of Leading Campings group.

Facilities

Five modern and one refurbished toilet blocks with washbasins (some in cabins) and controllable hot showers. Child size washbasins. Family shower rooms. Facilities for disabled visitors. Outdoor grill station. Motorcaravan services. Car wash. Shopping centre. Restaurants (self-service one has breakfast, lunch and evening menus). Several bars and kiosks. Water play area for children. Heated outdoor swimming pools. Mini-car track. Riding. Tennis centre. Trim track. Scuba diving. Professional entertainment team. Teen club. Games hall. Beach extension with climbing pyramids. Live shows on stage by the beach. Free WiFi. Off site: Historic towns of Nin 3 km and Zadar (parking difficult) 16 km.

Open: 30 April - 30 September.

Directions

From Rijeka take no. 2 road south or A1/E65 Autobahn leave at exit for Zadar. Drive north towards Nin, Zaton Holiday Resort is signed a few kilometres before Nin. GPS: 44.234767, 15.164367

Charges guide

Per unit incl. 2 persons and electricity	€ 24.60 - € 59.70
extra person	€ 6.00 - € 12.30
child (1-11 yrs. acc. to age)	€ 3.30 - € 9.70
dog	€ 5.00 - € 10.00

Novalja
Camping Strasko

Trg Loza 1, HR-53291 Novalia (Dalmatia) T: 053 661 226. E: strasko@hadria.biz
alanrogers.com/CR6776

Strasko is a very large and well managed site that can claim to be one of the best in Croatia. Positioned close to Novalja on the Dalmatian island of Pag, it has 1,900 pitches on level ground with good shade from mature oak, pine and olive trees. The 900 touring pitches all have water, drainage, 10A electricity and TV connection. A further 250 pitches for FKK Naturist Camping are located in a private area behind a high rock wall with its own designated beach. The site can accommodate up to 6,000 people and can get very busy in July and August, but all pitches are clearly defined and there always seems to be space around you. A superb 1,600 m. long Blue Flag beach is accessible from all parts of the site and almost every possible watersport is available.

Facilities

Thirteen traditional toilet blocks fitted out and maintained to a high standard provide toilets, washbasins and controllable hot showers. 24 private washrooms are for rent. Washing machines at six locations. Large supermarket and several retail kiosks. Bars, restaurant, self-service restaurant and pizzeria. New swimming pool. Sports centre. Trampolines. Aerobics. Minigolf. Motor scooter hire. Bicycle hire. Gymnastics. Games machines. Daily children's club. Evening entertainment. Small petting zoo. Bungalows to rent. Off site: Novalja with bars, restaurants and shops is close.

Open: 17 April - 11 October.

Directions

Take no. 2 coast road south from Rijeka and at Prizna take the ferry (check cost). From the ferry exit follow road for 5 miles, then turn right and follow signs for Novalja and site. GPS: 44.53883, 14.88627

Charges guide

Per unit incl. 2 persons and electricity	Kn 144 - 371
extra person	Kn 26 - 75
child (7-12 yrs)	free - 35
dog	Kn 38 - 68

Prices for pitches by the sea are higher.

For latest campsite news, availability and prices visit
alanrogers.com

Omis
Camp Galeb

Vukovarska bb, HR-21310 Omis (Dalmatia) T: 021 864 430. E: camping@galeb.hr

alanrogers.com/CR6860

Galeb is an attractive, grassy, beachside site set beneath mature trees. The River Cetina is just to the north of the site and the pretty port where river meets sea is a powerful attraction complemented by the ancient forts and pirate buildings above. A dramatic, 1,000-metre rock backdrop to the whole site reflects the light differently as the day progresses and the superb sunsets paint it with amazing orange and red hues. The 340 numbered touring pitches are level and most have some shade. However, in high season, units are very close together and there will be little privacy; 140 are fully serviced (16A Europlug). Some pitches are at the water's edge, from where there are views of the coast and the island of Brac.

Facilities

Two renovated sanitary blocks with plenty of hot water for showers and a regular cleaning routine. Facilities for disabled campers. Motorcaravan services. Shop selling basics, bar, restaurant, takeaway. Tennis. Play areas. Bicycle hire. Entertainment in high season. TV. Security boxes. Cold boxes. Currency exchange. Beach. Boat launching. Motor scooter and boat hire. Windsurfing. Sailing. Communal barbecue area. WiFi (charged).

Open: All year.

Directions

Site is on the main coast road 25 km. south east of Split. Site entrance is just after Omis town sign when coming from Split, and beside Studentac Shopping Center sign. GPS: 43.440617, 16.680283

Charges guide

Per unit incl. 2 persons	
and electricity	€ 21.20 - € 45.40
extra person	€ 5.60 - € 7.80
child (7-17 yrs)	free - € 5.80

Orebic
Autocamp Nevio

Dubravica bb, HR-20250 Orebic (Dalmatia) T: 020 713 100. E: info@nevio-camping.com

alanrogers.com/CR6875

This attractive, well designed, family run site fully optimises its quiet coastal location. Some of the 190 pitches are on the beach line, but most are at the top of the 50 m. high cliff with the swimming pool and the main building housing the restaurant and bar. The latter has a long, comfortable clifftop terrace from which there are superb views of the coast and islands. The water's edge pitches, new sanitary facility and small jetty are reached via well constructed roads. All pitches have 16A electricity, fresh and waste water supply. This is a site from which you can appreciate southern Croatia at its best.

Facilities

Two new, heated sanitary facilities with family shower rooms, washbasins in cabins, rooms for children and babies. Facilities for disabled visitors. Washing machine and dryer. Fridge hire. Beachside and other communal grills. Restaurant. Outdoor swimming pool with view (May-Oct). Boat launching. Mobile homes for hire. Off site: Supermarket 100 m. Bicycle hire. Boat launching. Orebic 1 km. Korcula within easy reach by local ferry.

Open: All year.

Directions

Site is 80 km. north west of Dubrovnik on the coast 1 km. east of Orebic. When approaching from the mainland site entrance (signed) is on the left opposite the supermarket 300 m. after passing the petrol station on the right. GPS: 42.9812, 17.1993

Charges guide

Per unit incl. 2 persons	
and electricity	€ 16.00 - € 38.20
extra person	€ 3.00 - € 6.60

Paklenica
Kamp Paklenica

Dr. Franje Tudmania 14, HR-23244 Paklenica (Dalmatia) T: 023 209 050. E: alan@bluesunhotels.com

alanrogers.com/CR6830

This is a relatively small site and is part of the adjacent three star Alan Hotel in Paklenica. It has 300 touring pitches, most with 16A electricity and 20 with water and drainage. Most are on level grass and gravel ground (firm tent pegs needed) under mature trees. The front pitches have beautiful views of the blue waters of the Adriatic. Paklenica is only 100 m. from the entrance of the Paklenica National Park and excursions to the Park and to the Zrmanja Canyon can be booked on the site. Paklenica has its own beach, paved with rock plates, that gives access to a sheltered lagoon for swimming and boating.

Facilities

Two good toilet blocks provide British and Turkish style toilets, open washbasins and controllable, hot showers. Area for children. Excellent facilities for disabled visitors. Motorcaravan services. Bar/restaurant and pizzeria. Oval shaped pool (150 sq.m) with paddling pool within hotel grounds. Playground (on gravel). Tennis. Minigolf. Fishing. Bicycle hire. Jet ski, boat and scooter hire. Children's club. Entertainment. Games room. WiFi (charged).

Open: Easter - 31 October.

Directions

From Rijeka, take no. 8 coast road south along the Dalmatian coast towards Starigrad-Paklenica. In town turn right at sign for Hotel Alan. Turn right to site. GPS: 44.287267, 15.447617

Charges guide

Per unit incl. 2 persons	
and electricity	€ 15.30 - € 34.50
extra person	€ 3.90 - € 9.50
child (3-12 yrs)	€ 1.60 - € 5.90

For latest campsite news, availability and prices visit
alanrogers.com

Pakostane

Camping Kozarica

Brune Busica 43, HR-23211 Pakostane (Dalmatia) T: 023 381 070. E: kozarica@adria-more.hr

alanrogers.com/CR6928

Camp Kozarica is situated directly by the sea. It has 325 well shaded touring pitches set on fairly level ground on the upper part of the site and on terraces towards the water's edge. All have 6A electricity and 56 are fully serviced. The small town of Pakostane is only a short, attractive walk from the site and has shops, restaurants, bars and watersports facilities. It is in a picturesque setting among the 100 small islands that comprise The Kornaten National Park. There is easy access from the coastal road, which makes this a convenient site to rest up for a few days and enjoy what this particular part of the coast has to offer. This is a comfortable site for campers of all ages with its close proximity to the town and the national park and is a quiet haven to return to in the evening. The site's beach has ample areas for sunbathing, either on the pebbles or on flat paved areas.

Facilities

Very good toilet blocks with facilities for children and bathrooms for disabled visitors. Controllable showers and washbasins in cabins. Family shower rooms. Bathrooms to rent. Laundry room. Dog washing area. Motorcaravan services. Mini-market. Pâtisseries. Bars, restaurant, takeaway (20/5-15/9). Outdoor paddling pool (1/5-15/10). Play area. Miniclub. Entertainment (high season). Beach volleyball. Windsurf school. Diving lessons. Boat and bicycle hire. Accommodation for hire. WiFi throughout (charged). Off site: Fishing 500 m. Riding 5 km. Lake Vrana with cycle path. Sibenik with UNESCO World Heritage cathedral.

Open: 5 April - 31 October.

Directions

The site is 30 km. south of Zadar on road to Sibenic. It is very well signed with a right turn just after yellow 'Pakostane' sign. GPS: 43.91107, 15.49968

Charges guide

Per unit incl. 2 persons and electricity	€ 17.90 - € 37.70
extra person	€ 4.90 - € 8.90
child (3-12 yrs)	€ 6.20
dog	€ 3.10 - € 6.10

Primosten

Camp Adriatic

Huljerat 1/a, HR-22202 Primosten (Dalmatia) T: 022 571 223. E: camp-adriatic@adriatic.com

alanrogers.com/CR6845

As we drove south down the Dalmatian coast road, we looked across a clear turquoise bay and saw a few tents, caravans and motorcaravans camped under some trees. A short distance later we were at the entrance of Camp Adriatic. With 530 pitches that slope down to the sea, the site is deceptive and enjoys a one kilometre beach frontage which is ideal for snorkelling and diving. Most pitches are level and have shade from pine trees. There are 212 numbered pitches and 288 unnumbered, all with 10/16A electricity. Close to the delightful town of Primosten, (with a taxi boat service in high season) the site boasts good modern amenities and a fantastic location.

Facilities

Four modern and well maintained sanitary blocks provide clean toilets, hot showers and washbasins. Facilities for children and disabled visitors. Washing machine and dryer. Kitchen facilities. Small supermarket (15/5-30/9). Restaurant, bar and takeaway (all season). Sports centre. Miniclub. Beach. Diving school. Sailing school and boat hire. Entertainment programme in July/Aug. WiFi in reception area (charged). Off site: Primosten 2.5 km. Riding 15 km. Sibenic 25 km.

Open: 1 May - 31 October.

Directions

Take the A1 motorway south and leave at the Sibenik exit. Follow the 33 road into Sibenik and then go south along the coast road (no. 8), signed Primosten. Site is 2.5 km. north of Primosten. GPS: 43.606517, 15.92095

Charges guide

Per person	Kn 37 - 68
child (3-12 yrs)	Kn 26 - 49
pitch incl. car and electricity	Kn 69 - 95
dog	Kn 34 - 50

For latest campsite news, availability and prices visit
alanrogers.com

Rakovica
Auto-Camp Turist

Grabovac 102, HR-47245 Rakovica (Dalmatia) T: 047 784 192. E: info@kamp-turist.hr

alanrogers.com/CR6915

Auto-Camp Turist is on the Zagreb - Split road, 125 km. south of Zagreb. It is well situated for visiting the beautiful Plitvice National Park. The site is surrounded by meadows, forests, mountains, lakes and waterfalls. There are 99 pitches for touring and some teepees for rent. Some of the average size pitches are on grass or hard ground, with many slightly sloping (levelling blocks useful). Some have part or full shade and all have 16A electricity. There is a good restaurant offering local and Croatian dishes along with an international menu. In high season, the site often gets full so early arrival is recommended. This is an ideal site for those seeking an active holiday but happy to make their own entertainment. There are many opportunities for cycling, mountain biking, quad biking, trekking, climbing, rafting, canoeing, riding and paintballing.

Facilities

Two modern toilet blocks with mainly open washbasins, could be stretched at times. Washing machine and dryer. Motorcaravan services. Small shop with fresh bread. Bar/restaurant. Small swimming pool (1/5-1/10). Play areas. Evening entertainment twice a week. Tennis. WiFi (free). Accommodation for rent. Off site: Rafting, canoeing, paintball, quad bikes, riding, cycling, trekking and hiking. Plitvice National Park 8 km. Historic Rastoke with watermills and ancient houses 21 km.

Open: 1 April - 1 October.

Directions

Leave Zagreb south west on the A1 autoroute for approx. 50 km. At Karlovac take Route 1 south for approx. 74 km. to Grabovac and site on right. GPS: 44.97098, 15.64705

Charges guide

Per unit incl. 2 persons	
and electricity	€ 19.50 - € 30.20
extra person	€ 7.00 - € 9.90
child (7-11 yrs)	€ 4.90 - € 5.40
dog	€ 3.00 - € 3.30

Simuni
Camping Simuni

Simuni bb, HR-23251 Simuni-Kolan (Dalmatia) T: 023 697 441. E: info@camping-simuni.hr

alanrogers.com/CR6778

Camping Simuni is landscaped on a gently sloping hillside with low rock walls alongside well maintained access roads. Many varieties of shrubs and flowers give it a pleasant, welcoming atmosphere. It is close to the fishing village of Simuni and just 10 km. from Pag on the island of Pag. There are 1,000 pitches, with 650 available for touring units. All have 16A electricity and a water tap between four pitches and 200 are fully serviced. Access is good and most plots are on level hardcore or gravel. Tent pitches are rather small. Good shade is provided by mature trees. The site has a private and very clean Blue Flag pebble beach and offers many sporting facilities.

Facilities

Three well fitted out sanitary blocks, plus a further three blocks without showers. Laundry service from reception. Supermarket and fruit kiosks, bakery and fish market. Bar, pizzeria and restaurants. Refurbished tennis and multisports area. Bicycle hire. Car and scooter hire. Aerobics. Boat launching. Trampolines. Miniclub. Nightly entertainment during high season. Mobile homes and bungalows to rent all season. Off site: Simuni (walking distance) and Pag 10 km.

Open: All year.

Directions

Take E65 road south from Rijeka to Prizna and take ferry to Pag. From ferry follow signs for Pag town and site. Alternatively, continue on E65. Before Zadar, follow signs to Pag. At petrol station in Pag town, turn left towards Novalja and follow signs to site (10 km). GPS: 44.46520, 14.96712

Charges guide

Per unit incl. 2 persons	
and electricity	€ 12.30 - € 50.00
extra person	€ 2.50 - € 11.50
child (3-12 yrs)	€ 1.50 - € 8.00
dog	€ 2.50 - € 8.00

For latest campsite news, availability and prices visit
alanrogers.com

Split

Camping Stobrec Split

Sv. Lovre 6, Stobrec, HR-21311 Split (Dalmatia) T: 021 325 426. E: camping.split@gmail.com
alanrogers.com/CR6855

Camping Stobrec is ideally located for those visiting Croatia and travelling down the coastal road or visiting Split (old town) – a must! The site has 272 touring pitches on a small peninsula, all with 10/16A electricity and some with water connections also. Some 37 of these are in a separate area reserved for tents. From the level pitches, which have ample shade from trees, there are views over the sandy beach and across the bay. Set on top of rocks at the point of the peninsula is a small, comfortable restaurant with terrace and wonderful views – an ideal place for a quiet drink or evening meal. Split, with its squares, streets and narrow alleys worn smooth by almost 2,000 years of continuous use (wear shoes with a good grip), really must not be missed. The campsite can organise trips and at reception there is plenty of tourist information as well as good personal advice available. Being close to the coastal road there is some traffic noise, especially during the day, however, it is not too obtrusive. A new wellness centre is due for completion in 2016 and will have sauna, massage and gym areas.

Facilities

Three sanitary blocks include free hot water, controllable showers and some washbasins in cabins. Facilities for disabled visitors (key) and children. Laundry facilities. Motorcaravan services. Beach bars and restaurant. Supermarket at entrance. Play area. Children's club and entertainment programme (15/6-15/9). Bicycle hire. Fishing. Internet access and WiFi throughout (free). Off site: Shops, cafés and restaurants within easy walking distance. Boat trips. Rafting on the River Cetina. Split city centre 5 km.

Open: All year.

Directions

Site is 7 km. south east of Split city centre close to No. 8 coastal road. Travelling north to south, bypass Split on No. 8 road, at bottom of hill on the descent to Stobrec, site is signed to right. Turn right and site entrance is almost immediately on left. GPS: 43.50333, 16.5275

Charges guide

Per unit incl. 2 persons and electricity	€ 20.00 - € 36.70
extra person	€ 3.90 - € 7.90
child (7-11 yrs)	€ 2.60 - € 5.40

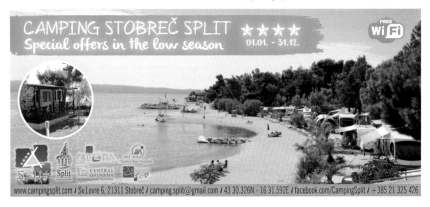

CAMPING STOBREČ SPLIT ★★★★
Special offers in the low season 01.01. - 31.12.
FREE WiFi

www.campingsplit.com / Sv.Lovre 6, 21311 Stobreč / camping.split@gmail.com / 43 30.326N - 16 31.592E / facebook.com/CampingSplit / +385 21 325 426

Sv. Filip I Jakov

Autocamp Rio

Put Primorja 66, HR-23207 Sv. Filip I Jakov (Dalmatia) T: 023 388 671. E: autocamp_rio@hotmail.com
alanrogers.com/CR6833

Autocamp Rio is a small, friendly family run site easily accessed from coastal road 8 and with direct access, via steps, to its own beach. There is a small harbour with moorings for 30 boats (up to seven meters). The 36 grass touring pitches are on sloping ground, mostly beneath olive trees, and have electricity (16A, 2-pin plugs). Those at the top of the small cliff have views over the sea to the island of Pasman, behind which is situated Kornati National Park with its 147 islands. The village of Sv. Filip I Jakov with its bars restaurants and shops is within strolling distance of the site.

Facilities

One well maintained sanitary block with roomy free showers. Washing machines. Dishwashing areas. Fishing. Marina. Sea swimming. Off site: Vransko Jezero bird reserve 10 km. Zadar 25 km. Komati Archipelago National Park. Biograd na Moru. Monthly market at Benkovac 18 km. (details at reception).

Open: Easter - 15 October.

Directions

Site is on coast 25 km. south of Zadar. Follow the coastal road 8 from Zadar towards Split. Turn right into village of Sv. Filip i Jakov then left for 800 m. following the campsite signs. Site is towards the end of village on right. GPS: 43.95604, 15.43521

Charges guide

Per unit incl. 2 persons and electricity	€ 18.00 - € 29.20
extra person	€ 4.50 - € 8.50

For latest campsite news, availability and prices visit
alanrogers.com

Trogir
Camp Seget

Hrvatskih zrtava 121, HR-21218 Trogir Seget Donji (Dalmatia) T: 021 880 394. E: booking@kamp-seget.hr
alanrogers.com/CR6850

Camp Seget is a pleasant site from where there are superb views over the water to the islands. The site has 120 touring pitches, all with 16A electricity (long leads may be necessary), on land that slopes down towards to the water. They are on grass with some terracing and enjoy shade from a mixture of palm, olive and pine trees. To the front of the site, a paved promenade gives access to the pebble beach and from there it is an easy five minute stroll to an interesting waterside village with restaurants and bars serving high quality, good value meals. The site is an ideal base for exploring this part of the Dalmatian Coast, or for visiting Trogir and Split.

Facilities

Two good and very well maintained sanitary blocks, one new (2014), contain toilets, washbasins and controllable, hot showers (free). Facilities for disabled visitors. Campers' kitchen. Fridge box hire. Shop (1/5-15/10). Bicycle hire. Motor scooter hire. Beach. Fishing. Boat rental. Barbecues permitted only on communal area. Off site: Bus at gate for touring. Boat launching 500 m.

Open: 15 April - 15 October.

Directions

Follow no. 8 coastal road south from Zadar towards Split. At Seget Donji, 2 km. before Trogir, keep to right and look for site signs, finishing in a right turn into the site. GPS: 43.5186, 16.224167

Charges guide

Per unit incl. 2 persons and electricity	Kn 221 - 237
extra person	Kn 50

Trogir
Camping Vranjica Belvedere

Seget Vranjica, bb Seget donji, HR-21218 Trogir (Dalmatia) T: 021 798 222. E: vranjica-belvedere@st.htnet.hr
alanrogers.com/CR6911

Camping Vranjica Belvedere is 30 km. west of Split, on the beautiful Dalmatian coast. This large terraced site lies on a wooded hillside with magnificent views across the crystal blue sea to the neighbouring islands. There are 333 average size, marked pitches, the majority with 10/16A electricity (long leads required), some have water and drainage. Rock pegs are advised. A stylish but small swimming pool with sunbeds overlooks the Adriatic Sea. There is a rocky and pebbly beach adjacent to the site offering many watersports. A small area of beach accepts dogs.

Facilities

Four modern toilet blocks located across the site were still being completed at the time of our visit (facilities for disabled visitors in one block at far end). Laundry. Motorcaravan services. Minimarket. Restaurant, takeaway and beach bar. New children's pool. Tennis. Minigolf. Boules. Multisports court. Watersports. Playground. Bicycle hire. Family entertainment and sporting activities. Communal barbecues only. WiFi (free). Off site: Beach 500 m. Deep sea diving 1 km. Fshing port of Ceget with boat trips, shops, bars, restaurants 2 km. Watersports.

Open: 27 March - 20 October.

Directions

Leave A1 motorway, exit 2, signed Prgomet. Continue south, approx. 12 km. to the D8 coastal route near airport. Take D8 west, signed Sibenik, for approx. 10 km. to site. GPS: 43.511572, 16.19377

Charges guide

Per unit incl. 2 persons and electricity	€ 18.00 - € 37.10
extra person	€ 5.00 - € 8.00
child (under 12 yrs)	free - € 4.80
dog	€ 2.40 - € 4.50

Zivogosce
Kamp Dole

Zivogosce bb, HR-21331 Zivogosce (Dalmatia) T: 021 628 749. E: auto-camp-dole@st.hinet.hr
alanrogers.com/CR6870

Kamp Dole is a spacious site with a long beach frontage in southern Croatia, close to the beautiful island of Hvar. It has 500 pitches, 400 are for touring units (10A electricity). The beachside pitches are numbered and marked, the remainder are used informally and are mostly in the shade of mature trees. There are great views of the sea from the pebble beach which stretches 500 m. in front of the site; at each end of the beach is a small harbour, palm-lined to the north west, and a restaurant. The pitches at the back have beautiful views of the impressive mountains. Close to reception is a welcoming bar with terrace. Facilities on site include a fruit and vegetable kiosk and there is a market.

Facilities

Four old but well maintained toilet blocks offer high quality British WCs, washbasins and controllable, hot showers (free). Fridge box hire. Several kiosks and supermarket. Bar. Jet ski hire. Paragliding. Pedalo and canoe hire. Full entertainment programme in high season. Excursions to Korcula. Barbecues only in communal area.

Open: 1 May - 30 September.

Directions

Site is 80 km. south oast of Split beside the No.8 coastal road 3 km. south east of Zivogosce. Well signed. GPS: 43.170833, 17.196333

Charges guide

Per unit incl. 2 persons and electricity	Kn 96 - 167
extra person	Kn 23 - 42

For latest campsite news, availability and prices visit
alanrogers.com

Accommodation

Over recent years, many of the campsites featured in this guide have added large numbers of high quality mobile homes and chalets. Many site owners believe that some former caravanners and motorcaravanners have been enticed by the extra comfort they can now provide, and that maybe this is the ideal solution to combine the freedom of camping with all the comforts of home.

Quality is consistently high and, although the exact size and inventory may vary from site to site, if you choose any of the sites detailed here, you can be sure that you're staying in some of the best quality and best value mobile homes available.

Home comforts are provided and typically these include a fridge with freezer compartment, gas hob, proper shower – often a microwave and CD player too, but do check for details. All mobile homes and chalets come fully equipped with a good range of kitchen utensils, pots and pans, crockery, cutlery and outdoor furniture. Some even have an attractive wooden sundeck or paved terrace – a perfect spot for outdoors eating or relaxing with a book and watching the world go by.

Regardless of model, colourful soft furnishings are the norm and a generally breezy décor helps to provide a real holiday feel.

Although some sites may have a large number of different accommodation types, we have restricted our choice to one or two of the most popular accommodation units (either mobile homes or chalets) for each of the sites listed.

The mobile homes here will be of modern design, and recent innovations, for example, often include pitched roofs which substantially improve their appearance.

Design will invariably include clever use of space and fittings/furniture to provide for comfortable holidays – usually light and airy, with big windows and patio-style doors, fully equipped kitchen areas, a shower room with shower, washbasin and WC, cleverly designed bedrooms and a comfortable lounge/dining area (often incorporating a sofa bed).

In general, modern campsite chalets incorporate all the best features of mobile homes in a more traditional structure, sometimes with the advantage of an upper mezzanine floor for an additional bedroom.

Our selected campsites offer a massive range of different types of mobile home and chalet, and it would be impractical to inspect every single accommodation unit. Our selection criteria, therefore, primarily takes account of the quality standards of the campsite itself.

However, there are a couple of important ground rules:

- Featured mobile homes must be no more than five years old

- chalets no more than ten years old

- All listed accommodation must, of course, fully conform with all applicable local, national and European safety legislation.

For each campsite we have given details of the type, or types, of accommodation available to rent, but these details are necessarily quite brief. Sometimes internal layouts can differ quite substantially, particularly with regard to sleeping arrangements, where these include the flexible provision for 'extra persons' on sofa beds located in the living area. These arrangements may vary from accommodation to accommodation, and if you're planning a holiday which includes more people than are catered for by the main bedrooms you should check exactly how the extra sleeping arrangements are to be provided!

Charges

An indication of the tariff for each type of accommodation featured is also included, indicating the variance between the low and high season tariffs. However, given that many campsites have a large and often complex range of pricing options, incorporating special deals and various discounts, the charges we mention should be taken to be just an indication. We strongly recommend therefore that you confirm the actual cost when making a booking.

We also strongly recommend that you check with the campsite, when booking, what (if anything) will be provided by way of bed linen, blankets, pillows etc. Again, in our experience, this can vary widely from site to site.

On every campsite a fully refundable deposit (usually between 150 and 300 euros) is payable on arrival. There may also be an optional cleaning service for which a further charge is made. Other options may include sheet hire (typically 30 euros per unit) or baby pack hire (cot and high chair).

IT64190 Camping River

▶ see report page 31

Localita Armezzone, I-19031 Ameglia (Liguria)

AR1 – BUNGALOW – Bungalow

Sleeping: 2 bedrooms, sleeps 5: 1 double, 3 singles, sofa bed, pillows and blankets provided

Living: heating, shower, WC

Eating: fitted kitchen with fridge, freezer

Outside: table & chairs, parasol, barbecue

Pets: accepted (with supplement)

AR2 – CH 4+2 A CN 6 – Mobile Home

Sleeping: 2 bedrooms, sleeps 6: 1 double, 4 singles, sofa bed, pillows and blankets provided

Living: heating, TV, air conditioning, shower, WC, separate WC

Eating: fitted kitchen with fridge, freezer

Outside: table & chairs, parasol, 2 sun loungers, barbecue

Pets: accepted (with supplement)

Other (AR1 and AR2): bed linen, cot, highchair to hire

Open: 27 March - 3 October

Weekly Charge	AR1	AR2
Low Season (from)	€ 203	€ 420
High Season (from)	€ 791	€ 1190

IT62630 Camping Bella Italia

▶ see report page 52

Via Bella Italia 2, I-37019 Peschiera del Garda (Lake Garda)

AR1 – ACACIA – Mobile Home

Sleeping: 3 bedrooms, sleeps 7: 1 double, 5 singles, pillows and blankets provided

Living: heating, air conditioning, shower, WC, separate WC

Eating: fitted kitchen with hobs, grill, fridge

Outside: table & chairs, 2 sun loungers, barbecue

Pets: not accepted

AR2 – OLEANDRO – Bungalow

Sleeping: 2 bedrooms, sleeps 6: 2 doubles, 2 singles, sofa bed, pillows and blankets provided

Living: heating, TV, air conditioning, shower, WC

Eating: fitted kitchen with hobs, microwave, fridge

Outside: table & chairs, 2 sun loungers

Pets: not accepted

Other (AR1 and AR2): bed linen, cot, highchair to hire

Open: 12 March - 23 October

Weekly Charge	AR1	AR2
Low Season (from)	€ 52	€ 64
High Season (from)	€ 175	€ 195

IT60020 Camping Aquileia

▶ see report page 73

Via Gemina10, I-33051 Aquileia (Friuli-Venézia-Giulia)

AR1 – B3/B1 – Bungalow

Sleeping: 1 bedroom, sleeps 4: 4 singles, bunk bed, pillows and blankets provided

Living: shower, WC

Eating: fitted kitchen with hobs, coffee maker, fridge, freezer

Outside: table & chairs, parasol

Pets: accepted (with supplement)

AR2 – MAXICARAVAN VENEZIA /MAUI – Mobile Home

Sleeping: 2 bedrooms, sleeps 4: 1 double, 2 singles, sofa bed, pillows and blankets provided

Living: heating, shower, WC

Eating: fitted kitchen with hobs, coffee maker, fridge, freezer

Outside: table & chairs, parasol

Pets: accepted (with supplement)

Other (AR1 and AR2): highchair to hire

Open: 1 May - 30 September

Weekly Charge	AR1	AR2
Low Season (from)	€ 420	€ 455
High Season (from)	€ 490	€ 525

IT60080 Camping Sabbiadoro

▶ see report page 75

Via Sabbiadoro 8, I-33054 Lignano Sabbiadoro (Friuli-Venézia-Giulia)

AR1 – TYPE H – Mobile Home

Sleeping: 1 bedroom, sleeps 3: 2 singles, pillows and blankets provided

Living: heating, air conditioning, shower, WC

Eating: fitted kitchen with hobs, fridge

Outside: table & chairs, parasol, 2 sun loungers

Pets: accepted (with supplement)

AR2 – TYPE L – Mobile Home

Sleeping: 2 bedrooms, sleeps 6: 1 double, 3 singles, sofa bed, pillows and blankets provided

Living: heating, TV, air conditioning, shower, WC, separate WC

Eating: fitted kitchen with hobs, microwave, fridge

Outside: table & chairs, parasol, 2 sun loungers

Pets: accepted (with supplement)

Other (AR1 and AR2): bed linen, cot, highchair to hire

Open: 19 March - 9 October

Weekly Charge	AR1	AR2
Low Season (from)	€ 350	€ 637
High Season (from)	€ 560	€ 1134

IT60110 Camping San Francesco

▶ see report page 80

Via Selva Rosata, 1, I-30021 Caorle (Veneto)

AR1 – PINETA/BEACH – Mobile Home

Sleeping: 2 bedrooms, sleeps 5: 1 double, 2 singles, sofa bed, pillows and blankets provided

Living: heating, air conditioning, shower, WC

Eating: fitted kitchen with hobs, microwave, fridge, freezer

Outside: table & chairs

Pets: accepted (with supplement)

AR2 – M50 COMFORT – Chalet

Sleeping: 2 bedrooms, sleeps 6: 4 singles, sofa bed, pillows and blankets provided

Living: heating, air conditioning, shower, WC

Eating: fitted kitchen with hobs, microwave, fridge, freezer

Outside: table & chairs

Pets: accepted (with supplement)

Other (AR1 and AR2): cot, highchair to hire

Open: 3 April - 30 September

Weekly Charge	AR1	AR2
Low Season (from)	€ 315	€ 427
High Season (from)	€ 1099	€ 1421

IT60200 Camping Union Lido Vacanze

▶ see report page 82

Via Fausta 258, I-30013 Cavallino-Treporti (Veneto)

AR1 – CAMPING HOME ROOF – Mobile Home

Sleeping: 2 bedrooms, sleeps 7: 1 double, 2 singles, bunk bed, sofa bed, pillows and blankets provided

Living: living/kitchen area, heating, TV, air conditioning, shower, separate WC

Eating: fitted kitchen with hobs, microwave, dishwasher, fridge, freezer

Outside: table & chairs, 2 sun loungers

Pets: not accepted

AR2 – CAMPING HOME VERANDA LARGE – Mobile Home

Sleeping: 2 bedrooms, sleeps 6: 1 double, 2 singles, sofa bed, pillows and blankets provided

Living: living/kitchen area, heating, TV, air conditioning, shower, separate WC

Eating: fitted kitchen with hobs, microwave, dishwasher, fridge, freezer

Outside: table & chairs, 2 sun loungers

Pets: not accepted

Other (AR1 and AR2): bed linen, cot, highchair to hire

Open: 21 April - 23 September

Weekly Charge	AR1	AR2
Low Season (from)	€ 707	€ 637
High Season (from)	€ 1162	€ 917

IT60560 Camping Miramare

 see report page 93

Via Barbarigo 103, I-30015 Sottomarina di Chioggia (Veneto)

AR1 – MAXICARAVAN – Mobile Home

Sleeping: 2 bedrooms, sleeps 5: 1 double, 2 singles, sofa bed, pillows and blankets provided

Living: living/kitchen area, heating, TV, air conditioning, shower, WC

Eating: fitted kitchen with hobs, fridge, freezer

Outside: table & chairs

Pets: not accepted

AR2 – CHALET BURSTNER – Chalet

Sleeping: 2 bedrooms, sleeps 5: 1 double, 2 singles, bunk bed, sofa bed, pillows and blankets provided

Living: living/kitchen area, heating, TV, air conditioning, shower, WC

Eating: fitted kitchen with hobs, fridge, freezer

Outside: table & chairs

Pets: not accepted

Other (AR1 and AR2): bed linen to hire

Open: 4 April - 24 September

Weekly Charge	AR1	AR2
Low Season (from)	€ 280	€ 315
High Season (from)	€ 840	€ 875

CR6731 Naturist FKK Camping Valalta

 see report page 203

Cesta za Valaltu - Lim 7, HR-52210 Rovinj (Istria)

AR1 – MOBILE HOME SUN 2 – Mobile Home

Sleeping: 1 bedroom, sleeps 3: 1 double, sofa bed, pillows and blankets provided

Living: TV, air conditioning, shower, WC

Eating: fitted kitchen with hobs, microwave, coffee maker, fridge, freezer

Outside: table & chairs, 2 sun loungers

Pets: not accepted

AR2 – MOBIL HOME LUX – Mobile Home

Sleeping: 2 bedrooms, sleeps 5: 1 double, 2 singles, sofa bed, pillows and blankets provided

Living: TV, air conditioning, shower, WC

Eating: fitted kitchen with hobs, microwave, coffee maker, fridge, freezer

Outside: table & chairs, 2 sun loungers

Pets: not accepted

Other (AR1 and AR2): bed linen, cot to hire

Open: 29 April - 3 October

Weekly Charge	AR1	AR2
Low Season (from)	€ 476	€ 525
High Season (from)	€ 959	€ 1085

CR6732 Camping Polari

 see report page 204

Polari bb, HR-52210 Rovinj (Istria)

AR1 – STANDARD – Mobile Home

Sleeping: 2 bedrooms, sleeps 6: 1 double, 2 singles, sofa bed, pillows and blankets provided

Living: TV, air conditioning, shower, WC

Eating: fitted kitchen with hobs, microwave, coffee maker, fridge, freezer

Outside: table & chairs, parasol, 4 sun loungers, barbecue

Pets: not accepted

AR2 – DELUXE – Mobile Home

Sleeping: 2 bedrooms, sleeps 6: 1 double, 2 singles, sofa bed, pillows and blankets provided

Living: TV, air conditioning, shower, WC

Eating: fitted kitchen with hobs, microwave, coffee maker, fridge, freezer

Outside: table & chairs, parasol, 4 sun loungers, barbecue

Pets: not accepted

Other (AR1 and AR2): cot to hire

Open: 22 April - 2 October

Weekly Charge	AR1	AR2
Low Season (from)	€ 450	€ 500
High Season (from)	€ 1300	€ 1600

CR6727 Camping Valkanela

▶ see report page 209

Valkanela, HR-52450 Vrsar (Istria)

AR1 – VALKANELA STANDARD
– Mobile Home

Sleeping: 2 bedrooms, sleeps 6: 1 double, 2 singles, sofa bed, pillows and blankets provided

Living: TV, air conditioning, shower, WC

Eating: fitted kitchen with hobs, microwave, grill, coffee maker, fridge, freezer

Outside: table & chairs, parasol, 4 sun loungers, barbecue

Pets: not accepted

AR2 – VALKANELA PREMIUM
– Mobile Home

Sleeping: 2 bedrooms, sleeps 6: 1 double, 2 singles, sofa bed, pillows and blankets provided

Living: TV, air conditioning, shower, WC

Eating: fitted kitchen with hobs, microwave, grill, coffee maker, fridge, freezer

Outside: table & chairs, parasol, 4 sun loungers, barbecue

Pets: not accepted

Other (AR1 and AR2): cot to hire

Open: 22 April - 2 October

Weekly Charge	AR1	AR2
Low Season (from)	€ 400	€ 450
High Season (from)	€ 1200	€ 1300

CR6765 Camping Kovacine

▶ see report page 211

Melin I/20, HR-51557 Cres (Kvarner)

AR1 – MOBILE HOME 4-6 PERSONS
– Mobile Home

Sleeping: 2 bedrooms, sleeps 4: 1 double, 3 singles, bunk bed, sofa bed, pillows and blankets provided

Living: heating, air conditioning, shower, WC

Eating: fitted kitchen with hobs, fridge, freezer

Outside: table & chairs, parasol

Pets: accepted (with supplement)

AR2 – MOBILE HOME 2 PERSONS
– Mobile Home

Sleeping: 1 bedroom, sleeps 2: 2 singles, pillows and blankets provided

Living: heating, air conditioning, shower, WC

Eating: fitted kitchen with hobs, fridge, freezer

Outside: table & chairs, parasol

Pets: accepted (with supplement)

Other (AR1 and AR2): bed linen to hire

Open: 19 March - 16 October

Weekly Charge	AR1	AR2
Low Season (from)	€ 385	€ 301
High Season (from)	€ 1029	€ 644

CR6782 Zaton Holiday Resort

▶ see report page 216

Draznikova ulica 76 t, HR-23232 Nin (Dalmatia)

AR1 – SHELBOX TAVOLARA – Mobile Home

Sleeping: 2 bedrooms, sleeps 6: 1 double, 2 singles, sofa bed, pillows and blankets provided

Living: TV, air conditioning, shower, WC

Eating: fitted kitchen with hobs, microwave, coffee maker, fridge, freezer

Outside: table & chairs

Pets: accepted (with supplement)

AR2 – PREMIUM – Mobile Home

Sleeping: 3 bedrooms, sleeps 7: 1 double, 4 singles, sofa bed, pillows and blankets provided

Living: TV, air conditioning, shower, WC

Eating: fitted kitchen with hobs, microwave, coffee maker, fridge, freezer

Outside: table & chairs, 2 sun loungers

Pets: accepted (with supplement)

Other (AR1 and AR2): cot, highchair to hire

Open: 30 April - 30 September

Weekly Charge	AR1	AR2
Low Season (from)	€ 385	€ 490
High Season (from)	€ 1274	€ 1610

Travelling in Europe

When taking your car (and caravan, tent or trailer tent) or motorcaravan to the continent you do need to plan in advance and to find out as much as possible about driving in the countries you plan to visit. Whilst European harmonisation has eliminated many of the differences between one country and another, it is well worth reading the short notes we provide in the introduction to each country in this guide in addition to this more general summary.

Of course, the main difference from driving in the UK is that in mainland Europe you will need to drive on the right. Without taking extra time and care, especially at busy junctions and conversely when roads are empty, it is easy to forget to drive on the right. Remember that traffic approaching from the right usually has priority unless otherwise indicated by road markings and signs. Harmonisation also means that most (but not all) common road signs are the same in all countries.

Your vehicle

Book your vehicle in for a good service well before your intended departure date. This will lessen the chance of an expensive breakdown. Make sure your brakes are working efficiently and that your tyres have plenty of tread (3 mm. is recommended, particularly if you are undertaking a long journey).

Also make sure that your caravan or trailer is roadworthy and that its tyres are in good order and correctly inflated. Plan your packing and be careful not to overload your vehicle, caravan and trailer – this is unsafe and may well invalidate your insurance cover (it must not be more fully loaded than the kerb weight of the insured vehicle).

There are a number of countries that have introduced low emission zones in towns and cities, including Germany, Czech Republic, Denmark, Italy and Sweden. For up-to-date-details on low emission zones and requirements please see: www.lowemissionzones.eu

CHECK ALL THE FOLLOWING:

- GB sticker. If you do not display a sticker, you may risk an on-the-spot fine as this identifier is compulsory in all countries. Euro-plates are an acceptable alternative within the EU (but not outside). Remember to attach another sticker (or Euro-plate) to caravans and trailers. Only GB stickers (not England, Scotland, Wales or N. Ireland) stickers are valid in the EU.

- Headlights. As you will be driving on the right you must adjust your headlights so that the dipped beam does not dazzle oncoming drivers. Converter kits are readily available for most vehicles, although if your car is fitted with high intensity headlights, you should check with your motor dealer. Check that any planned extra loading does not affect the beam height.

- Seatbelts. Rules for the fitting and wearing of seatbelts throughout Europe are similar to those in the UK, but it is worth checking before you go. Rules for carrying children in the front of vehicles vary from country to country. It is best to plan not to do this if possible.

- Door/wing mirrors. To help with driving on the right, if your vehicle is not fitted with a mirror on the left hand side, we recommend you have one fitted.

- Fuel. Leaded and Lead Replacement petrol is increasingly difficult to find in Northern Europe.

Compulsory additional equipment

The driving laws of the countries of Europe still vary in what you are required to carry in your vehicle, although the consequences of not carrying a required piece of equipment are almost always an on-the-spot fine.

To meet these requirements we suggest that you carry the following:

- FIRE EXTINGUISHER
- BASIC TOOL KIT
- FIRST AID KIT
- SPARE BULBS

- TWO WARNING TRIANGLES – two are required in some countries at all times, and are compulsory in most countries when towing.

- HIGH VISIBILITY VEST – now compulsory in France, Spain, Italy and Austria (and likely to become compulsory throughout the EU) in case you need to walk on a motorway.

- BREATHALYSERS – now compulsory in France. Only breathalysers that are NF-approved will meet the legal requirement. French law states that one breathalyser must be produced, but it is recommended you carry two in case you use or break one.

Insurance and Motoring Documents

Vehicle insurance

Contact your insurer well before you depart to check that your car insurance policy covers driving outside the UK. Most do, but many policies only provide minimum cover (so if you have an accident your insurance may only cover the cost of damage to the other person's property, with no cover for fire and theft).

To maintain the same level of cover abroad as you enjoy at home you need to tell your vehicle insurer. Some will automatically cover you abroad with no extra cost and no extra paperwork. Some will say you need a Green Card (which is neither green nor on card) but won't charge for it. Some will charge extra for the Green Card. Ideally you should contact your vehicle insurer 3-4 weeks before you set off, and confirm your conversation with them in writing.

Breakdown insurance

Arrange breakdown cover for your trip in good time so that if your vehicle breaks down or is involved in an accident it (and your caravan or trailer) can be repaired or returned to this country. This cover can usually be arranged as part of your travel insurance policy (see below).

Documents you must take with you

You may be asked to show your documents at any time so make sure that they are in order, up-to-date and easily accessible while you travel.

These are what you need to take:

- Passports (you may also need a visa in some countries if you hold either a UK passport not issued in the UK or a passport that was issued outside the EU).

- Motor Insurance Certificate, including Green Card (or Continental Cover clause)

- DVLA Vehicle Registration Document plus, if not your own vehicle, the owner's written authority to drive.

- A full valid Driving Licence (not provisional). The new photo style licence is now mandatory in most European countries.

Personal Holiday insurance

Even though you are just travelling within Europe you must take out travel insurance. Few EU countries pay the full cost of medical treatment even under reciprocal health service arrangements. The first part of a holiday insurance policy covers people. It will include the cost of doctor, ambulance and hospital treatment if needed. If needed the better companies will even pay for English language speaking doctors and nurses and will bring a sick or injured holidaymaker home by air ambulance.

An important part of the insurance, often ignored, is cancellation (and curtailment) cover. Few things are as heartbreaking as having to cancel a holiday because a member of the family falls ill. Cancellation insurance can't take away the disappointment, but it makes sure you don't suffer financially as well. For this reason you should arrange your holiday insurance at least eight weeks before you set off.

Whichever insurance you choose we would advise reading very carefully the policies sold by the High Street travel trade. Whilst they may be good, they may not cover the specific needs of campers, caravanners and motorcaravanners.

European Health Insurance Card (EHIC)

Make sure you apply for your EHIC before travelling in Europe. Eligible travellers from the UK are entitled to receive free or reduced-cost medical care in many European countries on production of an EHIC. This free card is available by completing a form in the booklet 'Health Advice for Travellers' from local Post Offices. One should be completed for each family member. Alternatively visit www.ehic.org.uk and apply on-line. Please allow time to send your application off and have the EHIC returned to you.

The EHIC is valid in all European Community countries plus Iceland, Liechtenstein, Switzerland and Norway. If you or any of your dependants are suddenly taken ill or have an accident during a visit to any of these countries, free or reduced-cost emergency treatment is available – in most cases on production of a valid EHIC.

Only state-provided emergency treatment is covered, and you will receive treatment on the same terms as nationals of the country you are visiting. Private treatment is generally not covered, and state-provided treatment may not cover all of the things that you would expect to receive free of charge from the NHS.

Remember an EHIC does not cover you for all the medical costs that you can incur or for repatriation - it is not an alternative to travel insurance. You will still need appropriate insurance to ensure you are fully covered for all eventualities.

Travelling with children

Most countries in Europe are enforcing strict guidelines when you are travelling with children who are not your own. A minor (under the age of 18) must be accompanied by a parent or legal guardian or must carry a letter of authorisation from a parent or guardian. The letter should name the adult responsible for the minor during his or her stay. Similarly, a minor travelling with just one of his/her parents, must have a letter of authority to leave their home country from the parent staying behind. Full information is available at www.fco.gov.uk

Travelling with dogs

Many British campers and caravanners prefer to take their pets with them on holiday. However, pet travel rules changed on 1 January 2012 when the UK brought its procedures into line with the European Union. From this date all pets can enter or re-enter the UK from any country in the world without quarantine provided they meet the rules of the scheme, which will be different depending on the country or territory the pet is coming from. Please refer to the following website for full details: www.gov.uk/take-pet-abroad

Low Cost Flights

An Inexpensive Way To Arrive At Your Campsite

Many campsites are conveniently served by a wide choice of low cost airlines. Cheap flights can be very easy to find and travellers increasingly find the regional airports often used to be smaller, quieter and generally a calmer, more pleasurable experience.

Low cost flights can make campsites in more distant regions a much more attractive option: quicker to reach, inexpensive flights, and simply more convenient.

Many campsites are seeing increased visitors using the low cost flights and are adapting their services to suit this clientele. An airport shuttle service is not uncommon, meaning you can take advantage of that cheap flight knowing you will be met at the other end and whisked to your campsite. No taxi queues or multiple drop-offs.

Obviously, these low cost flights are impractical when taking all your own camping gear but they do make a holiday in campsite owned accommodation much more straightforward. The low cost airline option makes mobile home holidays especially attractive: pack a suitcase and use bed linen and towels provided (which you will generally need to pre-book).

Pricing Tips

- Low cost airlines promote cheap flights but only a small percentage of seats are priced at the cheapest price. Book early for the best prices (and of course you also get a better choice of campsite or mobile home)

- Child seats are usually the same costs as adults

- Full payment is required at the time of booking

- Changes and amendments can be costly with low cost airlines

- Peak dates can be expensive compared to other carriers

Car Hire

For maximum flexibility you will probably hire a car from a car rental agency. Car hire provides convenience but also will allow you access to off-site shops, beaches and tourist sights.

Getting the most from off peak touring

£14.95 night outfit + 2 people

There are many reasons to avoid high season, if you can. Queues are shorter, there's less traffic, a calmer atmosphere and prices are cheaper. And it's usually still nice and sunny!

And when you use Camping Cheques you'll find great quality facilities that are actually open and a welcoming conviviality.

Did you know?

Camping Cheques can be used right into mid-July and from late August on many sites. Over 90 campsites in France alone accept Camping Cheques from 20th August.

Save up to 60% with Camping Cheques

Camping Cheque is a fixed price scheme allowing you to go as you please, staying on over 600 campsites across Europe, always paying the same rate and saving you up to 60% on regular pitch fees. One Cheque gives you one night for 2 people + unit on a standard pitch, with electricity. It's as simple as that.

Special offers mean you can stay extra nights free (eg 7 nights for 6 Cheques) or even a month free for a month paid! Especially popular in Spain during the winter, these longer-term offers can effectively halve the nightly rate. See Site Directory for details.

Check out our amazing Ferry Deals!

Why should I use Camping Cheques?

- It's a proven system, recognised by all 600+ participating campsites - so no nasty surprises.

- It's flexible, allowing you to travel between campsites, and also countries, on a whim - so no need to pre-book. (It's low season, so campsites are rarely full, though advance bookings can be made).

- Stay as long as you like, where you like - so you travel in complete freedom.

- Camping Cheques are valid at least 2 years - so no pressure to use them up. (If you have a couple left over after your trip, simply keep them for the following year, or use them up in the UK).

Tell me more... (but keep it brief!)

Camping Cheques was started in 1999 and has since grown in popularity each year (nearly 2 million were used last year). That should speak for itself. There are 'copycat' schemes, but none has the same range of quality campsites that save you up to 60%.

Ask for your **FREE** continental road map, which explains how Camping Cheque works

01342 336621

Order your 2016
Directory

campingcheque.co.uk

Open All Year

The following sites are understood to accept caravanners and campers all year round. It is always wise to phone the site to check as the facilities available, for example, may be reduced.

ITALY

Piedmont & Valle d'Aosta

IT65050	Gofree	25
IT65000	Gran Bosco	26
IT62200	Mombarone	27
IT65030	Valle Gesso	18

Ligúria

IT64010	Dei Fiori	35
IT64110	Miraflores	35

Trentino-Alto Adige

IT62010	Antholz	58
IT62110	Cevedale	61
IT61844	Naturcaravanpark Tisens	68
IT62000	Olympia	68
IT62030	Sexten	67

Veneto

IT60530	Fusina	90

Emilia-Romagna

IT60980	Castagni	100
IT66230	San Marino	97

Tuscany

IT66270	Boschetto di Piemma	123
IT66056	La Foce	118

IT66650	Soline	109
IT66610	Toscana Village	119
IT66073	Versilia Mare	116

Marche

IT65200	Mimose	138

Lázio

IT67790	Castelfusano	143
IT68140	Flaminio	146
IT67800	Roma	144
IT68100	Seven Hills	145

Abruzzo & Molise

IT67920	Vecchio Mulino	151

Campania

IT68250	Il Vulcano Solfatara	157
IT68300	Zeus	157

Puglia & Basilicata

IT68655	Masseria	160

Sicily

IT69170	Kamemi	171
IT69300	Marinello	170
IT69180	Nettuno	168
IT69350	Rais Gerbi	169
IT69215	Sabbiadoro	168
IT69190	Scarabeo	172
IT69175	Valle dei Templi	167

Sardinia

IT69670	Costiolou	179
IT69695	Telis	175

SLOVENIA

SV4250	Danica Bohinj	185
SV4400	Dolina Prebold	190
SV4150	Kamne	188
SV4270	Koren	186
SV4325	Lijak	191
SV4340	Ljubljana	187
SV4405	Menina	191
SV4320	Saksida	186
SV4410	Terme 3000	188
SV4415	Terme Catez	185
SV4455	Terme Lendava	187
SV4440	Terme Ptuj	190

CROATIA

CR6744	Brioni	202
CR6725	Porto Sole	208
CR6754	Cikat	212
CR6860	Galeb	217
CR6875	Nevio	217
CR6778	Simuni	219
CR6855	Stobrec Split	220

Dogs *(Please refer to the 'Travelling with dogs' notes on page 230)*

For the benefit of those who want to take their dogs with them or for people who do not like dogs at the sites they visit, we list here the sites that have indicated to us that they do not accept dogs. If you are, however, planning to take your dog we do advise you to contact them first to check as there may be certain restrictions.

Never – these sites do not accept dogs at any time

ITALY

Al Boschetto	87	Cisano & San Vito	45	Italy	82	Riva di Ugento	161
Alberello	102	Costiolou	179	Jesolo	91	Riva Nuova	151
Argentario	106	Dei Fiori	85	Lido (Bibione-Pineda)	78	Rubicone	103
Athena	156	Dei Fiori	35	Lido Village	141	Saint Michael	120
Baia di Gallipoli	160	Del Garda	51	Malibu Beach	90	Salinello	153
Baia Domizia	155	Delle Piscine	124	Marelago	81	Sant'Angelo	86
Bella Italia	52	Delle Rose	98	Masseria	160	Serenella	44
Bellamare	138	Delle Rose	47	Mediterraneo	86	Stella Maris	139
Belvedere	48	Europe Garden	152	Orlando	111	Telis	175
Ca'Pasquali	86	Framura	33	Paestum	156	Tenuta Primero	74
Ca'Savio	79	Garden Paradiso	87	PicoBello	137	The Garda Village	56
California	143	Grotta del Saraceno	153	Portofelice	89	Villa al Mare	84
Capalonga	77	Il Tridente	78	Pra' Delle Torri	81	Voltoncino	106
Cevedale	61	Internazionale	139	Punta Lunga	161		
Chiara	105	Isamar	94	PuntAla	122	**CROATIA**	
		Isuledda	177	Residence	84	Val Saline	205
						Valalta (Naturist)	203

Maybe – at certain times or other conditions

ITALY

Baia Verde	121	Costa Ponente	168	La Sorgente	120	Punta Indiani	65
Baia Verde	122	Dolomiti	61	Lago di Levico	64	Rais Gerbi	169
Baita Dolomiti	67	Dolomiti	88	Mareblu	112	Romantico	147
Butteri	125	Don Antonio	150	Marinello	170	San Nicola	160
Capo Ferrato	179	Europa	126	Miramare (Punta Sabb.)	88	Smeraldo	34
Cigno Bianco	181	International	152	Molino a Fuoco	128	Steiner	62
Conca d'Oro	21	Isolino	22	Perticara	137	Stella del Mare	109
		Italia	126	Pionier Etrusco	144	Tahiti	98
		La Pineta	176	Porticciolo	143	Tripesce	127

Town & Village Index